MW01504098

The Natural History Of Monkeys, Opossums And Lemurs

PUBLISHED UNDER THE SUPERINTENDENCE OF THE SOCIETY FOR THE DIFFUSION OF USEFUL KNOWLEDGE.

THE LIBRARY

OF

ENTERTAINING KNOWLEDGE.

THE MENAGERIES.

COMMITTEE.

THE LIBRARY OF ENTERTAINING KNOWLEDGE.

THE

MENAGERIES.

THE

NATURAL HISTORY

OF

MONKEYS, OPOSSUMS, AND LEMURS.

IN TWO VOLUMES.
VOL. I.

WITH ENGRAVINGS ON WOOD BY J. JACKSON,
AFTER DRAWINGS BY W. HARVEY.

LONDON:
CHARLES KNIGHT & CO., 22, LUDGATE-STREET.

MDCCCXXXVIII.

LONDON:
Printed by WILLIAM CLOWES and SONS,
Stamford Street.

CONTENTS.

CHAPTER I.

CHAPTER IX.

CHAPTER X.

CHAPTER XI.

CHAPTER XII.

ILLUSTRATIONS.

THE

NATURAL HISTORY

OF

MONKEYS, LEMURS, AND OPOSSUMS.

CHAPTER I.

On the Physical Structure, Habits, and Classification of the Cheiropeds.

OF all the scientific pursuits in which the human mind can be engaged, the history of the habits and economy of the lower animals is perhaps the most interesting and popular. From early youth to the latest decline of life it has charms for every age; it excites the wonder and gratifies the curiosity of the peasant, at the same time that it supplies to the moralist and the philosopher subjects of the highest interest and the most profound research. Natural history, it is true, has not yet arrived at the accuracy which characterises the mathematical and physical sciences; but its principles are every day becoming more fixed and certain; and a host of zealous observers, in every part of the habitable world, are accumulating a vast collection of valuable facts, which will in time change the whole face of the science, and eventually elevate it to an equality with the most forward and important branches of human knowledge. Within the last twenty years alone, the rapid strides which zoology has made in the career of advancement, are almost unexampled in the his-

B

tory of science; whilst the application of its principles to the study of fossil remains has opened up a
new and boundless field of investigation, and extended
the history of our planet perhaps millions of years beyond the creation of man! When Dr. Young and
M. de Champollion discovered the key to the hieroglyphics inscribed on the monuments and depicted
upon the tombs of the ancient Egyptians, the an-
tiquary and the historian hailed their researches as
the dawn of a new light, which was to dissipate the
darkness of ages, and dispel the gloom which had
hitherto concealed one of the most interesting and
important chapters in the progressive history of
human civilization. Yet what are the results of this
discovery, great and important as they undoubtedly
have been, compared with the mighty consequences
which have followed the late Baron Cuvier's splendid
application of the principles of zoology and comparative anatomy to the study of the fossil bones
and shells which we find every day imbedded in the
rocks and other superficial strata which compose the
solid crust of the earth! By these means we have
become acquainted with the forms and habits of
hundreds of animals, some of them of the most anomalous structure and gigantic magnitude, which inhabited this earth many thousand years before our
own creation; the condition of our planet, the nature
of the herbs and trees which covered its surface, and
the successive changes and catastrophes to which it
was subjected, have been likewise revealed to us, and
the great book of creation itself opened to our in-
quiring eyes. The hieroglyphics of Young and
Champollion have, indeed, partially raised the
curtain which concealed a small portion of this
earthly stage from the spectator's view, and that, too,
only during a single scene; but the discoveries of
Baron Cuvier have unveiled the whole face of nature,

and shown us, not the history of a small tribe or of
a single nation, but the great theatre of existence
itself, and the successive acts in the drama of creation
which have been performed upon it.

Nor should the light which these grand discoveries
have thrown upon the principles of natural and revealed religion be overlooked in a work like the
present.   Ignorant and bigoted men, who are either
too illiterate to appreciate truth, or too indolent to be at
the trouble of investigating it, may declaim, as they
have invariably done in all ages and in all countries,
against the innovations of science : they may hold up
to popular odium now the great truths of zoology
and geology, as heretical and anti-religious, in the
same manner that they formerly reviled the sub-
lime discoveries of Galileo, of Locke, and of
Newton ; and if they can no longer enforce their
arguments by means of the dungeon, the rack, and
the inquisition, it is not because their fanaticism has
settled down into christian zeal, but that the spirit of
the times is adverse to such modes of enforcing
opinions ; let it, however, be remembered, that truth,
whilst it demolishes the theories and fallacies of mere
human invention, can never be hostile to the revelations of infinite wisdom, but must necessarily
strengthen and support them.   Thus, when the
united doctrines of zoology and geology proved
that the present creation is but the last of a series of
similar epochs, through which our planet has already
passed, prejudiced and arrogant men immediately
raised the cry of irreligion and infidelity, because the
new doctrines appeared to contradict their own preconceived interpretation of the Mosaic cosmogony; but
they overlooked the important fact that the same doctrines, by demonstrating the recent origin of man,
and other important subjects of Divine Revelation,
established religion upon a foundation which it had

not formerly occupied, and confirmed the truth of
revelation by the evidence of our own senses, instead
of the questionable authority of human testimony.
But it is not our intention to enter further into these
matters : they are properly the subject of Dr. Buck-
land's Bridgewater Treatise, and to that work we
must refer such of our readers as desire further information upon this important and interesting subject.

Our object has a more limited and less ambitious,
though, perhaps, not a less entertaining or instructive
range. We propose to investigate the structure,
history, and economy of that group of animals
which the universal consent of mankind has recognized as occupying the next station to man himself,
in the scale of animated nature, and as forming a kind
of intermediate link between him and the inferior
animals. We allude, of course, to the various
tribes of monkeys, whether of Asia and Africa, or
of America ; but there are other groups, such as the
lemurs of the Old World, and the opossums of the
New, so closely associated with the monkeys of their
respective continents, in their habits and conformation, that they cannot be separated without breaking
the natural continuity of the chain which unites the
organic affinities of the animal kingdom. We shall
consequently treat of them all together, and after first
explaining the import of a few necessary terms, which
will frequently occur in the following pages, proceed
at once to detail the general characters of their structure and economy.

In the first place, then, as regards the word
mammal : it is a term derived from the Latin
mamma, a breast or udder, in the same manner as
animal is derived from *anima,* mind or spirit, and is
employed to denote those animals which are provided
with mammary glands for the purpose of suckling
their young, and which in ordinary conversation we

denominate beasts and quadrupeds. Both these col-
loquial terms, however, are highly improper, as being
deficient in the precision and accuracy required for
scientific purposes; the first is altogether vague and
indefinite; and the second, whilst it excludes man,
the monkeys, the bats, and the whales from all relation to their natural congeners, associates with the
common quadrupeds the tortoises, the crocodiles, and
the lizards, with which they have no real connection
or affinity. Under these circumstances it was that
the immortal Linnæus invented the word *mammal*—
a word which has the advantage of precisely limit-
ing and logically defining the class of beings to
which it is applied, and which is formed according
to the strict analogies of the Latin tongue. Yet
subsequent French naturalists, with that love of in-
novation which has even crept into their scientific
nomenclature, have rejected the classical denomination of Linnæus, apparently for no better reason
than because it was not of French origin, and substituted in its stead the uncouth and most inelegant
compound *mammifère*—a word as uncongenial to the
genius of the language as it is harsh and rugged in
sound and structure. It has, however, been recently
introduced into our own language by some writers
of no mean report, and we are shocked at finding
their pages encumbered with such barbarous and
uneuphonous words as *mammifère* and *mammifères*,
when the simple and classical terms of *mammal* and
mammals would have answered their purpose much
better. To some this may appear a matter of small
moment; but nothing that relates to the introduction
of a new word into our language should be viewed
with indifference, particularly where the choice is to
be made between a simple classical term and a barbarous, harsh, and inelegant compound: the vigour
and harmony of our language are both involved in

the question, and we shall, therefore, follow the great Linnæus instead of his French innovators, by invariably employing *mammal* and *mammals* instead of *mammifere* and *mammiferes*.

In the second place, we have to explain the origin and import of the word *cheiroped*, which stands at the head of the present chapter, and which will frequently occur in the course of the following pages. It is derived from the two Greek words χειρ (*cheir*) a hand, and πους (in the Latin *pes*), a foot, and is intended to signify that the feet of those animals to which it is applied are formed into hands, or have long, flexible, prehensile fingers, and opposable thumbs, calculated for grasping, handling, and various other operations besides the function of mere locomotion. In some cases these opposable thumbs are formed on the anterior extremities only, as in man, and then the animals are called BIMANA, or two-handed; in other cases they are found both upon the anterior and posterior extremities, as, for instance, in the common monkeys of Asia and Africa, and in the lemurs, which are thence collectively denominated QUADRUMANA, or four-handed; and finally the American monkeys, and the opossums of that continent and of Australia, have opposable thumbs only on the posterior extremities, from which circumstance they derive the appellation of PEDIMANA, or hind-handed; and these three families obviously include all the varieties which can possibly occur in the number and position of these remarkable and important organs. It only remains to be added, that we have invariably made use of the Latin form *cheiropeds*, instead of the Greek termination *cheiropods*, not only because the analogous word quadrupeds has made it more familiar to our language, and consequently less harsh and formal to the ear, but because the latter form is more particularly consecrated to the different classes and orders of mollusks, and such practical distinctions often save much lengthened explanation. In the last place, the words *Simiæ, Simiadæ, Lemuridæ,* and *Didelphidæ,* will occasionally occur in our subsequent investigations, and therefore require explanation. *Simiæ* will be invariably used in the ancient classical acceptation of the term, as applicable to those anthropomorphous animals of the old world which we usually denominate apes, monkeys, and baboons: *Simiadæ* will be restricted to the analogous tribes of the new continent, which commonly pass under the names of ring-tailed and American monkeys, and which, though differing from the kindred groups of Asia and Africa in some of their most important characters, yet resemble them more nearly in the general details of their structure than any other animals—a resemblance which it is endeavoured to convey in the name: the terms *Lemuridæ* and *Didelphidæ* offer no difficulties; the former is applied to the animals which Linnæus originally included in his genus Lemur, and the latter to those which the English inhabitants of America and Australia are accustomed to include under the general name of Opossums.

That the group thus characterised by the common possession of organic modifications — at once so marked and so influential in their bearings upon the habits and economy of animal life; the only philosophical principle of zoological classification, as the complete separation, length, and prehensile power of the fingers, and the opposable nature of the thumb — should present numerous important coincidences, not only in other parts of the physical structure, but likewise in the mental resources, habits, manners, and, what may be not improperly denominated, the moral character, of the animals which compose it, will be naturally expected

by those who are accustomed to investigate the relations which invariably and necessarily subsist between
structure and economy. Nor are these anticipations
deceived in the present instance. The great and
immutable law of philosophy, that *similar causes
invariably produce similar effects*, would naturally
induce us to conclude, even from *à-priori* considerations, that the identity of structure here pointed out
must necessarily induce a similarity of action and
character in the animals possessing it—modified, of
course, in different genera and species, by the modifications of their organic conformation, and always
in exact proportion to these modifications; and this
fact is abundantly confirmed by a comparative study
of the animals themselves. The monkeys, the
lemurs, and the opossums, however they may differ
in their dentition and other secondary characters of
organization, all exhibit a uniformity in the habits
and economy of their lives, and a variety and superiority of both mental and physical resources, which
assimilate them strongly to one another, and elevate
them manifestly above other mammals in the scale
of existence. These relations will be developed
more at large when we come to speak of the separate divisions of *Simiæ, Lemuridæ, Simiadæ,* and
Didelphidæ, of which the two main groups of *Quadrumana* and *Pedimana* are respectively composed:
and we shall only mention, at present, that the food
of all these animals is principally composed of wild
fruits, roots, and grain, more or less mixed with
animal substances, such as insects, eggs, birds, and
small reptiles—occasionally among the *simiæ* and
simiadæ, and habitually among the *lemuridæ* and
didelphidæ; that they are invariably sylvan or arborial animals, the conformation of their extremities
adapting them for climbing trees and grasping the
branches, rather than for walking upon the surface

of the ground ; that their extremities, instead of
being mere organs of locomotion, execute the still
more important functions of prehension and manipulation, and are endowed with a delicacy of touch
greatly superior to that possessed by any other tribe
of quadrupeds, or, indeed, by any other animal except man ; and, finally, that their mental capacity,
as testified by the variety and delicacy of their actions and resources, is greatly superior to that displayed by the rest of the lower animals.

These considerations will justify the union of the
monkeys, lemurs, and opossums, in the same group,
to all who have carefully studied the animals in
question, and whose minds are not too strongly en-
veloped in the trammels of system, to allow of their
perceiving and appreciating the truth and importance of the relations which we have here developed.
Upon this subject, however, as in almost all other
departments of zoology, much diversity of opinion
prevails among systematic writers—a diversity entirely occasioned by their neglect to study and explain the comparative value of the principles of
classification which they severally employ ; for,
where every student is thus left to follow the light
of his own experience, it is not surprising that we
should have almost as many systems as writers.
Every one possessing the most ordinary knowledge
of the subject can perceive the prominent defects of
any proposed arrangement ; but it requires a special
study, and a minute acquaintance with all its parts
and bearings, to appreciate its advantages, or estimate its real value. It is one thing to perceive a
defect, and another to apply a remedy ; every one
can observe a broken leg, but it requires a skilful
surgeon to set it, who has a thorough acquaintance
with the anatomy of the member, and with the
manner in which its different parts and organs har-

monize and act upon one another; and he who, without this necessary knowledge, attempts to perform the cure, is more likely to increase the evil than to remedy it. So likewise in zoological classification; no system is necessarily wrong merely because it happens not to suit the taste of a particular individual, who may have but a limited knowledge or experience of the subject; nor is any one justified in proposing alterations without a thorough acquaintance with the component parts of the group, and an ample and candid exposition of the comparative value of the principles upon which his proposed alterations are grounded. Such an exposition, it is true, may be the most difficult part of the business, because it necessarily implies a minute and accurate knowledge of the subject in all its branches and relations, but it is not the less necessary or useful on that account; and were it previously given in all cases, the science would be materially benefited, and its principles eventually become fixed and understood.

Influenced by these considerations, we shall, in the following pages, invariably precede the history of each particular group by a general discussion and exposition of the comparative value and importance of the characters by which its component subdivisions are either related to one another, or distinguished from other groups, and thus endeavour to settle the principles of its arrangement upon a rational and philosophical basis. The considerations which we have already offered upon this subject apply to the group of cheiropeds in general, and others will be found in the subsequent portion of the present chapter: they are intended to justify the union of all mammals with opposable thumbs, either upon one or both pairs of the extremities, into one great group, and to explain the relations and subordination of its minor constituent groups. These relations were originally perceived by the celebrated Buffon—of all the naturalists of the last century, the most successful in studying the habits and economy of animal life; and who, had he not been unfortunately biassed against all system, would have probably given us a more correct arrangement of mammals than any which has yet appeared. The little that he has attempted of this nature is almost perfect in its kind, and has never since been departed from. He was the first to introduce anything like order or generic distinction among the simiæ and simiadæ, more especially to distinguish these two groups from one another, and to point out their characteristic differences; he was the only zoologist of his day who made an especial study of the history and relations of these animals; and it is not a little to the credit of his sagacity, that, with the very imperfect materials which he possessed, he should yet have arrived at the knowledge of relations which have been more fully developed only within the last two or three years. "At the same time," says he, "as the apes, baboons, and monkeys, are only to be found in the Old World, we must consider the *sapajous* and *sagoins* (i. e. the simiadæ) as their representatives in the New; for these animals have nearly the same conformation, as well external as internal, as they have likewise many common traits in their natural habits. The same may be said of the *makis* (lemurs), of which no species inhabits America, but which, nevertheless, appear to be there replaced or represented by the *philanders*, that is to say, by the opossums and other quadrumana with elongated muzzles, which are found in great abundance on the new Continent, but on no part of the old." It is obvious from this, that Buffon not only perceived the mutual relations

which subsist between the simiæ and simiadæ, the
lemuridæ and didelphidæ, respectively, but that he
even considered all these groups as forming constituent members of the same great family : he calls
them all quadrumana, and though that term is a misnomer, as applied to at least one half of the animals
in question, the error is not to be wondered at, when
we recollect that it was only within the last few
years that the simiadæ were shown not to have opposable thumbs on the pectoral members, and that
the mistake of Buffon is repeated in the " *Règne
Animal* " of Cuvier, as well as in all zoological
works hitherto published.

The next zoologist who adopted and developed
these views with regard to the relations of the
cheiropeds was Storr, the first successful reformer of
the Linnæan genera, as far as regards the mammalia,
and the real author of the system which, with a few
unimportant modifications, and these not always
improvements, was afterwards propounded by MM.
Cuvier and Geoffroy St. Hiliare, and which has
since maintained its ground pretty steadily among
naturalists, both in this country and on the Continent.   Storr considers all mammals with opposable
thumbs as composing one grand group, which he
divides into three sections, as follows :—

Section I. .... Homo.

Section II. .... Simia.
                                   Prosimia.
                                   Procebus.
                                   Tarsius.
                                   Lemur.

Section III. .... Didelphis.
                                   Phalanger.

On referring to the table at the end of the present
chapter, it will be seen that the primary arrange-

ment there given differs from that of Storr, only in
the removal of the simiadæ, or *prosimia*, as he calls
them, from the second to the third section, in consequence of observations made since his time ; and the
coincidence is the more remarkable, inasmuch as the
arrangement of Storr, as well indeed as the passage
above quoted from Buffon, were unknown to the
author of that system till long after the publication
of his own views. Subsequent discoveries, by extending our knowledge to the marsupial quadrupeds
of Australia, and, adding the kangaroos and phasco-
lomes to the opossums of America, destroyed the
natural character of the Linnæan genus, didelphis,
and with it that of Storr's third section ; and this
appears to have been the reason that induced MM.
Cuvier and Geoffroy St. Hilaire, in adopting the
system of Storr, to remove his third section from the
quadrumana to the carnivora.   The object of these
zoologists was to keep all the marsupials together in
the same group, and it must be confessed that the
anomalous circumstances attending their production,
so uniform and so conspicuous throughout all the
animals which compose this family, appear at first
sight to justify such a measure ; but on the other
hand, it is to be observed, that these animals differ
widely in all the most important and influential
parts of their habits and structure, and that they
cannot be thus kept together without violating both
the logic and philosophy of systematic arrangement.
This was fully perceived by Illiger, the most classical
and judicious of modern systematists, who in his
celebrated *Prodromus Systematis Mammalium et
Avium*, has not only restored the didelphidous pedimana to the position assigned to them in the system
of Storr, but removed the only valid objection to
that arrangement, by separating the pedimanous
from the nonpedimanous marsupials, and including

these latter in a distinct group. It is obvious indeed
that the mode of generation, as exhibited in these
animals, must be either disregarded altogether as a
primary principle of their classification, or else considered as a co-ordinate character to the usual mode
of generation common to ordinary mammals, so as to
divide the whole of the mammalia into two prime
sections of monodelphine and didelphine mammals;
but such a distinction, however convenient to the
embryologist or the comparative anatomist, is totally
useless in its application to zoology, as is likewise
the group *Marsupialia*, as such, even in the subordinate station assigned to it by Baron Cuvier. So
predominant has this feeling become of late, that
the most recent systematists, however they may
differ on other points, agree in breaking up the order
Marsupialia, to distribute its constituent members
among other groups, and indeed the logical simplicity as well as the zoological utility of the system
equally justify this dismemberment. But the division of Illiger, however philosophical in bringing all
the cheiropeds together, is defective in many respects.
The five families into which he divides his primary
group of POLLICATA (including the quadrumana and
pedimana of the present volume), are neither co-ordinate with one another nor definitely characterised;
and his exclusion of the bimana, which under the
denomination of ERECTA he forms into an order
apart, is founded upon metaphysical rather than
physiological considerations, and destroys at once
both the harmony and the simplicity of his arrangement. The pride of intellectual superiority and
moral endowments has indeed frequently induced
naturalists to consider MAN as forming a distinct
and separate order by himself, and to fancy that it
would be degrading the Lord of the Creation to
associate him in the same group with the apes and

the monkeys; but such scientific weakness cannot destroy the numerous affinities which actually characterise the structure of these animals as compared with our own, or blind the unprejudiced observer to the obvious relations which subsist between the bimana and the quadrumana. The metaphysician and the divine may, without impropriety, consider man apart from the rest of the animal kingdom, and in relation only to his intellectual and moral nature; but the naturalist must view him in a different light: anatomical structure and organic conformation are the only principles which the zoologist can admit as the foundations of natural science; and in this respect, man is too closely connected with the apes and other simiæ, to admit of being placed so widely apart from them, as he has been in some recent classifications of mammals. But with man we have nothing to do at present, farther at least than concerns his general relations as a constituent member of the same group of cheiropeds; our proper business is with the simiæ, simiadæ, lemuridæ, and didelphidæ, or, as they are vernacularly called, the monkeys, lemurs, and opossums, composing the two great families of quadrumana and pedimana, and to these we shall henceforth confine our observations.

These four natural groups, then, the simiæ, the simiadæ, the lemuridæ, and the didelphidæ, or as they are rather arbitrarily called in ordinary conversation, the monkeys, lemurs, and opossums, will form the subject of the present treatise; and we shall now proceed to detail such points, in their general structure, habits, and economy, as appear to be most particularly deserving of notice.

General Structure of Quadrumanous and Pedimanous Mammals.

Notwithstanding the various discrepancies which
occur throughout the respective series of the quadrumana and pedimana, and give rise to the different
genera of which we shall hereafter have occasion to
describe the history and characters more at large, an
attentive examination of their general organic structure, and of the adaptations of which it is susceptible
to the great purposes of life, will convince us that these
animals are all formed upon the same model and intended to fulfil the same destiny in the inscrutable
wisdom of Creation.   Intermediate between man and
the common quadrupeds, between the proud heir of
immortality and the beasts that perish, they present
every degree of intervening form and character, from
the half-human chimpanzee to the viverrine dasyure;
nor is there any other group of mammals in which
this beautiful gradation of characters is at once so
obvious, so complete, and so uninterrupted. Like man,
they are invariably provided with complete and powerful clavicles, which serve to keep the anterior extremities apart from one another, throw them out to
some distance from the trunk, and by thus affording
free scope and a solid axis of revolution, enable the
animals to perform a vast variety of the most delicate
and complicated movements, which would be impossible without such mechanism. The bones of the fore-
arm likewise admit of complete rotation, as in the
human subject; the knees, elbows, ankles, and wrists
are constructed with an especial view to variety and
ease of motion, and the fingers are invariably long,
flexible, and prehensile.   Hence it is that the cheiropeds are by no means confined to the mere function
of progression; their extremities, in fact, appear to be
more especially formed for other purposes than loco-

motion, as, for example, for prehension, for the manipulation* or handling of objects, for delicacy of touch,
and a hundred other similar functions, which it is unnecessary to enumerate more particularly.

But there is one circumstance in which both the
quadrumana and pedimana differ from the bimana, and
which is too remarkable to be passed over without a
more detailed notice. In man, the perfection of his
mechanism is not more evinced by the delicacy of his
organic structure, and the variety and complexity of
motions and functions, which are performed by the
most simple contrivances, than by the fact that each
pair of his extremities is set apart for different purposes. The pectoral members, for instance, are never
used in progression, but reserved exclusively for the
more delicate functions connected with our intellectual
nature—for touch, for prehension, and for manipulation : thus the organs are preserved in a state of
constant delicacy, and their acuteness never impaired
by coming in contact with the rough surface of the
earth in walking : the abdominal members, on the
contrary, are entirely appropriated to the acts of progression and locomotion, and consequently require
to be differently modified from the anterior pair.
The extreme mobility which characterises the structure
of the latter would be a serious impediment to the
proper execution of the peculiar functions assigned to
the former ; and hence we find that whilst the shoulder,
fore-arm, and wrist, are formed with a view to varied
and complicated motion in every direction, the hip,
leg, and ankle are constructed upon a more solid and
rigid plan, so as to admit of free and easy motion

* We shall adopt this convenient term, applied by chemists
in a sense not very different from that in which we use it, to
express the actions of handling objects, carrying food to the
mouth, and other similar functions, besides mere locomotion,
which are occasionally performed by the extremities of animals.

only in the direction of the median plane of the body. Whilst the radius and ulna, the two bones of the fore-arm, admit of perfect rotation upon one another, the corresponding bones of the leg, the tibia and fibula, have no rotation whatever. Now this is not the case among the other two families of cheiropeds. The quadrumana and pedimana have not the functions of the respective extremities separated, and allotted to different pairs, as in man; all their extremities, both anterior and posterior, are devoted without distinction to the performance of the various acts of progression, prehension, manipulation, touch, &c., and consequently there is not the same difference of structure between their pectoral and abdominal members, which we have just seen to be so strongly characteristic of the human subject. Neither is there the same delicacy of function : they grasp, snatch, and hold with their hind feet equally as well as with their fore ; and some even seem better calculated to perform these functions with the posterior than with the anterior extremities, since, as we have already seen, one entire family have opposable thumbs upon the former and not upon the latter pair.

The conformation of the extremities which we have just detailed is the great instrument by which the habits and economy of the cheiropeds are governed and directed. The mobility of the different parts of the members, the length and weakness of the fingers, and the opposable nature of the thumbs, all disqualify these animals for progression on a level surface, like the face of the earth ; but the very qualities which incapacitate them for this species of locomotion are admirably calculated to facilitate their progress among the forests, where they grasp the branches with security, and swing themselves from tree to tree with astonishing precision and agility. The primeval woods and forests of tropical climates are consequently the appropriate habitats of the cheiropeds. They are peculiarly and exclusively a sylvan race; they find their food upon trees; they live, move, repose and bring forth their young among the branches, and enjoy, in the dense and impenetrable forests, the only opportunities of turning their peculiar organic conformation to advantage.

In the structure of the head and trunk, the quadrumana and pedimana offer the same general resemblance to the human subject as in that of the extremities; greatly modified, however, in different genera, according to the position which they occupy in the scale of organic perfection, and leading by an uninterrupted series of gradations from man himself to the actual quadrupeds. In the simiæ and simiadæ, for instance, the head has the same general form as in the human subject; the skull is round and capacious, the face short and proportionably of small dimensions, as compared with the capacity of the cranium, and the teeth, though sometimes differing in number, are exactly of the same form and relative dimensions; the ears likewise resemble the human; the nose is abridged and does not extend so far as the upper lip; the eyes are contiguous and directed forwards; and the mouth is comparatively small and incapable of great dilatation. In the lemuridæ and didelphidæ, on the contrary, all these characters are so changed and modified as to approximate them much more nearly to the common quadrupeds. The relative capacity of the skull is diminished; the face is prolonged and attenuated into a pointed muzzle; the nose lengthened beyond the extremity of the upper lip, and terminated by a truncated snout, with the nostrils opening beneath, as in the dog and other carnivora; the rictus or gape of the mouth extends almost to the ears backwards; the teeth differ from

those of man both in form and number, as they do
even in the different genera of the same family; the
eyes are for the most part directed sideways, and the
ears lengthened as in ordinary quadrupeds.

These varieties in the form of the head, and comparative length and development of the cranium and
face, have been eagerly seized upon by some naturalists and made the basis of generic distinctions
among the simiæ and simiadæ. By applying the
principle of the facial angle, employed by the celebrated Camper for the purpose of distinguishing the
different races of the human species, it was imagined
that an infallible measure could be obtained, not only
of the generic differences, but even of the mental
capacity of the cheiropeds; but the fallacy of the
principle, as a zoological character, is sufficiently evident from the circumstance of its being founded upon
modifications which confessedly differ not in species,
but in degree only; and even its practical utility is
seriously impaired by the fact that the form and relative proportions of the skull and face, among these
mammals, undergo so many and such extraordinary
changes in their progress from youth to maturity,
that the facial angle of the young individual is sometimes double the dimensions of that which distinguishes the adult of the same species. Thus it was
that MM. Cuvier and Geoffroy, misled by the application of their own principles, long placed the young
and aged orangs in two different genera, the former
next to man himself, and the latter even below the
baboons, with the whole series of the simiæ interposed
between them; and, were the same principles of
classification adhered to still, the orangs ought
unquestionably to occupy the lowest instead of the
highest station among the quadrumana. But the
principles which lead to such false results cannot be

natural, and we must consequently seek in other and more influential modifications for the true characters of generic distribution.

We have said that the teeth of the simiæ and simiadæ resemble those of the human subject in their general form and characters. The latter family, indeed, with the exception of a single genus, have a molar tooth more than man, on either side, both in the upper and lower jaw, and the greater number of the baboons and monkeys have a fifth tubercle upon the last inferior molar; but these are the only material differences which can be detected in the dental formulæ of these animals as compared with our own. They have invariably four incisors, two canines, and ten or twelve molars, as the case may be, in each jaw, of the same general form, and with the same blunt tuberculous crowns, as far at least as the cheek-teeth are concerned, as in man; nor is there any other marked distinction, except in the great development of the canines, more especially those of the old males— a circumstance which is necessitated by their condition, as a means of self-defence. In the lemuridæ and didelphidæ, however, the dental system undergoes a very remarkable change, and departs entirely from the anthropoid form, which it preserves throughout the entire series of the simiæ and simiadæ, to assume a character altogether anomalous and abnormal. The number of incisors varies from two to eight or ten, for there is no fixed rule here, as in the former two groups; it is even seldom that they are found of the same number in both jaws, and the molars are equally variable. These, however, as in the former instance, are essentially tuberculous, the only difference being that the tubercles are more prominently developed than in the simiæ and simiadæ, and consequently that the appetites become proportionally more carnivorous.

But however nearly they may approximate to the carnivorous type, none of the cheiropeds ever live exclusively upon animal food, or even prefer flesh when fruits or vegetables can be obtained with equal facility. The whole order are, in truth, essentially omnivorous, and, in a state of nature as well as in confinement, seek and thrive best upon a mixed diet. The apes, monkeys, and baboons, search after and devour the eggs of birds, locusts, and even small lizards, with great diligence and appetite, in their native forests, and when confined in menageries, enjoy their mutton-bone or leg of chicken with evident delight. So likewise the opossums : they are often fed exclusively upon animal substances, owing to the ignorance of their keepers ; but they invariably decline in health under such treatment ; and the satisfaction with which they receive and devour even a dry crust of bread is a manifest proof of the real nature of their appetites. All the details of their organization confirm these observations : the nature of their teeth, the structure of their stomachs and intestinal canal, and the general conformation of their digestive organs, prove that nature never intended them to subsist exclusively upon any one species of aliment, but rather upon a mixed and various food, and show the absurdity of those speculative theories which profess to restrain mankind to a vegetable diet, under the vain pretence of its being the appropriate food of an imaginary state of nature. Whatever may have been the original condition of man, previous to the development of his social and political relations, if indeed he can be supposed to exist at all without at least the germs of such necessary and congenial institutions, it is certain that he must have subsisted at all times and under all circumstances upon the same mixed regimen which nourishes him at present, unless it be supposed that his physical conformation has undergone the same

changes as his moral constitution. The question of
natural or appropriate food is not one which depends
upon the frame of the mind, but purely upon the
structure of the bodily organs, which it is designed to
nourish and support; and those who have argued it
upon contrary principles have but displayed their
ignorance of its real bearings.

The only other organ which it is necessary for us
to mention particularly, in relation to the general
characters of these animals, is the tail. This is a
very essential and important organ in the economy
of the cheiropeds. Man and the apes, which either
walk entirely upright, or in a semi-erect position,
have no tails, because such an instrument would
only serve to impede their motions without assisting
their progress; some species of baboons are likewise
without tails, or have them reduced to mere tubercles; for in these genera also they perform no
essential or important function, neither entering into
the elements of progression, nor assisting in the locomotion of the animals; but in all other cases, the
tails are long and powerful, and of material use
in balancing the body and guiding the direction,
during the various and rapid movements which the
quadrumana and pedimana habitually execute,
among the precarious habitats of their native forests.
Among many genera of the latter family, however,
this organ has a much higher and more important
office assigned to it. With the majority of the
simiadæ and didelphidæ it becomes a powerful instrument of prehension, and, by rolling firmly round
the branches, serves to secure the equilibrium of the
animal's station, whilst the hands are employed about
other matters. This singular organization, which,
with the exception of two or three other small genera
of arborial quadrupeds, likewise inhabitants of South
America, is exclusively confined to the pedimana,

appears to have been bestowed upon these animals
as a kind of compensation for the defective power of
their ordinary organs of prehension. We have already seen that the pedimana, including the simiadæ,
or American monkeys, and the didelphidæ, or opossums, have no opposable thumbs on the anterior
extremities; their power of grasping and holding by
these members is necessarily decreased in consequence, and the prehensile power of the tail, which
exists principally among these two tribes, seems to
have been especially designed for the purpose of
supplying the defect. But we shall enter more
fully into these considerations at a future period.
Let us in the meantime advert to a question which
was formerly much agitated among certain speculative philosophers, and which still attracts occasional
notice.

It is known to most of our readers that the late
Lord Monboddo, as well as the celebrated Jean
Jacques Rousseau, strenuously maintained that men
were but monkeys or orangs, which, by accidental
circumstances, succeeded in emancipating themselves
from the original debasement of their nature, and, by
the gradual development of their mental faculties
and physical structure, at length reached the high
degree of perfection which they at present enjoy.
Strange as this doctrine may appear, unsupported by
anything like fact or probability, and directly contradicted by revelation, it has nevertheless met with
its admirers, and there are still those who believe
that the living principle possesses within itself an innate capability of modification, which would account
for all the varieties of form and species observable
among animals and vegetables. The only thing
like facts which its authors have ventured to adduce
in support of this visionary hypothesis, is, in the first
place, that there is actually an uninterrupted grada-

tion of mental and physical qualities perceptible in
the animal kingdom; and secondly, that modifications, both of structure and intelligence, daily occur
under our own eyes, in the new varieties which are
constantly springing up among domestic animals.
Both these propositions are perfectly true; but it is
difficult to see how the first bears upon the question
at issue, or can be made to prove that each link in
the chain of gradation necessarily sprung from that
which preceded it, rather than that it had a separate
and independent origin, and that all were equally
due to distinct acts of creative power. The second
question requires a little farther consideration. It
is undoubtedly true that varieties are daily produced
among animals of all kinds, by the operation of external causes; but it is equally true that these
varieties are, by the fixed and immutable laws of organization, confined within certain prescribed limits,
which they cannot possibly transgress, or which, when
they do transgress, the result is not a new species,
but an individual malformation, a deformity, which,
not being a necessary condition of existence, disappears in the next or some succeeding generation.
How many varieties, for instance, do we possess of
the dog, the horse, or the ox, all differing from one
another in form of body and docility or sagacity of
mind, all adapted to different purposes, yet all unquestionably derived from the same original source;
but, on the other hand, all these different varieties,
however numerous, or however variously endowed,
are but dogs, horses, or oxen, after all, and, if continued to eternity, could never become anything else.
Who has ever seen a dog produced from a horse, or
a monkey from a dog? Yet this is just as probable
as that man could have originally derived his origin
from the orang-outan, or this from any of the inferior
monkeys.

c

But we shall examine the question a little more closely. If man was originally derived from the monkey, he must necessarily have possessed a tail, and walked upon all-fours; and Lord Monboddo and other advocates of this doctrine boldly meet the difficulty by admitting the fact, and endeavouring to account for the loss of these important attributes. M. Bory de St. Vincent, in a late work, written expressly upon the natural history of man, though he denies that our ancestors had tails, or walked upon their hands, is yet equally confident that they had the great toe opposable to the others, like the common quadrumana. He assures us that the inhabitants of the *landes* in the south of France, who are accustomed to collect resin in the extensive pine forests of the country, still retain this original character of pristine humanity, and affirms that the decline of his Parisian countrymen from the original perfection of their nature is attributable to their degenerate habit of wearing shoes, and not having a sufficient number of trees to keep up the practice of climbing. "Can it be denied," says M. de St. Vincent, "that four hands are better than two, as elements of perfectibility?" and consequently, that an animal possessed of four hands, is, on that very account, a superior being to the degenerate two-handed man of modern times? These extravagances only demonstrate to what lengths men will go in support of a favourite hobby. It may be very true that the inhabitants of the French *landes* have a greater facility of climbing and using their toes than the rest of their countrymen, just as individuals born without arms, or otherwise similarly mutilated, acquire such powers of prehension as to be even able to write with their feet; but this is far from proving that their great toes are opposable, much less that the whole structure of the legs can be so changed as to assimilate them to the arms and hands. For what would this imply? not only that the toes should be lengthened like the fingers, and rendered equally capable of being firmly folded up against the sole of the foot, not only that the great toe, now so much larger and placed on the same line with the others, should be diminished in size and thrown backwards and outwards, to admit of freer and more extensive motion, like the thumb, but that the whole structure of the leg should be equally modified ; that the heel should be entirely obliterated, the bones of the leg acquire an equal power of rotation as those of the arm, and the entire limb become adapted to the execution of free motion, instead of possessing its present strength and rigidity. All these various modifications would be necessarily induced by that primary law of harmony, or as Baron Cuvier calls it, that condition of existence, which ordains that the different parts and organs of the animal frame must accord with one another, and that none can be permanently changed without equally affecting all the rest. To those who can admit the possibility of all the changes which we have here enumerated, the doctrine of M. de St. Vincent may appear sound philosophy; but it is rather singular that his *quadrumanous* Frenchmen should have escaped the notice of all other observers, and not a little unfortunate for his opinions, that our sober-minded countrymen should never have detected an opposable great toe on the feet of the Australian and other savages, who are equally accustomed to climbing, and at least as little removed from " the state of nature" as the resin-gatherers of the *landes*. Our Anglo-Australian brethren, however, were not philosophers, and, having no favourite theories to support, saw nature with their own eyes : had they enjoyed the advantage of M. de St. Vincent's spectacles, we should doubtless have had a different account

As to the tails with which Lord Monboddo and others have endowed our ancestors, it is difficult to imagine what use they could have made of such appendages, or upon what circumstances so strange an opinion is founded, unless it originates in a spontaneous act of generosity, to prevent man from being behind-hand with his compeers the monkeys. The *Kakerlakies* of the old Dutch navigators, and other " homines caudati," whom certain travellers of the seventeenth century pretend to have seen or heard of among the islands of the great Indian Archipelago, will scarcely suffice to prove our original claim to this additional ornament. The lower orders in China firmly believe that all Europeans have tails, and that the capacious make of our sailors' trowsers is designed to stow them away more commodiously ; and during the war of the succession, and probably to a much later period, the same opinion was entertained by the ignorant Spaniards with regard to the English heretics. The accounts of early navigators were no doubt founded upon these absurd articles of Chinese belief; and if they imposed for a moment even upon the acute and logical mind of the great Linnæus, we need not be surprised that they should be pressed into the service of such speculative theorists as Rousseau and Monboddo.

The only remaining part of the hypothesis that requires particular notice, is the supposition that man " in a state of nature" originally went upon all-fours, and that his present erect attitude and biped progression are the effects of education and sophisticated habits. This opinion is attempted to be supported by the example of sundry poor idiots who have been occasionally lost in extensive forests on the continent, and, after wandering about for years in solitude, and supporting themselves on roots and wild plants, at length reappeared, to astonish the world and delight philosophers with a sight of "man in a state of nature." The latest and most authentic of these metaphysical God-sends was "Peter the wild boy," whom Swift has immortalised in his humorous piece, "*It never rains but it pours*," and whose appearance Lord Monboddo gravely assures us was of greater importance to mankind than the discovery of the Georgium Sidus. Peter was perfectly idiotic and dumb, apparently from a defect in the organs of voice: he was originally discovered in Hanover, and brought to this country by Caroline, Queen of George the First; but he can scarcely be considered as a fair specimen of the "state of nature," at least if quadruped station and progression be incident to that state, since he invariably walked upright, and never attempted to go on all-fours. Various other instances, however, are recorded, in which the quadruped progression is said to have been the natural pace; and Linnæus has even condescended to collect them together in the *Systema Naturæ*, under the epithet *Homo ferus, tetrapus, mutus, hirsutus*. Yet what is there in the history of these unfortunate beings, these accidental outcasts from society, to justify the attention which has been bestowed upon them? They are in reality but withered leaves which some rude whirlwind has shaken off from the tree of civilisation; and those who have mistaken them for the root of the plant itself, have reversed the order of nature, and preferred the dreams of fancy to the evidence of their own senses.

The rudest and most abject savages that have ever been discovered walked erect, nor was a single instance ever known to the contrary. This fact should be amply sufficient to satisfy any reasonable mind as to the natural pace and attitude of man; but it may be easily demonstrated, from his organic confor-

c 3

mation, that he could not possibly walk on all-
fours, and indeed it might be as rationally maintained, that the natural attitude of a cow or a horse
was erect. Were the advocates of this fanciful doctrine but to make trial of the quadruped pace themselves, if only for a few seconds, they would be at no
loss to discover the fallacy of their favourite hypothesis,
in the utter want of adaptation which they would soon
become sensible of in their organic structure to the
assumed position. They would discover that their legs
were too long, their arms destitute of sufficient
strength, and their heads connected with the body in
such a manner as to render it impossible for them to
see either before or on one side of them; even supposing that they could walk, which is impossible,
they could not make use of their organs of sense;
and, in short, to render the quadruped pace possible,
the entire structure of the head, trunk, and extremities,
must undergo a complete change. The anterior extremities must be consolidated, the posterior shortened, the skull provided with prominent occipital
crests, the position of the foramen magnum altered,
and even the spinous processes of the dorsal vertebræ
elongated. Those who believe that such changes are
the result of civilisation or external circumstances,
may be very good metaphysicians, but they are very
bad anatomists. However, we have spent more time
upon this subject than its intrinsic merits deserve, or
would have received, but that it still boasts an occasional disciple, and is naturally connected with the
subject of the present volume. We proceed to in-
quire into the geographical distribution of the quadrumana and pedimana.

The subject of the geographical distribution of existing animals over the face of the globe has of late
years acquired additional importance from its connection with fossil zoology, and the light which it

throws upon the condition of the earth previous
to the grand catastrophe which annihilated the former
world, and buried the animals of the then creation
in one common ruin. Yet its laws and principles
are but imperfectly understood ; and it is only in a few
instances that naturalists have hitherto succeeded in
pointing out the actual relations of natural groups
of animals to particular countries or climates. Among
these, perhaps, the most remarkable instance on record regards the geographical distribution of the
cheiropeds. It is a fact, which admits of neither
question nor doubt, that there are no pedimana in
the Old World, nor quadrumana in the New ; so
that these two great families are not less distinguished
by their organic structure than by their geographical
distribution ; and it becomes an interesting problem
to ascertain how far they are represented in fossil
zoology, and whether their analogies in a former
world were subject to the same laws of distribution
which govern existing races. Our present knowledge in this department of fossil zoology is unfortunately too limited to admit of a satisfactory solu-
tion of these questions : of pedimana we know but
a single fossil species, a small opossum, discovered
in the gypsum quarries of Montmartre, and described
by Baron Cuvier in the " Ossemens Fossiles ;"
whilst the quadrumana, like man himself, were supposed, till very recently, to have had no existence
previous to the present creation. Within the last
two years, however, undoubted fossil remains of
monkeys have been discovered both in France and
India, conjoined in both cases with the bones of
elephants, rhinoceroses, and other inhabitants of
tropical climates, and serving still farther to evince
the change which must have taken place in the distribution of heat over the earth, since the period of
their existence.

The second fact which we have to notice with regard to the geographical distribution of the cheiropeds is not less singular than that which has just
been mentioned. We have seen that the two primary
groups of quadrumana and pedimana are exclusively
confined to the eastern and western hemispheres respectively : but this is not all : the subordinate groups
which compose these two primary ones have themselves their appropriate localities, and, though not so
exclusively as the principal families, have nevertheless each its great central habitat, or head quarters,
from which it may occasionally diverge to the neighbouring continent or islands, but in which the great
majority of its genera and species are invariably con-
centrated. The simiæ, for instance, are common to
Asia and Africa ; but, as we shall afterwards find,
this group is itself divisible into the three subordinate groups of apes, monkeys, and baboons, of
which the former is, with one exception, confined
to Asia, whilst the latter two have representative
genera in both continents. The lemuridæ, again,
are chiefly found in the island of Madagascar, where,
as far as we at present know, they occupy the place
of the simiæ, which do not appear to exist in that
island ; the simiadæ are exclusively confined to
South America ; and, with the single exception of
the genus didelphis, likewise an inhabitant of tropical America, the didelphidæ are only found in
Australia and the neighbouring isles. These geographical facts are not a little singular in the history
of the cheiropeds, and are only equalled in importance by the similar fact of the almost exclusive
marsupial character of the Australian mammals.

It only remains for us to mention another fact
with regard to the geographical distribution of the
cheiropeds. It has been already observed that the prehensile power of the tail is a character almost peculiar

to the pedimana ; and it follows, therefore, from what
we have said above with respect to the habitat of that
family, that prehensile-tailed animals are confined to
the New World, to New Holland, and the continent
of South America ; and so true is this fact, that of
the only animals which possess the prehensile power
of the tail, besides the pedimana, viz., the small
genera, myrmecophaga, synætheres, and cerco-
leptes, the species are exclusively confined to South
America.

The following table exhibits these relations, and
the different genera which compose the respective
groups and families, in a regular and connected
series :—

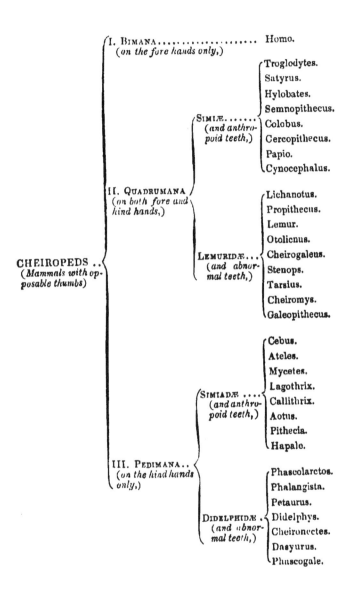

CHEIROPEDS ..
(*Mammals with opposable thumbs*)

I. Bimana.................... Homo.
(*on the fore hands only,*)

II. Quadrumana
(*on both fore and hind hands,*)

Simiæ.......
(*and anthropoid teeth,*)

Troglodytes.
Satyrus.
Hylobates.
Semnopithecus.
Colobus.
Cercopithecus.
Papio.
Cynocephalus.

Lemuridæ...
(*and abnormal teeth,*)

Lichanotus.
Propithecus.
Lemur.
Otolicnus.
Cheirogaleus.
Stenops.
Tarsius.
Cheiromys.
Galeopithecus.

III. Pedimana..
(*on the hind hands only,*)

Simiadæ ....
(*and anthropoid teeth,*)

Cebus.
Ateles.
Mycetes.
Lagothrix.
Callithrix.
Aotus.
Pithecia.
Hapale.

Didelphidæ .
(*and abnormal teeth,*)

Phascolarctos.
Phalangista.
Petaurus.
Didelphys.
Cheironectes.
Dasyurus.
Phascogale.

Chapter II.

The Simle.—Apes in general.

HAVING in the last chapter explained the organic structure and mental constitution of the cheiropeds in general, as well as their most remarkable habits and geographical distribution, we shall now circumscribe our views within a narrower compass, and confine ourselves more particularly to the consideration of the conformation and economy of the simiæ, the first and most important family of the whole group, and that which contains the species most nearly allied, in organisation and intelligence, to the human subject. It has been already observed that we confine the name of Simiæ, generally speaking, so greatly abused in its recent application, to the animals strictly and properly so denominated by the ancients, that is to say. to the apes, baboons, and monkeys of the Old World; for the Greeks and Romans were, for obvious reasons, totally unacquainted with the analogous forms of the western hemisphere, as well as with the didelphidæ, and, as far as they have left us any accounts, even with the lemuridæ of the remote parts of Asia and Africa. The name is generally considered to be derived from *simus* (flat-nosed), though it may perhaps be questioned whether this be not rather derived from *simia*, particularly since an extensive class of Latin derivatives from the same root, such as *simius*, a mimic, *simulo*, to counterfeit, *simulator*, a dissembler, &c., all refer to the root meaning of *simia*, and in no case to that of *simus*.

This family is composed of three minor groups,

definitely characterised by appropriate traits of organic development, and respectively distinguished, in
our own language, by the names of apes, monkeys,
and baboons—a division which has the rare advantage, seldom attendant upon mere popular classifications, of being in perfect accordance with scientific
principles, founded upon the structure and habits of
the animals. The apes have neither tails nor cheek-
pouches, and their ischial callosities are either defective altogether or developed only in a rudimentary
form ; though inhabiting the woods their pace is
semi-erect, and they walk on two legs even along
the branches, their extremely long arms compen-
sating the want of a tail, in steadying and directing
their motions. The monkeys have cheek-pouches,
callosities, and very long muscular tails ; they likewise are a pre-eminently sylvan race ; they walk on
all-fours, and their long tails become powerful and
efficient instruments in guiding their movements and
securing their equilibrium during the rapid and varied evolutions which they habitually execute, in
spite of the precarious nature of their footing. The
baboons have cheek-pouches and callosities, but tuberculous or short tails, never reaching beyond the
houghs, destitute of all muscular power, and incapable of entering as an efficient instrument into the
function of progression ; they go on all-fours, live
among rocks and mountains, and are seldom or never
found in the forests. But though these three primary groups of simiæ are thus definitely and essentially distinguished from one another by natural
modifications of structure, which exert a powerful
and obvious influence over their respective habits and
economy, the distinction has not always been recognized among zoologists with the same clearness as
by the world at large. This discrepancy relates
chiefly to the baboons : scientific writers, by attach-

ing an exaggerated importance to secondary characters, to the neglect of those which really influence
the habits and manners of these animals, have for
some time past been accustomed to confine this term
to the cynocephals; though the really essential characters of that genus are equally shared by the great
majority of the animals which they have called
macacs, and which, in direct violation of the most
prominent traits of their structure and habits, have
been hitherto classed among the monkeys. It is
true, that a small minority, some three or four species, of these so called macacs, have the long,
muscular, and efficient tails of the monkeys, and
agree in all their essential generic characters with
the ordinary cercopithecs; but in this respect they
differ entirely from the rest of their congeners, and
cannot be associated with them in any system
professing to be founded upon just and scientific
principles. They belong, in reality, to the genus
Cercopithecus, and will be included in that term
wherever it occurs in the present work; but as the
name of *macac*, or, as it is written by the French,
macaque, properly belongs to one of the species
thus excluded from the genus *Macacus*, to avoid the
confusion which might otherwise ensue, it will be
proper to suppress the latter term altogether, and
substitute that of *Papio*, as the generic name of the
short-tailed macacs of modern writers; a name formerly applied to some of these animals, and serving
very well to express the relations which they bear to
the cynocephals, or other baboons.

Each of these sub-families, the apes, monkeys,
and baboons, comprises two or more distinct genera; and all are exclusively restricted, as regards
their habitat, to the warmer regions of Asia and
Africa. The apes are, with one exception, confined
to the great islands of the Indian Archipelago, and

D

the Malay Peninsula : the monkeys are spread over
the tropical parts of both continents, though by no
means indifferently, since the Asiatic and African
species belong invariably to different genera, whilst,
of the two natural genera of baboons, one is appropriate to each of these continents. In describing
these different groups we shall follow this order of
their geographical distribution, because it has not only
the advantage of arranging the animals very nearly
according to their order in the scale of nature, but
likewise of keeping the inhabitants of the same regions together, and thus forming, as far as it goes,
an uninterrupted *Fauna* of each continent—an
object of no small moment to the practical observer.

The General Characters of the Apes.

The word *ape*, which exists with little variation in
all the modern European languages which have their
origin in the ancient Teutonic, as *aap* in Dutch, *affe*
in German, *apor* in Swedish, &c., is commonly sup·
posed to be derived from the German word *affen*, to
imitate (literally to *ape*) ; and in English is applied
indiscriminately to all simiæ without tails, which
are, on that account, generally considered to approach
most nearly to the human form.

Of all the inferior animals, the apes approach most
nearly to man, as well in their organisation as in
their habits and intellectual endowments. Zoologi-
cally considered, they are distinguished from the
other quadrumana by the total absence of tails and
cheek-pouches, of which we have already explained
some of the uses and functions, and which we shall
afterwards find to exercise a certain degree of influence upon the other simiæ, more or less apparent in
the manners and economy of different genera.   The

character arising from defect of tail, indeed, is not, strictly speaking, peculiar to the apes : certain other quadrumanous mammals, and those of groups greatly inferior, in point of structure and intelligence, such as the magot (*papio inuus*), called, from this very circumstance, the Barbary *ape*, and the *papio niger*, or black *ape* of the Philippines, are equally deficient in this organ ; even certain dog-headed baboons, as, for instance, the drill (*cynocephalus leucophæus*), and mandrill (*cynocephalus mormon*), have the tail so short as to be almost tuberculous ; so also have the *indris* and *nycticebi* among the lemuridæ ; but these instances can only be regarded in the light of casual exceptions to the general rule which obtains in their respective genera, whilst, on the other hand, the tailless character is a universal and distinguishing mark of the true apes. Nay, so appropriate is this character to the apes properly so called, that it has ever been considered by the world at large as the peculiar, if not the only diagnosis of these animals, and the term *ape* has been accordingly applied, universally in ordinary conversation, to designate a *monkey without a tail*, all quadrumanous mammals possessing this character being called indifferently apes.

The accuracy so necessary in scientific language, however, requires us to use the word in a more strict and limited acceptation ; for besides that, as we have already seen, the absence of tail is not peculiar to the apes, neither does it constitute their most marked or influential character. This is unquestionably found in their want of cheek-pouches, organs which exist universally in all the other simiæ, or monkeys of the Old World, the semnopithecs alone excepted, and which are a kind of natural wallet, in which these animals can stow away considerable quantities of fruits, grain, and other provisions, either in returning

from their predatory excursions into the gardens and
cultivated fields, when removing to distant parts of
the forest, or finally to preserve them for a future
occasion, after satisfying their immediate wants.
Being thus an influential as well as a peculiar attribute, the presence or absence of these organs becomes
a valuable character in the generic distribution of the
quadrumana, and more especially in defining the
natural groups of the simiæ, as distinguished from
the simiadæ and lemuridæ. No instance of cheek-
pouches, indeed, has ever been observed in any species
belonging to either of the latter two families ; nor,
for that matter, in any other animals, except the
ornithorhynchus, and a few genera of rodents, such
as the ground-squirrels (*tamia*), spermophiles (*sper-
mophilus*), hamsters (*cricetus*), &c.; but with the
exception of the true apes, and probably also of the
semnopithecs, a nearly-allied genus inhabiting the
same localities, these organs are common to all the
other monkeys of Asia and Africa.

There is another generic character, however, which
is even more peculiarly appropriate to the true apes
than the absence either of tails or cheek-pouches,
and, in its influence upon the economy of these animals, and more especially upon their mode of progression, of much greater consequence. This arises
from the extraordinary disproportion that exists between the length of the anterior compared with the
posterior extremities, and which is carried to such
a degree of apparent extravagance in some species,
that when the animals stand upright upon the hind-
legs they can touch the ground with the fingers of
the fore. The whole of the bat tribe (*cheiroptera*),
as well as the sloths of South America, exhibit an
equal excess in the development of the pectoral over
the abdominal members ; in so far a sort of analogy
may be traced between these animals and the real

apes; but here all kind of similarity ceases : the long limbs and slender prehensile fingers of the apes are differently constructed, and perform functions very different from those of the sloths and bats. Yet the analogy between these groups of animals, in other respects so widely separated from one another, is not altogether confined to the mere length of their anterior, compared with their posterior extremities; but extends in some degree to their mode of progression, and the natural habitat which the peculiarities of their organic structure compel them to seek. The long slender fingers of the bats are connected by a thin expansile membrane, continued along the flanks so as to unite the arms with the hind-legs, and present a great extent of surface compared with the absolute weight of the animal. This structure, united with the powerful muscles and perfect rigidity of the fore-arms, allows the bats to make the same use of their lateral membranes which birds do of their wings, for the purpose, namely, of supporting themselves in the atmosphere by a series of successive beats, and of passing through the air by a species of locomotion in all respects analogous to real flight. But in proportion as they are more perfectly organized for this kind of progression, in the same degree are they incapacitated for moving, with any sort of ease or facility, on the surface of the earth. In such situations they are consequently rarely, if ever found, except from accident; the boundless fields of air are their proper domain when in pursuit of food, exercise, or amusement; and when disposed to rest or retirement, they hang suspended by the hind-feet from the branch of a tree, or from the roof of some subterraneous cave or neglected building.

With respect to this part of their structure, the apes are, in some measure, intermediate between the bats and ordinary quadrupeds. Their long flexible arms, and separate prehensile fingers do not, it is true, permit these animals to elevate themselves into the air for the purpose of flight, but they equally incapacitate them for common quadruped progression on the surface of the earth. Did their organisation allow of it in other respects, biped station and biped progression are the only attitude and species of locomotion which would appear natural or proper to them under such circumstances; and, in fact, these are precisely, with slight modifications, the station and mode of progression which the apes assume when compelled to travel upon a level surface. But it must never be forgotten that such a situation is entirely foreign to their habits and organisation; their motions and carriage under these circumstances are constrained and awkward in the extreme, and though their attitude is partially erect, and they really walk upon the hind-feet like human beings, yet it is with a vacillating unsteady pace, which they are continually obliged to secure by touching the ground on one side or other with the long fingers of the fore hands. A celebrated French professor of zoology, M. Geoffroy St. Hilaire, compares the pace of the apes, when they walk upon a level surface, to that of a lame man who goes upon crutches. The cases, however, are not strictly parallel. The apes have perfect use of their hind-legs, which, though comparatively short, are strong and muscular; nor do they ever rest the entire weight upon the long forearms whilst they swing the body forwards, as is the practice of those whose infirmities compel them to make use of crutches. On the contrary, their pace is firm enough, though vacillating from the peculiar structure of their hind-legs, which, unlike those of the human subject, are better calculated for prehension than for walking; and if they use the fore-arms at all, it is not for the purpose of supporting the body,

but of steadying the motion, and recovering the
equilibrium, which is momentarily endangered by
the want of rigidity in the posterior members.

We have ourselves had frequent opportunities of
observing what is here described in various individuals of three or four different species of apes.
In no case, however, have we remarked them to
have recourse to the mode of progression ascribed
to them by M. Geoffroy St. Hilaire, not even when
their declining health and bodily infirmities might
naturally be expected to have reduced them to seek
such assistance and support. On the contrary, their
usual, we may even say, their natural station was
erect, with the knees, however, much more bent than
in the human species ; and when they walked, it was
on the hind-feet alone, touching the ground lightly
on either side with the knuckles of the fore-hands,
which were kept half closed for this purpose. This
was uniformly the case when the hands were free,
but when they were otherwise employed, as in grasping or carrying anything, the pace was purely biped,
and the station consequently erect, the knees, however,
being still very much bent ; nor did the animals appear to suffer as if the position were constrained or
unnatural. Little consideration is necessary to show
us the reason why the apes, in walking, lean rather
upon the backs of the half-closed knuckles, than
upon the under surface of the fingers. In this particular, in fact, they only take advantage of the
natural conformation of the bones and muscles of
the organ, as the reader may readily convince himself by pressing alternately upon the tips of his
fingers, and then upon the back of his bent hand ;
a contrary course would strain the fingers in the
direction opposed to their muscular power, and render
them liable to continual dislocation.

ˠ But, though thus capable of proceeding with sufficient ease and security upon a level surface, it is not
on the plain ground that the apes have an opportunity
of displaying the surprising force and agility with
which their organic structure really endows them.
As the conformation of their extremities is, in some
measure, intermediate between that of bats and
quadrupeds, so likewise do they occupy a habitat intermediate between the elements in which these two
different tribes of mammals are adapted to move and
execute the most important functions of their lives.
The apes are essentially an arborial or sylvan race;
every part of their conformation, every modification
of their organic structure, has a direct tendency to
this end; and those very peculiarities, which diminish
their powers of walking with ease upon the surface
of the earth, are admirably adapted to increase their
facility of climbing and grasping. The shortness
of their legs and thighs, by keeping the centre of
gravity always near to the surface upon which
they tread, necessarily secures a degree of equilibrium to the body, which it could not possess
were these organs of greater length; and no sooner
is this equilibrium in danger of being deranged than
the long arms are immediately employed to restore
it, either by grasping the nearest branches, or being
inclined upon either side like the balancing pole of
a rope-dancer. The legs, moreover, are not in the
same line with the thighs; the knees are turned
outwards, and the feet are articulated at the ankle in
such a manner that their soles turn inwards, so as to
face or be opposed to one another. By these means
the apes are enabled to embrace or grasp the trunks
and branches of trees with much greater force than
if their members were constructed like our own:
they thus become most essentially sylvan or arborial

animals, and never voluntarily abandon the forests, where they find at once the most congenial food and the most perfect security.

Their whole organisation peculiarly adapts the apes to these habits. Besides the conformation of the extremities just noticed, the fingers and toes are long, flexible, and deeply separated from one another; the thumb, though shorter, and placed farther back towards the wrist than in man, possesses, nevertheless, considerable power, and is completely opposable to the other fingers; and as this is equally the case on the anterior and posterior members, the apes become thus pre-eminently fitted for an arborial life. They are not *quadrupeds*, as has been justly remarked by Tyson, Buffon, and other naturalists, but *quadrumana*; not four-footed, but essentially four-handed animals. One part of their organisation, as we have already seen, renders them, in some degree, intermediate between the bats and ordinary mammals; but the great and leading details of their structure, their habits, actions, and superior intellectual endowments, make them, in reality, the connecting link between man and the inferior animals—the next grade to humanity in the descending scale of existence. As far, indeed, as the mere adaptation of their organic structure to purposes of prehension and locomotion is considered, they may be justly regarded as superior to all other animals, without even excepting the lord of creation himself; but it would be too much to say, with M. Bory de St. Vincent, that because the apes have four hands, and man only two, we are, therefore, an inferior and degenerate race, which, in acquiring the power of speech at the expense of losing our *hind-hands*, has only exchanged one advantage for another. Such dreams as these have already been noticed; and it is hoped that the reader is sufficiently convinced of

their illogical and unphilosophical nature, to spare
us the trouble of enlarging upon them at present.

It is unquestionable, however, that the superior
powers of prehension enjoyed by the apes greatly
enlarges their sphere of action. They are not confined to the surface of the earth like the generality
of mammals, and though they do not possess the
power of elevating themselves into the air like bats
and birds, they are, nevertheless, enabled to traverse
the intermediate regions of the woods and forests,
with an ease and velocity which can only be compared to actual flight. On the other hand, when
compelled by circumstances to pass over any part of
the earth's surface, their pace, as we have already
seen, is, properly speaking, neither that of a biped
nor of a quadruped; they do not walk upright with
the firm and portly attitude of man, but much less
can they be said to walk upon all-fours like the lower
animals, or even like the inferior tribes of monkeys
and lemurs. The oblique articulation of their ankles,
coupled with the opposable thumb-like great-toe,
which stands out almost at a right angle to the soles
of the posterior members—circumstances which are
manifestly well calculated to increase their powers
of prehension, compels them, in walking, to tread
only upon the outer edge of the hind-foot, and produces a rocking or waddling gait, precisely similar
to that of a ricketty child or bandy-legged man.
In their native forests, the extreme length of their
arms and hands is turned to the greatest advantage:
it not only extends their sphere of prehension, but
acts, as we have already observed, upon the principle of the rope-dancer's balancing-pole, and completely secures their equilibrium even with the most
precarious footing. Thus it is that travellers have
beheld the apes securely poised at the very extremity
of the slender trunk of the bamboo, balancing

themselves adroitly, and waving their long arms to and fro, with a gracefulness and ease of motion truly admirable.

The absence of a tail, which has already been slightly noticed as one of the most prominent characters of the apes, and which, in the estimation of the world at large, is usually considered as the distinguishing mark between them and the lower tribes of monkeys, is not altogether devoid of influence upon the habits and economy of these animals. Not that we consider this organ as generally exercising functions of superior or primary importance among the great majority of mammals; on the contrary, its uses are, in many cases, extremely obscure, if not altogether beyond the reach of observation: but among the arborial, aquatic, and some other tribes, its functions are at once obvious and important—too apparent, indeed, to be liable to the blunders which so often attend speculations upon final causes in some other departments of zoology. Though the presence of a tail, then, does not always indicate a corresponding function, and though its absence is not, strictly speaking, confined to the present group of quadrumanous animals, yet a long tail would seriously embarrass the nearly erect motion of the real apes; whilst its use is, in other respects, superseded by the length of the fore-arms, which appear intended to compensate its loss, and which supply its place in adjusting the proper balance of the body, the only function, an important one, no doubt, which the tail performs in the common monkeys.

A character, which is common to all the other known simiæ, is, nevertheless, found in some species only of the real apes, and absent in others: this is the possession of callosities, or naked callous patches on the buttocks, upon which these animals sit when fatigued by the violent and rapid movements which they habitually execute. These organs have been already partially referred to, and their functions will be described more at large when we come to speak of the baboons and other simiæ, in which their development is most remarkable. Among the apes they are confined to the gibbons, or *hylobates*, and even in them exist only in a rudimentary form; but their presence is, nevertheless, sufficiently important to become a legitimate generic character, to distinguish these animals from the chimpanzees and orangs, as the comparative length of the anterior and posterior extremities distinguishes these genera from one another. We shall find, however, that the gibbons, which possess these diminutive callosities, differ in no other particular from the chimpanzee and orang-outan, which are deficient in this respect; they have the same system of dentition, the same organs of sense, and the same singular modification of the organs of locomotion and prehension; their manner of life, also, is precisely similar; they take up their abode equally in the thickest and most solitary forests, inhabit the same countries, and live upon the same food; and, finally, their actions, character, and mental faculties are, in all respects, the same.

The teeth of the apes, as indeed those of all the other monkeys of the Old World, are of the same number as in man; nor, as far as the incisors and molars are concerned, do they present any difference of form in the chimpanzees and orangs, the two most anthropoid genera of the family; in the gibbons, however, the three posterior molars of the lower jaw have their crowns marked by five tubercles each, instead of four; and in the adults of all the species, more especially in the old males, the canines are developed in the same relative proportion as in the carnivora; the tusks of the full-grown orang-outan, at

least as large as those of the lion, are most formidable
weapons. Unfortunately, we know but little of the
manners of these animals in their adult state; but
this circumstance gives us strong reason to suppose
that the extreme gentleness and placidity observable
in the young individuals usually brought into Europe,
do not always continue to characterise them in their
native climates, but that their dispositions alter in
proportion to the development of their muscular
force; and that, in their adult state, they are as formidable and mischievous as the baboons themselves.

The characters and habits of the apes present individual differences, which we shall notice when
speaking of the several genera and species. As far,
however, as their general manners have been observed, they are of a gentle, and we may even say,
without exaggeration, of a grateful and affectionate
disposition, tinged, indeed, with an obvious shade of
melancholy, which may be owing, however, to the
confinement and other unnatural circumstances in
which they are necessarily placed when brought to
this country: their looks are expressive in the highest
degree; their eyes beam with intelligence; their actions are grave, circumspect, and deliberate; they are
seldom moved to violent passion, though occasionally
peevish and fretful when teazed or thwarted; and,
finally, they are totally free from that petulance,
caprice, and mischievous curiosity, which so strongly
characterise the monkeys properly so called. It must
be remembered, however, that these observations
apply to the apes only in the state of confinement in
which we have had an opportunity of seeing them in
Europe, when their spirits were, perhaps, broken
down by captivity, and absence from their native
woods and companions; those usually seen have
been, moreover, generally of immature age, and may
consequently be naturally supposed to have exhibited

a greater degree of gentleness and docility than what we may reasonably presume to be due to their adult condition, and the full development of their physical powers; but, on the other hand, the gibbons which we have observed had unquestionably attained their mature growth, as was manifest from the great development of their canine teeth, yet their character and disposition differed, in no respect, from what we have here described. The patience, circumspection, and docility of these animals, really approach more nearly to the attributes of human reason than our vanity may at first be willing to admit. They patiently endure clothing to defend them from the effects of our changeable climate, are readily taught to imitate or perform various actions, quickly learn to interpret the sentiments and emotions of those they are attached to, and almost seem to comprehend the language you address to them. If at any time they mistake your meaning when commanded to do a particular act, they hesitate with their hand perhaps on the object, look attentively at your face, as if to divine your meaning, and, in short, conduct themselves precisely as a dumb man would do under similar circumstances. Those which are deprived of callosities do not repose on their hams, after the fashion of ordinary monkeys, but stretch themselves on their sides like human beings, and support their heads upon their hands, or, by some other means, supply the want of a pillow.

We need not be surprised that animals approaching so nearly to the human form should have been at all times objects of intense interest to the philosopher, or of credulous and exaggerated relations among the common people. Accordingly we find that the inhabitants of Western Africa, the Indian Archipelago, and the south-eastern parts of Asia, universally regard the apes as a sort of wild men,

closely allied to the human species, and preserving
silence, not from any defect in the organs of speech,
but from motives of policy, that they may escape the
drudgery, servitude, and other evils incident to man
in a state of society. The credulous, and, for the
most part, ignorant travellers of the sixteenth and
seventeenth centuries, readily adopted these extravagant accounts, and, perhaps, embellished them
with additional colours from their own fertile imagina-
tions; they represented the apes as living in a kind
of regulated society, in the depths of the most
impenetrable forests, arming themselves with clubs,
expelling even the elephant from their cantonments,
always walking erect, sheltering themselves in caves,
or erecting rude huts to defend them from the in-
clemency of the weather, and occasionally kidnapping
the people of the country, when they happened to
meet them alone in the woods, and reducing them
to a state of the most revolting slavery. These and
similar narratives imposed upon the credulity of the
age, and even grave and learned philosophers began
to imagine that they had here a kindred and closely-
allied species, if not man himself in his original and
natural state. The great Linnæus himself long
hesitated as to the true affinities of these extraordinary
beings. In the earlier editions of his celebrated
Systema Naturæ he has invariably considered them
as *wild men*, and as such classed the only species
with which he was imperfectly acquainted, under
the name of *homo sylvestris* and *homo troglodytes*,
describing it as moving abroad only during the night,
and conversing in a kind of whistling sound; nor
was it till the publication of the twelfth edition of his
work, in 1766, that he began to entertain more correct ideas regarding the natural relations of the apes,
and, finally, degraded them from the rank of men,
to associate them with the other simiæ.

This little history might alone serve to convince us of the close approximation which the apes make to man, even were we ignorant of the physical and mental characters upon which it is founded, and which point out these animals as a kind of ambiguous beings, neither men nor monkeys, but sharing, in some measure, the attributes of both; partaking with the latter their quadrumanous formation, but resembling the former in their erect station and biped progression, as well as in the absence of tails, cheek-pouches, and callosities. In man the hair of the fore-arm is directed towards the elbow, and the incisor-teeth of the upper jaw are implanted immediately into the maxillary, without the intervention of intermaxillary bones: of all the simiæ, and, indeed, of all the lower animals, the apes alone resemble the human being in these particulars. Numerous other relations of equal importance, but which we cannot at present more particularly detail, will be found enumerated in Professor Owen's excellent paper on the Comparative Osteology of Man, the Chimpanzee, and the Orang-outan, inserted in the first volume of the Zoological Transactions.

The food of the apes, in a state of nature, consists of wild fruits, bulbs, and, probably, the inner bark and tender buds of certain trees. They likewise eat insects and small reptiles, and search after the nests of birds, of which they greedily suck the eggs, and devour the callow young. Of eggs they are passionately fond, even in a state of confinement, but they refuse beef or mutton unless it has been previously cooked. Milk or water is their favourite beverage; at first they will reject wine or spirits; but, like the savages of America and Australia, they soon overcome their aversion, and learn to enjoy their glass with the gusto of a connoisseur.

In point of geographical distribution, this group is

principally confined to the peninsula of Malacca and the great islands of the Indian ocean. One genus is, nevertheless, an inhabitant of Western Africa, and that too the most anthropoid of the whole, both in its intellectual faculties and physical conformation. It is, therefore, usually placed at the head of the series of apes, and we shall now proceed to relate its history and describe its manners.

CHAPTER III.

Apes *continued*—The CHIMPANZEE. (*Simia Troglodytes*).

THIS highly interesting animal, the *simia troglo-dytes* of Linnæus, and *troglodytes niger* of more recent naturalists, has been, with the exception of a single eminent zoologist, universally placed at the head of the brute creation; Baron Cuvier alone con-testing its right to occupy this rank in favour of the orang-outan. Subsequent observers, however, have satisfactorily established the pre-eminence of the chimpanzee; its form, its proportions, and its ana-tomical structure, as shown by the excellent memoir of Mr. Owen on the comparative osteology of both species, decidedly approximate more nearly to the human type than those of the orang; its attitude, its gait, and its habits are likewise more anthropoid, and even the character upon which M. Cuvier founded his preference of the Indian species, the apparently superior cerebral development, is so evanescent as to be confined to a very early period of the animal's life, and entirely disappears as it approaches to maturity. In other respects, the relative form and proportions of the extremities, those organs upon which the most important habits and functions of life depend, are in the chimpanzee very nearly the same as in man; the arms descend but a little below the knee when the animal stands upright; the heel is large and well proportioned; the sole of the foot broad, and capable of affording a firm support to the body in the erect posture; the legs and feet articulated nearly in a straight line with the thighs, the former being provided with a distinct though small calf; and the cranium plain, and without sagittal or interparietal crests. In the orang-outan, on the contrary, the arms nearly touch the ground in the upright attitude; the legs and feet are distorted, by being turned out-wards at the knee and inwards at the ankle, so that the soles are directly opposed to one another; the heel is narrow, the toes habitually bent inwards, the whole posterior members short even to deformity, and the skull provided with enormous crests, as large as those of the most formidable beast of prey. All these, and many other modifications of its structure, as well as the various traits of habit and economy which result from them, manifestly degrade the orang in the scale of existence, and vindicate the position which has been assigned to the chimpanzee, as the first link in the chain of gradation that unites man with the inferior animals.

We have been thus particular in detailing the most prominent circumstances of organic structure upon which the superiority of the chimpanzee over the orang-outan depends, because it is in itself an interesting inquiry, and one which has occupied a good deal of attention among zoologists, as to which of these extraordinary beings should occupy the next rank to ourselves in the scale of animal life. This question being disposed of, we shall proceed at once to the history and description of the chimpanzee; commencing with the young animal, because it is best known, and afterwards collecting the most authentic information contained in the relations of travellers who profess to have observed the manners and habits of the adult.

The young chimpanzees usually brought to Europe, and of which we have had opportunities of examining two very fine specimens, have generally varied from twenty-four to thirty inches in height, and been considered from eighteen months to two years old. The state of their dentition, however, accorded more nearly with that of the human child at the age of four or five, and the fact has been adduced in support of the supposition, that these young animals were really older than their importers represented; but as this hypothesis rests upon the .presumption that the average development and duration of life in the chimpanzee are the same as in the human species— an hypothesis unsupported by observation, though, perhaps, countenanced, in some degree, by the organic proximity of the animal—it is not entitled to any great weight, particularly as we know that the young of all the lower animals have their organs and faculties developed at a much earlier period than the human infant.

The skull of the chimpanzee, even in very young subjects, is flattened above, and presents a low retiring forehead, and prominent crest or ridge over the eye-brows. In this respect it is unquestionably inferior to the young orang-outan, which possesses a remarkable elevation of forehead, without any super-orbital crests, and a rotundity of cranium greater than even in the human infant; but its mental capacity does not correspond with these external appearances, whilst the great development of its face and muzzle degrade it to a close approximation with the baboons. The face of the young chimpanzee, on the contrary, is much less prolonged, in relation to the capacity of the cranium; the proportions of its different parts, the forehead alone excepted, more nearly assimilate it to those of the human face, and the mouth, even in the adult animal, wants the enormous canine teeth which distinguish the Indian orang. The projection of the jaws, however, is much greater than in the human subject, and gives the profile of the face a concave form; the nose is short and nearly flat, with the nostrils opening from above, but without giving rise to those ideas of disgust which attend the loss of this organ in man; the muzzle is prominent, the mouth large, the lips thin, and the ears like the human, but larger, thinner, and placed higher up towards the crown of the head. The chest, as in man, is broader from side to side than from front to rear, the shoulders are wide, the belly protuberant, and the whole body very similar to that of the human subject. The principal difference, indeed, is the want of hips, which form so conspicuous, and, at the

same time, so symmetrical a part of the human form,
and which are altogether peculiar to man: their
defect in the chimpanzee gives his figure a meagre
and ungainly appearance.

The body is covered with long coarse black hair,
thickest on the back and shoulders, and but thinly
furnished on the breast, belly, and extremities; the
hair of the head is partially divided in the centre,
and falls down on either side, surrounding the ear,
and forming long bushy whiskers on the cheeks; the
face and ears are dark brown, except the muzzle,
which is of a pale copper colour: these parts are
naked, with the exception of the lips, and space immediately surrounding the mouth, which are furnished
with a thin white beard; the hands and feet are likewise naked, dark brown on the backs, but copper-
coloured on the soles and palms; and the legs, as
already observed, are provided with small calves.
Finally, the hair of the fore-arm, which is thin and
scanty, is reversed, or directed backwards towards
the elbow—a character which this animal likewise
partakes with the human subject, and which we shall
afterwards find common to the orang-outan, and
some of the other apes. The eyes of the chimpanzee
are placed rather closer together than in man; they
are besides smaller, and of a deep hazel colour.

The first distinct and trustworthy account which
we possess of the habits and intelligence of the young
chimpanzee, as observed in a state of captivity, is
that of the celebrated anatomists, Tyson and Cowper,
who dissected and published an admirable memoir
on the anatomy of this species, in the year 1699.
The individual observed by these philosophers was a
gentle, affectionate, and harmless creature; in its
passage to England it would embrace its acquaintances
on ship-board with the greatest tenderness, opening
the breasts of their shirts, and clasping its arms
around them. It held some smaller monkeys, which

were brought home in the same vessel, in utter aversion, always avoided the quarter of the ship where they were kept, and appeared to consider itself as a being of a superior order. After it had been for some time accustomed to wear clothes, it grew extremely fond of them, would put on some of them without any help, and then carry the rest to some of the crew or passengers for their assistance. It lay in its bed, placed its head on the pillow, and wrapped itself in the blankets just like a human being.

M. de Brosse, during his voyage to Angola in 1738, procured two young animals of this species, said to have been but twelve months old, and of which he has given the following interesting account. "These animals," says he, "had the sense to seat themselves at table like men; they ate of everything without distinction, made use of a knife, fork, and spoon, to cut and carry their food to the mouth, and drank wine and other liquors indifferently. When at table, they expressed their wants by protruding the lips, and uttering a grave and gentle sound, and if refused would get into a passion, and bite or pinch the arms of their attendants. The male was attacked by sickness during the passage; he gave himself all the airs, and demanded the same care and attendance, as a human being in like circumstances; he was even bled on two occasions in the right arm, and afterwards, whenever he found himself indisposed, he would come and hold up his arm to be bound, as if conscious of the benefit he had formerly derived from the operation."

Some of the circumstances here detailed were undoubtedly the result of education; but the last and most important of all was unquestionably an act of natural judgment on the part of the animal himself, and shows the extraordinary intelligence which this young creature possessed, even at its early age. An individual observed by M. de Buffon, in 1740, was

rather more sophisticated; but his account of its manners is valuable, as showing the high degree of
instruction which the chimpanzee is susceptible of
attaining, and the facility with which it acquires the
habit of imitating the actions of civilised man.
" This animal," says M. de Buffon, " always walked
upright on its hind-legs, even when carrying heavy
burthens.   Its air was melancholy, its deportment
grave, its movements measured, its disposition gentle
and very different from that of the other simiæ; it
had neither the impatience of the magot, the ferocity
of the baboon, nor the extravagance of the monkey;
a sign, a word, was sufficient to render it obedient,
whilst the others yielded only to the fear of chastisement.   I have seen this animal present its hand to
conduct the company to the door, or walk about
gravely with them through the room; I have seen it
sit at table, unfold its napkin, wipe its lips, make use
of a spoon or fork to carry its victuals to its mouth,
pour out its drink into a glass, touch glasses when
invited, go for its cup and saucer, carry them to the
table, pour out its tea, sweeten and leave it to cool,
and all this without any other instigation than the
signs or commands of its keeper, and sometimes even
of its own accord.   It was gentle and inoffensive; it
even approached you with a kind of respect, and as
if only seeking for caresses.   It was passionately
fond of sugar-plums; but ate indiscriminately of
all things, only preferring ripe and dry fruit to most
other aliments.   It would drink wine, but in small
quantities, and gladly left it for milk, tea, or any
other milder beverage."

All these actions were of course the result of
education; but the following account given by Dr.
Traill, of a specimen which he observed and dissected
in the year 1817, will place the manners and intelligence of the chimpanzee in a more natural, and, on
that account, more interesting light.   The subject of

Dr. Traill's paper was a female, and had been procured at the Isle of Princes, in the Gulf of Guinea,
whither it had been brought by a native trader from
the banks of the Gaboon. It was represented as a
young animal, much inferior, in point of size, to the
specimens often seen in the recesses of its native
forests; and Captain Payne, who brought it to
England, observed that it was at least eight or ten
inches shorter than another which he had seen in the
Isle of Princes.

"'When first our animal came on board,' says
Captain Payne, 'it shook hands with some of the
sailors, but refused its hand, with marks of anger, to
others without any apparent cause. It speedily,
however, became familiar with the crew, except one
boy, to whom it was never reconciled. When the
seamen's mess was brought on board it was a constant attendant; would go round and embrace each
person, whilst it uttered loud yells, and then seat
itself among them to share the repast.' When angry
it sometimes made a barking noise like a dog; at
other times it would cry like a pettish child, and
scratch itself with great vehemence. It expressed
satisfaction, especially on receiving sweetmeats, by a
sound like ' hem,' uttered in a grave tone. In warm
latitudes it was active and cheerful, but became
languid as it receded from the torrid zone; and on
approaching our shores it showed a disposition to
have a warm covering, and would roll itself carefully
up in a blanket when it retired to rest. It generally
walked on all-fours; and Captain Payne particularly
remarked that it never placed the palms of the hands
of its fore extremities on the ground, but, closing its
fists, rested on the knuckles—a circumstance also
noticed by Tyson, which was confirmed to me by a
young navy officer, who had been for a considerable
time employed in the rivers of Western Africa, and

had opportunities of observing the habits of this species.

"This animal did not seem fond of the erect posture, which it rarely affected, though it could run nimbly on two feet for a short distance. In this case, it appeared to aid the motion of its legs, by grasping the thighs with its hands; it had great strength in the fore-fingers of the superior extremities, for it would often swing by them on a rope for upwards of an hour without intermission. When first procured it was so thickly covered with hair, that the skin of the trunk and limbs was scarcely visible, until the long black hair was blown aside. At that period the skin was free from any disease; but after it had been some time at sea, its body was attacked by a scaly eruption, attended by excessive itching. This might partly be owing to improper diet, as it was often fed on salted beef and biscuit. It ate readily every sort of vegetable food; but, at first, it did not appear to relish flesh, though it seemed to take pleasure in sucking the leg-bone of a fowl. At that time it did not relish wine, but afterwards seemed to like it, though it never could endure ardent spirits. It once stole a bottle of wine, which it uncorked with its teeth, and began to drink. It showed a predilection for coffee, and was immoderately fond of sweet articles of food. It learned to feed itself with a spoon, to drink out of a glass, and showed a general disposition to imitate the actions of men. It was attracted by bright metals, seemed to take a pride in clothing, and often put a cocked hat on its head. It was dirty in its habits, and was never known to wash itself. It was afraid of fire-arms, and, on the whole, appeared a timid animal."

To this interesting account we shall only add a few observations which we have ourselves had an

opportunity of making upon two individuals recently
exhibited in this country. The first of these animals, which were both males, was shown at the
Egyptian Hall about four or five years ago, and was
accompanied by a young female orang-outan, of
about the same age, which afforded a very favourable opportunity of comparing the form, habits, and
intelligence of the two species. The chimpanzee,
though in a declining state of health, and rendered
peevish and irritable by bodily suffering, displayed
very superior marks of intelligence to his companion.
He was active, quick, and observant of everything
that passed around him ; no new visitor entered the
apartment in which he was kept, no old one left it,
without attracting his attention. The orang-outan,
on the contrary, exhibited a kind of settled melancholy, and a disregard of passing occurrences, almost
amounting to apathy; and, though in the enjoyment
of better health, was evidently much inferior to her
companion in quickness and observation.

On one occasion, when these animals were dining
upon potatoes and boiled chicken, surrounded as
usual by a large party of visitors, the orang-outan
allowed her plate to be taken away without betraying
the least apparent concern: not so, however, the
chimpanzee. We took advantage of an opportunity,
whilst his head was turned to observe a person coming
in, to secrete his plate also ; for a few seconds he
looked about to see what had become of it, but not
finding it, began to pout and fret like a disappointed
child, till at length, perceiving a young lady, who
happened to be standing near him, laughing, he flew
at her with the greatest fury, and would probably
have bitten or scratched her, had she not got beyond
his reach. Upon having his plate restored, he took
care to prevent the repetition of the joke, by holding
it firmly with one hand, whilst he fed himself with
the other. He was very cleanly in his mode of

feeding, and always used his fingers to select the
morsels from his plate; the orang, on the contrary,
frequently bent her head down, and ate indiscriminately like a dog, and was, in other respects,
much less attentive to personal cleanliness and propriety. The chimpanzee was far advanced in that
catarrhal affection which never fails to carry off the
apes after a few months' residence in our moist and
changeable climate; and though it was fine summer
weather at the time, it was amusing to see with what
care he kept his small blanket rolled round his person, as if conscious of the benefit he derived from it.
When forced to throw it aside, for the purpose of
gratifying the curiosity of his visitors, the mild but
expressive looks with which he reproached what he
no doubt considered the harsh and cruel commands
of his keeper, conveyed his feelings as plainly as if
they had been expressed in the most eloquent language. He died a few days after these observations
were made, and his companion did not long sur-
vive him.

The second chimpanzee which we have had an
opportunity of observing, and which was, perhaps,
more deserving of attention than any other specimen
on record, since it was not only unsophisticated by
the arts which itinerant showmen often teach these
animals, for the purpose of exciting public curiosity,
but had withstood the effects of the changeable and
unhealthy winter of 1835-6 without injury, and was,
at the time of making these observations, in the enjoyment of the most robust natural health and
spirits, was brought to Bristol during the preceding
autumn by Captain Wood, who procured it at Grand
Bassan, near the mouth of the Gambia; whither it
had been brought from a place about a hundred and
twenty miles up the country. Tommy, for such was
the name by which this individual was distinguished,
was said to be about eighteen or twenty months old,

and measured two feet in height from the crown of
the head to the sole of the foot. The natives from
whom Captain Wood procured him reported that
they had found him in company with his mother, who
was nursing him in her arms at the time; they
described her as a robust powerful animal, about
four feet six inches high, but were obliged to shoot
her before they could obtain possession of the young
one. During his voyage to England this little creature
had the free range of the ship, was always healthy
and active, frequently amused himself by climbing
among the ropes and rigging, and exhibited strong
marks of affection towards those on board who
treated him kindly. He was afterwards purchased
by the Zoological Society.

In the Zoological Gardens he occupied a room in
the keeper's apartments, in which a large cage was
constructed for his accommodation, and which was
kept as nearly as possible at a uniform temperature.
Two artificial trees had been erected in the cage, and
a rope suspended between them, to afford him an
opportunity of amusing himself by climbing or swinging; but unless when commanded by his keeper, to
whom he invariably showed a ready and willing
obedience, he generally preferred running about the
bottom of the cage, or amusing himself with the
visitors. When moving quickly his pace was a kind
of brisk canter, and, unless when his hands were employed in carrying anything, he invariably walked on
all-fours, leaning on the knuckles of the half-closed
fist, as observed by Tyson and Dr. Traill. At the
same time, the entire sole of the hind-foot was
brought into contact with the ground in the act of
progression, and as the arms were not very much
longer than the legs, the body was stooped or bent
at the shoulders, though the attitude, nevertheless,
partook more of the erect than the horizontal. All

these circumstances accord accurately with the habits
of the specimen already noticed, as having been exhibited at the Egyptian Hall some years ago; but
as that individual, like most of those previously seen
in Europe, was suffering from acute disease, the
gait and attitude might have been assumed from
debility.   Tommy's case, however, admits of no such
doubts;   he was perfectly active, healthy, and
vigorous, and unquestionably exhibited the mode of
progression natural to his species, and which had
been previously inferred from their anatomical
structure.

But though, when perfectly free and unrestrained,
his most usual mode of progression was on all-fours,
Tommy could, nevertheless, adopt the biped pace and
station with great ease, when occasion required it.
His feet, and particularly his heels, were broader
and better adapted for this purpose than those of
the orang-outan, and in walking upright he was not
under the same necessity of stretching out his arms,
or moving them to and fro, for the purpose of
securing his tottering equilibrium: the soles of his
feet, however, were flat, and this circumstance, united
to the greater distance and freer movements of his
hind-legs, gave his gait a waddling motion, similar
to that of human beings whose feet are affected with
the same deformity.   In many of his other actions
Tommy likewise approximated nearly to the human
species.   He was, without exception, the only animal
we have ever seen that could leap, or jump upon
his hind-feet, like man;   and this feat he often performed, both on the floor of his cage, and in descending from his tree, or from the bars of the cage, up
which he often climbed for the purpose of seeing
over the heads of the spectators.   He frequently indulged, too, in a kind of rude stamping dance, perfectly similar to that of a child of three or four years

old, only that it was executed with greater force and confidence. All this arose from the uninterrupted spirits and buoyancy natural to the infant mind; he was at all times cheerful, lively, and perpetually in motion, from sunrise to sunset, either jumping, dancing, or cantering about his cage, romping and playing with the spectators, or amusing himself by looking out at the window.

He did not often climb up his tree, unless at the command of his keeper; he appeared, indeed, to be upon the whole but an indifferent climber, particularly when compared with the orang-outan, and generally preferred the level surface of the ground; whether it was that his tree was not properly constructed, or that he was too heavy and corpulent: but from his manifest awkwardness in performing this action, and his evident preference of the level surface, it is highly probable, as, indeed, most travellers have affirmed, that the progression and habits of the species are more terrestrial than arborial, and that they ascend trees principally, if not solely, in search of food. When ordered to seat himself in his swing, Tommy did so with great good humour, stretching out his foot to some of the company to set him in motion. We observed that he used the right hand in preference to the left, and had obviously greater power and facility of action with this than with the opposite member. In the human subject this has generally been attributed to the effects of education; but in Tommy, at least, it was a natural action, since he was perfectly unsophisticated in this respect: and it would be a highly interesting inquiry to ascertain whether the same preference may not be exhibited in other apes, and consequently how far it may depend upon some necessary and inherent principle of the animal conformation, rather than upon mere education. Dr. Traill mentions that when his animal walked upon

the hind-feet, "it appeared to aid the motion of the
legs by grasping the thighs with the fore-hands;"
Tommy never had recourse to this mode of assisting
his biped progression'; and we apprehend that Dr.
Traill's specimen resorted to it merely from the
weakness and debility incident to its declining health,
just as very old and infirm people are remarked to
do in similar circumstances.

Though not fond of being made the object of it,
Tommy dearly loved a practical joke, and played it
off with a great deal of cunning and circumspection.
On one occasion, when a carpenter was introduced
to make some necessary alterations in his cage, we
were greatly amused by witnessing the waggeries
which he practised upon the intruder; now pulling
his hair, or plucking off his paper cap, and again
running off with his tools, or even trying to trip him up.
All this was carried on with the utmost gravity, and
with an uncommon degree of cunning: he uniformly
pretended to be engaged at the farther end of the
cage, and took an opportunity of approaching suddenly when he thought he was unperceived. At
length, finding the carpenter's back turned, and apparently unable to resist the temptation, he seized
the occasion to administer him so sound a box on
the ear, that the keeper was obliged to interfere and
put an end to the sport. On another occasion he
had got a small dog into his cage, which he appeared
to have taken in hand with the intention either of
trying its temper, or improving its manners, and
which he was subjecting to very rough discipline.
He beat it, cuffed it, and pulled its ears and tail;
and when the poor brute exhibited any marks of resentment at such unprovoked and unmerited treatment, it was in the highest degree ludicrous to
witness the mock gravity and astonishment which
Tommy's countenance exhibited, as if he was actually

surprised at the dog's impudence, whilst at the same
time he held his uplifted hand over him in a
threatening attitude, and regarded him with a fixed
and angry look, projecting his lips and uttering a
deep guttural sound.

He was very fond of being tickled, and when
under the operation kicked about his arms and feet
in the greatest delight imaginable; he evidently
tried to laugh too; his eyes twinkled, his mouth
and lips were widely opened, the muscles of his
cheeks drawn up, and his whole countenance expressive of pleasure; but his face had not the peculiar expression which characterises the laughter
of the human subject. He appeared not to like
children, and never let slip an opportunity of
scratching or pulling the hair or clothes of such as
came in his way; but his conduct in this respect
was not accompanied with any signs of anger or
antipathy, and was perhaps the result of jealousy
rather than of hatred. Though generally good
humoured, he could not bear to be tantalised, or
refused anything he happened to take a fancy for;
he then lost his temper, tried to scratch or bite, and
uttered shrill and angry cries, at the same time
regarding you intently, whilst his whole countenance
was inflamed with passion; his resentment was,
however, soon over, and he would immediately
begin to romp and play again as if nothing had
happened. In his habits he was peculiarly cleanly,
generally climbed to the top of his tree to satisfy the
necessities of nature, and invariably pulled up his
swinging rope after him, and held it in his hand or
between his teeth to prevent it from being soiled.
He made a good deal of noise in eating, and the
act of swallowing was distinctly audible; we have
likewise seen him pick his teeth, clean his nails, and
perform many other similar acts which have been

generally considered as peculiar to the human species.

The mental powers of this young animal were of a very high order, as may be inferred from the foregoing history of his conduct and actions. His intelligence was altogether different from instinct, as well as from those qualities which we denominate sagacity in the dog and elephant. Where the common monkey acts from impulse alone, his conduct appeared to be prompted by prudence and forethought; and, in fact, the nature of his mind seemed to differ from that of man, not so much in species as in degree. The real, and as far as we have been able to observe, the only difference, leaving out of the question those qualities which belong to us as moral and accountable beings, consisted in the faculty of forming abstract ideas, which are altogether peculiar to the human race, and of which the invaluable gift of language is one of the immediate consequences. But with this exception, our young chimpanzee was unquestionably capable of forming very extensive combinations of ideas, and of reasoning with great quickness and accuracy upon the relations of material qualities and objects. All his actions were those of a human infant; and though his powers, both mental and physical, were, comparatively speaking, more developed, he had all the gaiety, playfulness, and curiosity of the child, the same innocence, the same gentleness, the same affection, and the same restless, pettish, and inconstant disposition; even his natural appetites and tastes were similar; he had the same natural fondness for sweets, the same propensity to eat at all times and of all substances, and equally preferred milk and tea to spirituous and fermented liquors.

In natural shrewdness and sagacity, however, Tommy greatly excelled the human infant, and,

indeed for that matter, many grown individuals.
The cerebral development of the chimpanzee's skull
has been compared with that of the human idiot;
but whatever similarity may exist in the crania, there
is certainly no resemblance whatever between the
respective intellects; and this is a strong proof of
the caution which should be observed, and the little
value to be placed, upon those analogical reasonings
which pretend to deduce mental phenomena from
material developments. But it is more particularly
in interpreting your wishes and intentions from your
looks, tones, and gestures, that this animal exhibited
the most wonderful quickness of apprehension, vastly
superior, indeed, to that of ordinary man, and only
equalled by what we observe in deaf and dumb
people, whose defect of speech is compensated by this
unusual acuteness of observation. We have seen
Tommy on one occasion, when commanded by his
keeper to bring him the core of an apple which he
had thrown down on the floor of his cage, manifest
the greatest anxiety to obey, though much perplexed
to discover what it was he was required to do, as
he evidently did not comprehend the nature of the
order. He moved towards the window, stopped and
looked back at the keeper, and then at the company;
perceiving by their looks that he was mistaken, he
returned, put his hand upon his swing as if to mount,
again looked round to see if he was right, and was
manifestly much puzzled what to do; at length one
of the spectators pointed to the core of the apple, he
stretched his hand towards it, looked inquiringly at
the keeper, hesitated for a moment till he received
the expected nod of approbation, and then lifted and
carried it to his attendant without farther hesitation.
The great interest attached to the chimpanzee, as
approaching so nearly to ourselves in the scale of
animal life, has induced us to dwell longer upon

this part of his history than we had originally intended, but we hope without either wearying the patience or exhausting the curiosity of our readers. A thorough acquaintance with the manners and intelligence of the young animal, as accurately observed and related by zoologists accustomed to such investigations, was besides necessary to enable us to form a just estimate of the habits and economy attributed to the adult in his native forests, and of the degree of credit to which the accounts of different travellers are entitled. On this part of the subject, however, we have to regret the scanty and imperfect nature of our information: we have, comparatively speaking, few accurate details relating to the natural habits of the adult chimpanzee; and this defect is the more to be lamented, as the character of their intellectual powers displayed in the young specimens whose history we have related, afford strong grounds for believing that the manners and economy of these animals would offer many curious points of resemblance with savage life, and perhaps afford some valuable data for illustrating the probable condition of man previous to the origin of civilised society. We are told, indeed, that in a state of nature, the wild chimpanzees erect rude huts by intertwining the branches and leaves of trees; that their stature approaches that of man; that they walk upright, arm themselves with clubs, live in a kind of rude society, unite to expel beasts of prey and other large animals from the cantonments which they occupy, attack and beat the negroes whom they find alone in the woods, and occasionally kidnap the young negresses, whom they carry with them to the deepest recesses of the forests, and subject to the most frightful and revolting captivity; but their domestic economy, the nature of the union or intercourse which subsists between the sexes, the bonds by which they are united in society, their passions, appetites, customs, and a thousand other inquiries of equal interest, have been totally neglected: nor is it probable, in the present state of African society, that we shall have much light thrown upon these subjects, at least for some time to come. The habitat of the species, as at present known, extends from the banks of the Gambia to the southern boundary of Benguela, thus comprehending the whole coast of the Gulf of Guinea, and embracing an extent of thirteen degrees of latitude on each side of the line. They are found chiefly in the interior of the country, and, as it would appear, more frequently upon hills of moderate elevation than in the level plains. The following brief extracts contain all the information we possess with regard to their history and manners.

The earliest account which we find of the chimpanzee,—and a highly interesting notice it is, though it has hitherto escaped the notice of zoologists, and even of the celebrated Camper, who has expressly written upon the history of the apes,—is contained in the *Periplus* of Hanno, an account of a voyage round the western shores of Africa, performed about five hundred years before the Christian era. "For three days," says the Carthaginian admiral, "we passed along a burning coast, and at length reached a bay called the Southern Horn. In the bottom of this bay we found an island similar to that already mentioned; this island contained a lake, that, in its turn contained another island, which was inhabited by wild men. The greater number of those we saw were females; they were covered with hair, and our interpreters called them *Gorilloi*. We were unable to secure any of the men, which fled to the mountains, and defended themselves with stones; as to the women, we caught three of them, but they so bit and scratched us, that we found it impossible to bring

F

them along; we therefore killed and flayed them, and carried their hides to Carthage." There can be no question as to the application of this curious passage; though Hanno invariably uses the terms ' men and women, it is no more than what many travellers have done since his time, whilst the hairy bodies of the animals, the nature of the resistance which they offered to their captors, and the final catastrophe, all identify them with the chimpanzee; and even the name *gorilloi*, dropping the Greek termination *oi*, bears a very close similarity to the word *drill*, which is still said to be the name of the species on some parts of the coast of Guinea.

When the natives of modern Europe began to hold commercial intercourse with this part of Africa, in the early part of the sixteenth century, the chimpanzee, as might be expected, was too extraordinary an animal to escape notice; and accordingly we find numerous accounts of his form and habits in the works of the earlier voyagers. These are for the most part meagre and credulous; but we unfortunately possess none more satisfactory, and must therefore content ourselves with a few short extracts from those which appear to be most authentic and trustworthy. Of these, the first in point of time is by Andrew Battel, an English sailor, who was taken prisoner by the Portuguese in 1589, and sent to their settlements in Angola, where he resided for many years. His adventures were afterwards published by Purchass, and bear every mark of truth. "There are two kinds of monsters," says Battel, "common to the woods of Angola: the largest of them is called *Pongo* in their language, and the other *Enjocko*. The pongo is in all his proportions like a man (except the legs, which have no calves), but he is of gigantic height. The face, hands, and ears of these animals are without hair; their bodies are covered, but not very thickly, with hair of a dunnish colour. When they walk on the ground, it is upright, with the hands on the nape of the neck. They sleep on trees, and make a covering over their heads to shelter them from the rain. They eat no flesh, but feed on nuts and other fruits; nor have they any understanding beyond instinct. When the people of the country travel through the woods they make fires in the night, and in the morning when they are gone, the pongos will come and sit round it till it goes out, for they do not possess sagacity enough to lay on more wood. They go in bodies and kill many negroes who travel in the woods. When elephants happen to come and feed where they are, they will fall on them, and so beat them with their clubbed fists and sticks, that they are forced to run away roaring. The grown pongos are never taken alive, owing to their strength, which is so great that ten men cannot hold one of them. The young hang upon their mother's belly with their hands clasped about her. Many of them are taken by shooting the mothers with poisoned arrows." Battel observes further, that when one of these animals dies, the others cover the body with leaves and branches; and Purchass adds, in a note to his narrative, that the author had informed him in the course of conversation, that he had known a young negro who had been carried away by the pongos, and lived an entire year in their society; and that on his return he reported that they had offered him no harm, and that they were of the stature of ordinary men, but much thicker and stouter.

This plain and unadorned account bears unquestionable marks of authenticity: but the author appears in some degree to have mixed up the history of the mandrill with that of the chimpanzee (if his pongo be not in reality a species hitherto undescribed)—a circumstance rendered more probable by the fact that his narrative was only written down from memory after his return to England, and many years after the events which it records took place. Of the enjocko, which appears to agree more nearly with what we know of the adult chimpanzee from other sources, he has given no farther account, nor is the name mentioned by any other traveller.

Francis Pyrard de Laval, a Frenchman, who published his travels in 1619, relates " that a species of animal called *Barris* is found in the province of Sierra Leone, which is large and muscular, and so sagacious, that if bred up and instructed from youth, it may be taught to perform all the duties of a household servant. These animals," continues he, " generally walk upright, upon the hind-feet only ; they will pound grain or any other substance in a mortar, go to the well, fill their water-jars and carry them home on their heads ; but, if some person be not at hand to relieve them from their burthen on their arrival, they let the jar fall, and begin to cry on seeing it broken."

M. de la Brosse, from whom we have already extracted a short notice relating to the manners of the young animal, and whose narrative appears to be entitled to every confidence, confirms many of the facts stated by Battel and Pyrard. " The *Quimpezés*" (for thus he writes the name), says he, " endeavour to surprise the negresses, whom they carry into the woods and force to live with them, feeding them plentifully, however, and in other respects doing them no injury. I knew a negress at Lowango who had lived three years among these animals. They grow to the height of six or seven feet, and are possessed of matchless strength and courage. They build huts and arm themselves with clubs ; their face is smooth, their nose flat, their ears without inverted rims, their body covered with long hair, thinnest in front, their belly large, their heel elevated about half an inch from the ground, and they walk either upon two feet or four, just as their fancy prompts them."

Smith, a man of sense and experience, who was sent by the African Company in 1744 to visit and report upon the state of their settlements on the Coast of Guinea, and who has left a very interesting account of his journey, writes of the chimpanzee in the following terms, calling it, however, by the name of mandrill, which indeed appears to belong more properly to this animal than to the baboon to which zoologists have applied it. "I shall now," says he, "describe a strange sort of animal, called by the white men in this country a mandrill; but why it is so called I know not; nor did I ever hear of the name before; neither can those who call them so tell, unless it be from their near resemblance to a human creature, though nothing at all like an ape. Their bodies, when full grown, are as big as a middle-sized man's, their legs much shorter, and their feet longer, their arms and hands in proportion. Their head is monstrously big, and their face broad and flat, without any other hair but on the eye-brows, the nose very small, the mouth wide, and the lips thin. The face, which is covered by a white skin, is monstrously ugly, being all over wrinkled as with old age, the teeth broad and very yellow; the hands have no more hair than the face, but the same white skin, though all the rest of the body is covered with long black hair like a bear. They never go upon all-fours like apes, but cry when vexed or teased, just like children. It is said that the males often attack and use violence to the black women whenever they meet them alone in the woods."

Our last quotation shall be from Lieut. Matthews of the Royal Navy, who resided at Sierra Leone during the years 1785-6-7, and whose letters, describing the country and its productions, were published in 1788. Of these animals he says, "The chimpanzees, or japanzees, are also natives of this country, and when caught young become very tame and familiar; extremely fond of clinging to those they like, and very sensible of good or ill treatment. I have now a young one in my possession who very readily comes when called by his name; but if I push him from me or strike him, or even do not regard his advances, by showing him encouragement, he turns sullen and sulky, will not take the least notice when called, or take anything from me till I put him into good humour again. Their appearance when they sit greatly resembles that of an old negro, except that the hair on their heads is straight and black like an Indian's. They generally take up their abode near some deserted town or village where the papau-tree grows in abundance, of the fruit of which they are very fond, and build huts nearly in the form the natives build their houses, which they cover with leaves; but these are only for the females and young to lie in; the males always lie on the outside. If one of them is shot, the rest immediately pursue the destroyer of their friend; and the only means to escape their vengeance is to part with your gun, which they directly seize upon with all the rage imaginable, tear it to pieces, and give over the pursuit."

We have preferred giving these extracts in the words of the original authors, that the reader may be the better able to appreciate their just value, and, by applying to them the authentic information which he already possesses on the subject of the habits and intelligence of the young animal, thereby judge of the credibility due to the accounts here given of the adult. Lieut. Matthews's relation is particularly valuable, not only from its being of more recent date than the others, but because it is written by a man of education and character, who was actually residing in the country at the moment, and who evidently describes what he himself had witnessed, and not the vague and exaggerated tales of ignorant and credulous native reporters. At the same time, it must be observed that, whilst it adds some new and interesting facts to those already recorded, it confirms in the fullest and most satisfactory manner the principal points in the narratives of former observers, and, combined with these, gives what we have every reason to consider as a tolerably accurate history of the habits and economy of this wonderful animal in his native forests.

All these accounts agree in representing the habits of the chimpanzee as terrestrial rather than arborial, thus fully confirming the conclusions which have been already deduced from the anatomical structure of the animal, and affording another and most important confirmation of his specific superiority, as compared with the orangs. In fact, the greater straightness of the legs, the breadth of the soles, the superior width of the pelvis, and above all, the approximate equality in the length of the anterior and posterior extremities, qualify the chimpanzee for walking and running upon the surface of the earth, as completely as they disqualify him for moving with facility or rapidity among the branches and trees of the forest; and it is therefore highly probable, that, in accordance with the universal testimony of travellers, he builds his hut, travels about and resides entirely on the ground, and only climbs trees for the purpose of procuring the fruits and nuts which serve him for food. In this respect, it will be afterwards seen that he differs essentially from the orangs, as he appears likewise to do in his more

active habits, social disposition, and superior intelligence. The circumstances of his building or inhabiting huts, residing on the ground, and living in
society, elevate this animal materially above the
sluggish, solitary, and arborial orangs of the Indian
isles, and countenance the probability of his occasionally erect attitude and biped progression, and
even of his presumed use of a club to attack or defend himself; a circumstance, perhaps, rendered
necessary, in consequence of the smaller development of his canine teeth, as compared with those
of the orangs and gibbons. In short, all his actions
and habits, as well as his physical structure and
mental endowments, combine to elevate him above
the other simiæ, and to place him in a station inferior only to that occupied by man himself, in the
scale of animated nature.

CHAPTER IV.

Young Orang-Outan.

Apes *continued.*—The ORANGS (*Satyrus*).

THE name "*orang-outan**," literally signifying "*wild man,*" is a Malay word, exclusively applied to the *simia satyrus* of Linnæus, the *pithecus satyrus*

---

* This word is often written *orang-outang*, but improperly; *outan* in the Malay language means *wild*, as *orang-outan*, wild man; *cambing-outan*, wild goat, &c.; *outang*, on the contrary, signifies a *robber*. *Utan*, which is also sometimes used, is the French form, and does not give the proper pronunciaton of the word in our language.

of more recent zoologists. The generic name of *pithecus* applied to the orangs by M. G. St. Hilaire is a misnomer : it properly belongs to the magot or Barbary baboon (*papio inuus*), and can only produce error and confusion by being transferred to the present species. The term *satyrus* is in all respects more appropriate, and free from objection : it was applied by the ancients to an indeterminate species of simia, and has always been the specific name of the orang-outan among modern zoologists. This species, long confounded with the chimpanzee, is, however, a very distinct animal, and greatly inferior, in the most important of those points of organic structure which constitute their common approximation to the human type, and upon which depends their respective positions in the scale of animal existence. We have already seen, in our review of the form and conformation of the chimpanzee, that, though unquestionably fitted for climbing trees, the *tout-ensemble* of structure, the comparative shortness of his arms, the breadth of his feet, the straight and muscular character of his legs, &c., all adapt him to terrestrial rather than arborial progression ; we have seen this inference borne out by the universal testimony of travellers, who have observed the adult animal in his native regions ; and finally, we have seen it confirmed by the habits of the various young specimens which have been at different times brought to this country. We have seen that, though these young animals do not habitually walk erect upon two feet, they are, nevertheless, perfectly capable of doing so when occasion requires it; and that their equilibrium is sufficiently steady in this attitude, without the assistance of the waving motions of the arms to which the other apes have recourse in similar circumstances: and we have seen that in the act of nursing their young, or when the hands are otherwise engaged, the adult chimpanzees, in their native climes, actually do adopt the erect posture and assume the biped pace. We have likewise seen, in the minuter actions of jumping, stamping, &c. how closely this animal approaches to man, and upon these traits of habit and structure we justified the pre-eminence which most zoologists are agreed in assigning to the chimpanzee over the rest of the lower animals.

But, though the structure and habits of the orangoutan do not raise him so high in the scale of animal life, though the great length of his arms, the narrowness and oblique articulation of his feet, and the general weakness and flexibility of his posterior extremities, degrade him from the human type, make the upright attitude and biped motion a matter of constraint and difficulty, and, by pre-eminently qualifying him for an arborial life, proportionally diminish his aptitude to move or travel on a level surface, it cannot be denied, at the same time, that he is second only to the chimpanzee in these qualifications, and that he as greatly excels the other apes in intelligence as he does in size and strength.

In detailing the natural history of the chimpanzee, we commenced with that of the young animal, because, from being frequently brought to Europe, its habits have been carefully observed, and its history is consequently more authentic than that of the adult : we shall pursue the same plan with regard to the orang-outan, and for the same reason, namely, that from the authentic manners of the young, as recorded by accurate and trust-worthy observers, we may be enabled to appreciate the degree of credit to which the relations of travellers are entitled, who profess to have observed and described the adult animal.

The first peculiarity which strikes us, in examining the orang-outan, is the singular disproportion which exists in the length of the anterior, compared with the posterior extremities. This is so great, that when the animal stands upright upon the hind-legs, it can almost touch the ground with the fingers of the pectoral members, whilst the abdominal are so short, that their whole length barely equals a third of the entire height. Upon closer examination, we find that the leg, instead of being in the same straight line as the thigh, is distorted in such a manner, that the knees are thrown outwards, and that the feet are so obliquely articulated at the ankles, that their soles are turned inwards and opposed to one another. This at once accounts for the great difficulty which the orang-outan has been observed to experience in preserving the upright posture, or walking upon the surface of the earth, but it equally demonstrates the amazing facility with which it has been observed to climb trees and make its way through the forests. In fact, its whole structure is pre-eminently adapted to an arborial life. The great length of the fore-arms vastly increases its sphere of action among the branches, whilst the perfect flexibility of the posterior members, and the extravagant length and curvature of the fingers and toes, which, even in the act of walking on a level surface, are habitually doubled inwards, increases its powers of prehension to such a degree, as well nigh to disqualify it for every other species of locomotion. The thumb of the fore and the great toe of the hind feet are opposable to the other fingers, but these members are still shorter and weaker than those of the chimpanzee; and it has been observed that, gene-rally speaking, the hind-thumb of the orang-outan is without a nail, and has but a single phalanx. The celebrated anatomist, Camper, who first remarked this peculiarity, found it in seven different speci-mens; Dr. Clarke Abel observed the same cha-

racter in three other individuals, and is strongly
inclined to consider it as a specific distinction between the orang of Borneo and that of Sumatra
and Java, hinting, that those described by MM.
Tilesius and F. Cuvier, which had the nail and two
joints of the hind-thumbs regularly developed, were
most probably from the latter locality. In favour of
this supposition may certainly be adduced the
instance of the adult Sumatran animal, which Dr.
Abel has himself described, and partly figured, in the
15th volume of the ' Asiatic Researches,' in which the
nails are very distinctly marked on the hind-thumbs of
the engraving, though they are not mentioned in the
text ; but, on the other hand, we have ourselves
ascertained that the adult female brought from Sumatra by Sir Stamford Raffles, and now in the
museum of the Zoological Society, is absolutely
deficient of thumb-nails, whilst the equally adult male
from Borneo, formerly described by Wurmb, in the
' Transactions of the Batavian Society,' had these
organs very perfectly developed, though they were
comparatively smaller than the nails of the other toes.
It is plain, then, that to whatever cause this singular
anomaly is to be attributed, it cannot be considered
as distinguishing the Bornean orang from that of
Sumatra ; much less can it be considered as a specific
character, since one of the individuals examined by
Camper had a perfect nail and unguinal phalanx on
the thumb of the right foot, whilst both were wanting
on that of the left. The most singular circumstance
attending this matter is, that the defect of nail is
always found to be accompanied by an equal defect
of the terminal or nail-joint, and that these defects
should be more common in female than in male specimens. In two very beautiful and accurate models,
taken from the living animals by a native artist at
Calcutta, and now in the collection of the Zoological

Society, the sexes are thus distinguished; but on the other hand, it is to be observed, that Dr. Abel's own specimen was destitute of thumb-nails, though a male, whilst M. F. Cuvier's, which was a female, possessed them. It is very evident, then, that this character is neither specific nor sexual, since it is found occasionally in specimens of both sexes, and from all localities. To what then are we to attribute so singular and apparently so capricious an anomaly, of which there is not another known example throughout the whole animal kingdom? Does nature, in this solitary instance alone, disregard the general laws of uniformity by which she has circumscribed the organic development of different species within certain pre-determined and invariable boundaries, and dispense, in the case of the orang alone, with those immutable forms and relations to which the rest of the animated creation has been subjected? Or does this variable and anomalous character arise from an intentional mutilation performed by these intelligent animals upon their offspring, for the purpose of counteracting some disadvantage in their economy, with which we are unacquainted? These are questions, which, however interesting, it is impossible for us to solve in the present state of our knowledge; we must therefore be contented with the truth of the fact, and wait patiently till more accurate and extensive observation gives us some certain clue to its cause. The simple fact of the matter most probably is, that the deficiency in question is natural to the orangs; and that being an exception to a general law of the animal structure, it is more frequently counteracted, and subject to greater anomaly, than in the case of the general law itself, owing to that innate power by which nature invariably tends to produce uniformity in all her laws and operations.

There is another character in the organization of the orang-outan, which it is necessary that we should briefly explain, since it has been supposed by many excellent anatomists, to be the principal, if not the only impediment that prevents this animal from uttering articulate sounds, and, in fact, from speaking as well, or nearly as well, as ourselves. That this idea is altogether gratuitous and unfounded might be very readily demonstrated ; it were easy to show that the faculty of speech is peculiar to man, not so much on account of the perfection of his organic structure, as of the superior constitution of his mind, and especially of that power of abstraction and generalization which he alone enjoys, and by which he is enabled to make his words the signs and interpreters of his thoughts. We shall not enter upon this purely metaphysical investigation at present ; but it is at least due to the talents of the celebrated men who have pro- mulgated these opinions, to examine what they are, and particularly as the structure in question, though unconnected with the faculty of speech, is no doubt an important agent in other parts of the animal's economy. It consists of one, or occasionally two*, laryngal sacks of large size, communicating with the lungs, and capable of being distended with air or contracted by its expulsion, at the will of the animal. When two exist, the one on the right side is always of large dimensions, occupying the whole extent of the neck, even beyond the collar-bone, and when distended appearing externally

---

* As it is now ascertained that there are probably more than one species of orang, this diversity of structure may possibly be found to characterise different species ; and we earnestly recommend future observers to be particular in ascer- taining whether this anomaly be not connected with the *habitat* of the specimen, or with the osteological differences pointed out by Professor Owen.

in the form of a large goitre, the resemblance being still farther increased by the nakedness and oily appearance of the skin of the neck in this part: the left sack is always small, and often united with the right so as to form but one, though in all cases it preserves a separate opening into the larynx. The immediate and most obvious effect of this conformation is in deepening the tone and increasing the volume of the animal's voice; but it is not improbable, that these laryngal sacks, communicating as they do immediately with the lungs, may serve the farther purpose of reservoirs to contain a sufficient supply of air for the necessities of the circulating system, during the partial impediments which the rapid flight of the animal among the trees of the forest must occasionally cause in the act of respiration. However this may be, it is certain the conformation in question is not confined to the orang-outan. It is equally conspicuous in the *siamang* (*hylobates syndactylus*); Dr. Traill found similar sacks, though of smaller dimensions, in the chimpanzee, whilst Camper mentions them as existing in the magot (*papio inuus*), and various other simiæ, the only difference being that they are single in the latter, and, most commonly, double in the real apes.

These general observations on the more important characters of the orang-outan being premised, we now come to the minor details of its structure, which, though less apparent, are not less essential, in the influence which they exert upon the habits and economy of its life. Among these must be noticed the extreme length of the fingers both before and behind, their character of being naturally bent or doubled inwards, and the remarkable shortness and backward position of the thumbs, modifications which, added to those already mentioned, all tend to increase the animal's powers of prehension, and

qualify it for an arborial life. The hips are without
callosities, and destitute of the large and powerful
muscles which give them their form and rotundity
in the human subject, and enable man to preserve
the erect attitude and biped progression ; the legs
likewise are without calves, and the whole posterior
extremities assimilate more nearly to the form and
proportions of our arms and hands than to those of
our legs and thighs. The head of the young orang-
outan bears a much nearer resemblance to that of
the human infant than the head of the chimpanzee ;
the forehead is broad and elevated, the capacity of
the cranium extensive ; but the neck is short and
thick, even to deformity, whilst the favourable circumstances which so strongly mark the cerebral
development of the young subject are speedily obliterated in the adult, and give place to a relative
contraction and flattening of the skull, and a proportional development of the bones of the face, scarcely
to be anticipated in the progress of any single species
from youth to maturity, and altogether unknown in
the case of any other animal. The muzzle is very
protuberant, the mouth large, the lips thin and ex-
tensible, the nose flat, and the ears remarkably small
and ill formed.

The singular changes, which the cranium of the
orangs undergoes as the animals advance in years,
are alone sufficient to demonstrate the insignificance
of the characters employed by MM. Cuvier and
Geoffroy St. Hilaire, for the purpose of distinguishing the different genera of the quadrumana. These
naturalists imagined that in the facial angle, employed by the celebrated Camper to distinguish the
different *varieties* of the human race, they had discovered the real key to *generic* distinction among
the simiæ and simiadæ ; but the absurdity into
which they were led by the practical application of

this principle, in considering the young and adult orangs, not only as distinct species, but even as different genera, is a sufficient proof of its worthlessness; since it places the young animal at the head of all the quadrumana, even before the chimpanzee, and degrades the adult to a level with the dog-headed baboons. It is evident, indeed, that so evanescent a character can never possess any value as a *generic* distinction: not only does it vary in *individuals* according to age and sex, but likewise in different *varieties* of the same *species*. It was in this latter sense alone that it was employed by Camper, and this we conceive to be its only legitimate application. It may be properly and usefully employed to distinguish the different *varieties* of the human *species*, or of domestic animals, which, like the dog, are subject to the same modifying influences, simply *because it is variable in the species, and constant in the variety ;* but this very reason renders it valueless as a principle of *generic* distinction, since its application would necessarily involve the absurdity of making all the mere varieties of the common dog, not different species, but actually different genera ; as was originally the case with MM. Cuvier and Geoffroy, in the instance of the young and adult orangs.

The whole body of the orang-outan is covered with long coarse hair, of a deep vinous red colour, thickest and longest on the head, back, and shoulders, but more sparingly furnished on the breast and belly. The face, ears, palms of the hands, and soles of the feet, are the only parts absolutely naked ; they are of a bright copper or brick colour, but the prevailing colour of the skin in general, as seen through the hair, is bluish grey, with a broad copper-coloured stripe, however, passing down each side from the arm-pits to the navel. The hair of the head is di-

rected forwards towards the face, and that of the fore-
arm reversed towards the elbow ; in other respects,
the disposition and quality of the hair and colours
offer no peculiarity.

In relating the history of the chimpanzee, we have
seen with what facility that animal can maintain the
erect posture, and walk upon two feet. The structure
of the orang-outan, as just detailed, will have already
convinced us of the difficulties which that animal
must encounter in performing similar acts, and the
most accurate and authentic observations confirm
our inferences upon this subject. Dr. Abel and
M. F. Cuvier both declare, that it was utterly impossible for the orangs which they describe to maintain a perfectly erect attitude, and those which we
have ourselves had an opportunity of observing
showed no greater aptitude in conforming to this
posture than a well-trained dancing-dog. All their
motions, whether standing or attempting to walk
upon the hind-legs, were constrained and awkward
in the highest degree : they trod only on the external
edge of the foot, whilst their long toes were invariably bent inwards along the sole, like a half-closed
fist, or like the claws of the *sloths, ant-eaters,* and
pangolins ; their long arms were elevated over the
head and waved from side to side, or occasionally
touched the ground lightly, for the purpose of recovering the tottering equilibrium of the body, momentarily
deranged by the vacillating and unnatural gait, and
their pace was altogether slower and more difficult
than the biped progression of many of the inferior
simiæ. When obliged to move along a level surface,
and left perfectly unconstrained, the orang-outan,
like the chimpanzee and other apes, prefers walking
on all-fours ; but there is an essential difference in
his mode of performing this action from what we
have observed in the case of any other species. He

does not tramp upon the whole sole of the foot like
the chimpanzee, nor has he either the confidence or
facility of that species in preserving an erect attitude.
M. Geoffroy says that, first leaning upon the knuckles
of the half-closed fore-hands, he raises both hind-legs
at the same time, and projects the body forwards
between the long arms; these, again, are advanced in
their turn, to support the body in a new projection,
and thus the progressive motion is performed by a
series of successive swings, in all respects similar to
the pace of a decrepid man moving upon crutches. It
was too hasty a generalization of these facts, as observed in the orang-outan, that led M. Geoffroy St.
Hilaire, and other naturalists, to attribute this mode
of progression to the apes in general; the truth is,
however, at least as far as our own observations extend, that it is entirely confined to individuals of the
present species when in the last stages of disease,
and that the weakness and constraint of motions are
to be attributed to the sickly and debilitated condition of the individuals observed. Individuals in
robust health never rest the entire weight of the
body upon the anterior extremities; but, like all the
other apes, walk upon the hind-legs, touching the
ground occasionally on either side with the fore-
hands, in order to preserve their equilibrium; and
so necessary is this action, that even when held by
one hand, the young orang is unable to walk upon
the hind-feet without occasionally assisting its progress
by resting upon the other. In a state of repose it
often sits cross-legged, in the manner of the orientals,
and when disposed to sleep stretches itself out at full
length, either on the back or side, draws the legs close
up to the body and crosses the arms upon the breast.
The reports of various travellers, confirmed in a
great measure by the interesting observations of
Dr. Abel, afford strong grounds for believing that

the orangs, in their native forests, construct rude
beds or huts in the trees, by intertwining the leaves
and branches, thus providing a secure retreat, equally
impervious to the ardour of the sun by day, and the
heavy dews of a tropical night. But the habits and
intelligence of these animals will be best learned
from the following extracts.

M. F. Cuvier, who has well described a young
female orang, brought to Paris in 1808 by a M.
Decaen, an officer in the French navy, has recorded
the following valuable observations relating to its
manners and economy. "This animal," says M.
Cuvier, " used its hands as we generally do our own,
but with rather less facility, arising from want of
experience ; it generally employed them to convey its
food to its mouth, but sometimes also made use of its
long lips for this purpose, and in drinking always
sucked up the liquid, as all long-lipped animals do. It
consulted the sense of smell upon all occasions, and
depended chiefly upon it in judging of the qualities
of any article of food with which it was not previously acquainted. Fruit, vegetables, eggs, milk,
and cooked flesh were eaten indiscriminately ; but it
was more especially fond of bread, coffee, and oranges,
and, on one occasion, emptied and swallowed the
contents of an ink-bottle, without appearing to be incommoded. It observed no particular order in its
meals, but, like a child, would eat at all hours whatever was presented to it.

" In order to defend itself, it bit and struck with
its hand ; it was only against children, however,
that it showed any kind of resentment, and then
apparently more from jealousy than anger. Generally speaking, it was gentle and affectionate, and
showed a natural propensity to live in society. It
was fond of being caressed, gave real kisses, and
appeared to experience great pleasure in the act of

sucking the fingers of its visitors, though it was never observed to make this use of its own. Its voice was shrill and guttural, but only heard when it ardently desired something that was withheld from it ; then all its actions became highly expressive, it knocked its head, pouted, and, when very angry, would roll upon the ground and utter loud and harsh yells.

" When first taken on board for the purpose of being brought to Europe, it showed great distrust of its own powers, or rather could not exactly appreciate the motion of the vessel, and exaggerated the dangers attending it. It never attempted to move without holding firmly by the ropes or some other part of the ship; it constantly refused to ascend to the rigging, in spite of every encouragement and temptation that could be held forth to it, and was at length induced to mount, only from that sentiment of affectionate attachment which nature seems to have strongly implanted in the whole species. Our animal indeed exhibited strong manifestations of this sentiment upon many occasions ; and this passion would be sufficient of itself to induce the species to live in society, and unite for mutual defence against common dangers. However this may be, our orang had not the courage to mount the rigging, till it saw M. Decaen ascend himself; it followed him without hesitation, and from that moment, would ascend alone whenever it had a fancy to do so.

" The means of defence employed by the orang-outan are in general such as are common to all timid animals, cunning and prudence ; but every thing announces that it possesses a very superior degree of judgment and foresight, which it employs occasionally to avoid its enemies. Our animal, while at liberty, was in the habit on fine days of frequenting a garden, where it found an opportunity of taking fresh air and exercise : it mounted the trees, and took a pleasure in sitting among the branches. One day, whilst thus employed, one of the attendants pretended to climb the tree for the purpose of securing him, but the orang began forthwith to shake the branches violently, as if his intention had been to frighten the intruder and prevent him from mounting. When the attendant desisted, he also ceased his exertions, but every renewal of the attempt was invariably followed by a similar exhibition, accompanied with such motions and gestures as strongly manifested his wish to deter the assailant, by impressing him with a fear of the consequences.

" When fatigued by being obliged to exhibit himself too often to his numerous visitors, he would cover himself with his little counterpane, so as to conceal himself effectually, nor would he come forth again till after the strangers had retired : he was never known, however, to act in this manner when surrounded only by those with whom he was acquainted.

" We have already seen, that one of the principal faculties of the orang is that which leads it to live in society, and attach itself by sentiments of affection to those who treat it kindly. The present animal had for M. Decaen an affection almost exclusive, and on many occasions gave remarkable proofs of it. One morning it entered his cabin before he rose, and, in the excess of its joy, threw itself upon him, embraced him with perfect transport, and applying its lips to his breast, began to suck his skin as it was accustomed to do the fingers of its most favourite acquaintances. On another occasion it exhibited a proof of still stronger attachment. It was in the habit of coming every day at meal-times, which it very well knew, to receive its share of the repast, and for this purpose invariably mounted upon the back of its master's chair, and there waited to receive whatever the company thought proper to bestow upon it. On approaching the coast of Spain M. Decaen was obliged to go ashore on duty, and another officer occupied his place at table; the orang as usual entered the cuddy, and immediately mounted the back of the chair which it believed, as formerly, to contain its master, but no sooner did it discover its mistake, and the absence of M. Decaen, than it refused every thing that was offered it, threw itself on the ground, rolled, beat its head and uttered the most lamentable cries. I have often seen it evince its impatience in the same manner, when refused any article it took a fancy to, and under circumstances that strongly incline me to believe that its conduct, on such occasions, was assumed from motives of cunning, and that there was more of pretence than reality in its passion; for in the midst of its anger it would lift its head from time to time, suspend its lamentations, and look attentively in my face to see what effect its cries had produced, and if I was disposed to yield to its wishes; always renewing its cries when it found no favourable symptoms in my looks or gestures.

"This principle of affection generally induced our orang to seek the society of those persons with whom it was acquainted, and to shun solitude, which was at all times displeasing to it: on one occasion it exhibited for this purpose a very remarkable degree of intelligence. It was kept in a small room off a larger saloon, usually occupied by the members of the family, and had frequently been observed to mount a chair which stood contiguous, for the purpose of unbolting the door and joining the rest of the company. At length the chair was removed to a distant corner of the room for the express purpose of preventing the intrusion; but scarcely had the

door been shut than it was again opened and the
orang seen in the act of descending from the identical chair, which he had carried back again to its
old situation, to enable him to mount up to the
height of the bolt. It is certain that the animal
had never been taught to act in this manner, nor
had he even seen others do so; the whole affair was
the result of his own natural reason, and differed in
no respect from what a human being would have
done in like circumstances.

"Nor are men the only beings besides their own
species to which these animals form attachments:
the orang here described had conceived an affection
for two kittens, which was sometimes attended with
considerable inconvenience; he generally employed
himself in nursing one or other of these favourites,
and sometimes amused himself by putting it upon
his head, but on such occasions he was sure to suffer
from the sharp claws of the kitten, and it was highly
amusing to witness the patience with which he resigned himself to the indulgence of this singular
fancy, and the rueful contortions of countenance
which accompanied it. Two or three times indeed
he was observed to examine the feet of the little
animals attentively; having discovered their claws,
he endeavoured to pull them out, but only used his
fingers in the operation, and was of course unsuccessful; ever after he resigned himself patiently
to his fate, and preferred enduring the pain to re-
signing the pleasure which this sort of enjoyment
afforded him. In other respects the action appeared
to be somehow connected with this animal's instinct,
for he was accustomed equally to place bits of paper,
cinders, earth, or any other light substance upon his
head in the same manner, but whether these actions
were peculiar to this individual or common to the
whole species, it is impossible to determine.

G

"I have said that in eating he used either the
hands or lips to take up his food. He was not very
handy at managing our table apparatus, but his intelligence amply compensated for his awkwardness.
When he could not manage to place the food properly upon his spoon, he would hand the instrument
to his next neighbour, with a look and gesture which
plainly conveyed his meaning. He drank very well
from a glass which he held in both his hands. One
day having replaced his glass on the table, but perceiving that it was not properly adjusted, and that it
was in danger of being thrown over, he placed his
hand under it so as to prevent its falling, thus evidently showing that he was not only aware of the
consequences, but likewise of the means of preventing them.

" Most animals in a state of nature are under
the necessity of resorting to some method of preserving themselves from the effects of severe cold;
and it is probable that the orangs have recourse to
some such means, particularly during the period of
the tropical rains. We are not acquainted with the
measures which these animals take in their natural
state, to guard against too-sudden changes of temperature, but that they do employ some means for
this purpose may be reasonably inferred from the
actions of the individual here described. He had
been accustomed to clothes, particularly on his bed
at night, and they became as indispensable to his
comfort as to that of a human being. Whilst on
ship-board he carried off whatever he met with capable of being turned to this use, and if the sailors
missed any little article of dress, they were sure to
find it in the orang's bed. This habit of carefully
covering himself before going to sleep afforded on
another occasion an admirable instance of his wonderful intelligence. His attendant was daily accus-

tomed to spread his little blanket on a lawn in front
of the dining-room, that it might be well-aired and
fresh by the time he usually retired to rest; this was
generally immediately after dinner, which meal he
commonly took with the family, and after it was
finished would of his own accord carry in his blanket,
and go to bed. One day, however, the blanket had
been hung upon a casement to dry; the orang
having missed it from its accustomed place, set
himself seriously to search for it, and having at
length discovered it, mounted up to the window and
brought it down as usual."

This interesting extract gives us a very favourable
view of the docility, gentleness, and intellectual capacity of the young orang-outan. We have ourselves observed four or five different individuals of
this species, and can confidently vouch for the
general accuracy of M. F. Cuvier's copious details.
But though in point of reasoning powers there may
be little or no difference between the orang-outan
and the chimpanzee, it must not be forgotten that
the awkwardness described by M. Cuvier is proper
only to the former animal, and arises entirely from
the malformation of his feet and hands, which, as we
have already repeatedly observed, are formed only
for grasping the branches of trees, and are but ill
adapted to any of the common purposes to which
those organs are applied in the human species. The
chimpanzee, on the contrary, more favourably organized in this respect than his Indian congener, can
handle his knife, fork, and spoon, as adroitly as
children much older than himself, but it must be
confessed, at the same time, that his superiority is
shown in his actions, rather than in his intellectual
faculties.

M. Vosmaer, a Dutch naturalist, contemporary with
Buffon and Pallas, published an admirable memoir

upon the habits of a young orang which lived for some months in the menagerie of the Prince of Orange, in 1776, and which was also observed and described by Allamand. M. Vosmaer's account contains some curious and interesting particulars which have not been mentioned by other observers, and of which we shall therefore present our readers with a short extract. "This animal," says M. Vosmaer, "was fond of society, without distinction of sex, only preferring those who had daily care of it and treated it kindly, to strangers; when its favourites retired, it would sometimes throw itself on the ground, as if in an agony of despair, uttering the most plaintive lamentations, rending its clothes and tearing them into small fragments, as soon as it was left alone. Its keeper was accustomed to sit down sometimes beside it on the floor; and to induce him to gratify it in this particular, it would often carry the hay from its bed, and arrange it on the floor, as if to invite him to be seated. On the approach of night it prepared to retire to rest by arranging the hay which formed its bed, shaking it well, and heaping an additional quantity at top by way of bolster; it then lay down, generally on the side, and covered itself carefully with the blankets. On different occasions I have seen it perform an action, which surprised me extremely the first time I witnessed it. After having prepared its couch in the ordinary manner, it took a piece of cloth which happened to be near it, stretched it very neatly on the ground, put a quantity of hay into it, and then rolling it up and fastening the four corners, carried and placed it carefully at the bed-head to serve as a pillow. On another occasion, observing me make use of a key for the purpose of opening the lock that fastened its chain, it got a small piece of wood, introduced it into the key-hole, turned and returned it in every direction,

and watched the operation with evident anxiety, in
expectation of being thus able to open the lock and
free itself from the chain. It has been likewise
known to pick the lock by means of a large nail,
which it introduced into the wards, and managed in
such a way as to shoot the bolts. When it observes
any water or other stain upon the floor of its sleeping
apartment it cleaned it carefully with a rag, and when
any of the visitors appeared in top-boots, it would go
up to them, as if to admire their polished surface, and
begin to rub and brighten them up. It had also a
trick of unfastening the buckles of people's shoes,
which it could do with the address of the most
accomplished footman, and could untie the knots on
cords, however tight and intricate they might be,
with the greatest ease and expedition.

"The ordinary pace of this animal was on all-
fours, like the other simiæ; but it could walk upright
on its hind-feet with tolerable ease, especially when
supported by a stick, and maintain the erect attitude
for a considerable period. At the same time, it
never placed the soles of the feet flatly upon the
ground, as men do, but kept them bent inwards, so
that it rested only on their external edges, whilst the
toes were doubled close along the foot, in such a
manner as to give the idea of perfect adaptation for
climbing and grasping, rather than for biped progression. With a glass or cup in one hand, and his
club in the other, it would have been difficult to deprive him of either, as he avoided all such attempts
with great address, or dexterously fenced and warded
them off with the stick. He was a remarkably powerful animal, and required four or five men to hold
him, for the purpose of having his chain fastened,
though he was then very young. I never heard
him utter any cry, except when alone, and then it
was a sound at first approaching to the howling of a

young dog, and afterwards assuming a harsh grating
tone, like the noise made by a saw in passing through
wood."

One more extract from Dr. Abel's valuable
memoir upon the young orang will put us in complete possession of its character and resources, as
compared with the chimpanzee, and enable us, at
the same time to reason more correctly upon the
habits and economy which travellers attribute to the
adult animal.   The specimen was procured in Java,
and the following observations were chiefly made
during the homeward-bound voyage.

" For the possession of this rare animal," says Dr.
Abel, " the scientific world is indebted to Captain
Methuen, who brought him from Banjarmassing, on
the south coast of Borneo, to Java; and, in the
hope of aiding the cause of science, placed him in
my possession for the purpose of being conveyed to
England.   The natives informed Captain Methuen
that he had been brought from the highlands of the
interior, and that he was very rare, and difficult to
take; and they evidently considered him a great
curiosity, as they flocked in crowds to see him.   The
orang-outan of Borneo is utterly incapable of walking
in a perfectly erect posture.   He betrays this in his
whole exterior conformation, and never wilfully
attempts to counteract its tendency.   His head
leaning forward, and forming a considerable angle
with the back, throws the centre of gravity so far
beyond the perpendicular, that his arms, like the fore-
legs of other animals, are required to support the
body.   So difficult is it for him to keep the upright
position for a few seconds, under the direction of his
keeper, that he is obliged, in the performance of his
task, to raise his arms above his head, and throw
them behind him, to keep his balance.   His progressive motion on a flat surface is accomplished by his

placing his bent fists upon the ground, and drawing his body between his arms : moving in this manner, he strongly resembles a person decrepid in the legs, supported on stilts. In a state of nature he probably seldom moves along the ground ; his whole external configuration showing his fitness for climbing trees and clinging to their branches. The length and plia bility of his fingers and toes enable him to grasp with facility and steadiness ; and the force of his muscles empowers him to support his body for a great length of time by one hand or foot. He can thus pass from one fixed object to another, at the distance of his span from each other, and can obviously pass from one branch of a tree to another, through a much greater interval.

" In sitting on a flat surface this animal turns his legs under him, in the manner expressed by the engraving. In sitting on the branch of a tree or on a rope, he rests on his heels, his body leaning forward against his thighs. This animal uses his hands like others of the monkey tribe. The orang-outan, on his arrival in Java, from Batavia, was allowed to be entirely at liberty till within a day or two of being put on board the Cæsar to be conveyed to England, and whilst at large made no attempt to escape ; but became violent when put into a large railed bamboo cage, for the purpose of being conveyed from the island. As soon as he felt himself in confinement, he took the rails of the cage by his hands, and shaking them violently endeavoured to break them to pieces ; but finding that they did not yield generally he tried them sepa- rately, and having discovered one weaker than the rest, worked at it constantly till he had broken it, and made his escape. On board ship an attempt being made to secure him by a chain tied to a strong staple, he instantly unfastened it, and ran off with the chain dragging behind ; but finding himself embarrassed by its length, he coiled it once or twice and threw it over his shoulder. This feat he often repeated, and when he found that it would not remain on his shoulder, he took it into his mouth. After several abortive attempts to secure him more effectually, he was allowed to wander freely about the ship, and soon became familiar with the sailors, and surpassed them in agility. They often chased him about the rigging, and gave him frequent opportunities of displaying his adroitness in managing an escape. On first start-ing he would endeavour to outstrip his pursuers by mere speed, but when much pressed, eluded them by seizing a loose rope and swinging out of their reach. At other times he would patiently wait on the shrouds or at the mast-head, till his pursuers almost touched him, and then suddenly lower himself to the deck by any rope that was near him, or bound along the mainstay from one mast to another. The men would often shake the ropes by which he hung with so much violence, as to make me fear his falling; but I soon found that the power of his muscles could not be easily overcome. When in a playful humour he would often swing within arm's length of his pursuer, and having struck him with his hand, throw himself from him.

"Whilst in Java, he lodged in a large tama-rind-tree near my dwelling; and formed a bed by intertwining the small branches, and covering them with leaves. During the day he would lie with his head projecting beyond his nest, watching whoever might pass under, and when he saw any one with fruit, would descend to obtain a share of it. He always retired for the night at sun-set, or sooner if he had been well fed; and rose with the sun, and visited those from whom he habitually received food: on board ship he commonly slept at the mast-head, after wrapping himself in a sail. In making his bed

he used the greatest pains to remove everything out
of his way that might render the surface on which he
intended to lie uneven ; and having satisfied himself
with this part of his arrangement, spread out the sail
and lying down upon it on his back, drew it over his
body. Sometimes I pre-occupied his bed, and teazed
him by refusing to give it up. On these occasions
he would endeavour to pull the sail from under me
or to force me from it, and would not rest until I had
resigned it. If it was large enough for both he would
quietly lie down by my side. If all the sails happened to be set, he would hunt about for some other
covering, and either steal one of the sailor's jackets or
shirts that happened to be drying, or empty a ham-
mock of its blankets. Off the Cape of Good Hope,
he suffered much from a low temperature, especially
early in the morning, when he would descend from
the mast, shuddering with cold, and running up to
any of his friends, climb into their arms, and clasping
them closely, derive warmth from their persons,
screaming violently at any attempt to remove him.

" His food in Java was chiefly fruit, especially man-
gosteens, of which he was extremely fond. He also
sucked eggs with voracity, and often employed himself in seeking them. On board ship his diet was
of no definite kind ; he ate readily of all kinds of
meat, and especially raw meat; was very fond of
bread, but always preferred fruits when he could
obtain them. His beverage in Java was water ; on
ship-board it was as diversified as his food. He
preferred coffee and tea, but would readily take
wine, and exemplified his attachment to spirits
by stealing the Captain's brandy-bottle: since his
arrival in London, he has preferred beer and milk
to any thing else, but drinks wine and other liquors.
In his attempts to get food, he afforded us many opportunities of judging of his sagacity and disposition.

He was always very impatient to seize it when held
out to him, and became passionate when it was not
soon given up; and would chase a person all over
the ship to obtain it. I seldom came on deck
without sweetmeats or fruit in my pocket, and could
never escape his vigilant eye. Sometimes I endeavoured to evade him by ascending to the mast-head,
but was always overtaken or intercepted in my progress. When he came up with me on the shrouds
he would secure himself by one foot to the rattlins,
and confine my legs with the other and one of his
hands, whilst he rifled my pockets. If he found it
impossible to overtake me, he would climb to a considerable height on the loose rigging, and then drop
suddenly upon me; or, if perceiving his intention, I
attempted to descend, he would slide down a rope
and meet me at the bottom of the shrouds. Sometimes I fastened an orange to the end of a rope and
lowered it to the deck from the mast-head, and as
soon as he attempted to seize it drew it rapidly up.
After being several times foiled in endeavouring to
obtain it by direct means, he altered his plan: appearing to care little about it, he would remove to
some distance, and ascend the rigging very leisurely
for some time, and then, by a sudden spring, catch
the rope. If defeated again, by my suddenly jerking
the rope, he would at first seem quite in despair,
relinquish his effort, and run about the rigging
screaming violently; but he would always return,
and again seizing the rope, disregard the jerk,
and allow it to run through his hands, till
within reach of the orange; but if again foiled,
would come to my side, and taking me by the arm,
confine it whilst he hauled the orange up.

"This animal neither practises the grimace and
antics of other monkeys, nor possesses their perpetual proneness to mischief. Gravity, approach-

ing to melancholy and mildness, were sometimes
strongly expressed upon his countenance, and seem
to be the characteristics of his disposition. When
he first came amongst strangers, he would sit for
hours with his hand upon his head, looking pen-
sively at all around him; or, when much incommoded by their examination, would hide himself
beneath any covering that was at hand. His mildness was evinced by his forbearance under injuries
which were grievous before he was excited to revenge; but he always avoided those who often teazed
him. He soon became strongly attached to those
who kindly used him. By their side he was fond of
sitting; and getting as close as possible to their
persons, would take their hands between his lips,
and fly to them for protection. From the boatswain
of the Alceste, who shared his meals with him, and
was his chief favourite, although, he sometimes pur-
loined the grog and the biscuit of his benefactor, he
learned to eat with a spoon, and might often be seen
sitting at his cabin-door enjoying his coffee quite
unembarrassed by those who observed him, and with
a grotesque and sober air that seemed a burlesque
on human nature. Next to the boatswain, I was
perhaps his most intimate acquaintance; he would
always follow me to the mast-head, whither I often
went for the sake of reading apart from the noise of
the ship; and having satisfied himself that my
pocket contained no eatables, would lie down by my
side, and pulling a topsail entirely over him, peep
from it occasionally to watch my movements. His
favourite amusement in Java was swinging from the
branches of trees, in passing from one tree to another,
and in climbing over the roofs of houses; on board,
in hanging by his arms from the ropes; and in
romping with the boys of the ship. He would entice
them into play by striking them with his hand as

they passed, and bounding from them, but allowing them to overtake him and engage in a mock scuffle, in which he used his hands, feet, and mouth. If any conjecture can be formed from these frolics of his mode of attacking an adversary, it would appear to be his first object to throw him down, then to secure him with his hands and feet, and then wound him with his teeth.

"Of some small monkeys on board from Java he took little notice, whilst under the observation of the persons of the ship. Once, indeed, he openly attempted to throw a small cage, containing three of them, overboard; because probably he had seen them receive food of which he could obtain no part. But although he held little intercourse with them while under our inspection, I had reason to suspect that he was less indifferent to their society, when free from our observation; and was one day summoned to the top-gallant-yard of the mizen-mast to overlook him playing with a young male monkey. Lying on his back, partially covered with the sail, he for sometime contemplated with great gravity the gambols of the monkey which bounded over him; but at length caught him by the tail and tried to envelop him in his covering. The monkey seemed to dislike the confinement and broke from him, but again resumed its gambols, and although frequently caught always escaped. The intercourse, however, did not seem to be that of equals, for the orang-outan never condescended to romp with the monkey as he did with the boys of the ship. Yet the monkeys had evidently a great predilection for his company; for whenever they broke loose, they took their way to his resting-place, and were often seen lurking about it, or creeping clandestinely towards him. There appeared to be no gradation in their intimacy; as they appeared to be as confidently familiar with him when first observed as at the close of their acquaintance.

" But although so gentle when not exceedingly irritated, the orang-outan could be excited to violent rage, which he expressed by opening his mouth, shewing his teeth, seizing and biting those who were near him. Sometimes, indeed, he seemed almost driven to desperation; and on two or three occasions committed an act, which in a rational being would have been called the threatening of suicide. If repeatedly refused an orange, when he attempted to take it, he would shriek violently, and swing furiously about the ropes; then return and endeavour to obtain it; if again refused, he would roll for some time like an angry child upon the deck, uttering the most piercing screams; and then suddenly starting up rush furiously over the side of the ship, and disappear. On first witnessing this act, we thought that he had thrown himself into the sea; but on a search being made found him concealed under the chains. I have seen him exhibit violent alarm on two occasions only, when he appeared to seek for safety in gaining as high an elevation as possible. On seeing eight large turtle brought on board, whilst the Cæsar was off the island of Ascension, he climbed with all possible speed to a higher part of the ship than he had ever before reached, and looking down upon them, projected his long lips into the form of a hog's snout, uttering at the same time a sound which might be described as between the croaking of a frog and the grunting of a pig. After some time he ventured to descend, but with great caution, peeping continually at the turtle, but could not be induced to approach within many yards of them. He ran to the same height, and uttered the same sounds, on seeing some men bathing and splashing in the sea; and since his arrival in England,

H

has shewn nearly the same degree of fear at the sight of a live tortoise.

" Such were the actions of this animal, as far as they fell under my notice, during our voyage from Java; and they seem to include most of those which have been related of the orang-outans by other observers. I cannot find, since his arrival in England, that he has learnt to perform more than two feats which he did not practise on board ship, although his education has been by no means neglected. One of these is to walk upright, or rather on his feet, unsupported by his hands, the other to kiss his keeper. I have before remarked with how much difficulty he accomplishes the first, and may add that a well-trained dancing dog would surpass him in the imitation of the human posture. I believe that all the figures given of orang-outans in an unpropped erect posture, are wholly unnatural. Some writer states that an orang-outan, which he describes, gave " real kisses," and so words his statement, that the reader supposes them the natural act of the animal. This is certainly not the case with the orang-outan which I have described. He imitates the act of kissing, by projecting his lips against the face of the keeper, but gives them no impulse. He never attempted this action on board ship, but has been taught it by those who now have him in charge."

Our knowledge of the adult orangs, like that which we possess of the adult chimpanzee, has been hitherto very imperfect. The recent return of the Dutch scientific mission, which has been so long occupied in investigating the zoology of the great islands of the Indian Archipelago, has, however, afforded us more correct and extensive information upon this subject. Much interesting matter, derived from this source, will be found in the sequel: in the meantime the following extracts contain the only trustworthy ac-

counts of the habits and economy of the adult orangs
which have yet been published. "I saw at Java,"
says Le Guat, "a very singular species of ape; it was
a female, of large size, and frequently walked quite
upright upon its hind-feet, upon which occasions it
invariably covered with its hand those parts which
modesty teaches us to conceal; the face was entirely
without hair, except on the eye-brows, and its countenance in general bore a likeness to those grotesque
faces which I have seen among the Hottentot women
at the Cape. It made its bed carefully every day,
and when it lay down, put its head on a pillow and
drew the counterpane over it. When it had a head-
ache, it bound its brows with a handkerchief, and it
was curious to see it thus prepare itself previous to
retiring to bed. I might relate many other little
actions which appeared extremely singular; but I
confess that I did not admire its proceedings so
much as others, because knowing its owner's intention
of bringing it to Europe, for the purpose of exhibition, I thought that there was more acquired than
natural in its conduct. This, however, was but my
own supposition. The animal died off the Cape of
Good Hope." Gemelli Carreri informs us that the
orangs live principally in mountainous and hilly
places, whence they descend to the sea-shores to fish
for crabs, oysters, &c., and that when they find the
oyster-shells open, they adroitly slip a small stone
between to prevent them from closing, and then
devour the fish at their leisure.

The Chevalier D'Obsonville communicated to
Buffon the following account of an adult orang which
he had an opportunity of observing. "One of these
animals," says he, "which I saw about two months
after its capture, was 4 feet 6 inches high; the eyes
were small and black, with a yellow tinge, and though
the countenance was haggard, it announced in-

H 2

quietude, embarrassment, and chagrin, rather than ferocity. The mouth was very large, the nose flat, and the cheek-bones projecting; the face was wrinkled, the skin tan-coloured, the hair of the head was some inches long, that on the back thicker than in front, and both of a brown colour; there was scarcely any beard, the breast was wide, the thighs not very fleshy, and the legs bent. I never saw this satyr except sitting or standing erect; but though habitually walking upright, I was told that he assists himself, in a state of freedom, with his hands as well as his feet, in the acts of running or leaping; and perhaps it may be this practice which encourages the extreme length of the arms in this species, for the end of the fingers touched the knees. The specimen was a male; I never saw the female. He sometimes heaved a long and deep sigh, and at other times uttered a harsh sound, but the modulations of his voice only expressed pain, ennui, or impatience. According to the Indians these animals wander in the woods or among mountains of difficult access, and live together in small societies. They are extremely wild, but apparently not savage, and soon learn to obey or perform whatever they are commanded. They can never, however, be bent to servitude; but always preserve a degree of ennui and profound melancholy, which degenerates into consumption, and soon terminates their lives. The people of the country told me this, and it was confirmed by my own observations on the individual here described."

M. Relian, a surgeon resident at Batavia, had likewise an opportunity of observing two adult orangs, of which he transmitted the following accounts to Allamand : " M. Pallavicini," says he, " took with him two living orangs, male and female, when he sailed for Europe in 1759 ; they were of the human size, and executed all the movements which men do, particularly with their hands. The breasts of the female were pendant; the breast and belly were naked, but much wrinkled; both were very bashful when you looked fixedly at them, and the female would then throw herself into the arms of the male and hide her head in his breast. This touching sight I have witnessed with my own eyes. They did not speak; but uttered a sound similar to that of a monkey, which they resemble in living only on fruits and inhabiting the thickest woods. They are called wild men, from the relation which they bear in outward form to the human species, particularly in their movements, and in a mode of thinking which is certainly peculiar to them, and which is not remarked in other animals; for their intelligence is quite different from that instinct, more or less developed, which characterises quadrupeds in general. It would be an interesting sight if one could observe these wild men in their native forests, without being seen, and become witness to their domestic occupations. They are said to be found in the inaccessible mountains of Java; but they are most abundant in Borneo, from which those exhibited here from time to time are for the most part brought."

Wurmb, to whom we are indebted for the only correct description of the adult orang, previous to that of M. Temminck, which will be found in the sequel, gives very little information regarding its habits. His specimen had been sent from Borneo by M. Palm, who reported that the animal defended himself so vigorously by means of large branches which he broke off from the trees, that it was impossible to take him alive.

Head of the Adult Sumatran Orang, from Dr. C. Abel.

But the most complete account on record of the adult orang is that given by the late Dr. Clarke Abel of the capture of a large male specimen in the island of Sumatra. "A boat party," says Dr. Abel, "under the command of Messrs. Craggyman and Fish, officers of the brig Mary Ann Sophia, having landed to procure water at a place called Ramboom, near Touraman, on the N.W. coast of Sumatra, on a spot where there was much cultivated ground and but few trees, discovered on one of these a gigantic animal of the monkey tribe. On the approach of the party he came to the ground, and when pursued, sought refuge in another tree at some distance, exhibiting as he moved, the appearance of a tall manlike figure, covered with shining brown hair, walking erect, with a waddling gait, but sometimes accelerating his motions with his hands, and occasionally impelling himself forward with the bough of a tree. His

motion on the ground was plainly not his natural
mode of progression, for even when assisted by his
hands, or a stick, it was slow and vacillating : it was
necessary to see him amongst the trees in order to
estimate his agility and strength. On being driven
to a small clump he gained by one spring a very
lofty branch, and bounded from one branch to another
with the ease and alacrity of a common monkey.
Had the country been covered with wood, it would
have been almost impossible to prevent his escape,
as his mode of travelling from one tree to another is
described to be as rapid as the progress of a swift
horse. Even amidst the few trees that were upon the
spot, his movements were so quick that it was very
difficult to obtain a steady aim, and it was only by
cutting down one tree after another that his pursuers,
by confining him within a very limited range, were
able to destroy him by several successive shots, some
of which penetrated his body and wounded his
viscera. Having received five balls, his exertions relaxed, and reclining exhausted on one of the branches
of a tree, he vomited a considerable quantity of
blood. The ammunition of the hunters being by
this time expended, they were obliged to fell the tree
in order to obtain him, and did this in full confidence,
that his power was so far gone, that they could secure
him without trouble, but were astonished as the tree
was falling to see him effect his retreat to another
with apparently undiminished vigour. In fact, they
were obliged to cut down all the trees, before they
could drive him to combat his enemies on the ground,
against whom he still exhibited surprising strength
and agility, although he was at length overpowered
by numbers, and destroyed by the thrusts of spears
and the blows of stones and other missiles. When
nearly in a dying state, he seized a spear made of a
supple wood which would have withstood the strength
of the stoutest man, and shivered it in pieces ; in the

words of the narrator ' he broke it as if it had been a
carrot.' It is stated by those who aided in his death,
that the human-like expression of his countenance and
piteous manner of placing his hands over his wounds,
distressed their feelings and almost made them question the nature of the act they were committing. When
dead, both natives and Europeans contemplated his
figure with amazement. His stature at the lowest
computation was upwards of six feet, at the highest
it was nearly eight, but it will afterwards be seen
that it was probably about seven.

" In the following description, which I give in the
words of my informant, many of my readers will detect
some of those external conformations which distinguish
the young Eastern orang-outans that have been seen
in Europe. The only part of the description in which
the imagination seems to have injured the fidelity
of the portrait regards the prominence of the nose
and size of the eyes, neither of which are verified by
the integuments of the animal's head, which are represented in Plate I. ' The animal was nearly eight
feet high, and had a well-proportioned body, with a
fine broad expanded chest and narrow waist. His
head was also in due proportion to his body ; the
eyes were large, the nose prominent, and the mouth
much more capacious than the mouth of man. His
chin was fringed from the extremity of one ear to the
other, with a beard that curled neatly on each side,
and formed altogether an ornamental rather than a
frightful appendage to his visage. His arms were
very long even in proportion to his height, and in
relation to the arms of men ; but his legs were in
some respects much shorter. His organs of generation were not very conspicuous, and seemed to
be small in proportion to his size. The hair of his coat
was smooth and glossy, when he was first killed, and
his teeth and appearance altogether indicated that
he was young, and in full possession of his physical

powers. Upon the whole,' adds his biographer, 'he was a wonderful beast to behold, and there was more in him to excite amazement than fear.'

"That this animal showed great tenacity of life is evident from his surviving so many dreadful wounds, and his peculiarity in this respect seems to have been a subject of intense surprise to all his assailants. In reference to this point, it may be proper to remark, that after he had been carried on board ship and was hauled up for the purpose of being skinned, the first stroke of the knife on the skin of the arm produced an instantaneous vibration of the muscles, followed by a convulsive contraction of the whole member. A like quivering of the muscles occurred when the knife was applied to the skin of the back, and so impressed Captain Cornfoot with a persuasion that the animal retained his sensibility, that he ordered the process of skinning to stop till the head had been removed. It seems probable that this animal had travelled some distance to the place where he was found, as his legs were covered with mud up to the knees, and he was considered as great a prodigy by the natives as by the Europeans. They had never before met with an animal like him, although they lived within two days' journey of one of the vast and almost impenetrable forests of Sumatra. They seemed to think that his appearance accounted for many strange noises resembling screams and shouts and various sounds which they could neither attribute to the roar of the tiger nor the voice of any other beast with which they were acquainted. What capability the great orang-outan may possess of uttering such sounds does not appear; but this belief of the Malays may lead to the capture of other animals of this species, and to the discovery of more interesting particulars of his conformation and habits.

"The only material discrepancy which we can detect

in the different accounts which have been given of this
animal regards his height, which in some of them is
vaguely stated at from above six feet to nearly eight.
Captain Cornfoot, however, who favoured me with
a verbal description of the animal when brought on
board his ship, stated, that ' he was full a head taller
than any man on board, measuring seven feet in
what might be called his ordinary standing posture,
and eight feet when suspended for the purpose of
being skinned.' The following measurements, which
I have carefully made of different parts of the animal
in the Society's museum, go far to determine this
point, and are entirely in favour of Captain Cornfoot's
accuracy. The skin of the body of the animal, dried
and shrivelled as it is, measures, in a straight line,
from the top of the shoulder to the part where the
ancle has been removed 5 feet 10 inches; the
perpendicular length of the neck, as it is in the preparation, $3\frac{1}{2}$ inches; the length of the head, from the
top of the forehead to the end of the chin, 9 inches;
and the length of the skin, still attached to the foot,
from its line of separation from the leg, 8 inches:—
we thus obtain 7 feet $6\frac{1}{2}$ inches as the approximate
height of the animal. The natural bending posture
of the ape tribe would obviously diminish the height
of the standing posture in the living animal, and
probably reduce it to Captain Cornfoot's measurement
of seven feet, whilst the stretching that would take
place when the animal was extended for dissection
might as obviously increase its length to eight feet."

Adult Bornean Orang, Male, from M. Temminck.

The principal facts mentioned in these different extracts, with respect to the habits, size, &c., of the orang-outan, were confirmed to us a few months ago, in a conversation which we had upon this subject at Leyden, with Dr. Muller of Heidelberg, a zoological traveller in the service of the king of Holland, who had just then returned to Europe, after fourteen years spent in investigating the natural history of the great Indian Archipelago. During his residence in Borneo, and the different excursions which he made, in every direction, through the primeval forests of that interesting island, Dr. Muller had frequent opportunities of observing the orang-outans in a state of nature, and of studying their manners in their native woods. He describes them as being in the highest degree unsociable, leading, for the most part, a perfectly solitary life, and never more than two or three being found in company. Their deportment is grave and melancholy, their disposition apathetic, their motions slow and heavy, and their habits so sluggish and lazy, that it is only the cravings of appetite, or the approach of imminent danger, that can rouse them from their habitual lethargy, or force them to active exertion. When under the influence of these powerful motives, however, they exhibit a determination of character, and display a degree of force and activity, which would scarcely be anticipated from their heavy, apathetic appearance; whilst their strength is so redoubtable, that, without the aid of fire-arms, it would be impossible to cope with them. The natives of Borneo hold them in especial dread, and carefully avoid those parts of the forest which they are known to frequent. They are never seen on the ground, but constantly reside in trees, among the branches of which they make their way with surprising agility. Here they build a kind of rude hut, by intertwining the branches, in which they spend most part of their time, and seldom move abroad, except when urged by the calls of appetite. They feed entirely on fruits, and are never known to eat flesh, or even eggs, though we have seen that young individuals, in a state of confinement, are readily taught to relish animal food. Dr. Muller never met with the orang-outan in Java or Sumatra; in the latter of which islands, however, he had heard of his existence, though he is seldom seen, and appears to be altogether of rarer occurrence than in Borneo.

It has long been suspected by zoologists that the orangs of Borneo and Sumatra were of different species. This supposition, though it must be confessed that, till of late, it rested upon very slender grounds, receives considerable support from certain peculiarities of structure which are found to be characteristic of the adult male of the Bornean animal, of which many fine specimens, in all stages of development, have been procured by Dr. Muller, and deposited in the *Museum des Pays Bas*, at Leyden. The following description of these animals, and of the peculiarities here adverted to, is from the monograph of the genus just published by M. Temminck: " The largest and oldest of our specimens is a male, of the height of four feet (French measure); but our travellers inform us, by letters from Banjarmassing, in the island of Borneo, that they have recently procured others of five feet three inches in height; the head is extremely large, and even appears of monstrous dimensions, in consequence of the cheeks being prolonged laterally by large and prominent excrescences, something in the form of a crescent, which, commencing on the temples, descend behind the orbits and in front of the ears, to extend themselves over the zygomatic arch, as far as the ascending branch of the lower jaw. This accessory tuberosity on each side of the face gives the physiognomy an appearance of deformity, which, added to the excessive prolongation of the muzzle, and the thickness of the lips, immediately above which a very minute nose is, as it were, grafted, contributes to give the whole expression of the countenance an appearance of hideous deformity unrivalled in the rest of the animal kingdom. The tuberosities in question are five inches long, and nearly two inches in thickness. They resemble the somewhat similar excrescences, of greater or less extent, which characterise certain species of the genus *sus* and all the known *phacochæres :* their texture is of an adipose substance, firm to the touch, and contained in a very abundant cellular tissue. Nothing is yet known of the functions which this singular organisation is intended to execute ; it is never developed but in the male sex, and even there only begins to show itself when the animal approaches near to its adult state, if our conjectures are exact, about the age of eight or ten years. A male specimen, known to have attained the age of between six and seven years, bears no trace of the organs in question, whilst another, much larger, and arrived at two-thirds of the adult size, already exhibits very prominent indications of their commencement: no appearance of them is to be observed in the females at any age.

" The forehead of the old male is almost entirely naked, the rims of the orbits are prominent, and the eyes a third less than in the human subject. There are no eye-brows, and but very small eye-lashes, formed of a few stiff hairs. The nose is depressed to the level of the cheeks, and is prominent only at the tip, where the nostrils open sideways ; they are separated by a cartilage, which ex-

tends beyond their termination, and is confounded
with the thick upper lip, which, as well as the lower
lip, is disproportionately large and fleshy. The
lower jaw ends in an extremely broad, truncated
chin, extending beyond the upper jaw, and covered,
in the male, with a long, bushy, pointed beard.
The mouth consists of a horizontal opening, sufficiently small for the size of the animal. All these
parts are nearly naked, with the exception of a few
scattered hairs of a yellowish-red colour, which are
observed on the temples. The lateral parts of the
upper lip are furnished with a sort of moustaches,
which extend from the nostrils to the commissure
of the mouth, on either side. The ears are small,
and of the same form as those of man, except that
the lobe is firmly united to the surrounding parts.
The posterior portion of the head is spherical; all
the hairs which cover this part appear to have their
origin in a common centre, from which they diverge
or radiate in every direction; the forehead is extremely flat and retiring, and terminates in a depressed occiput. All the proportions of the body
are heavy, thick, and totally deprived of symmetry,
by the extreme breadth of the hips and the prominence of the belly. The breast is nearly naked, or
only furnished here and there with a few scattered
hairs, which, however, become more abundant on
the sternum and belly, but still neither sufficiently
long nor copious to cover the parts completely, or
conceal the skin. The back, as far down as the
hips, is even less hairy than the front of the body,
but the sides are abundantly furnished with long
hair, which hangs down so as to cover the hair of
the thighs. The anterior extremities are out of all
proportion longer than the posterior; they nearly
reach the ground when the animal stands upright;
the fore-arm, more especially, is of extreme length.

All these members are thickly furnished with hair, though less so on the hands and fingers than elsewhere. The hair of the fore-arm is directed towards the elbow, where it meets that of the arm in a kind of pointed ruff. The fingers and toes, as well as the palms and soles, are much longer than in man, and hence the great distance to which the posterior thumb is thrown backwards behind the line of the other toes. This organ itself is short, completely opposable, and forms, with the corresponding index finger of the posterior members, a complete semi-circle—a conformation which affords a sufficient proof that the orang is not organized either for biped station or progression, but admirably adapted for climbing trees, mounting to their tops, and traversing the forests in every direction, without being often obliged to descend to the ground, where he would be necessarily embarrassed in his movements, whether he attempted to walk upright or on all-fours. We have examined six individuals of different ages, *all shot in their natural state of freedom*, without being able to discover the least trace of a nail on the posterior thumbs; even the skin which covers the unguinal phalanx of that member is neither thicker nor tougher than in other parts. A seventh individual, which we had known for many years *in captivity*, had no nail on the right posterior thumb, whilst the left was provided with one as perfectly developed as on any of the other fingers; two skeletons of young individuals, which had died in menageries, and now form part of the anatomical collection of the Museum des Pays Bas, have nails upon all the thumbs. To complete this observation, it would be necessary to ascertain whether individuals similarly furnished with nails upon all the toes occur in a state of nature; if such be really the case, there no longer exists a doubt as to the

anomaly to which this organ is subject, and the famous
question so long ago agitated among zoologists
is reduced within very narrow boundaries. In the
meantime, till an opportunity occurs of extending
this observation, we are justified by these facts in
affirming, that, in its normal state, the orang of
Borneo is without nails on the hind-thumbs*. All
the other fingers are furnished with black nails,
longer and more curved than in the human subject.
The fore-fingers preserve the same relative length as
in man; but the index of the hind-hands is constantly longer than the rest, and the length of the
other fingers diminishes gradually, so that the little
one is the shortest of all. The palms of the hands
exhibit the same disposition of the lines and papilla
as that which is observed in man; and as these papilla are extremely minute and fine at the tips of the
fingers, it is reasonable to suppose that the sense of
touch must be extremely delicate in the orang.

" All the naked parts of the head and body, with
the exception of the orbits and lips, are of a bluish,
or silvery-grey colour. The hair is generally of a
uniform deep chesnut-brown, more or less glossy,
but the beard and moustaches are of a rusty or yellowish-red. There is no difference of colour between
the male and female, nor even between adult and
young subjects: specimens of a year old, and those
presumed to be six, seven, or eight years of age, do
not vary in this respect from individuals of great
size and mature years; but there is a slight difference in the abundance or scarcity of the hair which
covers the head and body, according to the age of
the subjects, the young being always better clothed
than the adults.

" A second male, also of mature age, but smaller

* See this subject more fully discussed, at p. 85.

than that just described, has the beard much less developed, but the hair of the head longer, more abundant, and falling over the forehead. The upper lip is mutilated, and shows indications of a hare-lip—an anomaly which probably arises from a cicatrised wound. This individual has been given to the Museum of Paris. A third male, of a medium age, is upwards of three feet three inches, French measure, in height. The hair is of rather a deeper colour than in the two preceding specimens; the beard is already tolerably developed, but the callous protuberances of the temples have scarcely yet begun to appear: the eyebrows are formed of a few scattered hairs. A fourth male, much younger, probably about six or seven years old, exactly resembles the young females of the same age. It exhibits no indications either of the beard or of the temporal protuberances, and the muzzle projects but slightly in comparison with that of the adults. An adult, or nearly adult, female, of three feet seven inches, French measure, in height, resembles the males in general form and colour; but she has only a very small beard occupying the point of the chin, and neither so prominent, long, nor pointed, as in the other sex: the moustaches are totally wanting, and there exists not the slightest indication of callous development on the temples. The breasts are full, and the nipples long and flaccid; the belly is large and nearly naked, and there is no appearance of hair either on the breast or eyebrows. Another female, of the height of three feet, resembles the adult, but is better covered with hair, has the eyebrows more prominent, but is almost without beard on the chin. The colour is in all respects the same. A young male of the height of seventeen inches, and probably not more than five or six months old, has the whole body, with the exception of the face and hands, abundantly covered with long hair; that on the breast is short and thin; the forehead is furnished with scattered hairs, which, however, become more numerous between the superciliary arches, and longer on the temples and cheeks. The length of the hair on the arms and shoulders is five inches; the beard is feebly marked by a few hairs, which, as in the adult, are of a clear red colour; all the rest of the colours are precisely the same as in subjects of maturer years.

" None of our orangs has true callosities, but as the skin is generally very thick, especially on the hips, it follows that the epidermis, deprived of hair on these parts, is firm and hard to the touch. This species of rugosity is probably owing to the continual friction exercised upon this region during the act of sitting, which produces the same thickness and hardness of skin on the buttocks of the orangs as on the hands of labouring men and the soles of persons who go barefooted. Callosities, properly speaking—those, namely, with which the monkeys and baboons are provided—are of quite a different nature, being formed by salient prominences of the ischion, covered with an extremely callous skin. These excrescences alone, in the animals provided with them, are brought into contact with the ground in sitting, whilst the surrounding parts of the hips are covered with a soft and delicate skin; but the orangs, resting in this position upon the entire extent of the posteriors, it follows that the tubercles should be less developed, and covered, as in man, with the superincumbent muscles."

These elaborate details leave us little more to desire with respect to the orang of Borneo. Compared with the description of the adult Sumatran animal, above quoted from Dr. Clarke Abel, it will be observed that considerable discrepancies occur,

which have given rise to a very general belief that
the orangs of these two great islands belong to different species. The colour of Dr. Abel's animal,
for instance, is said to have been brown, and the
beard, instead of being long and peaked, is related
to have been short and curly; the height, also, of
the Sumatran animal, was very superior to the
largest-sized specimens of the Bornean variety which
have been hitherto recorded; but it is to be observed
that Dr. Muller has recently procured a specimen
from the latter locality, approximating much more
nearly to Dr. Abel's dimensions, and the colour and
beard are characters much too vague, or perhaps
too vaguely recorded, to merit particular attention;
more especially as the adult Sumatran female
brought home by the late Sir T. S. Raffles, and now
in the Museum of the Zoological Society, is perfectly similar, in this respect, to the Bornean ones at
Leyden. The presumed specific difference between
the two animals, therefore, which has been* hitherto
founded entirely upon these characters, is inadmis-
sible upon these grounds alone; but the description
above given of the adult Bornean male furnishes a
new and more important character, which may possibly be more decisive of this interesting question.
It will be observed, that Dr. Clarke Abel makes no
allusion to the existence of callous excrescences on
the temples of the adult Sumatran male, similar to
those which distinguish the Bornean specimens; nor
is there any appearance of these organs in the engraving of the head which he has given, and which
we have copied at page 114 ; and as it is scarcely possible that so acute and practised an observer would
have overlooked such prominent and singular developments, had they existed in his specimen, it seems
to be not improbable that they are peculiar to the
orang of Borneo. It may be, however, that these

organs were obliterated in Dr. Abel's specimen in the process of removing, and afterwards drying and stuffing, the skin; but, on the other hand, they are not even mentioned in the description of the living or recent animal, communicated by Dr. Abel's in·formant, though they could scarcely fail to have been noticed by the most careless observer, resembling, as they do, a pair of short, thick wings applied to either side of the face: at all events, the discrepancy is worth the attention of those who may hereafter have an opportunity of observing the adult male of the Sumatran orang.

The specific difference of these animals has recently been more strongly insisted on by Professor Owen, who, in the Zoological Transactions (vol. i. p. 380), and afterwards in the Proceedings (part iv. p. 91), distinguishes them by the names of *Simia Wurmbii* and *Simia Abelii* respectively. In the latter place he even describes the cranium of a supposed third species from Borneo, which, from its smaller size, he proposes to denominate *Simia Morio;* and though Dr. Muller, of whom we made particular inquiries on this point, had never been able to learn anything of the existence of a second species of orang in that island, his information may possibly have been deficient. The following is Professor Owen's description :—

" The size and form of the cranium of the simia morio at first suggests the idea of its being an intermediate stage of growth between the young and adult simia satyrus, or pongo ; but this is disproved by comparison of the teeth of simia morio with the permanent teeth in the adult pongo, and with the deciduous ones in the young simia satyrus, as well as with the germs of the permanent teeth concealed in the jaws of the latter: for while the teeth of simia morio are much larger than the deciduous teeth of the young simia satyrus, they have different relative sizes one to another from those which are observed in the permanent teeth of the full-grown : the molares and bicuspides of the simia morio being smaller, the canini much smaller, while the upper incisores have nearly, and the lower incisores fully, the same dimensions as those of the great pongo.

"The teeth in the jaws of a quadrumanous cranium may be known to belong to the permanent series, by the absence of the foramina, which, in an immature cranium, are situated behind the deciduous teeth, and which lead to the cavities containing the crowns of the permanent teeth. This character is very conspicuous on comparing the cranium of simia morio with that of a young simia satyrus, in which the deciduous series are present, together with the first permanent molares. The deciduous teeth in the young orang, besides their smaller size, are more or less protruded from their sockets, and thrust apart from one another by the *vis à tergo* of their huge successors, while the teeth of simia morio are lodged firmly in the jaws ; and, with the exception of the characteristic interval between the canines and incisores, are compactly arranged in close contiguity with each other.

"I have re-examined with much interest several crania of immature orangs, in order to ascertain if any of these might be the young of the species in question ; but they have all presented the crowns of the permanent molares of too large a size—of a size which shows that the great pongo, either of Wurmb or Abel, represents their adult state*. And these

* The permanent teeth in the Bornean and Sumatran pongos so closely correspond in size and shape, that I am unable to refer the crania of the immature orangs which I have hitherto examined to either species exclusively, from comparison of the crowns of the concealed permanent teeth ;

immature crania also indicate the condition to which
they are destined to attain by the size of the orbits,
which exceeds that of the orbits of the simia morio,
the eye having, like the brain, already in the young
pongos acquired its full size.

"That the cranium of the simia morio here described belonged to an adult is proved by the small
interval between the temporal ridges at the crown of
the skull, corresponding to the extensive surface of
origin of the crotophyte muscles, and by the obliteration of the intermaxillary sutures: that it belonged also to an aged individual is highly probable
from the extent to which the teeth are worn down,
and from the obliteration, notwithstanding the absence of interparietal and lambdoidal crests, of the
sagittal and lambdoidal sutures.

"The cerebral portion of the skull of simia morio
equals in size that of the pongo, and indicates the
possession of a brain at least as fully developed as in
that species, while the maxillary portion is proportionally smaller; so that, as the cranium rises above
the orbits, and is, like that of the pongo, more convex on the coronal aspect than in the chimpanzee,
and wants the prominent supraciliary ridge which
characterises the African orang, it presents in the
simia morio altogether a more anthropoid character.

in speaking of the immature specimens of the great pongo, I
therefore use the term simia satyrus; in comparing the simia
morio with the adult pongo, I would be understood as always
referring to the Bornean species, with cheek-callosities, or
the simia Wurmbii of Fischer. If the specific differences of
simia Wurmbii and simia Abelii be admitted, the term simia
satyrus must merge into a synonym, as having been applied
indiscriminately to the young of both these large orangs. In
each case, the generic term *simia* is applied in the restricted
sense in which it is used by Erxleben in his "Systema Regni
Animalis," 8vo. 1777, and with which the term *pithecus*, substituted by Geoffroy for the genus of orangs, is synonymous.

` "There are, however, the rudiments of the ridges,
which so remarkably characterise the cranium of the
mature pongo. Those which commence at the external angle of the frontal bone pass backwards, upwards, and slightly converge, but do not meet; they
gradually diminish in breadth, and, after passing the
coronal suture, subside to the level of the skull;
they are then only traceable by a rough line, which,
leading parallel to the sagittal suture, and gradually
bending outwards, rises again to be continued into
the lambdoidal ridges; thus circumscribing the ori-
gins of the temporal muscles. The lambdoidal and
mastoid ridges are broader and more developed than
in the chimpanzee, but inferior in both respects to
those of the pongo. The inial region of the occiput
is almost smooth, and is convex, without the mesial
ridge, and strong muscular impressions observable
in the pongo, where a preponderating weight in
front calls for the insertion of powerful muscles behind to counterbalance it.

"The temporal bones join the frontal in simia
morio as in the troglodytes niger; but this structure
occasionally is present on one or both sides of the
scull in simia satyrus.

" The *additamentum suturæ lambdoidalis* is present on both sides in the simia morio, and the beginning of the lambdoidal suture may be faintly
traced, but the remainder is obliterated.

" Directing our attention to the base of the scull
of simia morio, we observe the occipital foramen to
be less posteriorly situated than in the pongo, but
more so than in the chimpanzee. The plane of the
foramen is also less oblique than in the pongo; the
occipital condyles are as far apart anteriorly as in
the chimpanzee. The anterior condyloid foramina
are double on each side, as in the pongo: the carotid
and jugular foramina open within the same de-

pression; they are relatively further apart in the chimpanzee; the petrous portion of the temporal bone, as in the pongo, is relatively smaller than in the chimpanzee; and the articular cavity, or surface for the lower jaw, forms a larger proportion of the base of the scull.

"The other characters of the *basis cranii* correspond with those of the pongo; and the smaller size of the *meatus auditorius externus* is probably associated in both species with a smaller auricle, as compared with the chimpanzee.

"On the bony palate the relative position of the *foramen incisivum* corresponds with the development of the incisive teeth, showing the intermaxillary bones to be of larger size in the simia morio than in the chimpanzee: the situation of the sutures joining these bones to the maxillaries is indicated by vascular grooves, but otherwise obliterated; while, in the cranium of a young pongo of nearly the same size as that of the simia morio, the intermaxillary sutures still remain, corresponding to the non-development of the permanent laniaries. It will be interesting to determine at what period these sutures are obliterated in the more anthropoid simia morio.

"The *os nasi* is a single, narrow, long, triangular bone, slightly dilated at its upper end or apex, with the basal margin entire, presenting no indications of original separation into two parts, as has been observed in sculls of the chimpanzee.

"In the contraction of the interorbital space, and the general form of the orbit and its boundaries, the simia morio resembles the simia satyrus; but the orbital cavity, as before observed, is smaller. In the plane of the orbit and straight contour of the upper jaw, the simia morio resembles the Bornean species of pongo, or simia Wurmbii, rather than the simia Abelii or Sumatran pongo.

I

"The orbital process of the *os malæ* is perforated in the simia morio, as in the pongo, by several large foramina. There is one principal and two very small infraorbital foramina on either side; the upper maxillary bones are relatively smaller, as compared with the other bones of the face, and especially the intermaxillaries, than in the pongo—a structure which coincides with the smaller proportional development of the canine teeth. The nasal aperture has the same form as in the adult simia Wurmbii, being more elongated than in the immature orang.

"The main and characteristic difference then between the simia morio and the pongo, whether of Borneo or Sumatra, obtains in the size of the laniary or canine teeth, to the smaller development of which, in the simia morio, almost all the other differences in the cranium are subordinate or consequent. The laniary teeth, it may be observed, have little relation to the kind of food habitual to the orangs; had they been so related they would have been accompanied with a structure of the glenoid cavity fitting them, as in the true *carnivora*, to retain a living prey in their gripe, till its life was extinguished or resistance effectually quelled. But the flattened surfaces on which the condyles of the lower jaw rotate are in subserviency to the flattened tuberculate molars, showing the mastication of vegetable substances to be the habitual business of the jaws, and the application of the laniaries to be occasional, and probably defensive in most cases. We perceive the utility of formidable canine teeth to the orangs, whose stature makes them conspicuous and of easy detection to a carnivorous enemy; such weapons, in connection with the general muscular strength of the pongos, enable them to offer a successful defence against the leopard, and may render them formidable opponents even to the tiger; but in the smaller species,

which we have been describing, to which conceal-
ment would be easier, the canines are of relatively
smaller size, and those of the lower jaw are so placed
as to be worn down by the lateral incisors of the
upper jaw ; they were reduced in the specimen described to the level of the other teeth; and the
points of the upper canines were also much worn.
The size, forms, and proportions of the teeth which
relate more immediately to the food of the orangs,
viz., the molars and incisors, show indisputably that
the simia morio derives its sustenance from the
same kind of food as the larger orangs. The singular thickness or antero-posterior diameter of the
incisors, which are worn down to a flattened surface, like molar teeth, show that they are put to
rough work ; and it is probable that their common
use is to tear and scrape away the tough fibrous
outer covering of the cocoa-nut, and, perhaps, to
gnaw through the denser shell."

These observations of Professor Owen, though
still not perfectly decisive of the question, render the
existence of different species of orangs highly probable. It is only necessary to remark further, that
the name of pongo, as applied to the orangs, is a
misnomer, first employed by Buffon, and perpetuated
through the carelessness of succeeding writers. It
properly belongs to the chimpanzee, as may be seen
in the extract from "Battel's Narrative," given under
the head of that species.

Chapter V.

Apes *continued.*—The Gibbons (*Hylobates*).

Few groups among the *quadramana* are so definitely circumscribed, and distinguished by characters at once so appropriate and differential, as the genus *hylobates;* or, as the animals comprised in it are more commonly called, the *gibbons.* From the rest of the true apes, the *troglodytes* and the *satyri,* or orangs, they are readily known by the development, however partial or rudimentary, of naked callosities, —an attribute which sensibly degrades them in the scale of nature, and approximates them more nearly to the inferior tribes of *simiæ;* from which, on the other hand, they are distinguished by characters of still greater influence—by the absence of tails and cheek-pouches, the disproportion between the length of the anterior and posterior extremities, and the peculiarities of habit and progression which necessarily result from such modifications of organic structure. They thus occupy an intermediate station between the orangs and the common monkeys, the *semnopitheci, colobi,* and *cercopitheci* of modern zoologists; agreeing with the former in the conformation of their organs of locomotion and of mastication, and with the latter in the development of ischial callosities; more nearly related, however, to the true apes than to the inferior *simiæ,* and forming, with the *troglodytes* and *satyri,* a well-defined and clearly-circumscribed group, or sub-family of *quadrumana.*

The principal and most influential character of the

gibbons is unquestionably to be found in the conformation of the extremities, the organs of locomotion
and prehension; in the extravagant development of
the pectoral members, the length and separation of
the toes and fingers, and the oblique articulation
of the posterior hands, though, in this respect, they
are by no means so anomalous as the orangs. Hence
arise the sylvan residence, the arborial habits, and
the peculiarities of gait and attitude, which distinguish the gibbons when walking upon a level surface.
In an erect position their fingers almost touch the
ground; and, when they walk, their mode of progression, properly speaking, is neither that of a biped
nor of a quadruped, but of an intermediate kind,
partaking, in a great measure, of the qualities of
both, and yet perfectly distinct from either. The
weight of the body is supported upon the hind-feet
alone; but as the narrowness of the soles, and the
oblique articulation of the posterior members would
momentarily endanger their equipoise, if its security
depended only upon these organs, the long arms are
employed to counteract the natural tendency to vacil-
lation induced by these apparent defects, and by
lightly and rapidly touching the ground, from time
to time, on either side, with the fingers, as they proceed, they are thus enabled to restore their tottering
equilibrium, and preserve a tolerable degree of
steadiness in their motions. M. Geoffroy St. Hilaire
has compared the pace of the gibbons to that of a
lame man upon crutches; but the cases are not so
analogous in reality, as they appear to be at first
sight: the gibbons have the free and unconstrained
use of their posterior extremities, which, though
short and crooked, are, at the same time, muscular
and powerful; nor do they ever rest the entire weight
of the body upon the long pectoral members, as the
lame man does upon his crutches, in order to swing

the posterior simultaneously forward. Their pace,
on the contrary, more nearly resembles that of an
infirm person who walks with the assistance of two
staves; it is a species of quadruped progression, in
which the attitude is erect, and the weight of the
body rested upon the posterior extremities alone,
whilst the anterior are employed only to steady the
motion, and secure the equilibrium.

Such is the ordinary gait, not of the gibbons alone,
but likewise of the orangs and chimpanzees. We
have seen various individuals belonging to each of
these genera, but never observed them, even when
disease had reduced them to the last stages of debility, make use of the means of progression attributed
to them by M. Geoffroy; or, indeed, to proceed in any
other manner than that here described. And that
the anterior extremities do not enter into the means
of progression, on a level surface, as an essential and
indispensable component, nor execute the functions
which the French professor supposes, is sufficiently
proved by the fact that the animals occasionally dispense with their employment altogether, and invariably do so when the hands are otherwise occupied,
as, for instance, in carrying a burthen, and that, too,
without any serious derangement or apparent inconvenience.

But the truth is, that progressive motion, upon a
level surface, is no more the natural pace of the
orangs and gibbons than it is of the bats and cetaceæ.
M. Geoffroy, indeed, has been at considerable pains
to establish and point out analogies of structure between the locomotive organs of the apes and those of
the cheiroptera; but these analogies, to say the least
of them, are extremely partial, if not far-fetched;
they consist merely in the unusual development of
the extremities common to both these orders of
mammals, but as this common character of organic

structure, far from causing a corresponding similarity of function, is so modified as to produce effects of a directly opposite nature, the analogies in question must be regarded as matters of speculative curiosity rather than as subjects of legitimate philosophical inquiry. The boundless regions of the open atmosphere are the peculiar element of the cheiroptera: the gibbons, on the contrary, find their appropriate habitat in the dense woods and shady forests of tropical climes; there, the apparent incongruities of their structure vanish, and the very imperfections of organization which disqualify them for moving or residing upon the surface of the earth, become the powerful instruments of enlarging their sphere of action, and of adapting them, in the most perfect and beautiful manner, to the peculiarities of their situation. The comparative shortness of their hind-legs, by bringing the centre of gravity nearer to the surface, as they walk along the branches, secures the stability of their equilibrium, and leaves the hands at liberty to be otherwise employed; whilst the apparently extravagant length of the arms materially increases the sphere of their action, at the same time that these organs, by acting upon the principle of the rope-dancer's balancing-pole, enter as an important element into the function of locomotion. Even the bandiness of the legs and crookedness of the ankles are here turned to advantage, since they enable the animal to grasp the branches with more firmness, and to preserve its hold with less fatigue, and for a greater length of time, than it could possibly do were the limbs straight, or the joints articulated, as in the human subject. In their native forests, again, the trees stand so close together that the branches are frequently interwoven, and the gibbons are thus enabled to travel for many miles without once descending to the surface of the earth;

but, even where the trees are farther apart, these animals prefer leaping from one to another, rather than descending to the earth, where indeed their progress would be more impeded than facilitated by the thick jungle and underwood; and travellers assure us that they will, on these occasions, leap, with comparative ease, to the surprising distance of forty or fifty feet*.

The absence of tails and cheek-pouches are other characters which distinguish the gibbons from the ordinary simiæ; but as both these characters have been already described in speaking of the apes in general, it is unnecessary for us to insist farther upon them at present. Neither is it necessary to discuss the nature of the ischial callosities, farther than to remark a difference of habit between the gibbons and the rest of the real apes with which they seem to be connected. The object of these organs is to afford the simiæ a secure seat upon which they can repose without injury or fatigue, when wearied or exhausted by the rapid evolutions and complicated movements which they habitually execute. All those species, consequently, which possess ischial callosities, the gibbons among the rest, sleep and repose themselves in a sitting posture, with the arms folded across the knees, and the head reclined upon the breast, or supported by the shoulder. The chimpanzee and orangs alone, of all the simiæ, differ in this respect; they have no callosities, and when inclined to sleep or repose, lie down at full-length, like a human being, and lean the head upon the hand, or otherwise contrive to supply the want of a pillow. Hence they are obliged, in a state of nature, to construct huts or resting-places, by interweaving the small branches and twigs of trees, in which they can stretch themselves at their ease, and repose in se-

* Duvaucel in F. Cuv. Hist. Nat. des Mam. 4to edit., i., 22,

curity; or else to avail themselves of such cabins as
have been abandoned by the natives. Thus Dr.
Abel informs us that the young orang, of whose
habits he has given so valuable and entertaining a
description, when left to himself, previous to their
departure from Java, formed a rude kind of hut or
nest, by intertwining the slender branches of a
large tamarind tree in which he had taken up his
residence, and to which he invariably retired upon
the approach of night, or when a hearty meal, or the
fatigue attendant upon violent exercise, induced him
to repose: other observers assure us that this is the
common habit of the species, and it is universally
agreed by African travellers, that the chimpanzee
either builds a species of rude cabin for his own accommodation, or takes possession of the huts which
the negroes have abandoned in the woods. This
faculty of constructiveness, if we may be allowed to
borrow a term from the phrenologists, appears to be
mainly induced by the necessity under which these
animals labour of providing a secure and commodious
sleeping-place: we are farther of opinion that it may
be ultimately traced to their want of ischial callosities;
but to whatever cause it is to be attributed, it is unquestionably one of the most interesting and peculiar
of their habits, and one which they partake in common, neither with the gibbons, nor with any other
group of quadrumana.

But the characters here enumerated—the excessive
disproportion of the extremities, the possession of
callosities, and the absence of tails and cheek-pouches
—though undoubtedly the most important, are by no
means the only, nor the most appropriate, of those
which distinguish the gibbons: on the contrary,
these animals possess other characters, and some
which are altogether peculiar to themselves, at least
among the quadrumana. Such, for instance, is the

union of the index and middle fingers of the hind-
feet, which is found in many of the species of *hylobates*, and is not confined to the *siamang*, as was
supposed by Sir Stamford Raffles, nor yet indicative
of a mere sexual difference, as M. Duvaucel would
lead us to believe. Of the nine species here described, five unquestionably possess this peculiarity of
structure, and, perhaps, a sixth also; at all events,
three only are known, for certain, to be without it—
so that it may be regarded, with much greater propriety, in the light of a generic, than of either a
specific or sexual character. Indeed, the improbability of the latter opinion is sufficiently obvious,
from analogical considerations alone, and without
the contradiction which it receives from actual observation. It is most unlikely that the males and
females of the same species should differ, as M.
Duvaucel supposes, in so important a part of their
conformation as that which relates to the structure of
the organs of touch and prehension; there is no
known instance of such a sexual distinction throughout the entire range of vertebrated animals. In the
Australian marsupials, which exhibit a similar union
of the index and middle hind-toes, this character is
well-known to be uniformly generic, never sexual;
and, finally, we have ourselves ascertained, as carefully as an attentive examination of the prepared
specimens of seven species of gibbons, contained in
the collection of the Zoological Society, permits, that
it is found indifferently in both sexes, and invariably
common to the males, as well as to the females, of
those species which possess it at all. In other respects, though the character in question is sufficiently
curious, as existing in animals so elevated in the
scale of nature as the *hylobates*, it is by no means uncommon among other tribes: the majority of Australian marsupials, as has been already observed,

possess it in an equal, or even in a superior degree
to the gibbons, since their toes are united throughout
the whole length, whilst in the latter animals the
union takes place only throughout the first, or, at
most, part of the second phalanges; and it is well-
known that the entire order of *Incessores*, in ornith-
ology, are principally distinguished by the same
peculiarity of conformation.

The form of the head in the gibbons approaches
more nearly to that of the chimpanzee than it does
to that of the adult orangs, only that the forehead is
still flatter, and the brows less prominent than in that
animal; the scull is smooth and round, the occiput
particularly capacious, nor are there any indications
of the enormous sagittal and occipital crests, which
form so remarkable a feature in the sculls of the
orangs, and give to the head of these animals its singularly compressed and prismatic form. Except in
the great development of the canines, and this principally in the adult males, the nature of the dental
system is not materially different from that of man,
and the other simiæ. But the gibbons have another
character which approximates them more nearly to
the human type, than any other quadrumanous mammal, whithout even excepting the chimpanzee itself,
in other respects confessedly the connecting link between man and the inferior animals. We allude to
the form of the nose, and the position of the nostrils
in these creatures. In the chimpanzee and orangs
it can scarcely be said that there is any nose at all; the
large open nostrils are conspicuously placed in the
very centre of the face, and we look upon these animals with much the same feeling of loathing and
disgust with which we regard a human being whom
disease or accident has deprived of this important
and conspicuous organ. The nose of the gibbons,
on the contrary, though small and flat, is, neverthe-

less, sufficiently developed, and tolerably well formed ; the nostrils are small, and open at the extremity of the nose, very much as they do in the human subject, except that they are placed rather more towards the sides, and the whole organ possesses a degree of symmetry superior to anything of the same kind in many tribes of negroes and Hottentots. This characteristic trait imparts to the physiognomy of the gibbons a pleasing expression, and deprives it of that hideous appearance of deformity, which, in the orangs and chimpanzee, disgusts, whilst it humiliates us, as we view in it the degrading likeness, and compare it with the consequences of human disease or depravity. The eyes of the gibbons are, moreover, farther separated from one another, and less deeply sunk than in either the chimpanzee or the orangs ; the mouth is smaller and more neatly formed, the muzzle less projecting, and the chin more prominently developed ; in short, the whole contour and physiognomy of the head and face approach more nearly to the human form than those of other apes, confessedly their superiors in mental and physical endowments.

It is unnecessary to insist upon the less important characters of the gibbons. All those which have been carefully dissected, that is to say, *H. Lar.*[*], *H. Scyritus*[†], *H. Unicolor*[‡], *H. Choromandus*[†], and *H. Leuciscus*[§], were found to possess the vermiform appendix to the cœcum, as in the human species. With the single exception of the siamang (*H. Syndactylus*), they appear to be destitute of the laryngal sacks which distinguish the chimpanzee, orangs, and even some of the inferior simiæ ; at least, these organs have not been noticed in any other species of

* Buff. Hist. Nat., xiv., 98.
† Zool. Journ., iv., 109.
‡ Jour. Acad. Nat. Sci. Philad., v., 2.
§ Œuvres de P. Camper, i., 100.

the present genus, and Sir Stamford **Raffles** expressly denies the possession of them to any of the other gibbons with which he was acquainted*. The ribs vary from twelve to fourteen pair; the *H. Lar* has twelve pair† ; *H. Syndactylus‡, H. Agilis‡,* and *H. Leuciscus*§, thirteen ; and *H. Rafflesii‡,* and *H. Unicolor*‖, fourteen ; the number in the remaining four species of which the genus is at present composed has not been recorded. The fur is, generally speaking, of a fine woolly texture, soft, close-pressed, and erect; in *H. Syndactylus* and *H. Scyritus,* however, it is of a harsher and more silky quality, as it is likewise about the face, and on the hands and feet of the other species; these two animals, as well as *H. Rafflesii* and *H. Choromandus,* have the hair of the fore-arm reversed towards the elbow, as in the orangs and chimpanzee, though in the last-mentioned gibbons this character is less decidedly marked, owing to the woolly and more pliant quality of the fur. The face and ears are generally naked, or thinly covered with very short adpressed hairs ; the palms of the hands and soles of the feet are universally naked. The colours vary from the light ash of the *H. Leuciscus,* through almost every shade of brown, till we at length reach the deep and glossy black of the *H. Syndactylus*: the contour of the face, and the backs of the hands and feet, are, more or less, marked with white, or light grey, in many of the species ; and we are the more desirous of insisting upon this character, because we have found the nature and extent of these markings to be tolerably uniform in individuals of

---

* Lin. Trans., xii. 243.
† Buff. Hist. Nat., xiv. 104.
‡ F. Cuv. Hist. Nat. des Mam., 4to., i. 25.
§ Harlan in Jour. of Acad. of Nat. Scien. of Philadelphia, vol. v. part ii.
‖ Œuvres de P. Camper, i. 28.

K

the same species, and because we believe that ignorance of this fact has been the main cause of the doubts and disagreements which have hitherto prevailed among zoologists, with regard to the specific distinctions of these animals.

The history of our knowledge of the gibbons, and other true apes, ascends to a more remote period of antiquity than has been hitherto suspected. The name *gibbon*, indeed, though of ancient origin, is modern in its application to the animals which now bear it; since we learn from Aristotle that the κῆβος, κῆπος, κεῖπος, or *cephus*, of the ancient Greeks and Romans, (a word itself clearly derived from the Hebrew קוף, *koph*,) had a long tail; but though it may have been originally misapplied to the *hylobates*, custom has so sanctioned its use, that it would now be difficult, even were it desirable, to change it. The earliest unquestionable reference to any of the real apes, which we have been able to discover among classical writers, is to be found in the relation of a voyage along the western coast of Africa, performed about 500 years before the Christian æra, by the Carthaginian admiral, Hanno. This curious extract has been already given, under the head of the chimpanzee to which it was shown to refer; and it can scarcely be doubted but that the ancient fictions of pygmies, satyrs, cynocephali, cynoprosopi, &c., and other supposed tribes of human monsters, originated in vague accounts of different species of simiæ. Of these, the following passages from Pliny, in which are described three of these supposed races of human monsters, manifestly have their source in some imperfect descriptions of apes, properly so called, and not improbably refer to the two continental species of gibbons which will be hereafter described. " Sunt et satyri subsolanis Indorum montibus, (Catharcludorum dicitur regio,) pernicissimum animal: cum quadrupedes tum recte currentes, humanâ effigie, propter velocitatem, nisi senes aut ægri, non capiuntur. Choromandarum gentem vocat Tauron, silvestrem, sine voce stridoris horrendi, hirtis corporibus, occulisque glaucis, dentibus caninis. Eudoxus in meridianis Indiæ viris plantas esse cubitales, feminis adeo parvas ut struthopodes appellentur. Megasthenes gentem inter nomadas Indos narium loco foramina tantum habentem, anguium modo loripedem, vocari scyritas*." "In the tropical mountains of India, that is to say, in the country of the Catharcludi, are found satyrs, animals of surprising speed and activity. The face of these creatures resembles the human countenance; they walk sometimes on all-fours, sometimes on two feet only; and, owing to their great velocity, can only be captured through sickness or old age. Tauron mentions a savage tribe which he calls *choromandæ*, which have hairy bodies, amber-coloured eyes, teeth like dogs, and instead of articulate sounds utter only frightful screams. Eudoxus says that in Southern India the men's feet are a full cubit in length, but that the women have them so short, that they are called sparrow-footed. Megasthenes relates that, among the nomad Indians there is a tribe, which, instead of a nose, have only two open holes, and bandy legs which they can twist about in all directions, as serpents do their bodies; they are called *scyritæ*." Who does not at once recognize the principal characters of the gibbons and orangs in these descriptions? The surprising agility, the anthropoid features, and the pace indifferently biped or quadruped, which are attributed to the satyr; the hairy coats, amber eyes, long canine teeth—for this is unquestionably the true meaning of the phrase, "dentibus caninis"—and screaming voices of the *choromandæ*; and the mere "foramina" instead of regular nose, and

* Plin. Hist. Nat., lib. vii. c. 2.

obliquely-articulated limbs of the *scyritæ*, are all strictly applicable to the Asiatic apes, and so accurate, that we cannot help believing that the original describers derived them from actual observation of the animals. Not that it is probable that Pliny himself ever saw any of the animals which he here describes upon the authority of others; the satyr which he mentions from his own observation was a species of monkey[*]; Ælian assures us that it had a tail [†]: it is remarkable, however, that the passage which we have here quoted should have escaped the attention of the celebrated Camper, who has taken great pains, and with very indifferent success, to prove that the ancient Romans were acquainted with some species of true apes, and that some of the anatomical descriptions of Galen were derived from the dissection of orangs and gibbons. The passage indeed, whilst it proves that the ancients had heard of these animals, is unfavourable to the main supposition of Camper; for Pliny and Ælian both give their descriptions on the authority of others, and if they had ever seen the animals, would certainly not have classed them, as the former has done, among the varieties of the human species. Whether the animals intended were orangs or gibbons is a matter of little consequence; the continental habitat which is assigned to them makes it probable that they were *hylobates;* and it is for this reason that we have given the names of *choromandus* and *scyritus* to the two continental species here described. The allusion to the cramped feet of the Chinese ladies—for to them alone can the report of Eudoxus apply—proves that the ancients had already acquired some vague knowledge of these extraordinary people, and that the female fashions of the celestial empire are as immutable as its laws and ceremonies.

[*] Plin. Hist. Nat. lib. viii. c. 80.   [†] Æl. lib. vi. c. 21.

Up to a comparatively recent period, the knowledge which the civilized nations of Europe possessed of these animals was no less vague and unsatisfactory than that of the ancients. From the commencement of the Christian era to the time of Marco Polo, a period of nearly thirteen centuries, we are aware of no original mention of these animals. That early traveller informs us that the inhabitants of Basura, a province of Java, were accustomed to shave and embalm the bodies of the gibbons, and sell them, under the name of pygmies, to the stranger merchants, whom the commerce of drugs and spices attracted to their shores; nor is it at all unlikely that the knowledge of the ancients may have been thus acquired. The same practice is mentioned by other travellers as being exercised by the inhabitants of the Malabar coast. The early Portuguese and Dutch navigators, and the Jesuit missionaries to China and Malacca, occasionally mention some traits of their form and manners; but the first professed figure and description which have come to our knowledge are those by De Visme, in the 59th volume of the "Philosophical Transactions." These are of the hooloc (*H. scyritus*), a species since more perfectly described and figured by Dr. Harlan; but they are meagre in the extreme, and it was not till the appearance of the 14th volume of "Buffon's Histoire Naturelle," in the year 1756, with the accurate figures and descriptions of *H. Lar* and *H. Variegatus* therein contained, that zoologists could be said to possess any positive knowledge as to the real characters of the gibbons. From this time to the period of Sir Stamford Raffles's and MM. Diard and Duvaucel's researches in Sumatra and the neighbouring isles, the work of Buffon, with the exception of Camper's account of *H. Leuciscus*, was the only authentic source of original information upon this subject.

These meritorious observers added three others to
the list of species already known, viz. *H. Syndactylus*,
H. Agilis, and *H. Rafflesii*. Dr. Harlan has more
recently distinguished two others, the hooloc (*H.
Scyritus*), already figured by De Visme, but afterwards confounded with *H. Lar*, and *H. Concolor*, a
new species: and a ninth species has been recently
described in the "Memoirs of the Zoological Society."

The Siamang (*Hylobates Syndactylus*).

Having disposed of the chimpanzee and orang-
outan, the two animals which the universal consent
of observers admits to approximate most nearly to
the human species, we come now to describe the specific characters of a group of smaller apes, differing

from the former by the possession of rudimentary
callosities, and, on that and other accounts, considered as forming a distinct genus.   These, as has
been already observed, have been usually denominated *gibbons*, a word formed from the Greek name
kebus, kephus, or *keiphon,* applied by the naturalists
and historians of antiquity to some quadrumanous
animal which it is not now easy to identify.

The largest of this subdivision of the ape genus
is the siamang, *Pithecus Syndactylus*, which was
discovered by Sir Stamford Raffles and the French
naturalists, Diard and Duvaucel, during their zoological researches in the island of Sumatra.   The
skull of this animal is small and depressed, its
face of a deep black colour, and perfectly naked, with
the exception of a few red hairs, by way of beard,
upon the chin; the eyes are deeply sunk under
heavy projecting brows; the nose is broad and flat,
with wide open nostrils; the mouth is very large,
and opens almost to the articulation of the jaws;
the cheeks are sunk under high projecting cheek-
bones, and the chin is almost rudimentary.   The
hair over the entire body is extremely long, coarse,
thickly furnished, and of a glossy black colour; it
is much closer on the head, back, shoulders, and
extremities, than on the belly, which, particularly in
the females, is nearly naked.   Like that of the
chimpanzee, it is partially separated on the crown of
the head, and falls down towards each side so as to
give the appearance of whiskers on the cheeks.   The
scrotum of the male is furnished with a tuft of long
straight hair, which descends almost to the knees, and
readily distinguishes this sex from the females, which
on the other hand are easily known by their naked
breasts and bellies, and by their prominent mammæ
terminated by large black nipples.   The ears are completely concealed by the hair of the head; they are

naked, and like all the other naked parts, of a deep glossy black colour. Beneath the chin, there is a large bare sac, of a lax oily appearance, which is distended with air or emptied at the will of the animal, and when inflated, resembles an enormous goitre. It is in all respects similar to that already described in the orang-outan, and probably assists, if it be not the principal instrument, in swelling the volume of the voice, and producing those astounding cries which, according to the account of M. Duvaucel, may be heard at the distance of several miles.

But this is not the only point of resemblance between the siamang and the orang-outan. Like that animal, the present species has the hair of the head directed forwards so as to shade the temples, and that of the fore-arm reverted upwards, in the direction of the elbow, where, encountering the hair of the humerus, which grows in the opposite direction, it stands out in the form of a prominent ruff. The most extraordinary part of the organic structure of this species, however, consists in the union of the index and middle fingers of the posterior extremities, from which it derives its specific appellation of *syndactylus*, and which, being connected together nearly as far as the nail-joint, are necessarily destitute of separate or individual motion.

The following account of the habits and character of the siamang, from the pen of M. Duvaucel, is inserted by M. F. Cuvier in his " Histoire Naturelle des Mammifères," a work containing much valuable information relating to the apes of Sumatra. M. Duvaucel, and his companion, M. Diard, had been employed by Sir Stamford Raffles, at that time governor of Bencoolen, in the capacity of collectors of subjects of Natural History in the interior of the island ; and it is to the researches of these naturalists, and the liberality of their enlightened patron, that we owe our knowledge of this and the two following species.

"This species," says M. Duvaucel, " is very common in our forests, (those, namely, in the neighbourhood of Bencoolen, in Sumatra), and I have had frequent opportunities of observing it, as well in its wild state as in bondage. The siamangs generally assemble in numerous troops, conducted, it is said by a chief, whom the Malays believe to be invulnerable, probably because he is more agile, powerful, and difficult to attain than the rest. Thus united, they salute the rising and setting sun with the most terrific cries, which may be heard at several miles distance; and which, when near, stun, when they do not frighten. This is the morning-call of the mountain Malays, but to the inhabitants of the towns it is a most insupportable annoyance. By way of compensation, they preserve a most profound silence during the day-time, unless when disturbed in their repose or sleep. These animals are slow and heavy in their gait; they want confidence when they climb, and agility when they leap, so that they may be easily caught, when they can be surprised. But nature, in depriving them of the means of readily escaping danger, has endowed them with a vigilance which rarely fails them; if they hear a noise which is strange to them, even though they be at a mile's distance, fright seizes them, and they immediately take flight. When surprised on the ground, however, they may be captured without resistance, being either overwhelmed with fear, or conscious of their weakness and the impossibility of escaping. At first, indeed, they endeavour to avoid their pursuers by flight, and it is then that their awkwardness in this exercise is most apparent. Their body, too tall and heavy for their short slender thighs, inclines forwards, and availing themselves of their long arms, as crutches,

K 5

they thus advance by jerks, which resemble the hobbling of a lame man whom fear compels to make an extraordinary effort.

" However numerous the troop may be, if one is wounded, it is immediately abandoned by the rest, unless indeed it happens to be a young one; then the mother, who either carries it, or follows close behind, stops, falls with it, and uttering the most lamentable cries, precipitates herself upon the common enemy with open mouth and extended arms. But it is manifest that these animals are not made for combat; they neither know how to deal nor how to shun a blow. Neither is their maternal affection displayed only in moments of danger; the care which the females bestow upon their offspring is so tender, and even refined, that one would be almost tempted to attribute the sentiment to a rational rather than an instinctive process. It is a curious and interesting spectacle, which a little precaution has sometimes enabled me to witness, to see these females carry their young to the river, wash their faces in spite of their childish outcries, and altogether bestow upon their cleanliness a time and attention that, in many cases, the children of our own species might well envy. The Malays, indeed, related a fact to me, which I doubted at first, but which I believe to be in a great measure confirmed by my own subsequent observations: it is, that the young siamangs, whilst yet too weak to go alone, are always carried by individuals of their own sex, by their fathers if they are males, and by their mothers if females. I have also been assured that these animals frequently become the prey of the tiger, from the same species of fascination which serpents are related to exercise over birds, squirrels, and other small animals.

_ " Servitude, however long, seems to have no

influence in modifying the characteristic defects of this ape, his stupidity, his sluggishness, and his awkwardness. It is true, that a few days suffice to make him as gentle and contented as he was before wild and distrustful; but, constitutionally timid, he never acquires the familiarity of other apes, and even his submission appears to be rather the result of extreme apathy than of confidence and affection. He is almost equally insensible to good or bad treatment; gratitude and revenge are sentiments alike foreign to him. All his senses are dull and imperfect; if he regards an object it is manifestly without interest—if he touches it, it is involuntarily. In a word, the siamang exhibits an absence of all intellectual qualities; and if animals were to be classed according to their mental capacities, he would unquestionably occupy a very inferior station. Most commonly squatted on his hams, with his long arms twined round him, and his head concealed between his legs, a position which he also occupies while sleeping, he is seldom roused from his lethargy, nor does he break silence, unless at intervals, to utter a disagreeable cry, which in sound approaches to that of a turkey-cock, but which appears to be expressive of no sentiment, nor to declare any want, and which in fact expresses nothing. Hunger itself is insufficient to rouse him from his natural apathy: he receives his food with indifference, carries it to his mouth without avidity, and sees himself deprived of it without testifying either surprise or resentment."

This very unflattering and probably highly-charged picture conveys no very favourable impressions of the intellectual faculties of the siamang; though it may be observed that the latter part of the account is not exactly in accordance with the refined sentiments of affection which M. Duvaucel had formerly attributed to the females of the species, nor with the vigilance which he describes them as habitually employing in avoiding even distant dangers. The latter part of his observations, indeed, appears to have been made upon a subject in confinement, and probably in the last stage of disease, which is the only mode of accounting for the discrepancies of M. Duvaucel's own account, and reconciling it with the more favourable character of this animal's mental and physical faculties which has been given by Mr. George Bennett, and which, in justice to the siamang, we consider ourselves bound to present to the reader. Mr. Bennett's observations were made upon a young animal which he procured at Singapore, in the year 1830, and which had been brought from the interior of Sumatra. The Malays of Singapore, according to Mr. Bennett, called this animal *Ungka*, and denied that it was the siamang, which they described as a different species, distinguished by a circle of white hair round the face. The name siamang may perhaps be improperly applied to the present animal: it rests on the authority of Sir Stamford Raffles, who first described and named the species in the 13th volume of the " Linnæan Transactions ;" but on the other hand, it appears evident from Sir Stamford's paper, that the name of *Ungka* is generic in the Malay language, and is applied to at least two other gibbons, with an additional epithet to distinguish them, as *Ungka-puti*, *Ungka-etam*, &c.

After describing the specimen in question, Mr. Bennett proceeds : " He invariably walks in an erect posture when on a level surface, and then the arms either hang down, enabling him sometimes to assist himself with his knuckles; or, what is more usual, he keeps his arms uplifted, in nearly an erect position, with the hands pendent ready to seize a rope, and

climb up on the approach of danger, or on the ob-
trusion of strangers. He walks rather quick in the
erect posture, but with a waddling gait, and is soon
run down, if, while pursued, he has no opportunity
of escaping by climbing.

"His food is various: he preferred vegetable diet,
as rice, plantains, &c., and was ravenously fond of
carrots, of which we had some quantity on board.
Although, when at dinner, he would behave well, not
intruding his paw into our plates, yet when the
carrots appeared, all his decorum was lost in his
eager desire for them, and it required some exertions
to keep him from attacking them, whether we wished
it or not. A piece of carrot would draw him from
one end of the table to the other, over which he
would walk, without disturbing a single article, although the ship was rolling at the time; so admirably
can these animals balance themselves. This is well
seen when they play about the rigging of a ship
at sea: often when springing from rope to rope have
I expected to see him buffeting the waves, and as
often did I find that all my fears were groundless.

"He would drink tea, coffee, and chocolate, but
neither wine nor spirits. Of animal food he prefers
fowl; but a lizard having been caught on board, it
was placed before him, when he seized the reptile instantly in his paw, and greedily devoured it. He
was also very fond of sweetmeats, such as jams,
jellies, dates, &c., and no child with the 'sweetest
tooth' ever evinced more delight after 'bon-bons'
than did this little creature. Some manilla sweet-
cakes that were on board he was always eager to
procure, and would not unfrequently enter the cabin
in which they were kept, and endeavour to lift up the
cover of the jar: he was not less fond of onions, although their acridity caused him to sneeze, and loll
out his tongue; when he took one he used to put it

into his mouth, and immediately eat it with great rapidity.

"The first instance I observed of his attachment to liberty was soon after he had been presented to me by Mr. Bousted. On entering the yard in which he was tied up, one morning, I was not well pleased at observing him busily engaged in removing the belt to which the cord or chain was fixed, at the same time whining and uttering a peculiar squeaking noise. As soon as he had succeeded in procuring his liberty, he walked in his usual erect posture towards some Malays, who were standing near the place, and, after hugging the legs of several of the party, without, however, permitting them to take him in their arms, he went to a Malay lad, who seemed to be the object of his search; for, on meeting with him, he immediately climbed into his arms, and hugged him closely, having an expression, in both the look and manner, of gratification, at being once again in the arms of him, who, I now understood, was his former master. When this lad sold the animal to Mr. Bousted, he was tied up in the court-yard of that gentleman's house, and his screams to get loose used to be a great annoyance to the residents in the vicinity. Several times he effected his escape, and would then make for the water-side, the Malay lad being usually on board the proa, in which he had arrived from Sumatra. He was never retaken until, having reached the water, he could proceed no farther. The day previous to sailing I sent him aboard; as the lad that originally brought him could not be found, a Malay servant to Mr. Bousted was deputed to take charge of him. The animal was a little troublesome at first, but afterwards became quiet in the boat. On arriving on board, he soon managed to make his escape, rewarding his conductor with a bite as a parting remembrance, and ascending the rigging with such

agility, as to excite the astonishment and admiration
of the crew : as the evening approached, the animal
came down on the deck, and was readily secured.
We found, however, in a day or two, that he was so
docile when at liberty, and so very much irritated at
being confined, that he was permitted to range about
the deck or rigging.

"He usually (on first coming on board), after
taking exercise about the rigging, retired to rest at
sunset, on the maintop, coming on deck regularly at
daylight. This continued until our arrival off the
Cape, when, experiencing a lower temperature, he
expressed an eager desire to be taken to my arms,
and to be permitted to pass the night in my cabin,
for which he evinced such a decided partiality, that,
on the return of warm weather, he would not retire
to the maintop, but seemed to have a determination
to stay where he thought himself the most comfortable, and which I at last, after much crying and
solicitation from him, permitted.

"When sleeping, he lies along either on the side or
back, resting the head on the hands, and is always
desirous of retiring to rest at sunset; it was at this
time he would approach me, uncalled for, making a
peculiar begging, chirping noise, an indication that
he wished to be taken into the cabin to be put to bed.
Before I admitted him into my cabin, after having
firmly stood against his piteous beseeching tones and
cries, he would go up the rigging, and take up his
reposing place for the night in the maintop. He
would often (I suppose from his approximation to
civilization), indulge in bed sometime after sunrise,
and, frequently, when I awoke, I have seen him lying
on his back, his long arms stretched out, and with
eyes open, appearing as if buried in deep reflection.
He could not endure disappointment, and, like the
human species, he was always better pleased when he

had his own way: when refused or disappointed at anything he would display the freaks of temper of a spoiled child; lie on the deck, roll about, throw his arms and legs in various attitudes and directions, dash everything aside that might be within his reach, walk hurriedly, repeat the same scene over and over again, and utter the guttural notes of *ra, ra;* the employment of coercive measures during these pa-
'roxysms reduced him, in a short period, to a system of obedience, and the violence of his temper, by such means, became in some degree checked.

"When he came, at sunset, to be taken into my arms, and was refused, he would fall into a paroxysm of rage; but finding that unsuccessful and unattended to, he would mount the rigging, and, hanging over that part of the deck on which I was walking, would suddenly drop himself into my arms. The sounds he uttered were various: when pleased at a recognition of his friends, he would utter a peculiar squeaking chirping note; when irritated, a hollow barking noise was produced; but when very angry or frightened, or when chastised, the loud guttural sounds of *ra, ra, ra,* invariably followed. When I approached him for the first time in the morning, he greeted me with his chirping notes, advancing his face at the same time, as if intended for the purpose of salutation. His look was grave, and manner mild, and he was deficient in those mischievous tricks so peculiar to the monkey tribe in general. In only one instance did I experience any mischief from him, and that was in his meddling with my inkstand: he seemed to have an extraordinary *penchant* for the black fluid, would drink the ink (by placing his finger in the inkstand, and then sucking it), and suck the pens whenever an opportunity offered of gratifying this morbid propensity. There was a degree of intelligence in this animal beyond what is usually

termed common instinct. One instance of a very
close approximation to, if it may not be considered
absolutely an exercise of, the reasoning faculty, oc-
currred in this animal. Once or twice I lectured
him on taking away my soap continually from the
washing-place, which he would remove for his amusement from that place, and leave it about the cabin.
One morning I was writing, the ape being present,
in the cabin, when casting my eyes towards him, I
saw the little fellow taking the soap. I watched him
without his perceiving that I did so, and he occasionally would cast a furtive glance towards the place
where I sat. I pretended to write ; he seeing me
busily occupied, took the soap, and moved away with
it in his paw. When he had walked half the length
of the cabin, I spoke quietly without frightening him.
The instant he found I saw him, he walked back
again and deposited the soap nearly in the same place
from whence he had taken it. There was certainly
something more than instinct in that action : he evidently betrayed a consciousness of having done wrong,
both by his first and last actions, and what is reason
if that is not an exercise of it.

"When he walks in the erect posture, he turns
the leg and foot outwards, which occasions him to
have a waddling gait and to seem bow-legged. He
would pace the deck, being held by his long arms ;
and then had a resemblance to a child just learning
to step. The limbs from their muscular and strong
prehensile power, render the animal a fit inhabitant
for the forest, enabling him to spring from tree to
tree with an agility that we have frequently witnessed
him display about the rigging of the ship : he would
pass down the backstays, sometimes hanging by his
hands, at others walking down them in the erect
posture, like a rope-dancer balancing himself by his

long arms; or he would spring from one rope to a
great distance to another, or would drop from one
above to another below.   Being aware of his inability
to escape pursuit when running on a level surface,
his first object, when about to make an attack, was
to secure a rope and swing towards the object he was
desirous of attacking ; if defeated, he eluded pursuit
by climbing out of reach.

    " He has an awkward manner of drinking, by
which the liquid is much wasted : he first applies
his lips to the liquid, throwing the head up, which in
some degree may be attributed to the prominency of
the lower jaw ; and if the vessel in which the liquid
is contained should be shallow, he dips the paw into
it, and holding it over the mouth, lets the liquid drop
in.   I never observed him lap with the tongue when
drinking, but when tea or coffee was given him, the
tongue was carefully protruded for the purpose of
ascertaining its temperature.   This display of caution
was not confined to this species of ape, as I know of
several others which will do the same when hot tea
or coffee is given them, shaking their sapient head
violently if they are heated by the liquid, but still
undeterred will wait patiently until the hot liquid
becomes sufficiently cool for drinking.

    " He soon knew the name of Ungka, which had
been given to him, and would readily come to those
to whom it was attached, when called by that name.
His mildness of disposition and playfulness of manner
made him a universal favourite with all on board.
He was playful, but preferred children to adults.
He became particularly attached to a little Papuan
child (Elau, a native of Erromanga, one of the New
Hebrides group), who was on board, and whom it is
not improbable he may have in some degree considered as having an affinity to his own species.   They

were often seen sitting near the capstan, the animal
with his long arm around her neck, lovingly eating
biscuit together. She would lead him about by his
long arms, like an elder leading a younger child, and
it was the height of the grotesque to witness him
running round the capstan pursued by or pursuing
the child. He would waddle along in the erect
posture at a rapid rate, sometimes aiding himself by
his knuckles; but when fatigued he would spring
aside, seize hold of the first rope he came to, and
ascending a short distance, regard himself as safe
from pursuit. In a playful manner he would roll
on deck with the child, as if in a mock combat,
pushing with his feet (in which action he displayed
great muscular power), entwining his long arms round
her, and pretending to bite, or seizing a rope he
would swing towards her; and when efforts were
made to seize him, would elude the grasp by swinging
away; or he would, by way of changing the plan of
attack, drop suddenly on her from the ropes aloft,
and then engage in various playful antics. He
would play in a similar manner with adults; but
finding them usually too strong and rough for him,
he preferred children, giving up his games with them
if any adults joined in the sports at the same time.
If however an attempt was made by the child to play
with him, when he had no inclination, or after he
had sustained some disappointment, he usually made
a slight impression with his teeth on her arm, just
sufficient to act as a warning, or a sharp hint, that
no liberties were to be taken with his person, or as
the child would say, 'Ungka no like play now.'
Not unfrequently a string being tied to his leg, the
child would amuse herself by dragging the patient
animal about the deck; this he would good-naturedly
bear for some time, thinking perhaps it amused his

little playmate ; but finding it last longer than he expected, he became tired of that fun in which he had
no share except in being the sufferer ; he would then
make endeavours to disengage himself and retire. If
he found his efforts fruitless he would quietly walk up
to the child, make an impression with his teeth, in a
ratio of hardness according to his treatment : that hint
so terminated the sport, and procured him his liberty.

" There were also on board the ship several small
monkeys, with whom Ungka was desirous of forming
an acquaintance ; they treated him as an outcast,
and all cordially united to repel his approaches by
chattering and various other hostile movements.

" When dinner was announced by the steward, and
the captain and officers assembled, then Ungka, considering himself also one of the mess, would be seen
bending his steps towards the cuddy, and entering
took his station at a corner of the table, between the
captain and myself ; there he remained waiting for
his share. When, from any of his ludicrous actions
at table, we all burst out in loud laughter, he would
vent his indignation at being made the subject of
ridicule, by uttering his peculiar hollow barking
noise, at the same time inflating the air-sac, and
regarding the persons laughing with a most serious
look, until they had ceased, when he would quietly
resume his dinner.

" The animal had an utter dislike to confinement,
and was of such a social disposition, as always to prefer
company to being left alone ; when shut up, his
rage was very violent, throwing every thing about
that was lying near, or that he could move in his
place of confinement, but becoming perfectly quiet
when released. When standing with his back towards
the spectator, his being tail-less, and standing erect,
gave him the appearance of a little black hairy man ;

and such an object might easily have been regarded
by the superstitious as one of the infernal imps.
When he walks, to use a nautical phrase, 'he sways
the body,' and stepping at once on the whole of the
under surface of the foot, occasions a pattering noise,
like that which is heard when a duck, or any aquatic
bird, walks on the deck of a ship. When the weather
is cold, he may be seen huddled together, loses all
his lively and playful manner, sleeping much during
the day and giving up all exercise. The return of
warm weather imparted life to the animal, his activity
returned, his spirits revived, and his gambols and
sportiveness were resumed. Although every kindness
was shown to him by the officers and crew, and
sweetmeats and other niceties were given him by
them by way of bribes, to engage his confidence and
good opinion, yet he would not permit himself to be
taken in the arms or caressed familiarly by any
person on board during the voyage, except the com-
mander, the third officer, and myself, but with any
of the children he would readily gambol. It was a
strange fact that he in particular avoided all those
who wore large bushy whiskers. It was ludicrous
to behold the terrified looks of the animal, if his
finger was taken towards a cup of hot tea, as if to
ascertain the temperature, and his attempts at remon-
strating on the impropriety of such conduct, together
with his half-suppressed screams, were very diverting.
Among other amusements he would frequently hang
from a rope by one arm, and, when in a frolicsome
humour, frisk about, with his eyes shut, giving him
the appearance of a person hanging and in the
agonies of death. When we spoke a ship at sea, his
curiosity seemed to be much excited by the novel
object near us, for he would invariably mount up the
rigging, at a height sufficient to command a good

view of the stranger, and sometimes take up his position at the peak haul-yards, just under the flag— a signal difficult no doubt for the stranger to comprehend ; there he would remain gazing wistfully after the departure of the stranger until she was out of sight, 'give one parting lingering look,' and then come down on the deck again, and resume the sports from which her appearance had disturbed him.''

This more favourable character of the address and intelligence of the siamang is fully confirmed by Sir Stamford Raffles, who kept many individuals of this species for the express purpose of studying their manners, and whose situation, in other respects, gave him the best means of acquiring accurate information regarding their habits and economy. He describes them as bold and powerful, but easily domesticated, and so sociable and affectionate, that they are never content but when in company with those they are attached to. They grow to the height of three feet six inches, or upwards, and are very common in the forests about Bencoolen, where they associate in large companies, and make the woods resound with their harsh guttural cries.

CHAPTER VI.

Gibbons *continued.*—The WHITE-HANDED GIBBON, the, HOOLOO and the UNGKA-ETAM.

WE include these three species under the same head, not because there is any doubt of their being perfectly distinct from one another, but because they resemble each other so much in form and colours as to be distinguishable only by the greater or less extent of the white marking on the head and extremities, whilst their habits are so similar as to preclude the necessity of a separate notice. Their specific difference, however, though depending upon characters so slight and unimportant as far as regards their external conformation, is fully established by the more permanent and influential modifications of their internal structure. Specimens of the first two of these animals may be seen in the museum of the Zoological Society, and the third is described and figured in the " Histoire Naturelle des Mammifères," from the letters and drawings of MM. Diard and Duvaucel. The white-handed gibbon was formerly seen alive and figured by Buffon, and the hooloc, after having been cursorily noticed by many previous authors, has been at length accurately described and figured by Dr. Harlan in the " Transactions of the American Philosophical Society," vol. iv., new series. These sources, combined with our own original observations, have furnished the materials for accurately distinguishing and describing the species, as well as for relating whatever is most interesting and authentic in their manners and habits. Before detailing what is known of their habits and economy, we shall, according to our usual custom, briefly describe the species, and point out the prin-

cipal characteristics by which they may be most
readily distinguished from one another.

The White-handed Gibbon (*Hylobates Lar*).

1. The *white-handed gibbon*, the *simia lar* o.
Linnæus and Geoffroy St. Hilaire, is of a uniform
black colour, assuming an occasional shade of dark
brown, with the face surrounded by a broad circle of
pure white, and the backs of the hands and feet,
from the wrists and ankles to the extremities of the
toes, light grey. The white circle which encompasses
the face, is not very broad across the forehead, but
expands upon the cheeks into large whiskers, which
unite under the chin, so that the whole of the under
jaw is pure unmixed white. The face and hands
contrast strongly with the colours on the rest of the

body, which in the specimen we have ourselves
examined, as well as in that described by Buffon,
are uniform black, but tinged with a shade of very
deep brown in those described by M. Geoffroy, and
at present in the museum at the Jardin des Plantes.
The hair or rather fur has all the characters of common
wool; it is greasy to the touch, partially spiral in form,
readily separates into small locks or tufts, and stands
out from the skin in a perpendicular direction. Like
wool, too, it is very thick and closely pressed together.
These observations refer only to the black fur; the
white which surrounds the face, and covers the backs
of the hands and feet, is of a coarser quality, short,
harsh, and partaking more of the nature of common
hair, which it farther resembles in lying smoothly
along the skin. The fur of the fore-arm has the
same characters as that on the rest of the body, and
therefore cannot be properly said either to be directed
towards the wrist or reversed towards the elbow, as
in some other species of apes; it is very thick and
close on these parts, as elsewhere, and covers the
backs of the hands, feet, and fingers, down to the
very nails. The face, ears, and the palms of the
hands and soles of the feet are naked, and of a black
colour, and the eyes are fringed with long, stiff, black
lashes. All the toes of the hind-feet have a small
web interposed at their base, and extending about
half-way up between the first phalanges; that between
the index and middle toe unites them throughout
almost the whole of the first phalanx; but being
broad, allows the fingers to be widely separated, and
is indeed nothing more than an extension of the little
rudimentary web which is interposed at the base of
the human fingers. The specimen here described
is a female, and judging from the nature of the
dentition, evidently of immature age. The whole
length of the head and body is 15 inches; the length

L

of the anterior extremity 18 inches, and that of
the posterior 15 inches. It forms part of the
magnificent collection of Sumatran animals presented
by Sir Stamford Raffles to the Zoological Society.
The individual described by Buffon was brought from
Pondicherry, but it had probably come originally
from Sumatra, or some of the neighbouring islands,
since, though the contrary is asserted by some of the
ancient writers, modern travellers give us no reason
to suppose that any species of real ape exists in the
western peninsula of India*. M. Geoffroy has not
mentioned the locality from which he received the
specimens in the French museum.

2. The *hooloc, golok, hooloo*, or *voulock* (*hylobates
scyritus*), for travellers disagree about the orthography, was originally noticed in the 14th volume
of the " Philosophical Transactions," and has been
recently described and accurately figured by Dr.
Harlan. It inhabits the province of Assam, probably also other parts of the Eastern peninsula, and
attains the stature of four feet or upwards when full
grown and standing in an upright posture. The
whole animal is covered with uniform black hair of a
shining rigid quality, very different from the woolly
texture of the fur proper to the last species, and in
the absence of all other characters, alone sufficient to
distinguish them. A white band or fillet, about half
an inch in breadth, separates the face from the forehead; it passes immediately over the eyebrows, but
does not extend beyond the temples, leaving the
cheeks and chin of the same black colour as the rest

* We have since heard from an Indian officer of high
rank and celebrity, that there is unquestionably a real ape
(most probably the species in question) in the forests of the
Malabar coast: he had often heard the natives speak of it,
and not unfrequently heard its cry " *woo-woo* " in the woods
though he had never actually seen it.

of the body. The backs of the hands and feet are also black, and the hair of the fore-arms is reversed or directed towards the elbows. All these characters, common to both sexes, definitely distinguish the hooloc from the species last described, besides that the present animal has the toes of the hind-feet completely separate and without any appearance of the membrane that unites their first phalanges in the white-handed gibbon. The face of the preserved specimen here described, is of a dusky blue colour, sprinkled with short grey hairs; but it would appear from Dr. Harlan's description that the skin of the recent subject was uniform deep black; the nose is rather prominent, with a narrow septum, and the nostrils opening obliquely on the sides. We have already remarked that the noses of all the gibbons approach more nearly to the human form than those of the orang and chimpanzee; they are more prominently raised above the plane of the face, and of greater length, extending nearly to the edge of the upper lip, and having the nostrils opening a little sideways, but rather from below than above. The individual here described is a young female, which was presented to the Zoological Society by the late General Hardwicke, who received it from the continent of India. It is the same as that referred to under the name of *simia lar* in the 4th volume of the " Zoological Journal." Both the present animal and the white-handed gibbon have the vermicular appendix to the cœcum; and the latter species, at least, is furnished with twelve pairs of ribs only, as in the human species, though it has six lumbar vertebræ. Dr. Harlan mentions that the young of the hooloc is of a blackish brown colour, with the backs of the hands and feet sprinkled with grey, the buttocks greyish, a tuft of grey hair from the point of the chin, and a line of the same colour down the middle of the breast and belly; and that the superorbital

band is narrower in the adult than in the young, and
generally interrupted in the centre by a line of black.
The characters here attributed to the young are
probably but individual marks, as they do not exist
in the Zoological Society's specimen, unquestionably
a young animal, and of the same sex as that described
by Dr. Harlan. At all events, even supposing them
to be constant, the diagnoses above indicated will
be at all times sufficient to distinguish the young
hooloc from the white-handed gibbon.

3. The *Ungka-etam*, confounded by Sir Stamford
Raffles and M. F. Cuvier with the *simia lar* of
Linnæus, has been very properly distinguished by M.
Geoffroy St. Hilaire, who has dedicated it to the
memory of the distinguished individual who first
discovered it, by the name of *Hylobates Rafflesii*.
It was first made known by the description and
figures of M. Duvaucel, published in the "Histoire
Naturelle des Mammifères," the accuracy of which we
have ourselves confirmed by the examination of a
fine specimen in the British Museum, and of numerous others in the Museum des Pays Bas, at
Leyden. The hair of this species is thick, furry,
and of a uniform black colour, not so glossy as in
the siamang, and assuming in certain lights a
shade of deep brown, most conspicuous on the
loins and outer face of the thighs, which are manifestly of a lighter hue than the rest of the body, and
assume more of a pale coffee colour. The face, as in
the *simia lar*, is completely surrounded by a circle of
white hair, narrow across the forehead, but expanded
over the cheeks in the form of large bushy whiskers,
and extending beneath the chin so as to unite the
whiskers on either side. This circle, according to
M. Duvaucel, is reduced in the female to a narrow
white band across the forehead, the whiskers and chin
being of the same black colour as the rest of the
body; that sex is farther said to be distinguished by

the union of the index and middle toes of the hind
feet; but M. Duvaucel is unquestionably wrong in
considering this character to be a distinctive mark
common to all the female gibbons. The opinion,
indeed, was probably taken up hastily, and gene-
ralised without sufficiently extensive observation ; it
is contrary to all experience and likelihood that the
sexes of the same animal should present such an
anomaly of structure, and as M. Duvaucel is unquestionably deceived in attributing it to the ungka-
puti, it is natural to suppose that he is likewise
mistaken in the present instance. If any difference
really existed in this respect between the animals
observed by M. Duvaucel, it most probably arose
from his identifying the males and females of two
distinct species—a supposition countenanced by other
considerations, and which has been already entertained by M. F. Cuvier. The back of the hands and
feet of the ungka-etam are of the same uniform
black colour as the rest of the body, and judging at
least from the figures—for the text is silent on these
points—the face, palms, and soles, are dark blue, and
the hair of the fore-arm reversed towards the elbow.
The species consequently is distinguished from the
Hylobates lar by its black hands and feet; from the
hooloc by its white chin and whiskers, and by the
partial union of its toes; and from both by the colour
of the loins being sensibly lighter than that of the
breast, belly, and shoulders. It is farther distinguished not only from these species, but likewise
from all other known apes, by having fourteen pairs
of ribs—a fact which should teach us to appreciate
even slight external differences, since they may be
accompanied by interior characters of so much
importance.

The ungka-etam, called simply *ungka*, or *ounka*,
by M. F. Cuvier, is said to be so rare, that M.

Duvaucel never had reason to suspect its existence
during fifteen months spent in investigating the
zoology] of Sumatra; and it 'was only a short time
before leaving the island that he was fortunate
enough to meet with it in the neighbourhood of
Padang. He has given no account of its character
or habits; and the brief notice of Sir Stamford Raffles
merely informs us that this animal and the ungka-
puti, are of a timid, gentle disposition, and have
neither the size, strength, nor boldness of the siamang.
Buffon, contrary to the usual custom of that eloquent
writer, has left us an account of the manners of the
white-handed gibbon, little less meagre than that of
Sir Stamford or M. Duvaucel. He merely informs us
that the individual which he observed was of a mild
disposition, and peculiarly gentle manners, its movements measured and deliberate, and that it received
what was given it to eat with an air of meekness very
different from the precipitate and bold manner of the
common monkeys. It was fed upon bread, fruits,
almonds, &c., and had a great horror of cold and
moisture.

Of the habits and intelligence of the hooloc,
however, we possess more detailed and accurate
information, which will amply compensate for our
scanty knowledge of the other two species, whilst the
probable similarity of their manners leaves us little
cause to regret our ignorance upon this point.
Allamand, in his additions to the Dutch translation
of Buffon's works, inserts the following notice, which
he had received from Colonel Gordon, of an animal
of this species, which had been presented by the king
of Assam to Mr. Harwood, by whose brother it was
brought to the Cape of Good Hope and given to its
describer. "This ape," says Colonel Gordon, "called
voulock in its native country, was a female, and
remarkably mild in its disposition: small monkeys

alone were displeasing to her, and she could never endure their presence. She always walked upright upon her two hind-legs, and could even run very swiftly; when passing over a table or among china she was particularly careful not to break anything; she used her hands only in the act of prehension, and had her knees formed like those of the human species. Her cry was so acute, that when near it was necessary to stop your ears to avoid being stunned by it; she frequently pronounced the word *ya-hoo* many times consecutively, laying a strong emphasis on the last syllable, and when she heard any noise resembling this sound, she invariably answered it in the same manner; when expressing pleasure or content, however, she uttered a low guttural sound. When any way indisposed, she fretted like a child, and came to her acquaintances to be petted and comforted. Her food was milk and vegetables, and she had such a dislike to meat of all kinds, that she even refused to eat off a plate which had contained it. When thirsty she dipped her fingers into the liquid and then sucked them; she would not suffer herself to be dressed in any kind of jacket, but of her own accord would cover herself with any cloth she found at hand to keep out the night air. Her character was pensive and melancholy; but she would answer readily to her name, *Jenny*, and come to you when called."

But the most complete account which we possess of the character and habits of this species is contained in the following letter of Dr. Burrough, who had procured the specimens afterwards described and figured by Dr. Harlan. " These gibbons," says Dr. B., "were presented to me by Captain Alexander Davidson, of the Honourable Company's service, stationed at Goalpara, on the Burrampooter river in the kingdom of Assam. They are called *hooloc*

by the Assamese, and are met with on the Garrow
Hills, in the vicinity of Goalpara, between latitude
25° and 28° north, and the specimens in question
were taken within a few miles of the town of
Goalpara. The full-grown one was in my possession
alive from January to May. They inhabit more
particularly the lower hills, not being able to endure
the cold of those ranges of the Garrows of more than
four or five hundred feet elevation. Their food in
the wild state consists for the most part of fruits,
common only to the jungle in this district of country;
and they are particularly fond of the seeds and fruits
of that sacred tree of India, called the peepul tree,
and which on the Garrow Hills attains a very large
size. They likewise partake of some species of grass,
and also the tender twigs and leaves of the peepul,
and other trees, which they chew, swallow the
juice, and reject the indigestible part. They are
easily tamed, and when first taken, show no disposition to bite, unless provoked to anger, and even
then manifest a reluctance to defend themselves,
preferring to retreat into some corner rather than to
attack their enemy; they walk erect, and when placed
upon a floor or in an open field, balance themselves
very prettily, by raising their hand over their head,
and slightly bending the arm at the wrist and elbow,
and then run tolerably fast, rocking from side to
side; and if urged to greater speed, they let fall
their hands to the ground, and assist themselves
forward, rather jumping than running; still keeping
the body however nearly erect. If they succeed in
making their way to a grove of trees, they then swing
with such astonishing rapidity from branch to branch,
and from tree to tree, that they are soon lost in the
jungle or forest.

"The individual in question became so tame and
manageable in less than a month, that he would take

hold of my hand and walk with me, helping himself
along at the same time, with the other hand applied
to the ground, as described above. He would come
at my call, and seat himself in a chair by my side at
the breakfast table, and help himself to an egg, or the
wing of a chicken from my plate, without endanger-
ing any of my table furniture. He would partake of
coffee, chocolate, milk, tea, &c., and although his
usual mode of taking liquids was by dipping his
knuckles into the cup, and licking his fingers, still,
when apparently more thirsty, he would take up the
vessel from which I fed him, with both hands, and
drink like a man from a spring; his principal food
consisted of boiled rice, boiled bread and milk with
sugar, plantains, bananas, oranges, all of which he
ate, but seemed best pleased with bananas; he was
fond of insects, would search in the crevices of my
house for spiders, and if a fly chanced to come within
his reach, he would dexterously catch him in one
hand, generally using his right hand. Like many of
the different religious castes of this country (India),
he seemed to entertain an antipathy to an indiscriminate use of animal food, and would not eat of either
the flesh of the cow or hog, would sometimes taste a
little piece of beef, but never eat of it; I have seen
him take fried fish, which he seemed to relish better
than almost any other description of animal food,
with the exception of chicken, and even this he would
eat but very sparingly of, preferring his common diet,
bread and milk, and milk with sugar, fruit, &c. In
temper he was remarkably pacific, and seemed, as I
thought, often glad to have an opportunity of testifying his affection and attachment for me. When
I visited him in the morning, he would commence a
loud and shrill *whoo-whoo, whoo-whoo*, which he
would keep up often from five to ten minutes, with
an occasional intermission for the purpose of taking

a full respiration; until, finally, apparently quite exhausted, he would lie down and allow me to comb his head, and brush the long hair on his arms, and seemed delighted with the tickling sensation produced by the brush on his stomach and legs. He would turn from side to side, first hold out one arm and then the other, and when I attempted to go away, he would catch hold of my arm, or coat-tail, and pull me back again to renew my little attentions to him, daily bestowed. If I called to him from a distance, and he could recognise my voice, he would at once set up his usual cry, which he sometimes gradually brought down to a kind of moan, but generally resumed his louder tone when I approached him. This animal was a male, but showed no particular marks of the sex, and by a casual glance, might readily, if not examined more closely, have passed for a female. I have no idea of his age, but, judging from the size and length of his canine teeth, suppose him to have been advanced in life.

" The other large hooloc of which you have the cranium was also a male, and full-grown; he was likewise obtained from the Garrow Hills in Assam, and presented to me by my friend Captain Davidson, of Goalpara. He came into my possession in the month of April, and died at sea in July, just before getting up with the Cape of Good Hope, of a catarrhal affection. His death probably might have been hastened from the want of proper food, such as is not procurable on long voyages. This animal was similar in habit and general characters to the one already described, and may have been eight or ten years of age, or perhaps older, as I am informed by the natives of Assam that they live to the age of twenty-five or thirty years.

" The young specimen was also alive in my possession; this is a female, and was brought to me by a

Garrow Indian, at the same time the first was received, but died on the way from Goalpara to
Calcutta, of a pulmonary disease following catarrh.
This poor little creature, when first taken sick, suffered great pain and oppression at the chest, for which
I prescribed a cathartic of castor oil and calomel, and
a warm bath, which seemed to afford it some tempo-
rary relief, but she died after ten days' illness. The
animal appeared delighted with the bath, and when I
removed her from the vessel, she would run back
again to the water, and lie down again till again removed; she was like the others I had in my possession,
gentle and pacific in disposition, very timid and shy
of strangers, but in less than a week from the time
she was taken, would, if put down in an open space,
quickly run to me, jump into my arms, and hug me
round the neck: I supposed her to have been from
nine months to a year old. I fed her on boiled milk,
goats' milk diluted with water, and sweetened with
sugar-candy; she also would sometimes partake of
a little bread and milk with the older one; she soon
learned to suck the milk from a small bottle, through
a quill covered with a piece of rag."

In addition to the three gibbons whose distinctive
characters and habits have been here described, and
which differ from other animals of the same family,
by the dark brown or black colour of their fur, a
fourth species has been described and figured by Dr.
Harlan, in the "Journal of the Academy of Natural
Sciences of Philadelphia," vol. v. part 2: and though
the account there given is not sufficiently circum-
stantial to enable us to pronounce positively as to the
specific difference of the animal in question, or its
identity with some of the species already noticed, yet
we ought not to conclude the present part of our
subject without referring to it. The individual de-

scribed by Dr. Harlan was brought to New York in May 1826, from the island of Borneo. Its size, and the state of its dentition, evidently proved it to be a young animal; its total length from the crown of the head to the heel was two feet two inches, and it had only three molar teeth developed on either side of each jaw. The whole animal, except the face, ears, and palms and soles of the hands and feet, was covered with a thick frizzled coat of woolly fur, of a uniform deep black colour upon every part of the head, trunk, and extremities, without any indications of the white marks on the face and hands which distinguish the three species already described. The skin on the naked parts, viz., on the face, ears, palms, and soles, was likewise of a deep black colour ; the orbits of the eyes were prominent, the arms so long, that when standing erect the fingers nearly touched the ground, the nose more prominent, and the facial angle more elevated, than in the orangs.

In habits and manners, the individual in question displayed all the docility and intelligence characteristic of the apes in general ; when advancing on a plain surface he voluntarily assumed the erect attitude, climbed with great ease, and could walk with tolerable facility on the tight rope, balancing himself by means of his long arms ; he slept in a recumbent posture ; fed, in preference, upon ripe fruits ; and died at last of diarrhœa, brought on by an over-indulgence in this favourite luxury. Upon dissection this individual was found to be a perfect hermaphrodite ; it had large vermiform appendices, fourteen pair of ribs, five lumbar, five sacral, and five coccygeal vertebræ, and was without even a rudiment of the guttural sacks which distinguish some of the other species.

It will be readily observed that this account differs materially from the descriptions of all the other gibbons which have been hitherto noticed. From the white-handed gibbon (*H. lar*), it is distinguished as well by the uniform black colour of the cheeks and extremities, as by the number of ribs, of which there are fourteen pair in the one species, and only twelve in the other; the absence of the large guttural sacs separates it specifically from the siamang (*H. syndactylus*), but unfortunately its characters have not been described sufficiently in detail, to enable us to pronounce with equal certainty as to the specific distinction of this animal from the hooloc (*H. scyritus*), and ungka-etam (*H. Rafflesii*). The universal black colour which prevails over every part of the animal, forms, it is true, a sufficient external difference between it and both these species, but the woolly quality of the fur, and the remarkable number of the ribs, being fourteen pair in each, approximate it so closely to the ungka-etam, that a more extensive examination of its characters is desirable, particularly as regards the direction of the hair on the fore-arm, and the connection or separation of the index or middle hind toes. These, as we have already seen, are separate in the hooloc, and united in the ungka-etam. The number of ribs in the former species has not been recorded, but the harsh quality of the fur, as well as the difference of habitat, sufficiently distinguishes the *H. concolor* from that animal, as the uniformity of its colour does from the ungka-etam. Indeed, but for the peculiar circumstances of hermaphroditism observed in the only specimen of *H. concolor* hitherto met with, no reasonable doubt could be entertained of its claim to be considered a distinct species. The present notice will, it is hoped, be the means of directing further attention to this subject.

The Wouwou, Ungka-Puti, Variegated and Brown-whiskered Gibbons.

Having devoted the first part of this chapter to the history and specific descriptions of four gibbons, the common black or dark brown colour of whose fur renders them liable to be confounded without a careful and minute examination, we come now to perform a similar duty with respect to four other species, similarly circumstanced with regard to each other, but readily distinguished from the former group by their prevailing light brown or ashy grey colours. It is not our intention to enter so minutely into the remaining parts of our subject, but the elevated position which the animals hitherto mentioned occupy in the scale of existence, as the connecting links between man and the brute creation, would, we are convinced, justify us in the eyes of our readers, for the more extensive details which we have here given, even if this were not rendered imperatively necessary by the confusion and obscurity which has hitherto prevailed among the specific distinctions of the gibbons. No critical comparison, in fact, has been heretofore made of the differential characters of the various species of gibbons; the natural consequence was, that the ungka-puti (*H. agilis*), has been confounded with the wouwou (*H. leuciscus*), the variegated gibbon (*H. variegatus)*, with the white-handed species (*H. lar*) and this again with the ungka-etam, (*H. Rafflesii*), and with the hooloc (*H. scyritus*), whilst the brown-whiskered gibbon, (*H. choromandus*), was altogether overlooked, or strangely enough mistaken for the female of the *H. lar*. So long as the observed distinctions of animals depend only on the colours of the fur, such differences of opinion are unavoidable among naturalists; it is not to be wondered at, therefore, that the most recent catalogues enumerate only five out of the nine species of gibbons which are described in the present and last chapters; but an attentive and minute examination has enabled us to detect more permanent and influential characters among these animals, and which essentially distinguish the different species.

The Wouwou.

1. The wouwou (*H. leuciscus*), is covered with a very fine long fur of a woolly texture; the general colour is clear ash, except on the crown of the head, backs of the hands, and feet, which are brown, and there are a few long black hairs about the callosities. The whiskers are dirty white, and a very narrow band or fillet of the same colour, sometimes scarcely distinguishable, passes over the eyes; the wool of the fore-arm is erect, not reversed towards the elbow, as in some other species of apes; the naked parts of the face, hands and feet, are of a shining black colour, and the index and middle hind toes are separate throughout their entire length. This species, which was first described and dissected by the celebrated

M 2

Camper, inhabits Java and the Mollucca' islands.
Sir Stamford Raffles and M. F. Cuvier have confounded it with the ungka-puti (*H. agilis*), from
which, however, it differs, not only in the disposition
of its colours, but in the far more permanent and
important character derived from the connection of
the index and middle toes of the hind feet, so often
insisted on in the present and last chapters. In
the present species, as has been already observed,
these organs are perfectly separate, whilst in the
ungka-puti they are closely united throughout the
whole extent of the first phalanx.

2. The ungka puti (*H. agilis*). This remarkable
species of gibbon was first described by Sir Stamford Raffles, in the 13th volume of the "Linnæan
Transactions," and afterwards figured and more fully
described by M. F. Cuvier, from drawings and notes
forwarded by M. Duvaucel. The first of these
eminent naturalists, during his residence at Bencoolen,
as governor of Sumatra, possessed and ably availed
himself of facilities of observing and collecting objects
of Natural History, which rarely fall to the lot of
other men; and it is chiefly to his zeal and ability
that we owe our knowledge of the zoology of that
vast island, and more especially of the different
species of apes which inhabit its primeval forests.
He appears, however, to have mistaken the young of
the present animal, of which he possessed a living
specimen at the time he wrote the description already
referred to, for a different species from the adult;
at least his description differs in no respect from the
characters of the young *H. agilis*; and the other
variety which he mentions as being found in the
neighbourhood of Bencoolen, is unquestionably the
adult of that species. It is necessary to bear this
observation in mind whilst reading his paper, to
guard against the error of unnecessarily multiplying
or creating fictitious species.

The head, shoulders, inside of the arms, fore-arms,
legs and thighs, as well as the whole breast and
belly, are of a deep coffee colour, much darker on
the under than on the upper surface of the body,
contrary to the rule generally regulating the distribution and intensity of colours in other animals, in
which the darker shades generally prevail above and
the lighter below. The occiput, the whole extent of
the back and loins, from immediately behind the
shoulders to the extremity of the body, as well as the
outer face of the thighs, are of a light blond colour,
which contrasts singularly with the deep coffee-
coloured hue of the breast, belly and shoulders.
Large white whiskers cover the cheeks, and are
united by a narrow fillet of the same colour across
the lower part of the forehead; a few reddish brown
hairs surround the callosities; the first joints of the
index and middle hind fingers are united as in the
siamang (*H. syndactylus*); the face is of a bluish-
black colour, the eyes deeply sunk beneath large
projecting brows, the hair of the head directed
backwards, and the canine teeth remarkably long and
powerful. The female only differs by having the
face of a browner hue than the male, the whiskers
smaller and rather more obscure, the eyebrows less
prominent, and the breast and belly not so densely
covered with hair. The young exhibit nearly the
same disposition of colours as the adult, only less
marked and intense, sometimes even approaching to
a light yellowish or straw colour, but always darker
on the anterior than on the posterior surface of the
body. The quality of the fur at all ages is soft and
woolly.

M. Duvaucel extends his observation that the
female gibbons are distinguished from the males, by
the union of the index and middle hind fingers, expressly to the present species. However, notwith-

standing the positive terms in which he denies this
character to the male ungka-puti, we have found it
equally developed in both sexes; nay, it is moreover
extremely probable that the specimens which we
examined with the view of ascertaining this point,
were the very identical individuals observed by M.
Duvaucel himself, those, namely, formerly in the
possession of Sir Stamford Raffles, and at present in
the museum of the Zoological Society; nor can we
account for the error of M. Duvaucel otherwise than
by supposing it to be the result of a too hasty generalisation of ideas, which he wanted either time or
opportunity to confirm. We have already, whilst
describing the ungka-etam (*H. Rafflesii*), remarked
the extreme improbability of so important an organic
modification as that at present under consideration,
being a mark of mere sexual difference; and though
we have not had an opportunity of observing the
character in that species, yet the result of our
examination, as far as regards the ungka-puti, fully
justifies us in rejecting M. Duvaucel's observation in
the one case as well as in the other.

Sir Stamford Raffles goes further than even M.
Duvaucel in the erroneous account which he has
given of the character in question, since he not only
denies the union of the fingers in the male ungka-
puti, but in the female also. " In none of these
animals", says he, after describing the ungka-etam
and ungka-puti, " are there any naked folds of skin
under the throat (as in the siamang namely, with
which he is evidently comparing them), and all the
toes are separate." It is impossible to account for
this assertion of so able and candid an observer as
Sir Stamford Raffles, except on the supposition that
his mind was too strongly biassed by the previous
idea of the structure being the differential specific
character of the siamang, in which he had originally

observed it, to allow him to perceive it in any other species. At all events, M. Duvaucel contradicts it, as far, at least, as regards the female of the ungka-etam; and we can only refer to Sir Stamford's own specimens of the male, female, and young of the ungka-puti, to demonstrate that his assertion is equally inapplicable to that species.

We have already noticed M. F. Cuvier's error in confounding the ungka-puti with the wouwou; the specific distinction of these animals, as far at least as regards the different dispositions of their colours, had been already pointed out by M. Geoffroy St. Hilaire in his "Cours d'Histoire Naturelle des Mammiferes," but that eminent zoologist himself falls into another error not less grievous than that of M. F. Cuvier, in confounding the ungka-puti with the *petit gibbon* of Buffon, which had been already distinguished with some hesitation by M. Desmarest, under the name of *H. variegatus*. We shall return to this subject presently. It only remains farther to be observed, in order to guard against the possibility of confounding the ungka-puti with the ungka-etam, which might readily happen from the light colours which prevail on the back, loins, and whiskers of both these species, that besides the distinction in the ground colours, these animals differ in the number of ribs, of which, according to M. Duvaucel's dissection, there are fourteen pairs in the ungka-etam, and only thirteen in the ungka-puti.

3. The variegated gibbon (*H. variegatus*) was first figured and described by Buffon and Daubenton under the name of *petit gibbon*. These naturalists supposed it to be a mere variety of the white-handed species (*H. lar*), which they had figured and described by the name of *grand gibbon*, and more recent zoologists have either confounded it with this or some other species, or admitted it with doubt as

distinct. In the latter opinion, we believe M. Desmarest stands alone; he describes the *petit gibbon* of Buffon in a separate article, under the specific name of *variegatus*, but with a hesitation as to its specific distinction, arising most probably from having never had an opportunity of examining a specimen, and being consequently acquainted with the animal only from the description of Daubenton; and though M. Geoffroy St. Hilaire, no mean authority upon this subject, has more recently returned to the old opinion of the specific identity of the *H. variegatus* and *H. lar*, the examination of an individual in the museum of the Zoological Society has enabled us to confirm M. Desmarest's conjecture, and to establish beyond reasonable doubt the specific difference of these two animals. The specimen belonging to the Zoological Society, and which was brought from Sumatra by the late Sir Stamford Raffles, has the crown of the head, shoulders, arms, legs, and thighs, of a dirty brown, or light coffee colour; the back of the neck, loins, hips, breast, and belly, blond, or dirty white; a large white circle surrounds the face, forming a fillet of moderate breadth across the lower part of the forehead, expanding into large whiskers upon the cheeks, and uniting underneath so as to cover the entire region under the chin; the whole hands and feet, from the wrists and ankles respectively, are likewise white or light grey; and the index and middle toes of the posterior members are closely united throughout the entire length of the first joint, and even a little beyond, exactly as in the siamang (*H. syndactylus*). The individual appears to be a young female.

The distinctive points of difference between the *H. variegatus* and *H. lar*, as far at least as they regard the nature and disposition of the colours, will

be readily perceived from comparing this description
with that of the white-handed gibbon in the last
chapter. The grey colour of the hands and feet, and
the white circle round the face, are, in fact, the only
characters common to these two species; the ground
colours are different, being deep black in the one
and dirty light brown in the other, the back, loins
breast, and belly of the *H. variegatus* are blond, or
dirty white, whilst in the *H. lar* these parts are of the
same intense black colour as the rest of the body;
and, finally, the index and middle hind fingers are
united beyond the first joint in the former species,
and only throughout two-thirds of its length in the
latter. This last character is of itself abundantly
sufficient to prove the specific distinction of these
two animals; or, even admitting M. Duvaucel's
hypothesis of its being a sexual character, to the
fullest extent, it proves at least that they are not
the young and adult states of the same species,
because, upon that supposition, the character, if it
existed at all, would necessarily be developed to the
same extent in both: and that they are not merely
male and female varieties of the same species, is
manifest from the express declaration of Daubenton
that both his *grand* and *petit gibbons* were females,
as well as from the fact that the Zoological Society's
specimens belong to different sexes. We have
consequently arrived at the certainty that the same
shades and distribution of colours exist equally in
both sexes of the *H. variegatus;* and though the
only observed specimens of *H. lar*, whose sex has
been recorded, were both females, the probability
is, that the observation will apply to that species also.
Professor Geoffroy St. Hilaire, as has been already
remarked, has expressed a supposition that the
species at present under consideration may be
identical with the ungka 'puti (*H. agilis*), and the

M 5

light colour of the back and loins, the white circle round the face, and the union of the index and middle hind fingers, common to both, might at first sight tend to countenance the supposition; but these are in reality the only characters which they possess in common; the ungka-puti has neither the white hands and feet, nor the light colours on the breast and belly which distinguish the variegated gibbon; on the contrary, the under surface of the body in that species differs from what is observed in the great majority of animals, by having much darker colours than the upper, and that these characters are specifically distinctive is satisfactorily shown by the fact of their being permanent and invariable in both sexes and at all ages. The same observation applies with equal force to the *H. variegatus*; the shade and disposition of its colours depend neither upon age nor sex, and we are consequently justified in regarding it as a distinct and pure species.

4. The brown-whiskered gibbon (*H. choromandus*). This new species, the only observed specimen of which exists in the museum of the Zoological Society, was recently described at one of the scientific meetings of that body. It had been sent from the continent of India to the late General Hardwicke, together with a specimen of the hooloc (*H. scyritus*), of which it was said to be the female, an opinion sufficiently contradicted by the fact that both the specimens in question were of that sex, though they differed materially in colour, as well as by the express declaration of Drs. Harlan and Burrough, who, in their very complete description of the hooloc, inserted in the "Transactions of the American Philosophical Society," vol. iv. new series, assure us that the sexes in that species do not differ in colour, but that both are of the same uniform deep black upon every

part of the head, trunk and extremities, except the small fillet of white hair which passes over the eyebrows. These facts, independent of other characters which will be presently explained, are sufficient to prove the difference of the new species ; the name *choromandus*, by which it was proposed to distinguish it, is derived from that of an Indian tribe mentioned by Pliny, on the authority of one Tauron, and described as being covered with hair, having yellow eyes, teeth like dogs, and instead of articulated sounds, uttering nothing but frightful shrieks and cries ; a story, it was remarked, most probably originating in some confused and vague account of the present or some other continental species of gibbon. The following is the description of the new species. The specimen observed was an adult female, about the same size as the ungka-puti (*H. agilis*), and not very much differing in colour, except that it wanted the lighter shades on the back and loins, and that the cheeks, whiskers, and under part of the chin, instead of being white, as in that species, were of a deep coffee-coloured brown. All the upper parts of the body, the head, neck, shoulders, back, loins, hips, and outside of the limbs, are of an uniform dirty whitey-brown, with a shade of yellowish red, the breast, belly, and under parts, of a sensibly darker shade, as in the ungka-puti, but without any appearance of the light colour on the back and loins which distinguishes that animal ; the fingers and toes are covered down to the very nails with black hair, which contrasts strongly with the colour of the surrounding parts, and the hair of the cheeks forms large whiskers of a dark coffee-coloured brown, which likewise forms a strong contrast with the surrounding colours, and unites beneath the chin, so as to cover the whole under surface of the inferior jaw, but does not extend across the forehead, as the white colour of the cheeks does in some other species. In this respect the *H. choromandus* differs particularly from the hooloc, which with whiskers of the same black colour as the rest of the body, has a white band across the forehead, instead of which the present species has the forehead of the same unvaried whitey-brown as the other parts, and the whiskers so much darker as to form a very strong contrast with the surrounding colours. The ground colour of the two species is likewise essentially different, but they agree in having the index and middle hind toes completely separate throughout their whole extent, a character which is only found in one other species of gibbon, viz. the wouwou, or *H. leuciscus*, and which, therefore, definitely distinguishes these three species from their congeners. But the *H. choromandus* possesses other and peculiar qualities which will not allow it to be confounded with any other known gibbon. The face, instead of being naked and of a deep shining black, as in the *H. scyritus*, *H. leuciscus*, and *H. agilis*, the only species for which it could possibly be mistaken, is of a light greyish-brown colour, and, particularly on and about the nose, covered with short adpressed hair; the hair of the head is erect and bushy; the skull is larger and rounder than in any other species of gibbon; the nose, likewise, is considerably more prominent, extending to the edge of the upper lip, and having a remarkably broad septum, as different from the narrow contracted form of that organ in the other gibbons, as is the septum of the American *simiadæ* from that of the *simiæ* of Asia and Africa. It is this character which gives the nostrils of the *H. choromandus* the appearance of opening laterally instead of obliquely beneath, as is the case in the other species. The hair of the fore arm in the individual observed had the appearance of being partially reversed towards the elbow, though from its length and soft woolly quality, it might be readily made to assume any other direction. The detrition of the teeth proved the animal to be an adult individual of its species; the canines were smaller than is usually observed among the gibbons, but as the subject was a female, this will probably turn out to be a sexual rather than a specific character. It is said to be from the continent of India, but the precise locality is unknown: most probably the Malay peninsula.

The dispositions, habits, and intelligence of the gibbons included in the present chapter, do not materially differ from those of the species described in the last. Their size and habitats are likewise the same, all the known species being natives of the peninsula of Malacca and the large islands of the Indian Archipelago. The habits of the ungka-puti alone have been recorded with any sort of detail. "This gibbon," says M. Duvaucel in a letter which has been published by M. F. Cuvier, "which lives more frequently isolated in couples than in families, is the least common of the genus found in the neighbourhood of Bencoolen. Very different from the siamang (*H. syndactylus*) in its surprising agility, it escapes like a bird, and like a bird can only be shot, so to speak, flying; scarcely has it perceived the most distant approach of danger when it is already far off. Climbing rapidly to the tops of the trees, it there seizes the most flexible branches, and balancing itself two or three times to secure its equipoise, and acquire a sufficient impetus, it thus springs successively, without effort as without fatigue, to the distance of forty feet and upwards. As a pet or domestic animal it exhibits no extraordinary faculty. It is less clumsy than the siamang, its movements are more prompt and graceful, but its manners are less lively than those of the monkey tribes in general. Looking merely at the exterior development of its long slender arms, and short bandy legs, one would be far from supposing that its muscles were so vigorous, and its address so surprising. Nature, however, has not bestowed upon it a large portion of intelligence; in this respect it is in no way superior to the siamang; both species are equally deprived of that high and ex- panded forehead which indicates superior intellectual powers, and this is one of the principal points of coincidence between them. What I have myself seen, however, convinces me that our present animal is susceptible of a certain degree of education; it has not the imperturbable apathy of the siamang; it may be frightened or pleased; it flies from danger, and is sensible of good treatment; it is gluttonous, curious, familiar, and sometimes even gay and lively. Though deprived of the guttural sac so remarkable in the siamang, its cry is very nearly the same; so that it would appear that this organ does not produce the effect of increasing the sound usually attributed to it, or else, that it must be replaced in the present species by some analogous formation."

To this interesting account M. Duvaucel adds that the ungka-puti is known by various names to the natives of Sumatra; among others he says it is called wouwou, in imitation of its cry, which is said to resemble that word, but as this name, which is most probably a general term, has long been ap- propriated to a very different species, the *H. leuciscus*, we have thought proper to distinguish it by that of ungka-puti, under which it has been described by Sir Stamford Raffles, and which is most probably its real name after all. The account which Sir Stamford gives of the manners and character of the siamang and ungka-puti is so different from that of M.

Duvaucel, and agrees so well with Mr. George
Bennett's observations, that we cannot help sus-
pecting M. Duvaucel either to have drawn too
much from imagination, or to have observed these
animals only in the last stage of debility and disease.
"Both these species," says Sir Stamford, speaking
of the ungka-etam and ungka-puti, "are of a more
timid disposition than the siamang, and have neither
the strength nor boldness of that animal. With
regard to the ungka-puti, it is a general belief among
the people of the country where it resides, that it
will die of grief if it sees the preference given to
another; in confirmation of which I may add, that
the one in my possession sickened under these circumstances, and did not recover until relieved from
the cause of vexation by his rival, the siamang, being
removed into another apartment."

Little is known of the distinctive individual
manners of the other species. The wouwou described by Camper was obtained from the Mollucca
islands, where the species is said to frequent the
tops of bamboos, from the extremity of the long
slender trunks of which these creatures might often
be seen waving their long arms from side to side
with the most easy and graceful motions, or swinging
from branch to branch with a rapidity almost in-
conceivable. Camper's specimen often walked upright: its habits were active and its disposition
irritable and passionate. This statement agrees
with the manners of a specimen possessed by the
Zoological Society some years ago.

CHAPTER VII.

HAVING, in the previous chapters, described the three genera of simiæ which most nearly approach to the human subject in organic structure and mental endowments, we must now descend a step lower in the scale of animated nature, and introduce to the reader's notice those tribes of quadrumanous animals which partake more of the common quadruped form, and thus serve as the connecting link between the anthropoid apes and the dog-headed baboons. This numerous and very complicated group comprises the animals commonly and most properly denominated monkeys in the English language, a word apparently corrupted from the diminutive *manikin*, a little man, and serving to express the resemblance which they exhibit to the human being in their form and actions. They are readily distinguished from the true apes by their long tails, cheek-pouches, and ischial callosities, and by the habits and economy which necessarily result from these characters. Their length of tail, for instance, would be alone sufficient to make the semi-biped pace and station, which we have found to prevail so universally among the apes, a matter of great inconvenience, if not of absolute difficulty, among the monkeys, even did not the equality of their members reduce them to the common quadruped progression ; but this inferiority is amply compensated by the security which the same development affords them, in guiding their direction and steadying their motions,

during their frequent and violent gambols in the
forests ; and, in fact, so completely does their structure
incapacitate these animals for biped progression, that
the bear has as much facility of walking and standing
upright as the monkey, and resorts to that position
quite as frequently. It must be borne in mind,
however, that the surface of the earth is not the
natural stage upon which the monkey is designed to
act, any more than the ape ; perhaps he less frequently and more unwillingly appears on it than
even this animal, and consequently when he does, he
is out of his proper and natural sphere, and should
not be judged by those rules which apply to quadrupeds properly so called. His peculiar and appropriate province is found in the dense primeval forests
of tropical countries, Central Africa, Southern Asia,
and the islands of the Indian Archipelago ; he is
pre-eminently fitted for an arborial life, and as we
have just remarked, whilst his opposable thumbs
and prehensile fingers enable him to grasp the
branches securely, his long tail, like the pole of the
rope-dancer, serves as a balance to insure his equilibrium, when the hands are otherwise occupied, and
as a rudder to direct him in leaping and springing
from one tree to another. As compared with the
apes and baboons, this is unquestionably the most
important and influential organ of the monkey tribe.
Among them alone, of all the other simiæ, does it
execute any essential or assigned function, or fulfil
any efficient purpose, in the general economy of the
animals. The apes, as we have already seen, are
altogether deprived of tails, which would have embarrassed and impeded, instead of assisting, their
movements. We shall afterwards find that, in
the case of the baboons, though partially developed,
this organ is invariably too short and powerless to
become an efficient instrument of progression ; and,

in fact, it is only among the monkeys that it acquires the dimensions and executes the functions of an influential organ.

The next character which distinguishes the monkeys, and which, among cheiropeds, is peculiar to these animals and the baboons, is the possession of cheek-pouches, in which they stow away and carry off large quantities of nuts and fruits for future consumption, and are thus enabled to exercise a kind of provident foresight, which we rarely find among the lower animals, and not always among our own species. These organs are formed by a large cavity, or distention of the cheek, running backwards for a considerable distance behind the gums; they are likewise found in the hamsters, tamias, and some other genera of rodents, as well as in that singular and anomalous Australian animal, the *ornithorhynchus*, but with the exception of the cheironectes, or fishing opossum of South America, they are possessed by no other cheiropeds than the group at present under consideration. Yet this general rule is by no means without an exception; the organs in question are found in the great majority of monkeys, it is true, but they are not common to all, since in one entire genus they are either extremely minute or altogether deficient. The semnopithecs, in fact, have no cheek-pouches, and in this respect resemble the apes of the genus hylobates, with which, as we shall presently see, they very closely agree in other details of their organization.

But the most characteristic and appropriate attribute of the monkeys, and the only one which suffers no exception throughout the entire group, if we except the characteristic length of the tail, is the peculiar development of the ischial bones, which form an elongated process or protuberance, flattened into a round disk on the under face, and covered, ex-

ternally with a naked callous integument, which
serves these animals as a secure and commodious
seat when they are disposed to sleep or repose after
the violent and fatiguing motions which they
habitually execute. We have already had an instance of this peculiarity of structure in the case of
the gibbons; there, however, it was presented only
in a rudimentary form, but among the monkeys and
baboons it obtains its maximum of development,
and exercises a very powerful influence upon the
habits and economy of these animals. To them
also it is strictly peculiar, at least with the exception
of the rudimentary callosities of the gibbons, just
mentioned, no other known animal possessing
similar or equivalent organs. The apes, in which, as
we have already seen, the callosities are either
altogether absent, or but rudimentarily developed,
repose in a reclining posture, like human beings,
but the monkeys and baboons, in consequence of the
possession of these organs, take their rest in a
sitting position, and thus carry about with them a
seat of nature's own construction, always at hand
when it is required, and always comfortable. The
apes, or more anthropoid simiæ, deprived of these
organs, are obliged to construct rude huts and beds,
in which they can stretch themselves down at length
and repose at ease and in security; thither they
retire at the stated periods of rest and sleep, from
these they seldom wander to any considerable
distance; and, as they have not sufficient skill to
construct their dwellings on a large or commodious
scale, they lead in some measure a life of solitude,
being monogamous, and associating only in very
small families. The monkeys and baboons, on the
contrary, herd together in vast troops, scour the
mountains and forests in all directions, wherever
curiosity or the search of food may lead them, and

when overtaken by night, or overcome by sleep˜or
fatigue, seat themselves between the forked branches
of some convenient tree, or under the shelter of a
projecting rock, repose wherever they happen to be
at the moment, and thus avoid the necessity of
affixed or permanent dwellings.

We have already mentioned the equality, in point
of length, which subsists between the anterior and
posterior members of the monkeys, as a leading
distinction between the present group and the apes
which we have been hitherto describing, and as
being the immediate cause of the difference observable in the station and progression of these two
sub-families. It is unnecessary to advert farther to
this circumstance; its influence is, indeed, so obvious
that it cannot escape the observation of the most
casual inquirer; but there is another peculiarity in
the formation of these organs, which forms a remarkable exception to the general law; the more
remarkable too in the present instance, from its con-
tradicting one of the most important and essential
characters of the family now under consideration, and
which it is necessary to consider more at length. We
allude to the total absence or rudimentary form of the
thumb in a particular genus of monkeys, the *colobs*
(*colobus*), a defect which is altogether peculiar to
these animals, and which, in addition to its extreme
singularity, is particularly deserving of the attention of
zoologists, from the circumstance of its being an exception to the very structure which constitutes the
peculiar and influential character of the quadrumana,
the opposable power of the thumb to the other fingers. But it is not our intention, at present, to enter
into the consideration of this singular structure, and
the effects which it produces upon the habits and
economy of the animals which exhibit it; these subjects will be more appropriately treated of when we

come to speak of the colobs, and it is sufficient to have here indicated the existence of the anomaly in question.

The monkeys, like the apes, notwithstanding the general agreement which they exhibit in their structure and habits, nevertheless present various modifications of organization, and corresponding differences in their manners and ecomony, which definitely distinguish them into separate groups, and have been made the characters of distinct genera. One of these, the entire defect of thumb in the colobs, has been just adverted to; the absence or rudimentary form of the cheek-pouches among the semnopithecs is another and an important distinctive character, as is likewise the peculiar complication or sacculated form of the stomach in the same animals; but it may be justly questioned how far the existence of the fifth tubercle, which has been detected upon the posterior tooth of the lower jaw, in the generality of monkeys, ought to be considered as a generic character, not only because it exerts no assignable influence over the habits and economy of animal life, but, likewise, because it is not strictly confined to those genera which it has been assumed to cha-racterise, as we shall see when we come to speak of the cercopithecs and papios. That it may be of con-siderable value as a practical diagnosis is unques-tionable; other collateral and subordinate characters are equally so when they possess a tolerable degree of generality, but their introduction among the formula of generic characters is most mischievous, and has been the main cause of the doubt and uncertainty which prevail in that department of scientific zoology. We have already discussed the value of the character proposed by MM. Cuvier and Geoffroy, as dis-tinctive of the different genera of simiæ, derived from the facial angle, originally applied by the cele-

brated Camper for the purpose of differentiating the
various tribes and varieties of the human species:
we have shown that the principle cannot be applied
with the same success to distinguish the genera of
quadrumanous mammals from one another; it is
consequently unnecessary to insist farther upon the
subject, and we shall therefore proceed at once to
the detailed consideration of the first and most
elevated group of monkeys, those, namely, which
are comprised in the genus *semnopithecus* of M.
Frederic Cuvier.

Genus *Semnopithecus*—General Characters of the Semnopithecs.

The genus semnopithecus, originally founded by
M. F. Cuvier upon the very unsatisfactory and
trivial characters already referred to, the comparative
slenderness and elongation of the extremities, and
the existence of an additional or fifth tubercle upon
the posterior face of the last inferior molar, has,
however, been since established upon a more secure
and philosophical basis, by the subsequent discoveries
of Professors Owen and Otto, and is now universally
admitted by zoologists as a strictly natural and
scientific group. It is composed of a very considerable number of species, remarkable for the
slender, elongated form of their members, their want
of cheek-pouches, and a peculiar sacculated form of
stomach, which gives that organ something of the
appearance of a huge colon, and in all probability
indicates peculiarities of regimen, with which, however, we are at present but partially acquainted. Other
characters, less prominent it is true, but exercising,
nevertheless, a sensible influence upon the economy
of these animals, will be noticed in the sequel.

If we except the long, slender, but at the same time powerfully muscular, tail, with which nature has provided these animals, the exterior formation of the semnopithecs bears a very striking resemblance to that of the gibbons. They have the same elongated form of body, the same lengthened members, only, that the remarkable disproportion which exists between the anterior and posterior extremities of the apes is not reproduced in the present instance, the same round cranium and shortened face, the same diminutive callosities, and the same want of cheek-pouches. One species, indeed, the douc (*semno-pithecus nemeus*), was even thought to want callosities altogether, and has been considered by Illiger and others as the type of a separate genus, in consequence; but more recent observations have shown that the animal in question forms no exception to the general rule in this respect, and that it agrees with the rest of its congeners in the possession of these as of other generic characters. The manners and habits of the semnopithecs may consequently be presumed to resemble those of the gibbons as closely as their organic structure, and this induction is fully warranted by the observations afforded by such species and individuals as have been observed at different times in the menageries of France and England. The great length and slender form of their limbs manifestly incapacitate them for very prolonged or violent exertion; the fatigue resulting from such exertions necessarily precludes the attempt, and obviously places them at a great disadvantage when compared with the compact muscular members of the cercopithecs, macacs, and baboons. This appears to be the real and immediate cause of that indisposition to action which has been observed both among the gibbons and semnopithecs;

they are totally devoid of the petulance, mischievous curiosity, and restless activity of the cercopithecs, or common monkeys, and exhibit a sedate and even melancholy temperament, which has made M. Geoffroy St. Hilaire imagine that they are subject to ennui. It may be justly questioned, however, whether the learned French professor has sufficient grounds for this conclusion. The very apathy which so strongly characterises these animals, is of itself a sufficient antidote to the feeling which he has attributed to them, for it is only upon lively, restless dispositions that ennui can be successfully grafted; it grows and derives its nourishment from the suspension of active energy, and where the power or desire of active energy does not exist, it can never have being. The lively, curious, and restless Frenchman is of all other Europeans most subject to the intrusion of this unwelcome parasite; the phlegmatic and inert Dutchman the least so; and the infliction and the immunity are equally due to the vivacity of disposition in the one case and the gravity of demeanour in the other.

Connected with this subject there is another character which may be noticed as influencing the deportment of the semnopithecs; we allude to the disproportionate shortness of the thumbs on the anterior extremities, which scarcely surpass the rudimentary form, and prepare us in some degree to anticipate the total absence of this important organ in the colobs. This defect necessarily impairs the function of prehension in the semnopithecs, and helps to account for that sedateness of character and indisposition to violent activity for which they are so remarkable. The occipital foramen is situated, as in the gibbons, upon an elongated base, at about one-third of its distance from the posterior, and two-

thirds from the anterior margin. In the human
subject it is in the centre of the inferior plane of the
head, so that the line of gravity passes through it
and falls immediately upon the supporting vertebral
column; we are thus enabled to support the head
in an upright posture without fatigue, whilst the
monkey, like the rest of the lower animals, in consequence of the line of gravity falling considerably
in front of the supporting column, is thrown forward
upon the anterior members, and obliged to seek
their assistance in order to counteract the other
disadvantage.

The diminutive nature of the ischial callosities,
and the entire absence of cheek-pouches, at least as
far as we are at present aware,—for though Wurmb
has attributed these organs to the kahau (*semnopithecus nasalis*), there is reason to believe that the
observation originated in error,—have been already
slightly mentioned, and we have so often insisted
upon the influence and nature of these characters,
that it is unnecessary to repeat our observations
here. There is, however, one circumstance connected with the structure of the semnopithecs, so
remarkable in itself and so interesting from its
anomalous character, that we must not pass it by
without a more detailed notice; and as the subject
has been treated in the most ample and lucid manner
by Professor Owen, in the first volume of the
" Transactions of the Zoological Society," we shall
take the liberty of abstracting a few observations
from that gentleman's valuable paper.   It had been
originally observed by Professor Otto, in dissecting
the *semnopithecus leucoprymnus*, that the stomach
was of an enormous capacity, as compared with
the size of the animal, and presented a sacculated
appearance which had never been previously detected

in any other species of the quadrumanous family.
The descriptions of this curious and important
structure, as well as of the animal which furnished
the observations, were published in the 12th volume of
the "Nova Acta Academiæ Curiosorum," and though
the animal had been then marked, with some doubt
indeed, as a cercopithec, it was quickly recognised
as appertaining in reality to the present genus, and
naturalists, by a rather bold generalization, ventured
to extend the curious observation of M. Otto to the
rest of the semnopithecs. In this state the question
remained, from the publication of M. Otto's paper
up to the year 1833, when the collections of the
Zoological Society afforded to Professor Owen, of
the Royal College of Surgeons, opportunities of
dissecting two other species of this genus, the
semnopithecus entellus and *semnopithecus fascularis*,
and of thereby confirming, not only the previous observations of M. Otto, but, what is still more remarkable, the subsequent generalizations of zoologists.
Up to this time the title of the genus to the rank of
a natural and scientific group rested, it must be
confessed, upon a very insecure foundation; but the
beautiful observations in question at once established
it upon the basis of important and influential
characters, and fully entitle it to the rank which it
occupies among the natural genera of the quadrumanous family. Professor Owen's paper is published in the 1st volume of the "Zoological Transactions," and illustrated with figures of the structure
described, executed with all the accuracy of detail
and beauty which distinguish the engravings of that
valuable work.

The larger of the two stomachs described by
Professor Owen, was taken from a full-grown female
entellus monkey, which measured 1 ft. 8 in. in length,

from the nose to the origin of the tail. The dimensions of this stomach, when distended and dried,
were as follows :—

	ft.	in.
Length along the greater curvature, beginning at the left extremity	2	7
Length along the less curvature	1	0
Greatest circumference (a little to the right of the cardia)	1	0
Least circumference (at about two inches from the pyloris)	0	3¾

The following is Professor Owen's description of
its structure.

" This stomach may be regarded as consisting of
three divisions : 1st, a cardiac pouch, with smooth
and simple parietes, slightly bifid at the extremity ;
2nd, a middle very wide and sacculated portion ; and,
3rd, a narrow and elongated canal, sacculated at its
commencement, and of simple structure towards its
termination. The latter division, from its greater
vascularity, and the more abundant distribution upon
it of the nerves of the eighth pair, I regard as the
true digestive stomach; the preceding divisions
appear to be preparatory receptacles or reservoirs.

" The œsophagus enters into the left or cardiac
division, which is separated from the middle division
by a well-marked constriction. The diameter of this
aperture of communication, when the stomach has
been forcibly dilated, does not exceed two inches: so
that it seems highly probable, when no distending
force is operating at this part, that the circular fibres
which surround the constriction may, by the act of
contraction, render the separation complete, and thus
form the cardiac pouch into a distinct cavity. A
similar tendency to a separation of the cardiac from
the pyloric moiety of the stomach has been observed
to exist, in a greater or less degree, in stomachs of
a much more simple structure, as in those of man,

and of the carnivora. It is probably the possession of this power, in a greater degree, that enables some men to regurgitate at will a small portion of the contents of the stomach, or to ruminate. Such an action is therefore still more likely to take place, occasionally at least, in animals which possess the complicated stomach here described : and there is a provision in these stomachs for the passage of ruminated food, or such as is of a fluid or easily digestible nature, directly into the second or sacculated division.

" A ridge is continued along the pyloric side of the cardiac orifice obliquely to the fold in the middle division, which is situated beyond the constriction : a second ridge is continued from the right side of the cardiac into the lower part of the septum that separates the cardiac from the middle compartment : and, consequently, between these ridges a shallow canal is continued from the œsophagus to the middle division of the stomach. Supposing the circular fibres which form the two ridges to contract simultaneously with those forming the constriction above, then the communication between the œsophagus and middle division of the stomach would be cut off ; but, on the other hand, if these fibres were relaxed, the food, and especially liquid food, would pass along the oblique canal, directly into the middle compartment.

" Longitudinal fibres are continued from the œsophagus upon the cardiac division ; but they gradually converge towards its left extremity, and there begin to be collected into the narrow band which traverses nearly the whole of the greater curvature of the stomach. The extremity of the cardiac division is thus slightly indented, reminding one of the similar, but more marked, division of the same part in the stomach of the kangaroo, which in other respects bears so strong a resemblance to the present.

" The length of the cardiac division is three inches:
its greatest diameter, three inches four lines.

" The second or middle compartment of the stomach
is composed of a double series of sacculi of different
sizes,'puckered up upon the longitudinal band abovementioned.   Some of these sacculi have a diameter of
three inches; others of one inch.   They are formed
principally at the expense of the anterior parietes of
the stomach, and are eleven in number.   The septa
by which they are divided from each other, are of a
semilunar form, and project into the cavity of the
stomach to the extent of half an inch; and a few to
that of an inch.

" The length of this part of the stomach, in a
straight line, is five and a half inches; and its greatest
diameter, five inches.

" The third or pyloric division of the stomach
commences a little to the right of the œsophagus,
where the second longitudinal band begins.   It is a
narrow and almost cylindrical canal, gradually
diminishing in diameter to the pylorus, bent in a
sigmoid form, and terminating by making a complete
turn upon itself.   It is only this part of the stomach
which is puckered upon the two bands above
described.   The sacculi thus formed are, however,
by no means so large or so completely separated from
each other as in the preceding division ; and they
become gradually less distinct to within five inches of
the pylorus, where they cease altogether.   A similar
gradual disappearance of the sacculi is observable in
the stomach of the kangaroo.

" The whole length of this division, taken midway
between the two curvatures, is one foot six inches : its
greatest diameter, is two inches, its smallest diameter
one inch.

" In considering this stomach as being made up

of three principal divisions, I must not be understood
to suppose them as being equally distinct with the
different cavities of a ruminant or cetaceous stomach ;
they are not characterized by any essential difference
of structure, for none of them possess a cuticular
lining. These three divisions are, however, sufficiently obvious to justify their separate consideration
for the facility of a description of so complicated an
organ.

" In another species of semnopithecus, *Semn. fas-
cicularis*, (the croo of Sumatra, and *Semn. comatus*
of M. Desmarest,) the stomach presented precisely
the same structure as the preceding. Its dimensions
were not, however, quite so long in proportion to the
size of the animal The individual examined was
younger than the entellus, the stomach of which has
just been described.

" From the disproportionate size of the stomach in
these animals, some differences are met with in the
disposition of the other viscera of the abdominal
cavity. The liver, instead of crossing the epigastric
to the left hypochondriac region, extends downwards
from the right hypochondriac to the right lumber
region ; the whole of the opposite side of the abdomen,
with the epigastric region, being occupied by the
enormous stomach. The liver is proportionately
smaller in semnopithecus than in cercopithecus or
macacus. The spleen is of a more regular triangular
shape, and is attached to the omentum, continued
from the left side of the stomach. The pancreas,
on the contrary, is proportionately larger than in
these genera. Both the biliary and the pancreatic
secretions enter the duodenum together, about three
inches from the pylorus : were it not for the insertion
of these ducts, one might almost suppose that what
has been regarded as the true stomach was a portion
of the intestinal canal.

" With so complicated a stomach, it might also be expected that the intestines would not be so long as in those monkeys which have a simple stomach; this, however, is not the case. The small intestines are longer in proportion to the body in semnopithecus than in either cercopithecus or macacus, the ratio being respectively as 8 to 1, 6½ to 1, and 4 to 1. The latter genus evidently manifests in this respect its closer approximation to the carnivorous type.

" The following table exhibits the admeasurements : —

	Semnopithecus Entellus.		Semnopithecus Fascicularis		Cercopithecus Albogularis.		Macacus Cynomlogus	
	ft.	in.	ft.	in.	ft.	in.	ft.	in.
Length of the body from the nose to the root of the tail	1	8	1	2	1	9½	1	8
Length of the small intestines	13	6	9	10	11	6	6	9
Length of the large intestines	2	8	2	6	3	0	2	9
Length of the cæcum	0	4	0	2¼	0	3	0	3

As in all the preceding animals the intestines were prepared for admeasurement in the same manner, I believe the relative proportions may be relied upon. I mention this, because the admeasurements given by M. Otto of the *Semnopithecus leucoprymnus* would lead to the conclusion that the intestinal canal was much shorter. His admeasurements of that species, as published in the " Nova Acta, Bonn." tom. xii. p. 511, are

ft. in.

From the nose to the root of the tail . . . 1 8
Length of the small intestines 5 5
Length of the large intestines 1 8
Length of the cæcum . . . . 0 2."

In another part of his valuable paper, Professor Owen observes,

" With respect to stomachs of an analogous structure in the other animals of the class mammalia, I have hitherto limited my comparisons to that of the kangaroo, so well known for its remarkable resemblance to a sacculated colon and cæcum. Between this animal and semnopithecus there is a wide interval in the natural series. Stomachs, however, almost as complex as the preceding, are found in animals much more nearly allied to the quadrumana. In a large bat of the genus pteropus, *pteropus rubricollis*, Geoff., I found the cardiac moiety divided into two dilated compartments, of which the left is again subdivided, and plicated within, while the pyloric moiety is extended in an elongated tortuous form, proportionably exceeding in length that of semnopithecus entellus. It is to a pteropus, doubtless, and not a vampyrus, that is to be attributed a similarly complicated stomach, described and figured by Sir Everard Home, as belonging to the vampire bat, and from which he draws the rather hasty conclusions that "the vampire bat lives on the sweetest of vegetables; and all the stories related with so much confidence of its living on blood, and coming in the night to destroy people while asleep, are entirely fabulous." I suspect the stomach of the true vampire bat will be found to accord with the blood-thirsty habits so repeatedly ascribed to it, and in corroboration of which, Professor Grant, in his late lectures before the Society, gave some additional observations.

" The complicated stomachs of the bradypodæ are also well known; they approach in their external form more nearly to those of the true ruminants. The chambers into which the stomach of the sloth is divided, are not, however, characterised by the difference of texture of the lining membrane which exists in the ruminants: they present only a difference in the degree of vascularity and villosity, and in that respect are analogous to the complicated stomach of the quadrumanous genus."

Neither Professor Owen, nor the other anatomists who have treated of this peculiar structure, seem to be aware of the fact, that the observation had been already made by Wurmb in his description of the kahau. He does not indeed enter into any particulars with regard to the complications, but his expressions that " the stomach of the kahau was of unusually large size, and of a very irregular form," can refer only to the appearances since detected as generally characteristic of this organ in the semnopithecs*. The same structure has been since shown to exist in the *semnopithecus maurus* (Proc. of Zool. Soc. Part II. p. 6), in the douc (*S. Nemeus*), and in *S. Cucullatus* (*vide* ' Magazin de Zoologie,' 1836) ; so that we are now certain of its being common to seven species of the genus, and may conclude, with every probability, that it extends to all the others.

We have thought proper to give the above details of structure in Professor Owen's own words. That gentleman has treated the subject so fully, that it would be useless to insist upon it, farther at least than to direct the especial attention of the reader to the analogous structures which he has pointed out as existing in the kangaroos, sloths, and vampire bats. Professor Owen is inclined to believe, from the circumstance of these analogies, as well as from the peculiar modification of the stomach itself, that the semnopithecs may possibly feed upon the leaves and tender buds of trees, rather than upon the fruits and roots which constitute the food of the ordinary monkeys. Of this, however, it must be observed, that neither the accounts of travellers, nor the obser-

* This observation has been lately confirmed by Mr. Martin, in a description of the stomach of the kahau, read before the Zoological Society.

vations which have been made upon such specimens
as have been exhibited from time to time in our
menageries, afford any confirmation, though there
are other circumstances which have escaped Professor
Owen's notice, but which add some weight to the
conjecture. The teeth of the semnopithecs, in fact,
present analogous modifications to those which have
just been described as characteristic of their stomachs;
in short, the whole system of organs, which enter
either immediately or remotely into the function of
nutrition, appears to have undergone a simultaneous
change in these animals, and analogy and philosophy
equally forbid us to conclude that this change is
without an object, or unaccompanied by corresponding modifications of habit and economy. The
number of the teeth, as well as their composition, are
indeed the same as in all the simiæ, but their form
differs considerably from that of the other monkeys,
and like so many other details of their structure,
approximates them more nearly to the gibbons. In
the cercopithecs and baboons, the molar, or cheek-
teeth, are extremely tuberculous, and present a
number of mammilated points, which are scarcely
ever worn down by the effects of detrition; whilst,
on the contrary, these same teeth in the semnopithecs
become triturated at an early period, so as to present
a hollow cavity in the centre. This betokens a
corresponding motion of the jaws in the act of
mastication, that is to say, a longitudinal grinding
motion from front to rear, during the continuance
of which the teeth rub against, and wear one another
down. Now such a motion is clearly unnecessary to
an animal which lives upon nuts or soft pulpy fruits,
which require only to be bruised by opening and
shutting the mouth alternately, and not ground by
rolling the jaws upon one another; its existence,
therefore, in the semnopithecs, seems to betoken

some peculiarities in the regimen of these animals, with which we are at present unacquainted, more especially when taken in conjunction with the modifications already noticed as existing in the stomach and bowels; and it is hoped that this curious and interesting subject will attract the attention of some of our numerous countrymen resident in India, many of whom are so well qualified to investigate it, and who have already enriched the zoology of that country with many valuable observations. The additional, or fifth tubercle, which is found on the last inferior molar of the semnopithecs, as well as of the baboons, has been already mentioned. Another circumstance which appears strongly confirmatory of Professor Owen's conjecture is the fact reported by many travellers, as to the existence of bezoars in the stomachs and intestines of the Asiatic monkeys. These concretions, when genuine, are found only in the stomachs of ruminating animals, and of the genus of monkeys at present under consideration; for the analogous substances which are sometimes produced in the alimentary canals of other mammals, and even of men, and which have often been confounded with the true bezoar, appear to differ both in their mechanical and chemical structure. The bezoars produced by the monkeys of the Malay peninsula, and which can scarcely belong to a different genus from the semnopithecs, are described as being smaller, rounder, and more powerful in their qualities than those obtained from ruminating animals. It is certain, at least, that they are more highly prized by eastern nations; and the fact of their production, taken in connection with the complicated form of the stomach, in two groups of mammals, in other respects so widely separated from one another, offers a curious and interesting analogy between the semnopithecs and ruminants, and an additional argument in favour of the supposition advanced by Professor Owen.

The extremities of the semnopithecs are of great length, compared with the dimensions of the body; this is another instance in which the semnopithecs resemble the gibbons, as well as in the slender and elongated form of the body itself; but there is this remarkable distinction, that, whilst the anterior pair of extremities in the gibbons is beyond all proportion longer than the posterior, the proportions are reversed in the semnopithecs, and it is the posterior extremities which exceed the anterior in length. Still the disproportion is by no means so great as that which exists in the gibbons, nor does it in the slightest degree impede the quadruped motion of the animals, when they are forced to resort to that mode of progression; but it becomes an additional evidence, particularly when taken in conjunction with other traits, of the superior development of the abdominal over the pectoral members, and the consequent degradation of the animals in the scale of existence. This evidence is still farther strengthened by the very limited development of the thumb on the anterior extremities, which, as has been already observed, scarcely exceeds the tuberculous form, and enters but slightly into the functions of prehension and manipulation: thus, as it were, preparing the way for its entire disappearance in the colobs. The organ consists, nevertheless, of the ordinary number of phalanges of which it is composed in other cases, but they are greatly abridged in their dimensions, both as regards thickness and length, and form a remarkable contrast to the rather immoderate development which marks the rest of the members. The tails, likewise, are much longer in the semnopithecs than in any of the ordinary monkeys; though slender, however, they possess a very considerable degree of muscular power, and enter as a very important constituent into the motions and progression of the animals. When at rest and unemployed, they are allowed to hang down perpendicularly, and from their great length, which considerably exceeds that of the animal's body, have a very droll effect, which is heightened by the natural apathy and imperturbable gravity of the creatures themselves. This, when unemployed, is their ordinary position; they exhibit the very picture of sadness and melancholy, and appear as if perfectly regardless of every thing that passes around them; but when roused or excited, they are nevertheless capable of the most surprising exertions, and astonish the spectator by a rapidity, variety, and precision of movements, which could scarcely be anticipated from creatures apparently so apathetic in mind and delicate in body. They are in reality far from meriting the name of slow monkeys, which some zoologists have given them; their slowness is exhibited in disposition rather than in action, and is an attribute of character rather than of structure. When young they are readily domesticated; but being less petulant, curious, and restless than the cercopithecs and baboons, are supposed to exhibit less intelligence, though their mental qualities as well as their physical structure closely assimilate them to the real apes: the old males become morose, sullen, and mischievous. This genus contains numerous species, of which we shall notice such as are most remarkable for peculiarities of form, or interest attached to their history, reserving the complete enumeration of species, as in other genera, for the general synopsis at the conclusion of this work.

The KAHAU (*Semnopithecus Larvatus**.)

Is, in many respects, the most singular and anomalous species, not only of the present genus, but even of the entire family of simiæ. This extraordinary creature, of which the annexed engraving, taken from a fine specimen procured by the late Sir Stamford Raffles, and by him deposited in the museum of the Zoological Society, presents a very accurate likeness, is an inhabitant of the great island of Borneo, and, according to M. Geoffroy St. Hilaire, of Cochin China, and even of the western peninsula of India. It is probably the largest species of the genus, the body of

* Though the real name of this animal is *Bantanjan*, as we learn from Wurmb, yet the improper appellation of *Kahau*, bestowed upon it from the resemblance of its cry to that word, has been so long appropriated to it that it is now useless to change it.

the full-grown male attaining very nearly the size of an ordinary man, and evidently possessed of great muscular power. The females are considerably smaller, as is generally, if not universally, the case among the quadrumana; they likewise differ from the males in other respects, which will be noticed hereafter, and which at first sight appear so distinctive as to have led Messrs. Vigors and Horsfield to describe the sexes as different species.

The entire height of this animal, when standing upright, exceeds three feet six inches; the length of the body is two feet six inches, and of the tail two feet three inches. The body is large and robust; the head round and rather flattened, with a low forehead; the eyes are large and well separated from one another, and are unaccompanied either with brows or inferior eye-lashes; the mouth is very large, and furnished with long powerful canines, and strong broad incisor-teeth; the ears, though naked like the face, palms of the hands, and soles of the feet, and of the same dark blue colour, are concealed by the long hair of the head; and the neck is extremely short and thick, and apparently deformed by a goitre-like protuberance, in all probability caused by the laryngal sacks, which Wurmb informs us exist in this species as well as in the orangs, and which we have already seen reproduced in the siamang and others of the true apes. But the most extraordinary and anomalous trait in the physiognomy of the kahau is the enormous and disproportioned size of the nose, which has a most ludicrous appearance when viewed in relation to the dimensions of the animal, and almost impresses the spectator with the idea that nature intended it as an extravagant caricature upon that organ in the human subject. The nose of the kahau in fact is not flattened, and as it were rudimentary, as in

the other simiæ, but even more prominent than in
man, and prolonged beyond the mouth in such a
manner as to form a kind of small proboscis, a resemblance which has even procured it the name of
the proboscis-monkey from some naturalists. Such
indeed are the size and proportions of this organ in
the kahau, that, as M. Geoffroy St. Hilaire has
remarked, to suppose a man possessed of such an
organ, without being unnatural or disproportionate,
he must have a stature of at least ten feet. It
should be remarked, however, that it is only in adult
individuals that the organ acquires these extravagant
dimensions; the young have it little more developed
than the ordinary semnopithecs, but it increases
gradually with the age of the animal, and finally acquires the enormous proportions here mentioned.
In the female it is at all times much smaller than
in the male. The nostrils are placed at the extremity underneath, as in the human subject; they
are separated by a thin cartilage, and though at
all times large, are said to be capable of enormous
distention at the will of the animal. It is impossible to say what influence these circumstances
may exercise upon the habits and manners of
the kahau in a state of nature; naturalists, as far
as we are aware, have never had an opportunity
of observing the living animal even in confinement, but it is reasonable to suppose, from analogical
considerations, that the great development of the
organ of smell is accompanied by a corresponding
acuteness of function in that sense, though the
purpose which such increased sensibility may serve,
in the economy of a frugivorous animal, is not easily
conjectured. M. Geoffroy remarks that the cerebral
cavity likewise betokens a superior degree of intelligence, and that the forehead is more developed than
in the rest of the semnopithecs.

The body of the kahau is covered with hair of a reddish brown or dull chestnut colour, deepest on the back and flanks, light orange upon the chest, and greyish fawn on the belly, thighs, legs, and arms, as well on the outer as on the inner surfaces. These colours are less apparent, and not so strongly contrasted in the females as in the males, and the latter sex is likewise marked on the loins by a number of large rectangular spots, producing a bizarre variegation of which it is difficult to convey a clear idea in words, but which is very striking in the animal. The females are destitute of these diversified marks, the loins and back being of a uniform reddish brown colour; the nose also is much smaller in proportion, and less prominent than in the other sex, and has a recurved or puggish form, scarcely surpassing the mouth in length, whereas it has rather a drooping aspect in the males, and is very considerably prolonged beyond the upper lip. These considerations, added to the difference in size of body, which has been already noticed as character-istic of the two sexes, have caused Messrs. Vigors and Horsfield to describe the male and female kahau as distinct species. Their memoir upon this subject is inserted in the 5th volume of the Zoological "Journal," but that the distinction there made is really sexual instead of specific, is proved by the fact of the very specimens which they describe having been obtained at the same time and place, and presented to Sir Stamford Raffles as the male and female of the same species, as well as by the express testimony of Wurmb, as to the diminutive size of the latter sex. The recurved form of the nose, indeed, upon which these gentlemen so strongly insist, may be after all only an individual, and not even a sexual difference, if it be a natural character at all; for it is not unlikely to have been produced in drying and

mounting the specimen in question, and this conjecture receives some countenance from the fact, of
the circumstance not being mentioned by any of
the French naturalists who have described this
animal, though the national museum, at the Jardin
des Plantes, contains specimens of both sexes.   We
must therefore reject, as inconclusive, the reasoning
by which Messrs. Vigors and Horsfield have attempted
to support their opinion as to the specific difference
of the two specimens belonging to the fine museum
of the Zoological Society ; as we are equally bound
to oppose the establishment of the genus *Nasalis*,
which some foreign naturalists have proposed for
the reception of this animal, and which we shall
presently have an opportunity of demonstrating to
differ in no essential zoological character from the
rest of the semnopithecs.   The only other point
which it is necessary for us to notice in the description of the kahau, is the long hair which covers
the neck and shoulders, and which though not forming a marked mane, as in the wanderoo, tartarin,
and some other species, is nevertheless sufficiently
remarkable to attract the attention of the observer,
and to form a sensible contrast with the naked
bluish skin of the face.   The tail, contrary to the
general rule among animals of this genus, is not
quite so long as the body ; it is of a uniform white
colour throughout, as is likewise the under part
of the loins, below the maculated portion of the back,
and a remarkable line which passes transversely over
the shoulder, and contrasts strongly with the reddish
brown of the surrounding parts.

This very remarkable animal was first described
by the celebrated Daubenton, in a Memoir read
before the Academy of Sciences, which, however,
appears never to have been published ; and which, as
it was drawn up posterior to the breach between him

and Buffon, has not been inserted in the Supplements
to the "Histoire Naturelle," but is replaced by a very
meagre account in the posthumous volume, which
does not even mention the origin of the specimens
which it professes to describe. The species, however,
was very shortly afterwards described by Wurmb in
the "Memoirs of the Society of Batavia," from specimens which he had himself shot in the Island of Borneo; and as his account is the only one on record,
derived from original observations, or which professes
to relate the habits of the kahau in his native forests,
we shall give the most interesting part of it in his
own words. "These animals," says he, "associate
together in numerous companies : their cry, which is
extremely loud and grave, distinctly pronounces the
word *kahau*, and it is doubtless from this circumstance
that some Europeans, by changing *h* into *b*, have
supposed the name of the animal to be *kabau*. The
natives of Pontiana in Borneo, however, in the woods
surrounding which town they are sufficiently numerous, give them the name of *bantajan*, on account
of the peculiar form of their nose. They assemble
together morning and evening, at the rising and
setting of the sun, and always on the banks of some
stream or river : there they may be seen seated on the
branches of some great tree, or leaping with astonishing force and rapidity from one tree or branch
to another, at the distance of fifteen or twenty feet.
It is a curious and interesting sight; but I have
never remarked, as the accounts of the natives would
have you believe, that they hold their long nose in
the act of jumping ; on the contrary, I have uniformly
observed, that on such occasions they extend the legs
and arms to as great a distance as possible, apparently
for the purpose of presenting as large a surface as
they can to the atmosphere. The nature of their food
is unknown, which renders it impossible to keep

them alive in a state of confinement. They are of
different sizes; some are even seen which do not
exceed a foot in height, though they have already
become mothers and are engaged in nursing their
young. When seen from above, the nose of this
animal has some resemblance to a man's tongue,
with a longitudinal ray running down the centre. The
nostrils are oblong, and the creature has the power
of distending them with air to the extent of a full
inch or upwards. The brain is in all respects similar
to that of the human subject; the lungs are as white
as snow; the heart is surrounded by a great quantity
of fat, and this is the only situation in which that
substance is found. The stomach is of an extraordinary size, and of an irregular form, and there is a
sack beneath the skin of the neck which extends
from the lower jaw to the clavicles." Desmarest
adds, but upon what authority does not appear, that
this animal is of a violent and brutal nature, and
defends itself with a courage and perseverance allied
to ferocity. This is so much the character of all the
large simiæ, that it is probably true of the kahau as
well as of others; but it is to be regretted that we
have not a more detailed account of the manners of a
species which offers so many anomalies in its physical
conformation.

According to M. Geoffroy St. Hilaire it is a
native of the Malay peninsula as well as of Borneo, but we are equally ignorant of his grounds
for this assertion, which may, however, as well as
that of Desmarest, be derived from the original un-
published "Memoir" of Daubenton, if it be still
preserved in the archives of the Institute. Nay, it
would even appear from what M. Geoffroy has said
of the kahau, that it should be found in Mysore and
the western peninsula of India, since he relates
that the ambassadors sent to France by Tippoo Saib

when taken through the galleries of the National
Museum, at once recognised and pointed it out as
an animal of their country, and expressed a lively
pleasure at seeing in Europe a creature which they
regarded at home as endowed with every great
moral and intellectual quality. In this instance,
however, we suspect M. Geoffroy to be clearly mistaken; the kahau certainly is not found within the
limits of the British possessions in India, otherwise it
must have been noticed by some of the numerous
and zealous observers who have long successfully
employed themselves in investigating the natural history of that vast country. That it may be found in
Cochin China and other parts of the eastern peninsula
of India, is much more likely; though even of this we
have no express or direct evidence : but that it is not
found in the countries between the coasts of Malabar
and Coromandel is all but certain; and though the
ambassadors of Tippoo may have heard of or possibly
even seen specimens of the animal, it is unquestionable that they could not with truth have represented
it as an inhabitant of their own country. The precise
origin of the specimen in the French museum has
been nowhere stated. There is one specimen at
Leyden *said* to have been brought from Sumatra;
all the others in that magnificent museum, and
those belonging to the Zoological Society, as well as
the individuals procured and described by Wurmb,
were obtained in Borneo, so that this island is at
present the only certain habitat of the species.

The only other observation which it will be necessary to make upon this subject, regards the propriety
which some authors have urged of considering the
kahau as the type of a new genus, to which they
have proposed appropriating the name of nasalis.
This proposal was first advanced by M. Geoffroy
St. Hilaire in the 19th volume of the "Annales du

Museum," but was never adopted by the more judicious mammalogists, and has even been abandoned
in the present state of our knowledge at least, by
its eminent founder himself.   Notwithstanding this,
however, we find it reproduced in conjunction with
the pretended genus *Lasiopyga*, a still more unpar-
donable piece of ignorance, in numerous subsequent
compilations.   That the animal is a real semnopithec,
and nothing more, is demonstrated beyond contradiction by the details of its anatomy, which have been
furnished by Wurmb, and which, though they have
escaped the notice of Professors Otto and Owen, as
well as of M. Geoffroy, clearly show that the stomach
of the kahau exhibits the same structure which the
former naturalists have detected in the other species
of the genus. Its enormous size and capacity are expressly mentioned, and the *irregular form* attributed
to it can only refer to the sacculated structure described by Professor Owen[*].   The teeth also are
worn down by trituration in the same manner as
those of the ordinary semnopithecs, and the other
zoological characters are equally identical.   There
remains, then, no real difference but in the form and
dimensions of the nose, but this cannot be insisted
upon as a generic character, because it has no ap-
preciable influence upon the habits and economy
of the animal's life.

The Douc (*Semnopithecus Nemæus*),

One of the most beautiful of all the monkey tribe,
is well deserving of attention, not only on account of
the singular variety and brilliancy of its colours,
but likewise from the errors which long prevailed

[*] This, as already observed in a former note, has been
since shown from actual dissection by Mr. Martin, of the
Zoological Society.

concerning its structure, and which even now continue to be propagated by various compilations, though
accurate observation has long since cleared up all
doubt upon the subject. Buffon's description, which
first introduced the species to the knowledge of zoologists, happened to be taken from a badly mounted
specimen, in which the skin of the buttocks had been
contracted in the process of preparation in such a
manner as to conceal the callosities, at all times rather
diminutive in the semnopithecs; succeeding writers
found it more convenient to copy Buffon than to be
at the trouble of observing for themselves; the errors
of that brilliant but fanciful author were of course
not forgotten, and thus the mistaken notion was
grdaually propagated, and finally became fixed, as an
incontrovertible fact in zoology, that the douc formed
an exception to all the other true monkeys, in being
destitute of callosities. So universally did this idea
prevail for a long period after the death of Buffon,
and so firmly had it become established at one time,
that we find the greatest and most acute naturalists
admitting it without question, and even reasoning
about it as an undoubted fact. Thus Illiger and
Geoffroy St. Hilaire both proposed forming a distinct
genus for its reception, the one under the name of
lasiopyga, the other under that of *pygathryx*, both
names equally expressive of the supposed defect of
callosities, and the consequent hairy covering of the
buttocks. Even so late as the year 1820 we find
M. Desmarest falling into the same mistake, which
was however shortly after that period cleared up by
the arrival of numerous specimens, both alive and
dead, which had been procured by M. Diard during
his visit to Cochin China. Since that time there has
been no manner of doubt upon the subject : the
douc has taken its proper place among the other
species of semnopithecs; no author of any reputation
upon the continent has repeated the ancient mistake,

and yet we find it daily reproduced in this country, with a pertinacity which only shows how easy it is to propagate an error, and how difficult to eradicate it. In fact there exists in this, as in all their other organs, a perfect accordance between the douc and the rest of its congeners, and the differences which do exist are only such as are found among all species belonging to the same natural genus.

The douc, when full grown, is equal in size to the kahau already described ; the conformation of its parts and organs is in all respects the same as that of the other semnopithecs, and its principal distinction is found in the brilliancy and variety of the colours which spread over every part of the body and limbs, and which, did not its habitat differ so widely, would incline us to imagine that we recognized in this beautiful animal the *kepos* of the ancient Greeks as described by Ælian.   The head is brown, with a narrow band of a brilliant chestnut colour passing under the ears backwards; the face is naked, and of a lemon colour, the cheeks ornamented with long white whiskers directed backwards; the whole upper surface of the body and sides is of that annulated mixture of light and dark colours succeeding one another alternately upon the same hairs, which characterises so many of the cercopithecs, or common African monkeys, and produces that variety of greyish brown and green so generally prevalent among these animals. In the douc, however, the green tints do not appear, and the colours are of a shade resembling minever, rather darker on the upper than on the under surface of the body; the shoulders and thighs are black, as are likewise the hands and feet; the fore-arms white, and the legs deep chestnut colour.   The tail, and a large patch on the rump immediately at its origin, are pure white, and form a remarkable contrast to the deep black of the hips and thighs, and the clear minever of the body.   These colours are all decidedly marked, and do not blend gradually into one another; and their variety, brilliancy, and distinctness, taken all together, make the douc one of the most beautiful animals in nature.

The manners and habits of the douc are altogether unknown to naturalists. The only authentic and undoubted notice of the species, which we have been able to discover in the works of travellers, is contained in the following extract from the journal of M. Rey, a French captain of a merchantman, who made a voyage from Bourdeaux to Cochin China in the years 1819-20, and travelled for some distance into the interior of the country, with a quantity of fire-arms which he had been commissioned to procure for the king. It was during this inland journey that he met with the animal in question; and we transcribe the passage with the greater pleasure, as it contains the only recorded notice of the douc alive, and in its native forests. "Next morning early," says M. Rey, "we began to ascend the pass before mentioned, Tay-sons, and before we reached the breakfasting place, had killed a hundred monkeys, of a large species, peculiar to the country. Desirous to procure living specimens of this animal to carry to France, it was with great difficulty that I succeeded. In this operation many of them fell; for the more that were wounded the more collected around them; endeavouring to carry off into the woods the dead as well as the wounded. The three young ones which we captured held so fast round the bodies of their dams, that it required no small effort to detach them. This species of monkey greatly resembles the orang-outan in his stature and inoffensive manners, inhabiting the mountains and the tops of the loftiest trees, and living on fruit. The similarity of this creature to man is strikingly mortifying. His fur is exceedingly fine; the hands and feet are black, the shoulders and legs deep red, the belly white and the back grey. The face is flat, and of a white colour, the cheeks red, and the eyes large and black. Some of the males measured, when standing upright, above four feet four inches in height. In the country they are called *venan*, or men of the woods." M. F. Cuvier informs us farther, from an examination of the various specimens of all sexes and ages, which the late M. Diard procured during his visit to the same country, that there is no distinction of colours between the males, females, and young, all indifferently exhibiting the same marks which have been already described among the specific characters. The name of douc, by which this species has been so long known, would appear from M. Rey's account to be unknown in its native regions : it was given to Buffon by M. De Poivre as the native name of the animal, and though it may perhaps be improper, is now too well established to be rashly changed. The identification, however, which Buffon makes of this animal with the *sifac* of Madagascar, imperfectly described by Flaccourt, is manifestly wrong, and has indeed been universally rejected by all succeeding writers of judgment and authority. In another of his conjectures, and a very interesting one too, as things have turned out, it is probable that the great French naturalist has been more fortunate, and, though it was merely a random guess on his part, he still deserves the credit of having made it. Buffon supposes that the douc and the wanderoo are the species which produce the monkey bezoars, already noticed in the former part of the present chapter ; not because he was acquainted with the complicated form of the stomach in the former animal, but because these were the only two species which he knew to inhabit Southern India, from which these stones were said to be obtained. That these concretions should be produced in the stomach of a quadrumanous animal at all is sufficiently curious ; but the circumstance derives a lively interest from the discoveries of

Professors Otto and Owen with regard to the sacculated form of that organ in the semnopithecs; and
though it appears to have escaped their notice, it is
nevertheless worthy of farther attention, and, as before observed, will form another beautiful relation to
the ruminant order of mammals, if eventually found
to be characteristic of the semnopithecs, a result of
which there appears to be every probability. The
monkey bezoars are said to be smaller and rounder
than those produced by the goats, gazelles, and antelopes: they are highly esteemed in the East for
their supposed medicinal virtues, and sell for a much
larger price than any similar concretions.

The HOONUMAN (*Semnopithecus Entellus*).

Having in the last articles described two species of

semnopithecs, the one as remarkable for the singular
brilliancy and variety of its colours, and for the errors
which formerly prevailed concerning it, as the other
for its anomalous organic structure, we come now to
treat of a third species equally remarkable in another
point of view; not indeed on account of any peculiarities of form or colours which distinguish it from
the rest of its congeners, but from the historical interest which attaches to it as connected with the religious dogmas and traditions of a most singular and
remarkable people. The animal in question is the
entellus, the *hoonuman* of the Hindoos, and *lungar*
of the Hill Tribes, a native of Bengal and other parts
of continental India, which has from time immemorial
been held sacred by the inhabitants of that country,
and whose history is in many instances interwoven
with that of the Indian nation itself. It is not uncommon in our menageries, and has been frequently
and attentively observed by different zoologists. The
following description is principally extracted from
M. F. Cuvier. "The young entellus," says this
naturalist, "is at first remarkable for the disproportionate length and slenderness of its extremities, for
the deliberation of all its movements, and an eye and
physiognomy whose tranquillity nothing can disturb; it appears to bear in this respect the same relation to the cercopithecs that the ateles of America do
to the sapajous. It strikes the beholder at first
sight, by the contrast of its shining black face and
hands to the light grey or straw colour which is uniformly spread over the entire body and members,
and by the direction of the hair surrounding the face,
which forms a kind of projecting fillet over the eye-
brows, and a beard beneath the chin, the latter peaked
and directed outwards instead of falling perpendicularly downwards from the chin. The colour of the
fur varies from greyish white to pale orange, the

shade, however, being always darker on the loins and along the spine than elsewhere. The hands and feet as well on the backs as on the palms and soles, are black, and, in young individuals especially, strongly contrasted with the surrounding lighter colours. As the animals advance in age all these colours deepen in shade, till at length the fur becomes mixed with numerous black hairs, and assumes a uniform rusty brown colour, the weight and dimensions of the body at the same time increasing to such a degree as to deprive it entirely of that slender elongated character which marked it in youth, and in its stead to communicate an appearance of great muscular power and energy. In this state, that is, when it has arrived at its complete development, the entellus is at least equal in size to any of the species already described, measuring nearly four feet and a half in length from the extremity of the muzzle to the origin of the tail, and with a corpulence of body proportioned to its length. The tail is considerably longer than the body, but of the same general colour, and terminated by an obscure tuft of hair rather longer and darker than the rest."

The following account of the habits and history of the entellus was furnished by M. Duvaucel, to whom we have been already indebted for many interesting traits in the manners and economy of the gibbons. It is only necessary to observe that the name *houlman*, by which he says the animal is known to the Hindoos, is misspelt, the real orthography being *hoonuman*, and that by Gouptipara he appears to mean the city of Goalpara. "This species," says M. Duvaucel, "is highly venerated by the Hindoos who have even deified it, and assigned it one of the first places among their thirty millions of gods. It migrates from the upper provinces into Bengal towards the end of winter; yet, though sufficiently abundant, I had for some time a great difficulty in procuring a specimen, for however zealous I might be in my pursuits and endeavours, it was always to no purpose, the watchful care and perseverance of the Bengalees always preventing me from having an opportunity of killing an animal so highly esteemed, and after which, according to their superstitious belief, the perpetrator was certain to die within the year. As soon as I was seen to appear abroad with my gun in my hand, I was sure to be surrounded by crowds of the natives, who most assiduously employed themselves in chasing the monkeys out of shot; and during upwards of a month that a small family of seven or eight hoonumans remained at Chandernagore, and came freely every morning into the very houses to receive the offerings of the Brahmins, my house and compound were constantly surrounded by these pious religionists, who tormented me by an incessant beating of drums and tomtoms, for the purpose of scaring these four-handed divinities, and keeping them at a distance from so dangerous a neighbourhood. I entered the city of Goalpara (a holy place on the Hoogly river, inhabited by Brahmins, and covered with temples, in one of which is said to be preserved the hair of the goddess Douaga) something in the same state as we may suppose Pythagoras to have entered Benares, though for a different purpose; he went in search of men, I came in search of beasts, which are, generally speaking, more easily met with. I beheld the trees everywhere covered with their long-tailed godships, the hoonumans, which, on my appearance, betook themselves to flight, uttering loud cries. The Hindoos, perceiving my gun, guessed the object of my visit as well as the monkeys, and ten or a dozen of them quickly collected round me, and harangued me upon the danger which I should incur by molesting or injuring animals which were nothing less than great

princes and heroes metamorphosed. I would rather
have been spared the trouble of listening to these
charitable advocates; at the same time pretending
to be half convinced, I was in the act of passing on,
when I encountered in my way a princess so seduc-
tive, that I could not possibly resist the temptation of
cultivating a nearer acquaintance with her. I accordingly levelled my piece and fired, and it was then I
became witness to a scene which was truly touching
and pathetic; the poor animal, which had a young
one on her back, had been hit near the heart, she
felt herself mortally wounded, and uniting all her
remaining force for the effort, seized her young one,
and was just able to throw it up into the branches of
a neighbouring tree before she fell and expired at
my feet. An incident so touching and unexpected,
a trait so truly maternal, made a greater impression
on me than all the discourses of the Brahmins; and
the pleasure of obtaining a specimen of so beautiful
an animal was, for once, unable to contend against
the regret which I felt for having killed a being which
appeared to be tied to life only by the most estimable
and praiseworthy feelings."

The origin of the extreme veneration in which
these animals are held by the Hindoos is involved
in the obscurity of the early history of that wonderful
people. It may probably have arisen from the
doctrine of the metempsychosis or transmigration of
souls; for they firmly believe that the spirits of their
departed friends pass into these and other sacred
animals. But however this may be, it is certain
that it has subsisted among them from the earliest
periods. The superstitions and traditions of the
Brahmins upon the subject hold a prominent place
in the "Ramayan," one of the greatest epic poems
which the genius of any age or country has
produced, and of which we shall give a very brief

outline in so far as it is connected with the animal whose history we are now relating. The chief subject of the poem appears to be to celebrate the triumph of the good over the evil principle. These principles are typified by the Hindoo gods on the one hand, and a nation of demons on the other, who are called Rackschasas, and, who, under their king Ravana, are supposed to reside in the island of Lanka or Ceylon. The power of these demons had long been predominant over the earth; and, as the gods had made them invulnerable against the immortals, it followed that Ravana and his followers could only be subdued by a mortal adversary. The gods, compassionating the misery which prevailed on the earth, thus governed uncontrolled by the principle of evil, assemble a grand council, and agree to send Vishnu down in the form of a man to fulfil the decrees of fate by subduing the Rackschasas by human power. The incarnation is made in the person of Rama, the eldest son and successor to Dasharatha, king of Ayodhya (Oude), who thus becomes the hero of the poem, and though present on earth in the character of Rama, does not cease, in the mean time, to maintain his station among the gods in the character of Vishnu. In this latter capacity, he creates invulnerable tribes of apes and monkeys, all under their proper kings and generals, (of whom the chief is Hoonuman,) and endowed with the courage and intelligence necessary to creatures destined to be the allies of his earthly incarnation Rama, in the glorious enterprise against Ravana. Passing over the numerous previous incidents of the story, we come at once to the cause and consequences of the war between Rama and the Rackschasas. Its immediate origin arose out of the rape of Sita, the wife of Rama, who is carried off by Ravana and confined in the fortress of Lanka. The hero upon this contracts an alliance with Hoonuman, the king of the monkeys, who undertakes to go in search of the lost princess; and, having at length discovered her in Lanka, hastens back with the information, and rejoins Rama at Ayodhya. A grand expedition is immediately prepared against Ravana; a bridge is built from the continent to the island of Lanka, over which the army of the allies is marched, and the two princes sit down before the fortress. The feats of the warriors on both sides, and the conduct of the siege, fully equal, as we are assured by oriental scholars, if they do not surpass, the corresponding portions of the Iliad, both in the interesting nature of the events and the force and beauty of the description. The fight is not confined to the surface of the earth, the air is likewise filled with combatants; Rama and Ravana at length encounter one another in personal combat, the heavens resound, the earth trembles beneath their desperate contest, till at length, after seven days' struggle, Ravana is finally overcome, his forces scattered or destroyed, and Rama and Hoonuman enter Lanka in triumph.

Throughout the whole of this war Hoonuman is, next to Rama, the most conspicuous hero opposed to the demons, and signalises himself by numerous acts of strength, courage, and agility. Among others of his enterprises, the Hindoos still consider themselves indebted to him for the introduction of the mango, which he carried off from the gardens of a celebrated giant whom he had overcome, and which still continues to be especially grateful to the palates of his descendants. Such an act of theft, however, committed during the progress of so sacred a war, naturally drew down upon the perpetrator the supreme anger of the gods, and it was to evince their displeasure that they placed a mark upon himself and his race, by blackening their face and hands,

which continues to this day an unquestionable
evidence of the truth of these statements. Another
of Hoonuman's adventures had well nigh terminated
even more seriously. The hero conceived the
masterly project of setting fire to the whole island
of Ceylon, and thus destroying his enemies at once,
by means of a tar-barrel tied to the end of his tail.
The plan was no sooner conceived than it was
executed ; but, in the laudable act of thus burning
out his enemies, Hoonuman's own tail caught fire
also, a mischance upon which it appears the hero
had not calculated. Stung by the pain, and fearful
of losing this valuable and ornamental appendage
altogether, he was about to extinguish the flame by
plunging it into the sea ; but the inhabitants of that
element, apprehensive of the fatal consequence which
might ensue to themselves from such an unwarrant-
able proceeding, should the sea also be set on fire,
remonstrated strongly with him upon the subject, and
finally persuaded him to alter his intention. So far
all Indian histories agree in the relation of this important event, but the subsequent part of the story is
differently told by different authorities. Some learned
pundits say that Hoonuman upon this stretched his
tail out upon the shore, whilst his friend Sumunder
threw water over it and extinguished the flame ;
others, on the contrary, affirm that he proceeded
forthwith to the Himalayan mountains, and dipped it
into a lake at the source of the sacred river Ganges ;
and we must confess that we are ourselves most
inclined to credit the latter account, not only because
it is the most worthy of such an heroic action, and
most remote from the ordinary course of events, but
because the lake in question bears the name of
Bunderpouch, or "*monkey's tail*," to this very day,
as if to confound the audacious sceptics who venture
to question the truth of the legend. Moreover, all

the world (in Hindoostan) believe and affirm that a single monkey is deputed from the plains every year in the month of P'hagun, and ascending the hills by way of Hurdwar, takes his station on the snowy peak of a high mountain which rises majestically over the sacred lake, and there watches incessantly till relieved in the following season. In the execution of this sacred duty, as may be naturally expected from the inhospitable nature of the country and climate, he undergoes many privations, and returns to Bengal wasted to a skeleton by watching and fasting: but what will not men and monkeys suffer in support of a favourite dogma!

From these superstitious traditions, we learn to appreciate the force and origin of the high veneration and esteem which the hoonuman enjoys among the disciples of Brahma, wherever that system of worship extends. We see, in fact, that the animal is identified with the history of a great moral and religious doctrine, analogous to, if not identical with, our divine revelations regarding the fall and regeneration of man, though disguised and disfigured under the garb of an exuberant and extravagant allegory. Nor is the veneration of the people confined to the hoonuman; we have seen that the hoonuman tribe was only the chief, the Brahmins, as it were, of the many others created by Vishnu, for the purpose of assisting Rama in his enterprise of subduing the principle of evil, and we shall afterwards find that the bhunder (*papio rhesus*), and other species, enjoy the same degree of favour as the hoonuman itself. This favour is carried to the greatest height that religious fervour and zeal are capable of. Splendid and costly temples are dedicated to these animals; hospitals are built for their reception when sick or wounded; large fortunes are bequeathed for their support; and the laws of the

land, which compound for the murder of a man by a
trifling fine, affix the punishment of death to the
slaughter of a monkey! Thus cherished and pro-
tected, the entellus abounds over every part of India,
enters the houses and gardens of the natives at will,
and plunders them of fruit and eatables without
molestation ; the visit is even considered an honour ;
and the Indian peasant would consider it an act of
the greatest sacrilege to disturb or to drive them
away. They generally take up their residence in the
topes or groves of trees, which the people plant round
their villages for the purpose of screening them from
the too ardent rays of the sun, but they are permitted
to occupy the houses in common with the inhabitants,
when they feel disposed to change the scene, and are
described by a late traveller as to be seen by dozens
playing on the flat roofs, or perched with much
gravity at the open verandas to observe the passing
crowd.

The entellus, though a native of the hot plains of
India, is by no means incapable of sustaining the
rigours of a much more ungenial climate. It is
well known that they ascend the Himalayas where-
ever they can find wood : they are found in Nepaul ;
and Turner even informs us that he met with
them on the cold elevated plains of Bootan. The
following extract is from the works of that traveller,
which will be found to contain much valuable
information upon this subject :—" Wild animals,"
says he, " are so extremely rare in Bootan, according
to my experience, and as far as my information leads
me to conclude, that I must not pass by, without
particular mention, a multitude of monkeys which
we saw playing their gambols by the road-side.
They are of a large and handsome kind, with black
faces surrounded with a streak of white hair, and
very long slender tails. They are the honoumaunt

(*hoonuman*) of India, the largest in these regions,
and the gentlest of the monkey tribe. They are held
sacred by the Booteeas as well as by the Hindoos, and
have obtained a distinguished place in their miscellaneous and multifarious mythology. I once saw a
multitude of them at Muttra, in Hindoostan, which
I was informed, were daily fed on the produce of a
stipend, settled for their support by the Hindoo prince,
Madajee Sindia. I ventured amongst them with some
diffidence, for they were bold and active, which rendered it difficult to avoid any sort of liberty which
they might choose to take. Resentment was out of
the question, for I was informed that they were at all
times ready to unite in one common cause. One
amongst them was lame from an accidental hurt, and
it was surprising, in consequence of this resemblance
to his patron, what partial attention and indulgence
he had obtained, and of which indeed he seemed
perfectly sensible. I have also noticed multitudes of
the same species near Amboa, in Bengal."

The celebrated banian-tree called Cubbeer-bur,
from the name of a favourite Hindoo saint, which
grows on the banks of the Nerbuddah, in the province of Guzerat, and is believed to be the largest
specimen of that remarkable plant in India, is the
residence of a numerous colony of hoonumans.
The following is the account which Forbes, in his
" Oriental Memoirs," has given of the Cubbeer-bur
and its inhabitants. " High floods have at various
times swept away a considerable part of this extraordinary tree; but what still remains is above two
thousand feet in circumference, measured round the
principal stems; the overhanging branches, not yet
struck down, cover a much larger space; and under
it grows a number of custard-apple, and other fruit
trees. The large trunks of this single tree amount
to three hundred and fifty, and the smaller ones ex-

P

ceed three thousand: each of these is constantly
sending forth branches and hanging-roots, to form
other trunks, and become the parents of a future
progeny. It was much resorted to by the English
gentlemen from Baroche. Putnah was then a flou-
rishing chiefship on the banks of the Nerbuddah,
about ten miles from this celebrated tree. The chief
was extremely fond of field sports, and used to en-
camp under it in magnificent style, having a saloon,
dining and drawing rooms, bed-chambers, bath,
kitchen, and every other accommodation, all in separate tents; yet did this noble tree cover the whole,
together with his carriages, horses, camels, guards,
and attendants; while its spreading branches afforded
shady spots for the tents of his friends, with their
servants and cattle; and in the march of an army,
it has been known to shelter seven thousand men.

" This magnificent pavilion affords a shelter to all
travellers, particularly the religious tribes of Hindoos; and is generally filled with a variety of birds,
snakes, and monkeys: the latter have often diverted
me with their antic tricks, especially in their parental
affection for their young offspring, by teaching them
to select food, to exert themselves in jumping from
bough to bough, and then in taking more extensive
leaps from tree to tree; encouraging them by caresses when timorous, and menacing, and even
beating them when refractory. Knowing by instinct the malignity of the snakes, they are most
vigilant in their destruction; they seize them when
asleep, by the neck, and running to the nearest flat
stone, grind down the head by a strong friction on
the surface, frequently looking at it, and grinning at
their progress. When convinced that the venomous
fangs are destroyed, they toss the reptile to their
young ones to play with, and seem to rejoice in the
destruction of the common enemy. On a shooting

party under this tree, one of my friends killed a
female monkey, and carried it to his tent, which was
soon surrounded by forty or fifty of the tribe, who
made a great noise, and in a menacing posture advanced towards it; on presenting his fowling-piece
they retreated, and appeared irresolute. But one,
which, from his age and station in the van, seemed
to be the head of the troop, stood his ground, chattering and menacing in a furious manner: nor could
any efforts, less cruel than firing, drive him off. He
at length approached the tent-door; and, finding
that his threatenings were of no avail, he began a
lamentable moaning, and by every token of grief
and supplication seemed to beg the body of the
deceased. On this it was given to him. With tender
sorrow he took it up in his arms, embraced it with
conjugal affection, and carried it off in a sort of
triumph to his expecting comrades. The artless
behaviour of this poor animal wrought so powerfully on the sportsmen, that they resolved never
again to level a gun at one of the monkey race."

The same authority informs us, that the trees
which shade the houses at Cambay, in Guzerat, are
filled with monkeys, squirrels, doves, and parrots, of
which the monkeys alone are mischievous, occupying
the roofs of the houses, and swarming all over the
town, unmolested by the inhabitants. Of the monkeys at Dhuboy he gives the following account.
"The durbar, or governor's mansion, where I resided, with its courts and gardens, occupied seven
acres; it was almost surrounded by the lake, except
near the principal gate, communicating with the
town; a pavement of large flat stones, admirably
united, formed a dry walk at all seasons, above the
steps of the tank, shaded in most parts by lofty trees,
and adorned with fragrant shrubs; through which
only a few houses and towers on the walls were

visible; so that from the windows of the durbar,
overlooking the lake, everything had more the appearance of a rural village than a fortified city.
Near the durbar was a small woody island, affording
a nightly roost for cranes, kites, and crows, and
shelter for a number of those immense bats, not improperly called flying foxes. To finish this pic-
turesque scene, a ruined Hindoo temple, nearly
covered with moss, and the clematis, in great variety, terminated the terrace-walk in the garden,
where the animal creation had hitherto been so unmolested, that my orange and lime trees were filled
with peacocks, doves, and bulbuls; monkeys and
squirrels feasted on my pomegranates and custard
apples, while pelicans, spoonbills, and other aquatic
birds, occupied the lake. The intrusion of the
monkeys I could have dispensed with; their numbers were often formidable, and their depredations
serious. I believe there were as many monkeys as
human inhabitants in Dhuboy; the roofs and upper
parts of the houses seemed entirely appropriated to
their accommodation. While the durbar was re-
pairing, on my first arrival, I resided a short time
in one of the public streets; the back of the house
was separated by a narrow court from that of a principal Hindoo. This being the shady side, I generally retired during the heat of the afternoon to a
veranda, and reposed on a sofa with my book; small
pieces of mortar and tiles frequently fell about me,
to which, supposing them to be occasioned by an
eddy of wind, I paid no attention; until one day,
when I was so much annoyed by their repetition,
accompanied by an uncommon noise, and a blow
from a larger piece of tile than usual, that I arose to
discover the cause; and to my astonishment saw
the opposite roof covered with monkeys, employed
in assaulting the white stranger, who had unwit-

tingly offended by intruding upon their domain. Although my new situation invested me with considerable power, and made me the first man in the city, yet as I knew I could neither make reprisals nor expect quarter from the enemy, I judged it most prudent to abandon my lodging, and secure a retreat.

" I do not imagine that the inhabitants of Dhuboy protect the monkeys from any other motive than humanity to the brute creation, and their general belief in the metempsychosis: but, in Malabar and several other parts of India, Dr. Fryer's assertion is very true, that 'to kill one of these apes the natives hold *piacular*, calling them half-men, and saying that they once were men, but for their laziness had tails given them, and hair to cover them. Towards Ceylon they are deified ; and at the straits of Balagat they pay them tribute.' I cannot omit one singular employment in which the monkeys of Dhuboy are engaged. I believe among the higher castes of Hindoos, duelling is everywhere unknown, and the lower classes are equally ignorant of the art of boxing; but as even Hindoos do quarrel, though they do not often lose their temper, one principal mode of offence is that of abuse; not by calling a man a rascal or a villain, for that would neither lessen him in his own opinion nor in that of society ; but to abuse his mother, his wife, his sister, or his daughter, would be esteemed the grossest insult, and only to be reconciled by a more abusive retaliation. If that is not accomplished, it remains a subject for future revenge, which brings me to the point in question repecting the Dhuboy monkeys, who are the innocent agents of this revenge. Previous to the commencement of the periodical rains, about the middle of June, it is customary to turn the tiles on the roofs of all the houses in the towns and villages

in Hindostan, both of Europeans and natives.
These tiles are not fixed with mortar, but regularly
laid one over the other, and by being adjusted immediately before the setting-in of the rains, they keep
the roof dry during that period ; after which, their
being misplaced is of little consequence, in a climate
where not a shower falls for eight months together.
At this critical juncture, when the tiles have just been
turned, and the first heavy rain is hourly expected,
the injured person, who has secretly vowed revenge
against his adversary, repairs by night to his house,
and contrives to strew over the roof a quantity of
rice or other grain ; this is soon discovered by the
monkeys, who assemble in great numbers to pick up
this favourite food ; when finding much of it fallen
between the tiles, they make no ceremony of nearly
unroofing the house, at a time when no turners of
tiles are procurable ; nor can any remedy be applied
to prevent torrents of rain from soaking through the
cow-dung floors, and ruining the furniture and de-
positories of grain, which are generally formed of
unbaked earth, dried and rubbed over with cow-
dung."

These animals frequently become the prey of the
leopard and tiger, which even appear to capture them
by a kind of fascination. " While the mischievous
monkey," says Mr. Forbes, in another part of his
amusing and instructive memoirs, " as well as the
innocent dove, found an asylum within the walls of
Dhuboy, the adjacent country was infested with
tigers and savage beasts; which, in defiance of Py-
thagorean systems and Brahminical tenets, waged
perpetual war against the antelopes and innocent
animals near the villages ; even the monkeys, with
all their wily craftiness, could not escape them. The
peasants in the wilds of Bhaderpoor confirmed the
stratagem used by the tiger to effect his purpose, as

mentioned by Dr. Fryer. 'The woodmen assert, that when the tiger intends to prey upon the monkeys he uses this stratagem: the monkeys, on his first approach, give warning by their confused chattering, and immediately betake themselves to the highest and smallest twigs of the trees; when the tiger, seeing them out of his reach, and sensible of their fright, lies couchant under the tree, and then falls a-roaring; at which they, trembling, let go their hold, and tumbling down, he picks them up to satisfy his hunger. That monkeys are their food their very ordure declares, scattered up and down, where is visible the shaggy coats of these creatures.'"

The doctrine of the metempsychosis, so characteristic of the Hindoo religion, though unquestionably the principal, is by no means the only motive which actuates these singular people in their veneration of the lower animals. On his first arrival at Dhuboy as chief magistrate of the district, the Brahmins entreated Mr. Forbes not to permit the officers or soldiers of the garrison to molest the monkeys, or fire at the wild fowl, which resorted to the lake, urging not only the doctrine of the metempsychosis, but dwelling particularly upon their utility in keeping the city and tank free from dirt and nuisances. When remonstrated or reasoned with on the necessity of killing animals intended for food, they, however, opposed the doctrine of the metempsychosis to every argument; it was fruitless to argue with them upon such subjects; their pride and self-sufficiency militating against every attempt to convince them of their errors. "The Brahmins of Malabar," says Mr. Forbes, "usually treated such kinds of conversation with arrogance and contempt; those of Dhuboy affected either an air of superiority or indifference."

Captain Williamson, in his " Oriental Field Sports,"

gives the following information on the subject of the
hoonuman :—" Monkeys," says he, " abound almost
everywhere ; their usual haunts are in thick mango
topes, near to cultivated spots. They are of various
sizes. The loongun is at least equal to a lad of
fourteen, and when erect stands five feet and a half
or upwards in height. [This is rather exaggerated,
but we have seen very old males which were
certainly five feet high.] They are extremely mischievous, and have, in many instances, been guilty of
the most brutal violence. Nothing can surpass their
boldness. If in numbers, they will strip a moderate-
sized maize plantation during a few hours, in spite of
the opposition of a small party of men. Their disposition is so libidinous, that where they exist, women
cannot pass their haunts in safety. They are of a
curious appearance, being of a greenish-dun colour,
with black faces and paws, and a grey rim of hair
surrounding their foreheads, so as to resemble a small
toopee wig. I have at various times seen these
gentry in a field of vegetables, where until approached
very nearly, I mistook them for natives weeding."

We shall conclude the history of this interesting
animal with the following extract from Johnson's
" Sketches of Indian Field Sports :"—" There are,"
says this author, " two species of monkeys common
throughout Hindoostan. One of them is of a large
kind, with a black face and brown body ; the other
is a small brown monkey, such as we often see in
this country with dancing bears. I believe there are
many other species in the Thibet mountains, and
other large forests, but I have never seen any of
them in a wild state. Although all the monkeys in
India are wild, they are not much afraid of men,
which I attribute to their never being molested by
the natives. They often follow boats along the
banks of the Ganges and other rivers, in expectation

of having bread or fruit thrown to them, which is often done; but if a gun be presented they instantly decamp. Ramah, one of the Hindoo gods, according to their mythology, conquered India and other countries, delivering many nations from tyrants, with an army of monkeys; their general was named *Hunamat* (described by Sir William Jones to be the Grecian Pan), and the large monkeys with black faces are now called *Hunamans*, and are much venerated by the Hindoos; every other kind of monkey is held by them in veneration, but in a less degree."

The BUDENG (*Semnopithecus Maurus*).

This species, long known to systematic writers by the name of *Simia Maura* and *Cercopithecus Maurus*, has been accurately figured and described by Dr. Horsfield, in his "Zoological Researches in Java," of which and the neighbouring island of Sumatra it is a native. The latter locality is, indeed, the head quarters of many different species of semnopithecs, and, among others, of the lutung (*S. Pyrrhus*), mentioned in the following extract from Dr. Horsfield's work. M. F. Cuvier calls the *S. Maurus* tchincoo. The whole body is covered with long, silky, black hair in the adult animal, partially tipped or intermixed with silvery-white in old age, and uniform reddish-brown in the young. The face is naked, and surrounded by a tuft of upright hair; the hair of the cheeks is directed backwards, and passes under the ears in the form of pointed whiskers; the under surface of the body is less densely covered than the back, and the abdomen is nearly naked.

" The *Semnopithecus Maurus*," says Dr. Horsfield, " is distinguished, among the Javanese, by the
name of *budeng*, from another species which has
the same form and habit, but a different external
covering. The name of the latter is *lutung;* but
the Malays and Europeans apply this name to both
species, and distinguish them by the epithets of
black and red : the budeng being denominated
lutung itam (black lutung), and the lutung of the
Javanese, *lutung mera* (red lutung). In Sumatra
the name of the *S. Maurus* is lotong.

" The budeng, or black species, is much more
abundant than the lutung, or red species; and the
latter, both on account of its rarity and comparative
beauty, is a favourite with the natives. Whenever
an individual is obtained, care is taken to domesti-
cate it, and it is treated with kindness and attention.
The budeng, on the contrary, is neglected and de-
spised. It requires much patience in any degree to
improve the natural sullenness of its temper. In
confinement, it remains during many months grave
and morose ; and, as it contributes nothing to the
amusement of the natives, it is rarely found in their
villages or about their dwellings. This does not
arise from any aversion on the part of the Javanese
to the monkey race; the most common species of
the island, the *Cercocebus Aygula* of Geoffroy, or
Egret monkey of Pennant, is very generally domesticated : and a favourite custom of the natives is to
associate it with the horse. In every stable, from
that of a prince to that of a mantry, or chief of a
village, one of these monkeys is found ; but I never
observed the budeng thus distinguished.

" The *Semnopithecus Maurus* is found in great
abundance in the forests of Java : it forms its dwellings on trees, and associates in numerous societies.
Troops, consisting of fifty individuals and upwards,

are often found together. In meeting them in the
forests, it is prudent to observe them at a distance.
They emit loud screams on the approach of a man,
and by the violent bustle and commotion excited by
their movements, branches of decayed trees are not
unfrequently detached, and precipitated on the spectators. They are often chased by the natives for
the purpose of obtaining their fur. In these pursuits, which are generally ordered and attended by
the chiefs, the animals are attacked with cudgels
and stones, and cruelly destroyed in great numbers.
The skins are prepared by a simple process, which
the natives have acquired from the Europeans ; and
they conduct it at present with great skill. It affords
a fur of a jet black colour, covered with long silky
hairs, which is usefully employed, both by the natives
and by the Europeans, in preparing riding equi-
pages and military decorations."

There are various other species of semnopithecs,
but their history possesses little interest : they will be
enumerated in the synopsis, at the end of the second
volume.

Chapter VIII.

Monkeys *continued.*—African Monkeys—Genus Colobus—its Characters
and various Species.

Africa may be justly considered as the head
quarters of the monkey tribe: no other portion of
the earth swarms with these animals to such a degree
as the western coasts of this vast continent, whether
we consider the immense troops of individuals or
the countless variety of species, which every where
spread over the face of the country.   Between
twenty and thirty different kinds are known to inhabit the west coast alone, and the undescribed
varieties in all probability amount to as many more,
if not to double that number.   Almost every new
arrival presents us with species before unknown, and
it is probable that, were we equally acquainted with the
productions of the opposite coasts and of the interior,
the number would amount to a hundred or upwards.
The habitats of the different species appear to be
local, and circumscribed to a comparatively small
extent of country; but it is to be regretted that we
have few details upon this part of the subject, and
are in most cases unable to fix the precise locality in
which particular species may be found.   One thing
at least is certain, namely, that nine-tenths of the
numerous cercopithecs, or small long-tailed monkeys,
brought to this country, and exhibited in our different menageries, come from the Gambia, Sierra
Leone, and the countries round the Gulf of Guinea;
but the dealers through whose hands they pass, take
little interest in their origin or previous history, and

it rarely happens that we can ascertain the port from which they were obtained. All travellers, however, attest the immense multitudes of monkeys which abound in these countries. Monkeys of different species, we are assured by Jobson, are innumerable along the banks of the Gambia, and may be seen in troops of three or four thousand, assembled each according to its species. It is pretended that they maintain among themselves a kind of republican form of government, in which the strictest order and subordination are enforced; that they travel about from place to place, under the orders of particular chieftains, which are always the oldest and most powerful of the tribe, and maintain a kind of rude discipline upon the march; that the females carry their young under their bellies when they have only one, but that when they happen to have twins, which sometimes takes place, the second is mounted upon the mother's back; that the females and young always travel in the centre during a march, a troop of the old males leading the van, and another bringing up the rear of the party. In his progress up the river Gambia, the same old traveller was remarkably struck with the numbers and temerity of the monkeys, which covered the trees at every step along the banks, shook the branches violently, and by their incessant chattering and grinning, seemed desirous to menace the travellers and deter them from proceeding. Barbot makes nearly the same report as to the vast abundance of these animals in Guinea. Atkins says that at Sierra Leone they are of all imaginable species and colours, except white, and swarm in such incredible numbers, that the natives are obliged to keep a constant watch, and to employ poison, fire-arms, and other devices, to preserve their plantations of yams and millet from the depredations of these unwelcome visitors; and, finally,

Smith, a very credible and well-informed traveller, assures us that, on the Gold Coast alone, there are upwards of fifty different species of monkeys, and that they are so numerous that it would be a very difficult matter to distinguish or describe all the various kinds.

These African monkeys are neither so large nor so mischievous as their Asiatic congeners. Generally speaking, they are remarkable for the agreeable variety and intermixture of their colours, their playful, lively dispositions, and their greater attention to cleanliness and propriety than the baboons, whose filthy habits render them as obnoxious as their morose and intractable tempers. Two very distinct genera of these animals inhabit Africa, one of which appears to be peculiar to that continent, whilst the other, though principally an African genus, is represented in Asia by certain species hitherto confounded with the papios under the common name of macacs. The first of these we shall now proceed to describe.

Genus *Colobus.*

Till within the last two or three years, the materials with which this genus was constructed were of a very scanty and imperfect nature. They consisted merely of the rude figure and very brief descriptions which Pennant gives of two monkeys, formerly preserved in the museum of Sir Ashton Lever, and which offered the remarkable character of having no thumbs on the anterior hands. The defect of so important and influential an organ, in a group of animals principally characterised by its perfect development, and the functions which depend upon its opposable power, was justly regarded by Illiger as a legitimate generic character; and he accordingly formed the animals observed by Pennant, and which had been previously confounded with the ordinary cercopithecs, into a distinct genus to which he gave the name of *colobus*, from the seeming mutilation of the hands, and which was quickly adopted by other zoologists. The want of thumb, however, was well nigh the only known character of the new genus; the presence or absence of cheek pouches and callosities, the nature of the teeth, and other equally interesting particulars, were unknown; nor was it for many years afterwards that naturalists had an opportunity of ascertaining these particulars, or even of confirming the accuracy of Pennant's original observation. In fact, so much doubt hung over the genus colobus, that Baron Cuvier was long disposed to consider the absence of the thumbs in Pennant's animals as arising from an accidental or intentional mutilation; and as he had never met with the character in any of the old world simiæ, which came under his notice, he refused to admit it into the "Règne Animal." In this state of uncertainty the genus continued to be involved, till the exhibition of a specimen in Bullock's Museum put an end at last to the doubts which might have reasonably attached to it before, and afforded an opportunity of making some farther observations upon the characters of these anomalous animals. This specimen afterwards passed into the possession of M. Temminck; it belonged, indeed, to a different species from either of the animals described by Pennant, but it satisfactorily confirmed the accuracy of that naturalist's original observations, as far as related to the primary generic character of the colobs, and was shortly afterwards described by Kuhl under the name of *colobus Temminckii*. Nothing farther however was known of these animals, and M. Temminck's specimen continued to be unique in the museums of

Europe,—those in the Leverian collection having been long since destroyed,—till about the middle of 1832, when the mutilated skins of two species, one at first supposed to be identical with the *colobus Temminckii* of M. Kuhl, the other referred to the *colobus polycomus*, or full-bottomed monkey of Pennant, were received and exhibited at the Zoological Society. Three years afterwards the skins of another and still more distinct species were brought from the Gambia, and exhibited before the same Society; and as these were in perfect condition, the occasion afforded a favourable opportunity of ascertaining the real characters of the genus, and comparing the different skins and fragments already in the Society's possession. The result of this examination, which is published in the third volume of the Proceedings of the Society, clearly established the existence of six distinct species of colobus,—two, namely, described by Pennant; one by Kuhl, which was shown to be distinct from the *colobus ferruginosus*, with which it had been previously confounded; a fourth, just then announced by Dr. Rüppell; a fifth, founded upon the Gambian specimens; and a sixth, upon the mutilated skins above mentioned, as having been erroneously referred to *colobus polycomus*. Still more recently, a seventh has been added to the catalogue; whilst this work was passing through the press, two other magnificent species have been received from Fernando Po; and we have no doubt but that the number may be doubled or trebled by the researches of future inquirers.

Yet, notwithstanding the great and rapid accession of knowledge which we have acquired on the subject of these animals within the last few years, it must nevertheless be admitted that our materials for the complete illustration of the genus are still of a very imperfect nature. Of the nine species above

enumerated, six only are at present known from
complete specimens; the other three are described
from imperfect skins, or founded upon the figure and
original description of Pennant; but, with the exception of the few facts furnished by Dr. Rüppell,
we know nothing of the osteology or internal anatomy of the genus; and indeed the chief materials
which we possess are three or four perfect skins
and a number of fragments. These fragments consist of the skin of the body and great part of the
extremities, but want the head, hands, and belly; yet,
notwithstanding their mutilation, there can be no
doubt as to the propriety of their reference to the
present genus, since the quality of the fur is alone
a sufficient character to distinguish them from all
other monkeys. The colobs, in fact, may be divided
into two sub-genera or inferior groups, according to
the length and quality of the hair and the general
distribution of the colours. In the first of these
minor groups, the fur is six or eight inches in length,
either over the body generally, or at least upon the
head, neck, and shoulders; and the colours universally, as far as at present known, are black and white,
not minutely intermixed with each other, but disposed
singly or occupying particular members; in the
second, the fur is everywhere short, and the colours
different shades of red, combined with black or
light blue, disposed in the same manner. The
nature of the long, soft, silky hair of the first group,
which are unquestionably the handsomest monkeys
in existence, causes the animals to be much sought
after by the negroes, who make their tie-tie caps of
the skins, and purchase them for this purpose at the
rate of twenty or thirty shillings a piece. This
economical use of the fur probably accounts for the
fact of our receiving none but mutilated specimens;
the hunters will not be at the trouble of skinning and

preparing the head and limbs, so long as the body is
the only part to which they attach a commercial
value.

But there is another observation which we have
to make concerning the nature of the fur of the
colobs, and it applies equally to both the small
groups which have just been characterised,—namely,
that the hairs, considered individually, are of the
same colour throughout their whole extent, and not
annulated with alternate rings of different colours,
as is the case, less or more, with all the known
cercopithecs. This character, however subordinate
and unimportant in a zoological or scientific point
of view, is of great practical value, since it serves at
once to distinguish even the most imperfect fragment
of a colob's skin from that of all other African
monkeys. The two genera of Asiatic monkeys,
the small section of the cercopithecs (the long-tailed
macacs of authors) which inhabit that continent, and
the semnopithecs, are distinguished in precisely the
same manner; the Asiatic cercopithecs have the
hair more or less annulated, like their African congeners, and the colours minutely speckled or mottled in consequence; the semnopithecs, on the other
hand, resemble the colobs, in having the individual
hairs of the same shade throughout, and the colours consequently disposed in patches and not finely
grained or intermixed with one another. Nor are
these the only analogies which these respective genera bear to each other: we shall find, as we proceed, that almost all the characters of the one are
reproduced in the other; and it is a singular and
interesting fact in the history of the quadrumana, that
the two Asiatic genera of monkeys should have each
its representatives in Africa, as we shall presently
find that the baboons of the latter continent are
equally represented in the former; but as far as

the monkeys are concerned, each continent is inhabited by two distinct genera, which, whilst they agree
together in some of their characters, are in other
respects related to those of the opposite continent in
such a manner as to become their veritable geographical representatives.

But the most peculiar and distinctive character of
the colobs arises from the defect of thumb on the
anterior hands; a fact which deserves the greatest
attention, on account of the important functions
which this organ performs in the actions and
economy of the animals, and of the indirect influence
which it necessarily exerts over their mental faculties.
We have already had many occasions of observing
the extent to which Nature pushes her power, and
makes use of the vast resources which she has at
command, for the purpose of modifying the different
organic systems of the animal frame; we have
already seen her, in the case of the semnopithecs,
verge upon the very boundaries of the great and
leading character of the quadrumana, in abbreviating
the thumb to such a degree as to render it but a
feeble instrument of prehension, and almost to
deprive it of all power of executing its ordinary
functions; but here she altogether oversteps the
limits of her own general law, and actually forms
an entire genus of quadrumanous animals without
the organ which mainly characterises their kind, and
which, without ceasing to be quadrumana, are yet
deprived of thumbs on the anterior members! Some
species, nevertheless, have this organ still represented
by a minute rudimentary tubercle—in one instance
even furnished with a small nail, as in the analogous species of the genus ateles; but, as among the
latter animals, it never rises above the skin, is totally
destitute of motion, and never enters into the functions of prehension or manipulation. In the semno-

pithecs, on the contrary, though short, it still possesses
the motions natural to the organ, and is capable of
being effectively opposed to the other fingers.   Many
instances of the same kind of degradation might be
adduced in the history of organic modification,—instances in which the leading and most influential character is abolished, without, at the same time, destroying the relations of the animal to the group of which
it forms in other respects a constituent member ; and
these remarkable exceptions to great general laws
are the very instances which have puzzled and tormented naturalists ever since zoology was studied
as a branch of science.   The truth is, and it is the
only explanation we can give of the phenomenon,
that Nature is not bound in the creation by the same
strict rules of logic to which we are obliged to
conform in studying and classifying her works : her
only law is to modify every organ of the animal
frame in succession, so far as modification is possible,
and consistent with the harmony of structure necessary to the production of some preconceived
object, or the compassing of some special end ; and
to this systematic modification not only must the
minor and subordinate characters submit, but the
primary, leading, and most influential characters are
subjected to it in their turn, and obliged to undergo
a gradual degradation in different groups, till at last
they disappear altogether.

Such is exactly the case in the present instance.
We find the anterior thumbs of the monkeys abbreviated to such an extent in the semnopithecs as to
become almost tuberculous ; proceeding a little farther we find it disappearing altogether in the colobs ;
and, if we pursue our researches still farther, we shall
find it reappear in a much inferior tribe of animals,
in the papios, cercopithecs, and cynocephals, with a
degree of force beyond what might be reasonably ex-

pected. But it may be here asked, what are we to
infer from an anomaly at once so strange in itself and
apparently contradictory of the general plan and laws
of creation? What inference are we to deduce from
the fact that two genera of monkeys, on all hands
allowed to be superior to the remainder of the group
in the general details of their organic structure and
intellectual capacity, are at the same time infinitely
inferior to them in the most important and influential character of the order,—that, namely, upon
which the very existence of the order depends, and
to which the animals composing it are indebted for
the elevated position which they occupy in the scale
of existence? We know that Nature does not proceed
by a uniform and uninterrupted chain of organic
and mental degradation, in which each link is absolutely superior in every respect to those that
follow; we know that the animal frame, being
composed of a great variety of different organs, each
adapted to its own especial function, and admitting
of every degree of variety consistent with the
difference of circumstances and design, actually
undergoes various modifications, in different animals,
whilst all the other characters remain unchanged.
We know, besides, that any attempt to arrange the
works of Nature according to a conceived plan,
whether in a straight line or circle,—which latter was
some time since the more fashionable mode, and
still continues to be so with some naturalists,—must
necessarily be inconsistent with this general law,
since either plan will be attended with at least as
many exceptions as accordances; or, in other words,
with innumerable instances in which beings undoubtedly superior in the scale of existence will be
postponed to others as manifestly inferior.

Such we apprehend to be precisely the case with
regard to the monkeys at present under considera-

tion. Were we to judge of them only according to
the leading traits of their organization, or compare
them with the monkeys alone, we should be obliged
to place them at the very bottom of the list; but if
we extend our views a little farther, and include the
apes in our comparison, we quickly perceive that
both the semnopithecs and colobs present striking
affinities to these animals, and are, in fact, to all
intents and purposes, gibbons so modified, as to be
converted into monkeys. They have the same
slender bodies and lengthened extremities as these
animals; the same mild and gentle dispositions; the
same round cranium and short face; the same abbreviated fore-thumb and lengthened fingers, and
even the simple and unannulated nature of the fur is
the same,—a character which is found in none of the
other simiæ. These animals, consequently, are to
be considered rather as a modification of the ape
than of the monkey type; a view of the case which
puts an end at once to the anomalous position which
they appear to occupy in the series of monkeys, by
showing that, whilst their long tails alone ally them
to the cercopithecs and macacs, all their other
characters approximate them to the gibbons.

But the absence of the thumb in the colobs, and
its tuberculous form in the semnopithecs, is not
altogether without compensation; for, though these
animals are not furnished with the prehensile tails
which compensate a similar defect in the ordinary prehensile organs of some of the American simiadæ, they
have, nevertheless, like these animals, the remaining
fingers of the mutilated members prolonged to a most
unusual extent,—a structure which enables them to
grasp bodies of very considerable size, by wrapping
the long fingers round them, and making the back part
of the palm in some degree answer the purpose of a
thumb. The same may be observed in the ateles;

but whether the defect of opposable power in the organs of prehension, by rendering their grasp less certain and their equilibrium less secure, imposes upon the colobs the slow pace and wavering gait of the American animals, is a question upon which we have no direct evidence. The manners and habits of these interesting monkeys, in fact, have never been observed in a state of nature, except in the instances of the *colobus guereza,* nor are we aware of any instance of their having been introduced alive into Europe; but it is reasonable to conclude, from the peculiar circumstances of their structure, that they can neither be so confident, nor so petulant, as the more favourably organized cercopithecs; and it is probable that, as they possess the external form, so likewise they enjoy the mild disposition and gentle manners of the semnopithecs.

There is one character, however, in which they differ materially from these animals. The semnopithecs, as we have already seen, like all the Asiatic simiæ, with the exception of the papios, are destitute of cheek pouches, a character invariably found in the African genera, and in the colobs, among the rest. Of the existence of these organs, in the present genus, there can be no doubt. M. Geoffroy St. Hilaire asserts it, we presume, on the authority of M. Temminck; and they are distinctly visible in the various specimens of *colobus rufo-fuliginus* belonging to the Zoological Society. The callosities are equally developed in both genera; and in the great length of the limbs and tail, as well as in the slenderness of the body and small round form of the head, they are perfectly similar. But what is still more remarkable, and highly interesting, in a physiological point of view, is, that the teeth of the colobs, like those of the semnopithecs, are subject to the same kind of detrition as those of herbivorous animals, and in old individuals may be observed worn down to the very gums. This detrition seems to take place in a longitudinal direction, indicating thereby a corresponding motion of the jaws, something similar to what takes place in rats, squirrels, and other rodent animals; at least the peculiar manner in which the teeth are worn leads to this conclusion, there being a longitudinal furrow in the centre, with an elevated and rather sharp rim on each side. The molar teeth of the semnopithecs present exactly the same appearances, and are in every respect similar to those of the colobs, without even excepting the fifth lobe or tubercle, common to the last inferior molar of all the Asiatic monkeys, and which, though not generally found in African species, has been observed by Dr. Rüppell in the Abyssinian colob; we have ourselves detected it in *colobus rufofuliginus*, and it no doubt exists in the other species of that genus. This, however, is a character altogether destitute of influence; and though it serves a useful purpose as a practical diagnosis, is merely such, and does not enter into the list of elements which modify or control the habits or economy of the animals.

But the detrition of the molar teeth is a character of a far different description. We have seen it in the case of the semnopithecs, as well as of other mammals, connected with a corresponding modification of the organs of digestion, and indicating peculiarities of regimen, which cannot fail to have a very powerful effect upon the habits of the animals; and the question naturally presents itself, have the colobs, in addition to the worn-down teeth of the semnopithecs, their complicated stomachs likewise, and do they equally feed upon the leaves and buds of trees in preference to fruits, roots, and grain? To this question, unfortunately, the present extent of our knowledge will not permit us to give a positive answer. Except the guereza, no species of this genus has ever been

dissected; and Dr. Rüppell's account of the viscera
of that animal is not so much in detail as could have
been wished. But, reasoning from the analogy of the
case, it is extremely probable that, when we become
better acquainted with the internal structure of the
colobs, we shall find them possessed of the same
capacity, if not of the sacculated form of stomach,
which distinguishes their Asiatic prototypes. In fact,
the functions of the teeth and digestive organs are so
intimately related to one another, that no modification can well take place in the one without
equally affecting the other; and it is therefore but
reasonable to conclude that, since the teeth of the
colobs indicate a decided change of function, the
form of the stomach will be found to correspond.

Dr. Rüppell indeed, distinctly mentions that the
stomach of the Abyssinian species is of very large
dimensions compared to the size of the animal, and
that it forms a long sack, bent upon itself in the
manner of a semicircle, and having small cords or
bundles of muscular fibres passing through it; but
he does not expressly mention the existence of any
sacculation or complicated structure, though he may
possibly mean so, from the expressions of which he
makes use. The cæcum was rather small and shaped
like a nine-pin; the small intestines measured 9 feet
7½ inches; and the colon and rectum 3 feet 11
inches; making the whole length of the intestinal
canal rather better than 13½ feet, which compared with the length of the body, gives about the
same proportion as Professor Owen's comparative
table of the viscera in the semnopithecs. Dr.
Rüppell enters at greater length into the osteological
structure of the *colobus guereza;* he informs us
that the molars are tuberculous, as in the ordinary
simiæ, and that the last inferior molar has the fifth
or supernumerary tubercle, both of which characters

we have ourselves verified in the *colobus rufo-fuligi-nus*, though, as already mentioned, the tubercles are worn down and obliterated in old specimens; and lastly, that the metacarpal corresponding to the thumb has a small sesamoid-like bone articulated to its extremity, but entirely concealed within the flesh, and forming no external projection. This rudimentary representation of the thumb no doubt extends to the other species of the genus, and, as has been already observed, has a greater development in some species than in others, as in the analogous case of the American ateles; there may possibly be such degrees of development in this respect, as to unite the colobs and semnopithecs by a gradual and uninterrupted series of gradations; but, even so, the two genera can never be united, as some zoologists have proposed, since, notwithstanding their numerous affinities, the existence of cheek-pouches in the one, and their absence in the other, must necessarily keep them apart.

As to the tuberculous form of the teeth, described and figured by Dr. Rüppell, it must have arisen, notwithstanding the apparent development of the canines, from the youth of the specimen; as the molars of the adult female specimen of *colobus rufo-fuliginus*, belonging to the Zoological Society, are worn down to the very gums, and M. Temminck describes the same detrition as apparent in the specimen of the same species which belongs to the museum of Leyden. It is to be observed, however, that this species belongs to the second sub-genus which we have characterised above, whilst the *colobus guereza* of Dr. Rüppell belongs to the first; and it is just possible that the structure of the teeth may differ in these two small groups. The stomach of the guereza, also, would appear, from Dr. Rüppell's description, to be of an intermediate

form between that of the semnopithecs and that of
the common monkeys—a fact which, according with
the tuberculous character of the teeth, may prepare
us to expect a greater complication of this viscus, in
those species which have the teeth more subject to
detrition. These questions, however, can only be
satisfactorily answered by actual dissection. In the
mean time, with an expression of regret that our
materials are so scanty, we proceed to describe the
specific distinctions of these highly interesting but
still imperfectly known animals.

1. Colobus Ferruginosus.

This is one of the species described by Pennant
from a specimen originally in the collection of Sir
Ashton Lever. It had been brought from Sierra
Leone together with the *colobus polycomus*, and, like
that species, was remarkable for the great length and
slenderness of the extremities, and the spare, meagre
form of the body. The crown of the head was
black, as were likewise the tail and external face of
the limbs; the back and upper surface of the body
were of a deep bay colour; and the cheeks, belly,
legs, and under parts, of a very bright bay. The
hands had only four fingers, and the feet five very
long toes.

Such is the very brief description which Pennant
has given of his bay monkey, the *simia ferruginosa*
and *colobus ferruginosus* of systematic writers; a
description, however, sufficiently explicit to enable us
to characterise the species and distinguish it from its
congeners. It is not a little remarkable that neither
this species nor the *colobus polycomus* should have
been observed since the time of Pennant; nor do we
find any distinct allusion to them in the works of the

numerous travellers who have written on the West
Coast of Africa. It is probable, indeed, that, like
the other African monkeys, these species are rather
local in their distribution, and confined for the most
part to particular cantons or districts; but the
animals in question are found at Sierra Leone, or
perhaps rather in the interior of the country contiguous to that settlement, that is to say, on the very
spot with which our countrymen have the most
direct and constant intercourse; and it is to be hoped
that some of the many competent observers connected with that colony will at least procure for our
public museums perfect skins of this and other
interesting animals of the country, if they cannot
send us living specimens. It too often happens that
those who have opportunities of serving the cause of
science in this way, and are very well inclined to
make use of them, neglect to do so under the idea
that what is most common and of every-day occurrence with themselves must be equally well known
in Europe; but they could not fall into a greater
fallacy, for the same error being entertained by others,
it constantly happens that no one ever thinks of
sending home the plants or animals most commonly
found in their own neighbourhood, and consequently
these common things are above all others the things
least known to scientific men, and most rare in museums or cabinets of curiosities.

2. Colobus Pennantii.

Closely allied to the *colobus ferruginosus*, but differing from the original description of that species,
as recorded by Pennant, is an animal of which numerous skins were recently received in the city, from
Fernando Po; of these two were presented to the

Zoological Society, and described by Mr. Waterhouse, the active and zealous curator of that establishment, under the name of *colobus Pennantii.*
The whole length of these skins, from the nose to
the origin of the tail, was two feet and an inch, the
length of the tail two feet three inches, and of the
head about four inches. The dried and wrinkled
state of the skins, however, renders this last measurement uncertain. All the upper and outer parts
are of an intense purplish red or maroon colour,
deepening upon the head, back, and tail, into dark
brown, but so gradually that no distinct line of separation is to be observed between the two colours,
which seem to fade into each other; the brown,
however, occupying but a very narrow stripe along
the median line of the back, whilst the deep maroon
spreads over all the rest of the shoulders, sides, and
outer face of the limbs. In this respect the animal
is very distinct from the two following species, which
not only have the upper and lower colours definitely
separated from one another, but in which the colour
of the back likewise descends down the outer face of
the arms and thighs, and covers the whole of the
shoulders, sides, and flanks. The front of the shoulders, the breast, belly, and interior surface of the
members are dirty yellowish white, as in *colobus
rufo-fuliginus;* but this colour is not separated from
the maroon of the sides by the pale red band along
the flanks, which is so characteristic of that species.
The cheeks are furnished with long thick whiskers,
of a white colour, and directed backwards. The
outer face of the thighs, arms, and fore-arms are purplish red, like the sides and body ; but the hind legs,
from the knee down, are of the same brown hue as
the head, back, and tail; the hairs of the tail are
very obscurely annulated, and the brown colour of
this organ and of the back are rather lighter than

that of the head, which, indeed, almost approaches
to black.

3. Colobus Rufo-fuliginus.

This species, of which we are enabled to give a
very characteristic engraving from the pencil of Mr.
Harvey, was first fully described in the Zoological
Proceedings for 1835, under the name of *colobus fuliginosus;* but as the epithet of *rufo-fuliginus* more
accurately expresses the colours of the animal, and
contains within itself a short but very accurate definition of the species; and as it has been since ascertained to be identical with the animal there de-

scribed under the name of *colobus Temminckii*, we
have determined upon suppressing both the specific
names there given, and substituting that here proposed, in order to avoid the confusion which might
otherwise attend the double synonym. Such changes
are seldom admissible ; but they are often, as in the
present case, of real advantage to the science, by
uniting the name and the definition in such a manner as to render it impossible to separate them afterwards, or to mistake the species to which they refer.
The individual specimen, from which the original
description of *colobus rufo-fuliginus* was taken, has
been deposited in the museum of the Zoological Society. It was an adult female, brought from the
Gambia, together with a well-grown cub, which resembled the mother in every respect, except size ;
and which has been since deposited in the Museum
of the Jardin des Plantes. Still more recently we
have had an opportunity of examining no fewer than
forty or fifty skins of the same species, and comparing them with the Leyden specimen ; so that we
have no doubt as to their identity, or as to the specific characters of the animal.

The Society's specimen measures two feet five
inches from the upper lip to the origin of the tail,
which organ is itself two feet eight inches in length.
All the upper parts of the body are of a light smoky
blue colour, very similar to that of the common
mangaby (*cercopithecus fuliginosus*,) rather darker
on the shoulders than elsewhere, and copiously
tinged with red on the occiput : the colour of the
back extends some way down on the external face of
the fore-arms and thighs, and also for a short distance,
but more obscurely, on the upper surface of the tail.
With these exceptions, all the rest of the extremities,
the arms, fore-arms, thighs, legs, hands, feet, and tail,
are of a uniform light or brick red, deepest on the

paws; and a more intense shade of the same colour extends up the fore-part of the shoulders, and spreads over the breast, throat, and whiskers, which latter are long, directed downwards on the cheeks, and backwards into long pointed tufts behind the ears, which are small, round, naked, and furnished with a distinct helix, in all respects similar to that of the human subject. The belly and under parts are of a dirty white, separated along the flanks and thighs from the smoky blue of the upper parts by a distinct line of clear yellowish red; and a circle of black stiff hair passes over the eyes. The face, palms of the hands, and soles of the feet, are naked and of a violet colour; the callosities are of moderate size; the thumbs of the anterior extremities are wanting, but their situation is marked by a small nail-less tubercle; the middle and ring fingers, both on the fore and hind hands, are of equal length, as are likewise the index and little fingers; and it is to be observed that the latter are united to the contiguous middle or ring fingers respectively, through the greater part of the first phalanx, as in the siamang and certain other gibbons. The face is short, the head round, and the whole form and habit of the animal similar to those of the semnopithecs. The teeth are of the usual form and number, and there are pretty large and very distinct cheek-pouches. The teeth, incisors, canines, and molars, indifferently, are worn down almost to the very gums. This species is very common along the banks of the Gambia, and, like most of the monkey kind, keeps generally in the vicinity of running streams. It leaps with great force and agility among the trees, but is rarely or never known to descend to the surface of the earth. The only notice which we find taken of it in the works of travellers is to be found in the voyages of Francis Moore, a factor in the service of the African

Company, who, about a century ago, resided for
many years at the Gambia, and during his frequent trading excursions up the river, often encountered troops of this and other species of monkeys.
He calls it the blue and red monkey, and mentions
having found it on the banks of a small stream,
which falls into the Gambia about three or four days'
journey from the mouth of that great river, close to
the native town of Damasensa.

---

4. Colobus Rufo-niger.

The species described by Kuhl and Desmarest
under the name of *colobus Temminckii* is, as remarked in the last article, identical with the *colobus
rufo-fuliginus*, as we have ourselves ascertained from
an examination of the original specimen observed by
Kuhl. This specimen, already mentioned as having
been formerly exhibited in Bullock's Museum, afterwards passed into the hands of M. Temminck, and
is at present deposited in the museum at Leyden;
but an error in the description of Kuhl, who says
that the upper and outer parts are *black*, whereas they
are really *blue*, made us originally confound it with
the present species; and it was only upon visiting
Leyden, and seeing Kuhl's specimen, that we ascertained their actual difference. Owing to this error
in the original description of the species, the skins
mentioned in the proceedings of the Zoological Society (Part III., p. 99) were erroneously referred to
the *colobus Temminckii:* they belong, however, to a
very distinct species, which we shall now proceed
to describe by the name of *colobus rufo-niger*.
These skins are unfortunately in an imperfect and
mutilated condition, the head and paws having been
amputated; but enough still remains to enable us

to characterise the species, and recognise its principal characters. The size of the *colobus rufo-niger* is about equal to that of *colobus rufo-fuliginus*, and the tail and extremities appear to bear about the same proportion to the length of the body. The entire upper surface of the body, consisting of the head, neck, back, shoulders, and outer surface of the thighs, is of a deep, dead, black colour; the flanks, limbs, and tail, are of a uniform maroon, or clear purplish red; the face, hands, and feet are wanting, but are probably of the same shade as the rest of the extremities; and the maroon of the tail is much more intense than that of the legs and flanks, approaching almost to black, and, in the older of the two specimens, actually replaced by that colour on the terminal half of the tail. It will be observed that this general distribution of colours is pretty much the same as in the last species; the black of the back and sides descends similarly down the outer face of the arms and thighs, but the whole of the under parts are very deep maroon, not separated along the flanks by a pale yellowish red band, as in *colobus rufo-fuliginus*, and much darker and more intense than the bright red in front of the shoulders in that species. The tail, almost black, is only slightly shaded with maroon, and there is no white or yellow on any part of the animal, in which respect it differs essentially from that last described. The origin of the skins in possession of the Zoological Society has not been satisfactorily ascertained, though they were reported to have been brought from Algoa Bay in South Africa. There is great reason, however, to doubt the accuracy of this habitat. The country about Algoa Bay has been too long the residence of an active and enterprising colony of British subjects, and its natural productions are too well known to admit the supposition of such curious animals existing in the neighbourhood, without having been long since seen and recognised by the numerous authors who have lately published accounts of that part of Africa. We know, besides, that South Africa contains only two quadrumanous animals, the common Cape baboon, *cynocephalus porcarius*, and a small species of monkey, *cercopithecus pygerythrus ;* these are the only simiæ found south of the Gareip or Orange River, and we must therefore seek for some other habitat for the present species, and the *colobus ursinus,* of which skins were procured at the same time and in the same locality. It is possible that there might have been some confusion between Algoa Bay and Delagoa Bay, and that the skins in question were brought from the latter locality ; and the supposition may perhaps receive additional countenance from the fact of our very imperfect knowledge of the animals inhabiting the eastern coasts of Africa ; but, on the other hand, we have no certain knowledge whatever as to the existence of any species of monkey on the eastern coasts of this continent ; and, for our own parts, we are of opinion that the skins in question were obtained at Sierra Leone,[*] or from some other part of the Western Coast ; a supposition which is greatly strengthened, if not confirmed by the fact of skins of *cercopithecus Diana,* which is known to be a native of the west coast, having been procured in the same locality.

The four species just described belong to the second sub-genus, which we have pointed out among the colobs ; the five following appertain to the first,

[*] The truth of this conjecture has been since fully established by Major Campbell, late Governor of Sierra Leone, who has recently presented the Zoological Society with a perfect skin of *colobus ursinus* from that colony, a species which, as we shall afterwards find, was originally procured from the same locality as that at present under consideration.

and are distinguished by the length and fineness of their fur, and the distribution of their colours. Of these the best known and most celebrated is

5. THE GUEREZA (*Colobus Guereza*),

long known as an inhabitant of Abyssinia, but only described and figured within the last few years by Dr. Rüppell, who procured many specimens during his recent travels in that country. Of these, individuals are deposited in the British Museum, in the museum of the Zoological Society, and in various continental collections. The colours of the animal are most remarkable; the head, nape of the neck, back, as far as the loins, breast, belly, extremities, and radical half of the tail, are covered with short hair of the most intense black; the cheeks, throat, chin, and a narrow line across the forehead, are clothed with the same description of short hair, but of a pure snowy-white colour; whilst the whole of the sides, from the shoulders on each side backwards over the rump, are furnished with very long, silky fur, of the most brilliant and unmixed whiteness, which hangs down over the body, and gives the animal the appearance of being covered with a loose white garment; the terminal half of the tail is of the same white colour and considerably tufted; and the face, ears, palms, and soles, are naked and of a bluish-black colour. It is difficult to convey an idea of the singular distribution of these colours by mere words; perhaps the reader might acquire a more accurate notion of its appearance, if we were to say that the whole animal was of a black colour, with the cheeks, throat, sides of the neck, and latter half of the tail white, and an abundance of long silky hairs, of the same colour, growing from the shoulders, sides, flanks, and rump, and hanging loosely down, so as to conceal the under parts of the animal.

This species has long been celebrated, being
mentioned in the earliest accounts of Abyssinia, where
its skin is an article of commerce among the natives,
and used for both useful and ornamental purposes.
No warrior appears in the field without having at least
some portion of these skins attached by way of ornament to his shield, and the princes and great men of the
country have them formed into mantles and coverlets
of the richest and most beautiful description. From
the very imperfect knowledge which we had of the
animal previous to Dr. Rüppell's journey, it was
generally supposed to be a species of lemur, and most
commonly confounded with the vari (*lemur macaco*),
to which indeed it has no very remote resemblance
in the distribution of its colours; but the researches
of that distinguished traveller put zoologists in
possession of its real affinities, and proved it to be
even a more singular animal than had previously
been supposed. Dr. Rüppell's excellent figure, too,
is the only one of the species ever published; for
that given by Ludolf in his 'History of Ethiopia,'
is altogether apocryphal as regards the animal, being
in reality taken from a species of jaccus or marmoset,
apparently the *jaccus penicillatus* of systematic
writers, an animal only found in South America,
and having no relation whatever to the guereza.
Ludolf's account of the animal, however, is interesting, as being the first on record. "There is a sort
of creature," says he, "very harmless and exceeding
sportive, called in the Ethiopic language *foukes*, in
the Amharic dialect *guereza*, which is a kind of
marmoset, and in Latin *cercopitheculus*, of which
the following rhyme is common in several parts of
Ethiopia:—

> Hominem non lœdo,
> Frumentum non edo,
> Oderunt me frustra.

R

"I give no man pain,
I eat no man's grain,
They hate me in vain!"

They are party-coloured, or blue mixed with grey;
India breeds them white and beautiful, but so tender,
that unless they are wrapped very warm, and carried
in the bosom, they cannot be brought into these parts.
Whether they be the callitrices of the ancients I leave
others to judge." The popular saying, so quaintly
expressed in these rude verses, expressing the harmless and inoffensive manners of the guereza, as
compared with other monkeys, which break into the
fields and gardens to plunder the fruits of the husbandman's labour, and the unmerited persecution
which it endures on account of the beauty of its
fur, notwithstanding its innocence, appears to allude
to some similarity in the food of this animal to what
is believed to characterise the semnopithecs; and
thus, in some measure, to corroborate the conclusions already deduced from the detrition of the
teeth, and other characters, viz., that the food consists rather of the tender leaves and buds of trees,
than of hard fruits and grain. The conjecture as to
the identity of the guereza with ·the callithrix of
the ancients, is by no means devoid of probability :
at all events it appears to be much nearer the truth
than any other we have met with on the same subject, more especially than that of Buffon, which
identifies the callithrix with the *cercopithecus sabæus*, or green monkey of western Africa, with
which the ancients could scarcely have been acquainted. " Callitrices, dicit Plinius, toto pene
aspectu differunt; (id est de cynocephalis et sphin-
gibus) ; barba est in facie, cauda latè fusa primori
parte. Hoc animal negatur vivere in alio quam
Æthiopiæ, quo gignitur cœlo." "The callithrices
are altogether different in form and appearance

from the cynocephals and sphinxes. The face is bearded, and the tail largely tufted : this animal can only live in Ethiopia, its native country." Five facts are here mentioned with respect to the callithrix : 1st, that the fur is handsome and valuable ; for this is the meaning of the name, which is compounded of the Greek words καλος *beautiful*, and θριξ *hair* or *fur ;* 2nd, that the animal differs generically from the cynocephals ; 3rd, that the face is bearded ; 4th, that the tail is tufted ; and 5th, that the animal is a native of Abyssinia ; for this country was the Æthiopia of the Greeks and Romans. Now, exclusive of the baboons, we know of only two other species of simiæ, besides the guereza, which inhabit that country, of which the zoological productions have been so carefully explored by the recent travellers, Rüppell, and Hemprich and Ehrenberg. The two species in question are the patas, or red monkey (*cercopithecus ruber*), which we shall afterwards show to be the *cebus* of the ancients, and the grivet (*cercopithecus griseus*) of M. F. Cuvier ; neither of which fulfils the first, third, or fourth of the abovementioned conditions. The Guereza, however, perfectly answers to all these essential requisites in Pliny's description, as will be readily observed by referring to its description. The beautiful quality of the fur, the short white beard on the chin, the large tuft which terminates the long bicoloured tail, for the expression " latè fusa" can bear no other interpretation, and the habitat of the animal, which its describers to this day agree in representing as too delicate and sensitive to be transported beyond its native country, or even kept alive in confinement, all identify the guereza with the callithrix, and establish, upon the surest foundation, the truth of Ludolf's happy though random conjecture. Poncet, in his ' Journey to Abyssinia,' speaks rather obscurely of these animals in the following terms :— " I saw an animal," says he, " of an extraordinary species in this country. It is not much larger than a cat, but has the face of a man and a white beard. I suppose it is of the monkey kind. Its voice is like that of a person's bewailing himself. This animal keeps always upon a tree, and, as I was assured, is brought forth and dies upon it. It is so very wild that there is no taming it. If a man catches one of them, and endeavours to preserve it, though he takes ever so much pains, the creature wastes, and quite pines with melancholy until it dies. One of them was taken down before me; the creature, fixing itself to the bough of a tree, by twining its legs one within the other, died some days after."

The account which Pearce has given in his " Life and Adventures in Abyssinia," is rather more recognisable. " *Focha*," says he, " in Amharic, and *grazer*, in Tigré, is the name of a monkey or lemur, most common in the Galla districts to the southwest, and in Agow Mudda, though frequently found in the Kolla or warm parts between Samen and Walkayt. The head and back are covered with fine short black hair; the hinder part and sides with long fine white hair. The tail is very long. When taken alive it will be for some days sulky, and will not eat. Great numbers of their skins are brought to market for ornaments." But the most complete and detailed account of the animal which we possessed previous to the publication of Dr. Rüppell's observations, was from the pen of the late celebrated Mr. Salt, and is to be found in the Appendix to his ' Second Journey into Abyssinia.' " The faunkus, or guereza," says he, " is an undescribed species of maki or lemur, of which an imperfect drawing has been given by Ludolf. This animal is about the size of a cat, and is commonly seen among the

branches of trees : it has a long tail, faintly striped
black and white, with white bushy hair at the end ;
the hair on the body is long and of a clear white colour
throughout, except on the back, which is marked
with a large oval spot of short hair, of the deepest
black. The skins of these animals are brought out
of Damot and Gojam, and are commonly found in the
markets, selling for about half a dollar each ; every
man in Tigré wearing a piece of this skin as an
ornament on his shield. When a number of them
are sewed together, they form a very splendid covering for a couch, which I never met with except in
the house of the Ras: one of these was presented
to me by the Ras himself, which is at present in the
collection of his Royal Highness the Prince Regent."

The brief notice which Dr. Rüppell has given of
the osteology and internal structure of this species
has already been referred to, in speaking of the general
characters of the genus, and need not be repeated here.
Of its habits, this author informs us that it constantly
resides in the loftiest trees, living together in small
families, and mostly in the neighbourhood of running
water. Though silent and never heard, it is, he
says, a restless, lively animal, perpetually in motion,
but perfectly harmless in its nature, and unlike some
other species of baboons and monkeys, never committing depredations upon the gardens and plantations of
the natives, or ravaging the fields of the husbandman.
Its muscular force and activity are so great that
Dr. Rüppell saw one, which had been taken by a
hunter, leap down from the branches of a tree at
least forty feet high. Its food consists of wild fruits,
seeds, and insects ; in collecting which, according to
the same authority, it spends the entire day, indeed
the whole of its waking life, and retires at night to
sleep among the loftiest branches of the forest. It
is only to be found in Gojam, Damot, and the Kolla ;

R 3

in the province of Damot, it is hunted for the sake
of the fur, and the skins are sometimes sold in the
market of Gondar for the price of five shillings a-piece,
for the purpose of covering the ornamented shields
of the native soldiers.

***

6. *Colobus Satanus.*

This magnificent species was described by Mr.
Waterhouse, at a recent meeting of the Zoological
Society, from skins procured at Fernando Po, at the
same time with those of the *colobus Pennantii,*
already mentioned. The species is easily distinguished from all the other colobs hitherto discovered, by the uniform intense black colour which
covers every part of its body, both above and below,
on the head, throat, belly, and tail, as well as on the
back, sides, and extremities. There is not a white
or coloured hair to be seen on any part of it; the
hair also is much longer and coarser than in any
other known species of colobus; in quality and appearance it exactly resembles that of the *ursus
labiatus,* or sloth-bear of India, being coarse and
shaggy, and without the smooth glossy appearance
which, notwithstanding the length of the fur, is so
remarkable in the *colobus ursinus* and *colobus leuco-
merus.* The hair of the head and limbs is equally
long and coarse, like that of the body; on the tail
alone it is somewhat shorter. The species is of very
considerable size; the body measures, from the nose
to the origin of the tail, 2 ft. 8 in., and the tail itself
is no less than 3 ft. 4 in. in length. It is to be
regretted that we know nothing of the habits or
economy of this singular animal; or indeed, for that
matter, of any other species of *colobus* except perhaps the *guereza.*

7. *The Colobus Polycomus.*

This is the species originally figured and described by Pennant, from the specimen already observed as having been formerly deposited in the Leverian Museum. The figure and description were both copied by Buffon, and afterwards published in the Seventh volume of the Supplement to his ' Histoire Naturelle,' and these materials, with the equally brief description of Shaw, long formed the only data which zoologists possessed for studying the characters or investigating the history of these animals. The species in question measures about three feet from the crown of the head to the sole of the foot. The body, legs, and tail, are very long and slender, the head small and round, and the face short and rather flat. The whole of the body, both above and below, the legs, thighs, arms and feet, are covered with very short hair of a deep glossy black colour; the face likewise is black, and the head, neck, cheeks, and shoulders are covered with long, flowing, coarse hair, of a dirty yellowish-white colour, thinly mixed with black hairs, and compared, by Pennant, to a full-bottomed periwig, though his figure would rather suggest a resemblance to the mane of a lion. The face, hands and feet are naked and black, and the tail is of a snowy whiteness throughout its entire extent, and tufted with a bunch of the same colour at the extremity. There was no thumb on the fore-hands, and the toes were remarkably long and slender. The specimen was brought from Sierra Leone, and the animal was said to be common in the forests about the Gulf of Guinea, where it was reported to be called the bey or king monkey. The negroes were said to hold the skins of these creatures in high estimation, and to use them for the purpose of making pouches, and covers for the locks of their guns.

Such is all the information which we possess with
regard to this species, perhaps the most interesting
of the genus from having been the first noticed ; and,
up to the year 1835, when Dr. Rüppell published
his 'Neue Wirbelthiere,' the only one that had
ever been figured. It is singular that, since the
time of Pennant, neither the live animal, nor even
its skin, should have been brought to Europe, though
from the reported use which we are informed the
negroes make of their skins, they would appear to
be by no means rare in Western Africa.

8. Colobus Ursinus.

Three skins of this species, at present in possession
of the Zoological Society, were procured at the same
time and in the same place as the skins of the
colobus rufo-niger, already described, and, like them,
were equally mutilated. At first they were considered to belong to the *colobus polycomus* of Pennant,
described in the last article ; but a more attentive
comparison and examination of their characters,
satisfactorily established the specific difference of the
two species. The *colobus ursinus*, in fact, has very
long, glossy, black hair over the whole body and
extremities ; the tail alone, which is somewhat longer
than the body, being of a snowy whiteness throughout, and terminated by a tuft of long shining hair of
the same colour. The head, hands, and feet were
cut off from the specimens here described, but a
very few greyish brown or light dun-coloured hairs,
intermixed with the long black hair on the anterior
face of the shoulders, render it probable that the
head and neck of the animal may be of a different
colour from the body. The late Mr. Bennett, who
first noticed these skins, considered them referable

to the *colobus polycomus;* and the general colour of
the body and tail, as well as the slight appearance
of grizzled grey hair about the neck, just where the
head had been cut off, would at first sight appear to
justify his views; but the words of Pennant, the
only original describer of the species, imply that
the long, dirty, yellowish hair, which he compares
to a full-bottomed periwig, grows from the shoulders
and neck as well as from the head, and he expressly
declares that the hair on the rest of the body, as well as
on the legs, is very short. His figure, also, perfectly
confirms these points of the description, and places its
accuracy beyond a question. Now, in the specimens
here described, and upon which the characteristic distinctions of the present species are formed, the very
reverse of all this is observable. The black hair of
the shoulders, as already observed, has a partial mixture of silvery white or grey on the anterior face, just
where the head has been cut off, but it is not longer
than the hair upon the rest of the body and limbs,
which is moreover five or six inches in length, and
in texture and appearance not unlike the hair of the
Bhaloo or sloth-bear of India, (*ursus labiatus,*) except
that it is of finer texture and still more glossy.
The whole animal, in fact, must very closely resemble
a small bear; the body being covered with the same
kind of uniform, long, black, and glossy fur upon
every part, except the tail, which, at the root more
particularly, is furnished with much shorter hair.
Whether or not this species, like the polycomus, has
the head of a different colour from the body, is a
subject which must be left for further observation;
the greyish white or silvery intermixture of hairs,
which, however few in number, still remain about the
shoulders, renders it extremely probable that it has;
but even supposing this to be the case, it can never
form the striking contrast in length, nor present the

long flowing mane or wig-like appearance, ascribed to the animal observed by Pennant.

It has been already observed in the article on the *colobus rufo-niger* that the skins, from which our descriptions of that and the present species have been taken, were reported to have been brought from Algoa Bay, on the borders of Caffraria, in Southern Africa. Reasons were assigned at the same time which rendered this habitat more than improbable; and it was suggested, that from some confusion arising perhaps from the similarity of sound, the name of Algoa Bay might by some mistake have been substituted for Delagoa Bay, and the native country of the animals consequently be found some distance farther up the Eastern coast. It was, however, intimated at the same time, that our own opinion was altogether adverse to this habitat, and that we rather supposed the skins in question to have been brought from some part of Western Africa. The principal reason upon which that opinion is founded arises as well from the identity of its habitat with that of the Diana monkey, as from the following notice which Bosman gives of a monkey found in Guinea, and which we think clearly refers to the present species. "The third sort of monkeys," says this author, "are very beautiful, and generally grow to the height of about two feet. The hair is as black as pitch and above a finger's length; they have a long, white beard, whence they are called bearded little men, or bearded monkeys. Of their skins are made the 'tie-tie' caps, mentioned in another letter of mine. The negroes sell these monkeys to one another for about eighteen or twenty shillings, and when they bring them to us, we do not refuse them at that price." If our conjectures be well founded as to the proper application of this passage to the present species, a fact which we see no reason to doubt, unless, indeed, it be more properly referable to the following, it furnishes us with some additional and valuable information regarding the characters of the species. We are told, for instance, that the animal has a long white beard, and this mode of expression is alone sufficient to differentiate it from the *colobus polycomus*, the "long, dirty, yellowish hair," upon whose head, neck, and shoulders, would never have been called a *beard* by an observer so accurate and well-informed as Bosman. Had the Dutch traveller intended to have described that species, and it must be observed that, having resided for many years in the country, he described from personal observation, and long and intimate acquaintance with its productions, he would have made use of the word mane, instead of beard; since the long hair which covers the fore parts of the *colobus polycomus*, in reality more nearly resembles the mane of a lion than the beard of a man, and could never, with any semblance of propriety, procure for that animal the name of "bearded little man," which Bosman bestows upon his species. Besides, the long hair which he mentions as covering the body of his animal, is not found in the *colobus polycomus*, which, according to the express words of Pennant, has short hair, both upon the body and extremities; and we may consequently conclude with tolerable certainty, that Bosman's species is in reality the *colobus ursinus;* and that instead of inhabiting the country round Algoa Bay, that species, as well as the *colobus rufo-niger*, must be sought for in the neighbourhood of the Dutch settlement of Elmina, on the Coast of Guinea.*

* Since this article was printed, we have had an opportunity of examining a perfect skin of the *colobus ursinus*, brought from Sierra Leone by Major Campbell, late governor of that colony, and by him presented to the Zoological Society. We are thus enabled not only to confirm the above reasoning as to the habitat of the species, but to complete our description of its characters, and establish its specific distinction from the *colobus polycomus*. The face is naked and of a light bluish

9. *Colobus Leucomeros.*

This species, the last, and probably one of the most beautiful, of the whole genus, is founded upon a skin, like all the rest, unfortunately deprived of the head, hands, and feet, lately sent to the Zoological Society, and said to have been brought from the brown colour; the forehead and whole region between the ears and eyes, the cheeks, sides of the head and neck, from the ear downwards, are covered rather thinly with silvery or greyish white hair, much shorter than that on the body; the long hair of the shoulders is likewise partially tinged with the same silvery hue, and the entire tail is of a pure unmixed white. From between the ears backwards over the occiput, neck, &c., the hair is long and intensely black, as likewise on the thighs: a few long, stiff, black hairs, surmount the eyebrows, as in the semnopithecs, and the callosities are partially surrounded with white. The length of the head and body is 2 ft. 7 in., that of the tail, to the end of the vertebræ, 3 ft. 3 in., and including the tuft 3 ft. 6 in.

Gambia. In the nature of the long, silky fur, which covers the body of the animal, it bears a striking resemblance to the *colobus ursinus*, but the hair is still longer, finer, and, if possible, of a more deep and glossy black colour. But the chief distinction is in the hair of the thighs, which, instead of being of the same long, silky quality, and glossy black colour, as that on the body, is remarkably short, and of a beautiful silvery white, and the point of each shoulder has a small patch of short curly hair, of a pure snowy whiteness, the middle part of the neck being black; thus rendering it probable that the short white hair overspreads the throat, chin, and cheeks, as in the *colobus guereza*, which the white hair of the shoulder precisely resembles in its short, frizzled character. There is nothing of this observable in the *colobus ursinus*, in which the few light-coloured hairs visible about the junction of the neck and body are thinly mixed among the black hairs of the surrounding parts, and of the same length and straight silky quality. The tail is unfortunately wanting, but the short hair and silvery whiteness of the thighs, independently of all the other characters, will be at all times sufficient to distinguish this beautiful new species from the rest of its congeners.

Since the original description of this species, founded upon the imperfect skin here mentioned, was published in the Memoirs of the Zoological Society, we have had opportunities of examining two perfect specimens, one of a young animal, preserved in the Leyden Museum, and the other of an adult, at the Jardin des Plantes. The whole animal is covered with long silky black hair, except the chin, throat, cheeks, and sides of the neck, which are furnished with shorter bushy hair, of a yellowish white colour and woolly texture, rather longer on the chin,

s

where it forms a pointed beard, and passing in a narrow fillet over the eyebrows, to unite the white colours on either side of the head. The tail is very long, of a snowy whiteness throughout its entire length, with the exception of about an inch of black at the root, and partially tufted. The thighs of the old specimen are of the clear silvery grey above described; but this character, though still sufficiently apparent, is less strongly marked in the young. The hair of this part, in both specimens, is shorter than that on the body. With these exceptions all the rest of the body, the head, back of the neck, back, and sides, are of the intense glossy black already mentioned. The anterior thumb is marked externally by a small tubercle, furnished with a nail, but perfectly immovable. The origin of the Parisian specimen is unknown: that belonging to the Museum des Pays Bas was brought from the coast of Guinea. Besides the shorter hair and silvery grey colour of the thighs, this species differs from *colobus ursinus* in the black portion of the root of the tail, and the absence of white about the callosities, which a pure border of this colour renders very conspicuous in that species.

We have already observed that the skin from which this description is taken was said to have been brought from the river Gambia; and if this be the proper habitat of the species, which there seems no good reason to doubt, it follows that, of the eight species of colobus now known to inhabit the western coast of Africa, four are found at Sierra Leone, two at Fernando Po, and two on the banks of the river Gambia; and what is not a little singular, it would appear, that of the two small sub-genera which we pointed out as composing the principal group, one species of either sub-genus is found at each of these places. Thus the *colobus leucomeros* and *colobus rufo-fuliginus* are known to be found in the neighbourhood of the Gambia; the *colobus polycomus*, *colobus ursinus*, *colobus rufo-niger*, and *colobus ferruginosus*, are reported by Pennant and Major Campbell to inhabit the vicinity of Sierra Leone; and we have unquestionable evidence that the *colobus satanus* and *colobus Pennantii* come from Fernando Po. In these localities the respective species must be sought for by future inquirers; and it is to be hoped that, having now ascertained the exact spots where they are to be found, and having pointed out their great scarcity and the consequent curiosity which attaches to them, we shall be more fortunate than we have hitherto been, in obtaining specimens of these beautiful animals for our public museums and menageries.

CHAPTER IX.

Monkeys *continued.*—Genus *Cercopithecus.*—Its Characters—Different Species of Cercopithecs.

IT is only within the last twenty-five or thirty years that zoologists began to have distinct ideas of the limits and characters of the different genera of simiæ. Previous to that time the whole group had been considered as a single genus, or subdivided into the three minor groups of apes, monkeys, and baboons, and even these not free from serious confusion ; but no writer of the last century dreamt of the necessity of further subdivision, or of comparing the component parts of these several groups. The first step towards this necessary reform was made by Illiger in 1811, by the formation and accurate definition of the genera hylobates and colobus. With the exception of the latter group, however, the whole of the monkeys and baboons were included in the genera cercopithecus and cynocephalus, for the proposed genus lasiopyga is purely nominal, being founded upon an erroneous character; but so indefinitely were these two genera distinguished, that the author himself doubts the propriety of their separation ; and indeed the arbitrary nature of Illiger's genus cynocephalus may be judged of from the fact of its uniting three such incongruous species as the wanderoo, the magot, and the adult orang-outan. Next in succession came M. Geoffroy St. Hilaire, who, in the 19th vol. of the "*Annales du Museum,*" published one year after the appearance of Illiger's "*Prodromus,*" reviewed the whole of the groups *simiæ, simiadæ,* and *lemuridæ*, and endeavoured to divide them into natural genera. In so far as the simiæ are concerned this was by no means a happy attempt : many purely nominal genera were proposed, such as *pongo*, *pygathrix*, *nasalis*, *cercocebus*, and *inuus*; the genera cercopithecus and cynocephalus were retained as Illiger had left them, with the exception of the separations necessary to form the fictitious genera just mentioned ; and, in fact, the only positive benefit resulting from M. Geoffroy's labours upon this group was the generic distinction of the orangs and chimpanzees, which had been united by Illiger. Even this advantage, however, was counterbalanced by his suppression of the genus hylobates of the latter author, and his union of the gibbons with the orangs.

Five years after the publication of M. Geoffroy's Memoir (1817), appeared the first edition of the " *Règne Animal*," and here it was, for the first time, that the illustrious Baron Cuvier definitely characterised and distinguished the genus cynocephalus ; his brother, M. F. Cuvier, a few years subsequent to that event (1821), made a still happier and more important step towards the final elucidation of the simiæ, by the definite separation of the semnopithecs from the other monkeys, with which, up to that period, they had been confounded. There still remained, however, a large number of species divided between the two genera macacus and cercopithecus, but distinguished by no appropriate or influential characters, and for which, indeed, no definite generic characters have been hitherto proposed. The principle derived from the facial angle has been repeatedly shown to be fallacious : its application in the present instance is, moreover, insufficient, even as a practical artificial test, to distinguish the macacs of authors from the larger species of cercopithecs ; whilst the distinction formerly imagined to subsist between these two

genera, from the absence of the fifth tubercle of the
last inferior molar in the latter group, has been recently destroyed by the discovery of that character
in the mangabey (*cercopithecus fuliginosus*), and its
probable existence in other species. The destruction
of characters so perfectly trivial and uninfluential as
these is not to be regretted by the scientific zoologist; so long, however, as they remained uncontra-
dicted, and were believed to be general and appropriate, they afforded an excuse for continuing the
genera *macacus* and *cercopithecus* as hitherto constituted; but, deprived of the frail support which
has heretofore upheld them, they must now submit
to be tested by more important principles.

These vicious and insufficient characters then
being abstracted, it may be asked, what others remain by which to differentiate the macacs from the
cercopithecs, as these groups are at present constituted ? As at present constituted, absolutely none ;
but a little attention to the function performed by the
tail in these animals, a most efficient organ, as we
have often had occasion to remark, in the economy
of the simiæ, will lead us to more just and accurate
notions. Experience and observation teach us that,
wherever this organ is developed to the extent that
we find it in the cercopithecs and colobs, it becomes
a powerful and efficient adjunct to the ordinary instruments of locomotion, by guiding the direction
and securing the equilibrium of the animals during
their rapid and varied motions among the trees of
the forest ; it serves at once the purposes of a rudder
and a balancing-pole, and indicates the habits of the
animals more clearly than any other part of their
structure. Here then we get into the path of fair
and legitimate induction, by following which we
shall undoubtedly arrive at a just and philosophical
distinction between the macacs and cercopithecs. We

shall find, by pursuing this route, that, whilst a few of the species hitherto included in the genus maca- cus agree with the larger-sized cercopithecs in all the most important details of their habits and struc- ture, they differ in almost every essential particular from the rest of their presumed congeners ; that their long and powerfully muscular tails, their infe- rior size, their sylvan habitat, and even the annulated nature of their hair, distinguish them from the lat- ter animals, and approximate them to the former; and that, in fact, they possess no character of suf- ficient influence to separate them from the ordinary cercopithecs.   The species thus rendered so anoma- lous by their present unnatural association, are the common *macaque* of Buffon (*macacus cynomolgus* of authors), the black-faced macaque of M. F. Cuvier (*macacus carbonarius*), the *macacus pileatus* and the *toque*, or bonnet monkey (*macacus radiatus*) ; all of which have the tail as long, or even longer than the body, and use it precisely in the same manner as the cercopithecs.   The remaining species of the ge- nus macacus, on the contrary, as that genus has been hitherto constituted, have tails most commonly tuberculous, never reaching lower than the hough, and perfectly powerless as instruments of progressive motion, or of any other function in the animal eco- nomy ; their habits and structure approximate them closely to the cynocephals, of which they are the Asiatic representatives ; and all the details of their conformation and economy pronounce them to be baboons instead of monkeys.   With the anomalous species above enumerated they only agree in their geographical habitat, and in the additional tubercle on the last inferior molar ; but habitat is no generic character, and the tubercle in question, even if it were unexceptionable in other respects, has been shown to exist in some, and will probably be found in others, of the acknowledged African cercopithecs.

By means of this necessary reform, founded, as we have here shown, upon important physical distinctions, the two groups in question become as clearly distinguished, and as definitely characterised, as any of the other genera of simiæ; the one including all those species, without distinction of habitat, which nature has furnished with long muscular tails, capable of guiding and steadying their motions; and the other all such as have this organ so short or tuber- culous as to be unfit for the execution of that or any other function. The first of these groups is natu- rally allied to the monkeys, and the second to the baboons, which, as we have already seen, are chiefly distinguished by this difference of function in the tail: but as the generic name, *macacus*, by which the latter group has been hitherto known, properly belongs to one of the rejected species, it will be ex- pedient, in order to avoid the confusion which might otherwise ensue, to substitute in its place the less ex- ceptionable term *papio*, by which some of the species were formerly designated, and which has the addi- tional advantage of expressing the intimate relations which they bear to the cynocephals. These animals will form the subject of the following chapter; in the mean time we proceed with the history and description of the cercopithecs.

The genus *cercopithecus*, as here defined, will con- sequently comprehend all the *monkeys* properly so called, which have cheek-pouches and perfectly de- veloped thumbs on the anterior extremities. The first of these characters differentiates them from the semnopithecs, and the second from the colobs; their long tails and ischial callosities are common to the other monkeys, as the latter character is to the baboons and most of the apes. This distinction, so simple and appropriate, founded upon characters at once so obvious and so influential, accomplishes a great desideratum in the history of the cercopithecs, and places that genus on an equality with the semnopithecs and colobs, or any other natural group of simiæ, in point of logical precision and exclusive propriety of character. As for minor modifications, it has been already observed that the absence of the fifth tubercle of the last inferior molar tooth, hitherto supposed to be peculiar to the cercopithecs, is not a universal character of the genus. The tubercle' in question was discovered on examining the skull of a mangabey (*cercopithecus fuliginosus*), which died some time since in the Zoological Gardens; it will probably be found to exist likewise in the *collared mangabey* (*cercopithecus Æthiops*), and other similar species among the larger-sized cercopithecs; and, upon the whole, the adoption of its absence, as an exclusive generic character in this group of simiæ, appears to have been the result of a too hasty and inconsiderate generalisation. Were the existence of this tubercle a character of any importance, it might countenance the re-formation of M. Geoffroy St. Hilaire's suppressed genus *cercocebus*, to include the Asiatic species which we have here dissevered from the old genus *macacus*, and the African species of acknowledged cercopithecs, in which it has already or may be afterwards found; but it is neither sufficiently influential, nor even sufficiently general, for this purpose; its adoption would place the green monkey (*C. sabæus*), the white-throated monkey (*C. albogularis*, and their allied species, in a different group from the mangabey (*C. fuliginosus*), the macac (*C. cynomolgus*), and the bonnet-monkey (*C. sinicus*), and could only lead to arbitrary and artificial distinctions. The genus cercopithecus, there-

s 3

fore, as it is here defined and limited, admits of no
further subdivision : it is founded upon important
and influential modifications of structure, and is consequently entitled to be considered as a perfectly natural and scientific group.

The annulated nature of the fur is another secondary character which is very generally found among
the cercopithecs, and serves at a glance to distinguish
them from all other monkeys. It is equally common to the acknowledged African animals, and to
those anomalous Asiatic species which have been
heretofore associated with the true papios, in the arbitrary and artificial genus *macacus*; and its existence in the latter is no small confirmation of their
generic identity with the true cercopithecs, which has
been here founded upon more important and influential characters. This annulated character of the
fur produces a pleasing variety and intermixture of
colours, and gives the animals a minutely-mottled
or speckled appearance; it is not, however, confined
to the cercopithecs, being equally found in the greater
number of the cynocephals; but, with the exception
of the few Asiatic species of the former genus, it is
more peculiarly appropriate to the African simiæ,
though without being absolutely universal even
among these. The colobs, and even some species
of cercopithecs, such as the white-eyelid monkeys,
resemble the Asiatic simiæ in the unannulated nature of their hair; but, generally speaking, this character will be found to be a ready practical distinction between the simiæ of the two continents.

The cercopithecs are of a lighter and more active
make than the papios; their heads are rounder, their
faces shorter, and their eyes less deeply sunk beneath
projecting superorbital crests; their limbs are longer,
their bodies more slender, and their whole proportions destitute of that massive and powerful structure

which characterises the latter animals. Neither have they the gloomy, morose, and saturnine disposition common to all the baboons. They are capricious, petulant, and inconstant, rather than intentionally mischievous or malicious; they substitute vivacity, impetuosity, and restlessness, for the mild, gentle, and almost apathetic manners of the semnopithecs and colobs; and if they possess the activity and impetuosity of the papios and cynocephals, they are at the same time free from their sullen and intractable dispositions, and from the disgusting propensities which they sometimes display.

Like all the other monkeys, the cercopithecs are a pre-eminently sylvan race; they never abandon the forests, where they live in society under the guidance of the old males: they appear even to be extremely local in their habitat. Each tribe or family has its own particular district, into which individuals of other tribes or species are never allowed to intrude, the whole community uniting promptly to repel any aggression of this nature, either upon their territory or upon their individual rights. So strongly is this propensity implanted in the cercopithecs, that they carry it with them even into our menageries; nothing is more common or more pleasing than to see monkeys of the same species uniting to defend one of their brethren against the tyranny of a more power ful oppressor, or to resent any insult offered to a member of their little community. They are highly gregarious, never leave the recesses of the forest, generally take up their quarters in the vicinity of a running stream, and seldom approach the habitations of men, or invade the cultivated grounds of the gardener and husbandman. It is, no doubt, this spirit of union and mutual defence which prompts the monkeys to collect round travellers, and, by their chattering, grimace, and every other means in their power, endeavour to prevent them from intruding into the little territory which they regard as their especial property. That their minds are capable of entertaining this idea of the right of property, all their actions plainly demonstrate; and the fact gives us a high idea of the superior order of their intelligence. They feed indiscriminately upon wild fruits, the seeds and buds of trees, insects, birds' eggs, &c., but appear, on the whole, to be less carnivorous in their appetites than either the apes or baboons—an observation, indeed, which may be extended to all the true monkeys.

The geographical distribution of the genus cercopithecus has been generally believed to be confined to the continent of Africa; and, with the exception of the four species heretofore confounded with the papios, this is no doubt true. If, as is commonly admitted, we assume the Asiatic papios to be the legitimate representatives of the African cynocephals, and consider the colobs as the proper analogues of the semnopithecs, it will follow that the cercopithecs, which are still a pre-eminently African genus, have no appropriate representatives peculiar to the eastern continent or its dependent islands; but, the truth is, that these animals are no more exclusively proper to Africa than the papios are to Asia, or the cynocephals to the former continent; each of these genera having representative species in both localities, and the colobs and semnopithecs alone being confined to one or other. Thus the genus cynocephalus, which has its head-quarters in Africa, is nevertheless represented in Asia by the *C. hamadryas*, which is found on all the mountains of Arabia; the genus papio, pre-eminently an Asiatic group, is represented in the neighbouring continent by the *P. gelada* and *P. inuus*, the latter of which even extends into Europe ; and so likewise the genus cercopithecus, though the

vast majority of its species inhabit the western continent, has equally its representative species on the
mainland of Asia, and in the great islands of the
Indian Archipelago.   There is consequently no argument to be derived from the geographical distribution of the animals, against the union of the Asiatic
cercopithecs with their African congeners, though
this has been hitherto one of the main supports, and
probably the original motive, of the arbitrary distinction between the cercopithecs and the so-called
macacs.

By far the greater number of cercopithecs with
which we are acquainted come from the west coast
of Africa, where, we are assured by different travellers, that they swarm in countless multitudes and
varieties between the parallels of the Senegal and
Cape Negro, or about fifteen degrees on each side
of the Equator.   One species, *C. pygerythrus*, inhabits South Africa, and extends up the eastern coast
as far as Port Natal; the *C. albogularis* is, in all
probability, a native of the same coast, a little higher
up; the *C. ruber* and *C. griseus* inhabit Abyssinia
and the neighbouring countries; but, with these exceptions and that of the four Asiatic species, all the
known cercopithecs are brought from the western
coast of Africa.   Not that we are to suppose the
opposite shores of this vast continent less abundantly
supplied with appropriate and perhaps peculiar species.   On the contrary, Dos Santos assures us that
apes and monkeys of many different sorts are to be
found without number about Sofala and throughout
the whole of Eastern Ethiopia; but the fact is, that
our limited commercial intercourse with this part of
Africa has hitherto kept us in ignorance of its natural
productions in this as in various other departments.
Some travellers mention having found monkeys in
Madagascar and the Comoro Islands; but we have

the express testimony of Sonnerat that there are no
simiæ in the former locality. Prior, indeed, assures
us that *common monkeys* are found in the island of
Johanna; but we know from other sources that the
Comoro Islands abound in different species of lemuridæ, and it was probably from confounding the animals of these two kindred groups that the mistake
originated. M. Desjardins again informs us that
the *C. cynomolgus* is at present found wild in the
Isle of France; but it is unquestionably a recent introduction, since we know that the species is an
inhabitant of the Island of Java; besides which the
old navigators assure us that there were originally no
quadrupeds in the Mauritius, except rats and tortoises. The opposite shores of India, however, are
inhabited by one, or perhaps two, species of cercopithecs. The common bonnet-monkey (*C. radiatus*)
is found all along the coast of Malabar, from Bombay to Cape Comorin, if it be not replaced towards
the south by the *C. pileatus*, a species not so frequently seen in collections, and of which the exact
habitat has not been ascertained. Java and Sumatra,
again, contain each one species of cercopithec; the
former locality produces the common macac (*C. cynomolgus*), and the latter the black-faced macac (*C.
carbonarius*). These are the species so often referred to as having been hitherto confounded with
the papios in the arbitrary genus macacus; they
are the only cercopithecs known to exist out of
Africa.

The number of species belonging to this genus,
which are already known to zoologists, is very considerable, and will no doubt be greatly increased
when we become better acquainted with the productions of Eastern Africa. Even from the west coast
new species are occasionally received, and the una-
nimous testimony of all travellers in these regions

gives us good reason to believe that many undescribed species still exist in the extensive forests of
Guinea and Angola.   Those which we already know
differ considerably in size, strength, and consequent
boldness of character; the larger species have more
elongated muzzles, flatter skulls, and more prominent
superorbital crests than the smaller; but these are
only modifications of degree, not of kind, and are
consequently insufficient for the purpose of generic
characters.   The proposed genus *cercocebus* of M.
Geoffroy St. Hilaire, founded upon these slight degrees of modification, has therefore been very properly suppressed by succeeding naturalists; and if
M. Desmarest, who first effected this reform, had
united the Asiatic cercopithecs, above enumerated,
with the rest of their congeners, as he did the African species which M. Geoffroy had joined with them
in his proposed genus, instead of confounding them
with the papios, we should not have been so long
ignorant of the true relations of these animals.   But
M. Desmarest failed to appreciate the real distinctive
characters of these groups; instead of breaking up
the pretended genus *cercocebus*, to divide its species
between the cercopithecs and the macacs, he ought
to have simply united it to the former genus; and
the impropriety of the opposite course, as well as the
purely arbitrary nature of the genus macacus, is sufficiently evinced by the fact that he has included one
single species, the *guenon couronnée* of Buffon, in
both his genera, first as *cercopithecus pileatus*, and
afterwards as *macacus sinicus*.   The same error had
been formerly committed by M. Geoffroy, and it has
since been adopted by succeeding writers—a very sufficient proof, if any further proof were wanting in
addition to those already adduced, of the unnatural
character of the genus macacus, since even its pro-
posers mistake the species which belong to it.

But, though the differences between the larger and smaller-sized cercopithecs are not of sufficient importance to warrant their generic distinction, they may be conveniently employed to divide these animals into small artificial groups, for the purpose of facilitating description. The mangabeys, or white-eyelid monkeys, for instance, may be united with the four Asiatic species hitherto confounded with the papios, to form one sub-genus, which will be readily characterised by the obscurity or total absence of annuli on the fur, and by the existence of the fifth tubercle on the last inferior molar. Another little group will consist of those larger species allied to the common green monkey (*C. sabæus*), which have but four tubercles on the last inferior molar, and the fur brilliantly and minutely annulated; whilst the smaller species, with similar characters, may be included in a third division. We have more than once had occasion to notice the difficulty of discriminating between the different species of monkeys, owing to the close approximation which they often make to one another, and the impossibility of describing through the ear characters which address themselves to the eye. In no other group is this difficulty so sensibly felt as in the cercopithecs; and it is only by arranging them in still smaller sections, and describing some three or four species in reference to a particular type, that we can hope to arrive at anything like clearness or precision in this matter.

The TOQUE, or BONNET-MONKEY (*Cercopithecus radiatus*),

Is a native of the Malabar coast, and not of China, as the very objectionable name of Chinese bonnet, applied to it by Buffon, would seem to indicate. Colonel Sykes informs us that it is called *waanur* by the Mahrattas, and inhabits the woods of the western ghauts in small troops or families. It is probably this species which extends throughout the whole of the peninsula of India, and is held in the same veneration in these parts as the entellus and rhesus in Bengal and the upper provinces. No species is more commonly brought into England, and exhibited about the streets or in our menageries, than the toque. It is of a uniform greenish-dun colour on the upper parts of the body; the breast, belly, and inner face of the arms and thighs being light dun or grey, and the face, ears, and hands naked and of a dirty flesh colour. But the mark which immediately distinguishes the species is a copious and peculiar tuft of long dark hair, which grows from the crown of the head, and spreads round on all sides like rays from a common centre. This hair does not stand erect in the toque, but lies flatly along the head like the diminutive wigs called scalps, which bald persons sometimes wear on the centre of the crown; and it is the peculiar appearance which it gives the animal, that has suggested the name of the bonnet-monkey, by which it has long been known.

Great confusion prevails in the synonyma of this species, even among the best and most careful writers on zoology. It was originally described and figured by Buffon in the 14th volume of his celebrated "Histoire Naturelle," under the name of *bonnet Chinois*, and admitted into the system of Linnæus, Erxleben, and others, by the specific appellation of *simia sinica*, from the presumed habitat suggested by the very objectionable name of Buffon. In the mean time a second species, in some respects allied to the bonnet Chinois, was observed and figured by this latter naturalist in the 7th volume of the Supplement to his great work, under the name of *guenon couronnée*, and reproduced, in the General Zoology of Dr. Shaw under that of *simia pileata*. Thus the matter rested up to the year 1812, when M. Geoffroy St. Hilaire published his *Tableau des Quadrumanes*, in the 19th volume of the *Annales du Museum*. In this paper we find the *guenon couronnée* of Buffon introduced twice; first, under the name of *cercopithecus pileatus*, as authority for which the author quotes Buffon and Shaw; and secondly, as a macac, under the name of bonnet Chinois (*cercocebus sinicus*), which he thus transfers from the original owner to a very distinct species, the real bonnet Chinois being described under the name of *toque* (*cercocebus radiatus*). Such is the origin of all the confusion which has since prevailed upon this subject. M.

Desmarest, who, it must be observed, is not generally
so inattentive in matters of this kind, adopted the
errors of Geoffroy, without change or observation,
not only as regards the confusion of names introduced by that zoologist, but likewise in the
duplication of the species, which is twice introduced
into his valuable work, first, as the *cercopithecus
pileatus*, marked with an asterisk, as a doubtful
species; and secondly, as the *macacus sinicus*: thus,
like Geoffroy, counfounding it with the bonnet
Chinois, or *simia sinica*, of preceding authors, and
substituting the names of toque and *macacus radiatus*
for that of the real bonnet Chinois. Next in succession came M. F. Cuvier, who, having taken his
descriptions from the living animals, could not fail to
remark the misapplication of names by M. Geoffroy;
yet, instead of correcting, he has adopted the error,
and given still farther currency to the confusion: so
that we now find two very distinct animals described
by different naturalists under the same name, and
one of them even described twice by the same
naturalist under two different names.

Under these circumstances, the best thing we can
do to clear up the confusion is, in the first place, to
retain the specific appellation of *pileatus* for the
guenon couronnée of Buffon, about which there never
has been any mistake or confusion; and, secondly,
to suppress altogether the vicious and improper
name of *sinicus*, as liable to mislead the inquirer
regarding the habitat of the animal, and to substitute
that of *radiatus*, as proposed by M. Geoffroy. By
this means we shall avoid mistake in future; and
indeed the animals are too distinct to be confounded
by those who have an opportunity of comparing their
characters. British naturalists, in particular, have
no excuse for falling into this error, for our intimate
relations with India bring both species frequently into

this country; and we have ourselves seen at least
ten living specimens of the *cercopithecus pileatus*,
and probably five times that number of *cercopithecus
radiatus*, in the different British menageries, within
the last eight or nine years. Their colour at once
distinguishes the two animals: the toque, or bonnet
Chinois (*cercopithecus radiatus*), is, as we have already seen, of a greenish-dun colour, and has the long
hair on the crown diverging from a common centre,
and closely applied to the skull; the *cercopithecus
pileatus*, on the contrary, is of a deep chestnut or
rusty-brown colour, with the long hair of the head
standing erect like an upright crest; besides which it
has a peculiar and appropriate character, in the rim
of the under lip being of a deep black colour, which
forms a remarkable contrast with the light tan colour
of the surrounding parts, and is alone sufficient to
distinguish this animal from all others of the monkey
tribe. The foreheads of both species are curiously
furrowed with deep transverse wrinkles, which are
even more apparent in young than in aged specimens, and give the animals a singularly ludicrous
resemblance to an old Indian woman; a resemblance
still further increased, in the toque especially, by the
habit of squatting upon its hams and crossing the
arms upon its breast or resting them on the knees.

No monkey affords greater amusement in menageries than the bonnet Chinois; and the imperturbable gravity with which it accompanies all its
actions is truly diverting. When young, it is sufficiently gentle and familiar, and may be instructed
to perform every action that monkey genius is
capable of aspiring to. It is indescribably droll to
see these animals, when two or three of them are
together, hugging and nursing each other, or kindly
performing the office of combs, and searching
through one another's fur, with the most laudable

assiduity, for fleas and other vermin, which they take
effectual means to prevent from giving farther
annoyance, in the mode equally adopted by the
Hottentots, Esquimaux, and Australians, in similar
circumstances,—namely, by forthwith eating them on
the spot. Happy, no doubt, does the monkey consider himself whose good fortune it is to pounce
upon a fine fat jumper, and he evidently devours it
with the gusto of an accomplished gastronome.
But the penchant of the toque for nursing is not
confined to its own species: when only one of these
animals happens to be possessed by a menagerie, a
kitten is very frequently given to it as a companion,
and nothing can exceed the ridiculous caricature of
humanity which it presents,—petting, nursing, and
hugging the unfortunate kitten, at the imminent
risk of choking it, with all the gravity and fondness
that a little child will display in similar circumstances.
Thus it will continue for hours together, to the
manifest annoyance of the object of its solicitude,
who, however, is in no condition to escape from the
loving embrace, as the least attempt at resistance to
the arbitrary will of the toque, is followed by prompt
and sometimes severe punishment. We recollect in
one instance witnessing a singular and laughable
instance of this description. A bonnet-monkey,
exhibited in a travelling caravan, had a cat of considerable size to keep it company in its confinement.
Puss, at the moment when our story commences,
happening to feel somewhat drowsy, as cats will
sometimes do, even in the presence of their betters,
had retired to the back and quietest part of the cage,
and composed herself to have a comfortable nap.
Pug, however, was neither inclined to sleep himself,
nor to let any one else do so within his range; he
therefore selected a stiff straw and amused himself
by poking it up the cat's nose, which, after bearing

this annoyance for some time with exemplary stoicism, at length lost all patience and gave her tormentor a smart scratch on the face with her not very velvet paw. This was more than the offended dignity of the monkey could brook : he seized the unfortunate culprit by the tail, and flying like lightning to the top of the cage, there held her suspended between heaven and earth, like Mahomet's coffin, and with something worse than the sword of Damocles over her, whilst he inflicted upon her such a series of cuffs and pinches, as no doubt warned her in future to be on her better behaviour.

But though, generally speaking, thus gentle and amusing in youth, the toque is extremely irascible, and ever ready to take offence on the slightest occasion. This is particularly apparent when it is tantalised by offering and then withholding any species of food; and it is ludicrous upon such occasions to witness the serious anger which is depicted in its countenance, whilst it pouts with its lips, looks fixedly in your face, and mutters a low complaint, or suddenly darts out its hand and endeavours to scratch you.—Even when not thus provoked, however, it is always precipitate in its actions, and snatches with hasty rudeness the food which is offered to it, never pausing to eat it at the moment but stowing it away in its capacious cheek pouches, and begging with pouting lips and out-stretched arms for a farther supply. So long as the visitors continue to give, it never refuses to receive; and it is only when the offerings are exhausted that it retires to a corner, and, emptying its reservoirs with the assistance of the bent knuckles pressed upon the outside of the cheeks, devours their contents piece-meal, and is ready to fill them again from the liberality of the next comer.

When adult, the toque becomes excessively sullen

and morose, and the deeply sunk eyes, and projecting superorbital crests, give him an aspect of gloomy ferocity which accords but too truly with his natural disposition, and warns the visitor against attempting a familiarity which is not likely to be reciprocated. . Of the *cercopithecus pileatus* we have never seen the adult male, nor do we even know the particular locality which the species inhabits. It is most probable, however, that its habitat is either more remote or less frequented by Europeans than that of the toque, since the animal is more rarely brought to England. In youth it resembles the toque in manners and disposition, but is gentler and less petulant, and in this respect appears to approach the smaller African cercopithecs and semnopithecs. It may possibly be this species which inhabits Ceylon, and which has given origin to the supposition that the toque, like the wanderoo, is found both in that island and on the continent.

We know little of the habits of the toque in its wild state, if it be not the species mentioned by Buchanan in his admirable "Journey through Mysore, Canara, and Malabar," and which he describes as a great nuisance to the gardens and plantations of the natives. "The monkeys and squirrels," says he, " are very destructive, but it is reckoned criminal to kill either of them. They are under the immediate protection of the *dáséries*, who assemble round any person guilty of this offence, and allow him no rest until he bestows on the animal a funeral that will cost from one to two hundred fanams, according to the number of *dáséries* that have assembled. The proprietors of the gardens used formerly to hire a particular class of men, who took these animals in nets, and then by stealth conveyed them into the gardens of some distant village; but as the people there had recourse to the same means of getting rid of them, all parties have become tired of this practice. If any person freed the poor people by killing these mischievous vermin, they would think themselves bound in decency to make a clamour, but inwardly they would be very well pleased; and the govern- ment might easily accomplish it by hiring men whose consciences would not suffer by the action, and who might be repaid by a small tax on the proprietors."

There is at present (May, 1836) a white specimen of *cercopithecus radiatus* in the gardens of the Zoolo- gical Society. It is of a uniform unmixed white over the entire body, head, and extremities, the naked face, hands and paws being of the same colour; but the eyes instead of the pink hue generally observed in animals affected with albinism, are of the ordinary brown colour natural to the species. There is, however, one singularity about the vision of this specimen which is worthy of record; it is the only one of the monkey tribe, or, indeed, of the lower animals in general, in which we have ever observed a decided squint. Yet, notwithstanding this mani- fest obliquity, and the consequent sinister expression which it communicates to the countenance of the individual, he is in reality an exceedingly well tempered animal, though it is impossible to refrain from smiling at the absurdly comical expression of face produced by this optical phenomenon.

The next species which we shall notice among the Asiatic cercopithecs is the animal to which the name of macac is most commonly appropriated, and which passes in zoological catalogues by the names of *macacus cynomolgus*, and *simia aygula*. This, as we learn from Dr. Horsfield, is the most common species of monkey in the forests of Java, and a great favourite among the natives of that island, by whom it is very generally domesticated. A common custom

of theirs is to keep at least one of these monkeys in
the stable with their horses, in the same manner as
goats are often kept in England, under the impression
that the smell of them is grateful to these animals.
" In every stable," says Dr. Horsfield, " from that of a
prince to that of a mantry, or chief of a village, one
of these monkeys is found;" and a recent traveller
relates the same thing, and adds that so highly are
they esteemed for this purpose that a native often
thinks more of the monkey than of the horse, and
would as soon part with the one as the other.
Sumatra has been likewise given as a habitat of the
common macac; and it is certain that Sir Stamford
Raffles had specimens in his collection which are now
deposited in the Zoological Museum, but whether
they were originally obtained in Sumatra or brought
from Java has not been mentioned. It is not
improbable, however, that the macac may be an
inhabitant of both these islands; their contiguity
favours the supposition; and M. F. Cuvier and other
naturalists expressly assign Sumatra as the principal
habitat. This, however, is a question which, though
of the utmost importance in the history of animals,
can only be satisfactorily settled by competent
travellers, or by the direct receipt of well-authenti-
cated specimens. At all events, it is certain that a
very closely allied, though distinct species, does inhabit
the island of Sumatra, where it was obtained both
by Sir Stamford Raffles and M. Duvaucel. Both
species have been described and figured by M. F.
Cuvier; the former under its ancient name of *macacus
cynomolgus*, and the latter, under the specific denomination of *macacus carbonarius*.

The common macac is of a form more heavy and
compact, and has shorter and more robust limbs, than
almost any other monkey which we recollect having
observed; more so even than the rest of its Asiatic

T

congeners; a group of which these qualities are
among the leading characters; the head is large and
flat above; the muzzle is short and obtuse; the nose
flat; and the eyes sunk beneath the very prominent
and projecting crests of the frontal bones. All the
upper and outer parts of the body are of a greenish-
brown colour, resulting from a mixture of yellowish
and black hair upon a light dun ground; the under
parts and interior faces of the four members are
greyish white. The tail is brown and as long as the
body, when not injured, but there is no species in
which this member is so often seen truncated, nor
have we observed any other monkey so much given
to gnawing the end of the tail as the common macac:
the hands and feet are entirely black, the face livid,
the eyes brown, and the canine teeth of the aged
males very long and powerful. But the most marked
character of the species consists in a small crest or tuft
of hair, forming a narrow, peaked, longitudinal ridge
along the middle of the crown, and arising from
the arrangement of the hair on each side of the head,
which appears as if it had all been brushed upwards
towards the centre. This arrangement of the hair
of the head is not observed equally in all individuals;
some display it much more prominently than others;
and this circumstance has given rise to a duplication
of species, among naturalists who see no difference
between individual and specific distinctions, though
both Buffon and Daubenton, the original describers of
the animal, expressly declare that those with and those
without the crest were specifically identical. Others
have supposed that the crest was a sexual mark
appropriate to the females; but, among the numerous
specimens which we have seen at different times in
the various British menageries, we have observed it
equally conspicuous in both sexes; and M. F. Cuvier
informs us that it is even found in the young at the

period of birth. These observations are sufficient to demonstrate the propriety of suppressing, as indeed the most judicious naturalists generally have done, the fictitious species which Gmelin and M. Geoffroy St. Hilaire have introduced, under the name of *simia* and *cercocebus aygula*, a species founded entirely upon the accidental presence or absence of the crest here described. It is likewise said that the *atys* of Audebert is but an albino variety of the common macac, and that the *simia cynocephalus* of Gmelin is in no respects different. Of these animals we have no personal knowledge*; but whether the *atys* be an albino of this or of any other species,—since it seems to be agreed on all hands that it is only an albino— it is clear that it ought never to have been admitted into the system at all; and as for the *simia cyno-cephalus*, it is a species founded upon a bad plate of the old naturalist Johnston, and entitled to no credit whatever; at least, if it do not refer to the common macac, which, from the description of Brisson, with which it is identified, seems most probable. Johnston was a Dutchman, and therefore likely to have seen an animal so common in Java and Sumatra; and though both he and Brisson assign Africa as the habitat, it is certain that they must have been mistaken, as the colours show clearly that the animals which they describe were macacs, and not common cercopithecs.

The common macac has another character by which it may be at all times readily distinguished from the rest of its congeners. Many of the monkeys, and more especially those of the genus cercopithecus,

* Since this passage was written the Author has had an opportunity of examining the original specimen of the *atys*, which is still preserved in the Museum of the Jardin des Plantes. It is an albino variety, not of the common macac, but of the bhunder (*P. Rhesus*), as is proved by its shortish hairy tail, and the habitat " India" upon the label.

are furnished with long copious whiskers, mostly
white, or at least of a different shade from the colour
of the surrounding hair, and, as it were, combed
smoothly along the cheeks in a backward direction,
so as to cover the ears.   In the macac, these whiskers
are very apparent, but they are of the same colour as
the rest of the hair; and, instead of being smoothly
applied along the cheeks, stand out in a bushy
manner, greatly increasing the apparent size of the
head, and giving the animal altogether a singularly
grotesque appearance.   This mark will in general be
sufficient to distinguish the *cercopithecus cynomolgus;*
but the most infallible diagnosis in this, as in all other
cases, by which to recognise the different monkeys,
is the peculiar expression of countenance proper to
each species, and which, however modified in individual cases, is invariably found to be perfectly
characteristic.   An acquaintance with this character,
it is true, can only be acquired by observing and
studying the living animals, or by the assistance of
such drawings as a Harvey or a Landseer only can
supply; but this knowledge once acquired, it is
impossible afterwards to forget the animal, or confound it with any other species.   Let the reader
compare the different engravings which the unrivalled
pencil of the first-named eminent artist has furnished
for the illustration of the present work, and which
have been, for the most part, taken from the living
animals; let him compare, for example, the bonnet-
monkey of the present article with the green monkey
of the following, and he will at once perceive the
importance of the character which we allude to, and
the peculiar traits of physiognomy appropriate to
each.   Further, it is an undoubted fact that this
expression of physiognomy corresponds with and
indicates the disposition and temper of each species,
as clearly as it does in the different races of man-

kind; and Lavater himself might have studied with advantage the relations between the countenance and character of the different monkeys.

The macac is often brought to Europe, and is very common in our menageries. When young it is sufficiently gentle, and even indulges in as frequent gambols as the generality of its congeners; but the old males become morose, sullen, and spiteful. This species occasionally breeds in confinement, and such instances have occurred both in the French National Menagerie and in that of the Zoological Society; but the mother, in all these cases, invariably deserted her offspring,—the strongest instinct of nature thus appearing to cede to the unnatural circumstances of the animal; or, perhaps, the maternal passion being at no time very strong in the present animal, since other species, as for instance the bhunder, have not only produced in confinement, but nursed their young with an affection and solicitude truly wonderful. The young macac is at first black, and only acquires the adult colours of its species at the period of changing the hair; the face, however, is livid, as in the old animal, and there is a remarkable white spot between the eyes, which is never completely obliterated, though it becomes more obscure as the animal advances in age. The *cerco-pithecus carbonarius*, already mentioned as an inhabitant of the same countries as the common macac, is so similar to it in form and colour, that it can scarcely be distinguished, except by its black face. It is nevertheless a very different, though certainly a very nearly allied species, as is proved by that infallible test to which we have already referred, the expression of the physiognomy. This species, however, is not so frequently brought to Europe, and we have never had an opportunity of seeing more than two specimens.

Three distinct species of cercopithecs pass under the common name of white-eyelid monkeys. Though differing in no essential character from the rest of their African congeners, they are more particularly related to the Asiatic species just described, by the presence of the supernumerary tubercle on the last inferior molar, which has been detected in one of them, and probably extends to all three, and by the nature of the fur, which is almost of uniform colour, and without annuli. Two of these animals, *cercopithecus Æthiops* and *cercopithecus fuliginosus,* were first described by Buffon, who, however, confounded them together under the common name of mangabey, believing the collared species to be a mere variety of the common white-eyelid monkey, with which, indeed, it agrees in many of the most prominent details of its external form and disposition, and especially in the dead white colour of the upper eyelids, a character almost confined to the cercopithecs of the present section, and by which they may be at all times readily distinguished from the rest of the monkeys. The third, which approaches still more nearly to the *cercopithecus fuliginosus,* or common white-eyelid monkey, was distinguished by Kuhl, in the Leyden Museum, under the name of *cercopithecus lunulatus;* but has not, as far as we are aware, been described by him, or even so much as mentioned by succeeding writers. All three are natives of the west coast of Africa, the head-quarters of the genus *cercopithecus :* the common white-eyelid monkey was indeed said by Buffon to have been brought from Madagascar, on which account he called it *mangabey,* from the name of a province in the interior of that island ; but he was unquestionably mistaken in this matter. M. F. Cuvier has clearly ascertained the habitat of the present and following species to be Western Africa. The *collared monkey*, again, from its Linnæan name of *Æthiops*, has been universally taken for an inhabitant of the countries south and south-west of Egypt, though that name was in reality given it, not on account of its habitat, but to express the deep brown shade of its colours : we know, moreover, that it does not exist in Ethiopia; at least it is not mentioned either by Rüppell or Ehrenberg, and it can scarcely be supposed to inhabit a country so carefully explored by these scientific travellers, without having come to their knowledge.

The white-eyelid monkey, properly so called, is of a uniform deep smoky blue colour on all the upper parts of the body, and ashy-dun beneath. The face is livid, with dark-brown blotches about the eyes and on the nose, muzzle, and cheeks ; the ears, palms of the hands, and soles of the feet are deep and unmixed brown ; the head and occiput are still darker than the rest of the body ; and the tail, which is of uniform thickness throughout its whole length, is kept habitually turned over the body in a manner peculiar to the present species, and which, far from being an individual trick, has been universally remarked in all specimens. The *cercopithecus lunulatus* of Kuhl is very nearly allied to this species, and indeed appears to have been confounded with it by all other observers. It is, however, a distinct species, bearing the same resemblance to the common mangabey which the *cercopithecus pileatus* of the last article bears to the *cercopithecus radiatus*, or the black-faced to the common macac. We have seen four living individuals at the Surrey Zoological Gardens, and prepared specimens in the Museum of Leyden, where they are labelled with the name here given, and ascribed to Kuhl, though there is no allusion to the species in the "*Beiträge zur Zoologie*" of that author, and it appears, indeed, to be hitherto undescribed. It differs from the *cercopithecus fuliginosus*, in being of a much lighter or more ashy-grey colour, the face and ears, instead of dark brown, are of a livid flesh colour, and there is a remarkable patch of white on the crown of the head, which is invariable in all the specimens we have seen, and probably gave origin to the name of *lunulatus*, though it is not very descriptive of the character.

The collared white-eyelid monkey, *cercopithecus Æthiops*, has the back and outer surface of the limbs of the same dark sooty-brown colour as the *cercopithecus fuliginosus*, but of a still more intense shade; the under surface of the body is equally of an ashy-dun colour, the face and ears smutty-brown, and the proportion of the members in all respects similar, as well as the white colour of the eyelids: but the head is of a beautiful deep chestnut-brown, and the neck surrounded by a broad and conspicuous collar of pure white, which spreads over the throat and cheeks, and gives the animal too marked a character to allow of its being readily confounded with any other species. The fur of all the three species comprised in the present article is of a different quality from that of the rest of their congeners, and approaches more nearly to the fur of the semnopithecs and colobs. It is of a finer and more silky texture, and, instead of being annulated with alternate rings of different colours, as among the generality of the cercopithecs, is of a uniform colour throughout its whole length. In this respect the white-eyelid monkeys resemble the Asiatic cercopithecs described in the last article, in which, though the fur is partially annulated, this character is by no means so conspicuous as in the rest of the genus. Whether all the white-eyelid monkeys are still more nearly related to their Asiatic congeners, by the common possession of the fifth tubercle on the last molar tooth of the lower jaw, has not yet been ascertained for certain ; but the character is known to exist in the common mangabey, and will very probably be found in the other two species.

These species, particularly the *cercopithecus fuliginosus* and *cercopithecus Æthiops*, are not uncommon in our menageries and exhibitions of animals. They are, generally speaking, docile and good-tempered, and more amenable to instruction than most other species of the larger cercopithecs. A specimen of the common mangabey, which lived for many years in the Zoological Gardens, was unusually gentle and intelligent ; he was a lively, grimacing, good-tempered fellow, and a most importunate beggar ; but instead of snatching the contributions of his visitors with violence or anger, like the generality of mon-

keys, he solicited them by tumbling, dancing, and a
hundred other amusing tricks.   He was very fond of
being caressed, and would examine the hands of his
friends with great gentleness and gravity, trying to
pick out the little hairs, and all the while expressing
his satisfaction by smacking his lips, and uttering a
low suppressed grunt. Many other specimens which
we have since observed had the same habit, which,
indeed, appears to be characteristic of the species,
though we have seen none that had arrived at the
same degree of intelligence as the individual here
commemorated.   He died two or three winters
ago ; and it was on the occasion of his post-mortem
examination that the observation was made with
regard to the existence of the additional tubercle
on the last inferior molar, which, by destroying
the only diagnosis till then supposed to be peculiar
to, or generally distinctive of, the cercopithecs, removed the only assignable line of demarcation between these animals and those hitherto included in
the arbitrary genus *macacus*, and made it necessary
to seek for the true limits of these groups in more
important and influential characters.   The live specimens of *cercopithecus lunulatus* which we saw at
the Surrey Zoological Gardens were equally lively
and good-natured as the common mangabey, but
appeared to be less docile and familiar.   They occupied a large cage in common with a number of
other monkeys of different species; among the rest
was a frolicsome young callitrix, or green monkey,
which exhibited a trick well worthy of being recorded, and which we have, since that time, frequently seen performed by individuals of the same
species.   When he wished to induce his associates
to play with him, he would steal quietly behind one
of them, and, giving him a smart but gentle tap with
the hand, dart off to a distant quarter of the cage, fol-

lowed by his playmate, who continued the pursuit in all directions till he succeeded in touching the callitrix ; the pursuer then fled in his turn, followed by the first-named monkey, and thus the game continued, precisely as we have a thousand times seen children perform it. The circumstance has often struck us forcibly : the similarity of mental phenomena here exhibited between these animals and the human species is both curious and interesting, and we are often tempted to ask whether the mental principle be really so uniformly constituted that, as far as their organic structure permits, the very amusements of the lower animals are thus similar to our own ?

CHAPTER X.

Genus *Cercopithecus continued.*—The CALLITRIX (*Cercopithecus Sabæus*).

THE name of callitrix, significant of the varied and beautiful colours of the fur, was applied by the ancient Greeks to a species of monkey which has not been satisfactorily determined hitherto. As regards the present animal, the appellation was first given by Buffon, and is unquestionably a misnomer, since it is not likely that the ancients were acquainted with an animal only found in Senegal and the Cape de Verd Islands. The true callitrix, as has been shown in a former chapter, was, in all probability, the *colobus guereza*, a native of Abyssinia, equally

remarkable for the purity and contrast of its colours,
and for the commercial value of its beautiful long and
silky fur; but, however this may be, the name is at
present universally restricted to the animal to which
it is here applied, and which is one of the species
most commonly seen in Europe, where it passes indifferently by the names of callitrix, green monkey,
and Cape de Verd monkey. It is a handsome species, about the size of a large cat, but, when old,
highly capricious in its disposition, and not to be
trusted. All the upper and outer parts of the body
are a mixture of very dark-green and brown, with a
shade of deep yellow; the under and inner parts are
bright yellow, and the whiskers long, copious, and of
a beautiful orange colour. The face, ears, palms of the
hands and soles of the feet are naked and pure black,
and the tail and limbs long, and of the same colour
as the body, only of a rather lighter shade, the end
of the tail being furnished with a small and not very
apparent tuft of long yellowish hair.

This species is very frequently seen in menageries and exhibitions of animals; it is restless, lively,
and petulant at all times; in youth full of gaiety and
good-nature, but capricious, indocile, and full of malice in old age. It is one of the hardiest of the cercopithecs, and bears the vicissitudes of our changeable
climate better than most other species; but, owing
to its indocile and unfamiliar disposition, it is more
admired for its colours and lively habits than for its
social qualities. The individual described by M. F.
Cuvier, though adult, was perfectly gentle and good-
natured; it was fond of being scratched and petted
by its acquaintances; seldom got into a rage or attempted to bite, and expressed its pleasure or con-
tentment by a low gentle kind of purring noise. Of
the many specimens which we have ourselves observed in the gardens of the Zoological Society and

U

other British menageries, we never remember to
have heard any attempt to emit a sound; and, indeed, for that matter, we have uniformly remarked
that the cercopithecs in general are more silent than
the papios and cynocephals; in this as in other respects, resembling the semnopithecs, which, like
them, are seldom known to emit any kind of sound
in confinement.   In other respects, the different individuals which we have seen, varied as much in
character and disposition as so many human beings
would have done ; and this is universally the case
with individuals of all species, not of monkeys alone,
but of every other kind of animal.   There can be no
greater fallacy than that which is involved in the too
common practice of deducing the character and disposition of entire species from the observation of single individuals, and that generally in unnatural circumstances, if not labouring under actual disease.
The characters and dispositions of animals, as well
as the features and expressions of their countenances,
are as varied and as diversified as those of men ; and
if we fail to perceive the nicer shades of difference, it
is not because they do not exist, but because we have
not enjoyed sufficient opportunities for observation
and experience.   Who does not know that every
dog, horse, or ox, besides the broad and general nature of his kind, has an individual and appropriate
character of his own, and differs in his social and moral qualities from other individuals of the same species ?   The shepherd, it is well known, can tell every
sheep in his flock by the expression of its face ; and
the Irishman was not forsworn who deposed to the
identity of his stolen pigs, though slaughtered and
scraped, from the peculiar expression of their countenances.
    Of the habits and manners of the callitrix in a
state of nature, our only knowledge is derived from

the following interesting passage contained in Adanson's Travels in Senegal. After having previously informed us that the trees were filled with *green monkeys*, and thus identified the species to which he refers with that at present under consideration, he proceeds : " But what struck me most was the shooting of monkeys, which I enjoyed within six leagues this side of Podor, on the landes (downs ?) to the south of Donai, otherwise called Coq; and I do not think there ever was better sport. The vessel being obliged to remain there one morning, I went on shore to divert myself with my gun. The place was very woody, and full of green monkeys, which I did not perceive but by their breaking the boughs and the tops of the trees, from whence they tumbled down on me ; for in other respects they were so silent and nimble in their tricks that it would have been difficult to perceive them. ·Here I stopped and killed two or three of them before the others seemed to be much frightened; however, when they found themselves wounded, they began to look about for shelter, some by hiding themselves behind the larger boughs, others by coming down upon the ground, others, in fine, and these were the greatest number, by jumping from one tree to another. Nothing could be more entertaining, when several of them jumped together on the same bough, than to see it bend under them, and the hindmost to drop down to the ground, whilst the rest got farther on, and others were still suspended in the air. As this game was going on, I continued still to shoot at them ; and though I killed no fewer than three-and-twenty in less than an hour, and within the space of twenty fathoms, yet not one of them screeched the whole time, notwithstanding that they united in companies, knit their brows, gnashed their teeth, and seemed as if they intended to attack me."

The *tota*, or grivet, of M. F. Cuvier, *cercopithecus*

griseus, is a species closely allied to the callitrix, but readily distinguished from it by the clearer grey or ash colour of its upper parts, the pure white of its large whiskers, and the bright orange mark which passes from the root of the tail forwards between the thighs. The naked parts of the face and hands also are rather brown than black; a white band passes across the forehead; the thighs and arms are of a much lighter and clearer grey than the rest of the body, and the scrotum is of a beautiful light verdigris colour. In this last respect it resembles the callitrix; but differs materially from the three following species, which have the scrotum of a deep indigo-blue colour—a mark by which, as has been already observed, these animals are most readily distinguished from one another, and which, with a little ordinary attention, may even be preserved in skins and mounted specimens. The grivet is a native of Nubia, where it was observed by Caillaud, and of Senaar, Kordofan, and the lower provinces of Abyssinia, as we learn from Dr. Rüppell. In the latter country it is called *tota;* in Senaar and Egypt, where it is frequently kept in the houses of the natives, it is called abellan. Salt says that tota is the Amharic name, the animal being called *alesteo* in the language of Tigré, and that it is a small species with a black face; whilst Bruce describes the tota as a small beautiful green monkey with a long tail, and informs us that all the plantations of corn about Deber are much infested by it. It is not unfrequently brought to Europe in vessels trading to Alexandria and the Levant; whither it arrives from Upper Egypt, being often brought to Cairo along with various other species of animals, by the trading caravans or pilgrims from the interior and distant parts of Africa, who yearly resort to that capital on their way to the shrine of the prophet at Mecca. In confinement its manners differ in no respect from those which have been already described as common to the larger cercopithecs of the present section. Its temper is not at all times to be trusted; and though the females and young are generally playful and good-natured, the adult males usually become capricious and mischievous. Such, at least, is the character which M. F. Cuvier, its first describer, has drawn of the different individuals of this species which he observed in the menagerie of the Jardin des Plantes, and the few specimens which we have ourselves seen in this country, for the species is not so commonly brought to England as some of the other monkeys, exhibited no difference in this respect.

The *vervet* of M. F. Cuvier, *cercopithecus pygerythrus*, is another species closely allied to the callitrix. Its colours are an intimate mixture of grey, brown, and green, producing a dark greenish-grey tint on the upper and outer surface of the body, and unmixed white on the whiskers and under parts; a white line, like a fillet, passes across the forehead, and the feet, hands, and terminal third of the tail are of an intense and unmixed black colour, which is a character peculiar to the vervet among the monkeys of the present section, and which readily distinguishes it from the proximate species. The face and other naked parts are dark brown, the scrotum, as in the tota, is of the purest verdigris colour, surrounded with white hairs, and a small tuft of deep red marks the situation of the anus and junction of the tail, and gives its specific appellation to the animal, though it is only visible when the tail is elevated. The general shade of colour which pervades the superior parts of the body in this species is of the same intense brownish-green as in the callitrix; but it may be readily distinguished from that animal by the pure white of the under parts and the black of the paws and tail. From the tota, again, it

is distinguished by the deeper shade of its colours
and the same black marks on the extremities, though
in other respects it approaches much nearer to this
species than to the callitrix. The vervet inhabits
the southern parts of Africa; it is the only cercopithec, or, indeed, with the exception of the chacma,
cynocephalus porcarius, the only quadrumanous
mammal found south of the tropic of Capricorn.
The woods throughout the colony of the Cape of
Good Hope, more especially along the sea-coast
from Cape Town to Algoa Bay, and thence through
the whole extent of Caffre Land and Natal, abound
with this species. It is often mentioned by Barrow,
Lichtenstein, Thunberg, and other travellers in that
country; and Patterson informs us that it feeds
principally upon the gum arabic which exudes from
the *acacia nilotica* and other species of the same genus, which abound in South Africa, and which are
called by the Dutch colonists rhinoster-bosh and
camel-doorn, from being browsed upon by the rhi-
noceros and giraffe. Though so common in one of
the nearest and most frequented British colonies, this
species is rarely brought alive to England, and we
do not remember to have seen more than three or
four individuals in the menageries during the last ten
years. The manners and disposition of the species
are in all respects similar to those of the callitrix, which
it further resembles in the size and proportions of the
body and extremities.

Lieutenant-Colonel Sykes, on his return from
India some years ago, brought a new species of cercopithec from Bombay, whither it was said to have
been originally imported from Madagascar, and
which lived for a considerable time in the collection
of the Zoological Society. It was afterwards described by Colonel Sykes, in the proceedings of that
body for 1831, under the specific name of *cercopi-*

thecus albogularis, and is remarkable as being much the largest known species of the genus. In its proportions and the general distribution of its colours, this animal resembles the group of monkeys at present under consideration, and is, in all respects, a true cercopithec; for though the gallant and estimable officer who originally described it was at first inclined to consider it as a species of semnopithec, the dissection of the animal afterwards proved it to belong to the present genus. The following is Colonel Sykes's description: "Its canines are remarkably long, slender, and sharp; the incisors very short and even. The head is rounded and short; the ears very small, nearly rounded, and for the most part concealed in the long hair about the head. The eyes are deeply seated, and shaded by a continuous arch of long hair directed forwards; the irides broad, and of a brown ochre colour. The hair forms a bunch on each cheek resembling whiskers, and there is no beard. The cheek-pouches are rudimentary only (?) and not observable externally, even, when filled, being concealed by the long hair of the cheeks. The thumbs of the anterior hands are short and distant, those of the posterior long. The whole upper surface of the body is of a mingled black and yellowish ochre colour, each hair being banded black and ochre, the black prevailing on the shoulders, and the ochre on the back and flanks. The under surface is grizzled white and black; the anterior limbs uniform black, and the posterior black, with a little of the dorsal colour. The chin and throat are pure white, and the tail half as long again as the body, and black."

" The manners of this monkey," continues Colonel Sykes, " are grave and sedate. Its disposition is gentle, but not affectionate; free from that capricious petulance and mischievous irascibility which charac-

terise so many of the African species, but yet resenting irritating treatment, and evincing its resentment
by very sharp blows with its anterior hands. It
never bit any person on board ship, but so seriously
lacerated three other monkeys, its fellow-passengers,
that two of them died of the wounds. It readily
ate meat, and would choose to pick a bone, even
when plentifully supplied with vegetables and dried
fruits." This account fully agrees with our own observations of the same individual whilst it lived in
the possession of the Zoological Society. It had a
gravity in its demeanour, which certainly resembled
the disposition of the semnopithecs rather than that
of the African monkeys, and, whilst less petulant and
curious, was at the same time less irritable and mischievous than the rest of its congeners. We have
seen a second individual in the possession of a travelling showman, which strongly exhibited the same
antipathy towards other monkeys, that Colonel Sykes
has recorded in the case of his specimen. It even
flew upon a stuffed skin, which its owner threw
down to it, and worried it with all the hatred and
fury of a terrier against a rat. In other respects,
and towards its master and visitors, it appeared to be
as docile and good-natured as the individual observed by Colonel Sykes, and this is no doubt the
natural character of the species. The exact habitat
of this animal has not been satisfactorily ascertained.
Colonel Sykes's specimen was reported to have been
brought to Bombay from Madagascar; this may
certainly have been the case, but we have no certain
knowledge of any species of real monkey inhabiting that great island, so singular and exclusive in
its mammal productions, more especially as regards
the quadrumana, and we think it not improbable
that the animal may be one of the monkeys said to be
found on the eastern coast of Africa, or perhaps the

species of common monkey mentioned in Prior's
Voyage as an inhabitant of the Island of Johanna ;
a conjecture which receives some countenance from
the fact that the Bombay vessels frequently touch at
the Sechelles, and very seldom at the Mauritius,
from which, moreover, it would probably find its
way more frequently to this country, were it a native
of the neighbouring island of Madagascar.

The last species of the present group of cercopithecs which we shall notice, and that, principally, for
the purpose of clearing up the confusion which has
been lately introduced into its synonyma, is the animal which Buffon, Scopoli, M. F. Cuvier, and others,
have described and figured under the name of malbrouk. The species was originally described and
figured under that name by Buffon and Daubenton,
and admitted into the catalogues of systematic
writers by the specific appellation of *simia faunus*,
and afterwards by Scopoli under the name *simia cynosurus*. On the formation of the French School of
Zoology, when Baron Cuvier, M. Geoffroy St. Hilaire, and other eminent naturalists, undertook the
task of reforming the errors and confusion which
Gmelin and other compilers had introduced into the
Systema Naturæ, the descriptions of Buffon and
Scopoli were very properly referred to the same species, and united with the *cercopithecus faunus* of
Linnæus. It does not appear, however, that these
zoologists had an opportunity of examining the living
animal; but specimens were subsequently obtained
and figured by M. F. Cuvier, who expressly identified them with the malbrouk of Buffon and the *cercopithecus faunus* of systematic writers. The animal,
however, is not so frequently brought to England as
some other species, and, consequently, its distinctive
characters were less generally known than those of

most other cercopithecs, till the arrival of a specimen at the gardens of the Zoological Society, some years ago, afforded to British zoologists the means of comparing it with other closely-allied species and of thus becoming acquainted with its differential characters. The specimen in question was at first taken by the late Mr. Bennett to be entirely new, but its identity with the real malbrouk was pointed out to him, when he was about to notice it as an undescribed species; notwithstanding which, he has described it in the proceedings of the society, under a new name—a proceeding which has caused great confusion in the synonyma of the species, and to which Mr. Bennett appears to have been induced by the error of considering Buffon's animal as a distinct species from that afterwards figured by M. F. Cuvier. Even had this been the case, however, the proper and legitimate course should have been to have left the specific name of *cercopithecus faunus* to Buffon's animal, to which it had been invariably applied by previous writers, and to have given a new name to the new species, supposed to be confounded with it by M. F. Cuvier, instead of sanctioning this zoologist's error, and transferring both the trivial and specific names of the real malbrouk, to an animal which had no legal right to bear them. This was making confusion still more confounded; but the truth is, that Mr. Bennett was altogether mistaken in this matter, and consequently his name of *tephrops* must be altogether suppressed. Of M. F. Cuvier's identification of his own animal with that of Buffon and Daubenton there cannot be the slightest doubt ; we have ourselves examined the original specimens deposited in the Paris Museum, and are fully satisfied as to their specific identity with the animal described by Mr. Bennett. The names of *cynosurus* and *lephrops* must consequently be both suppressed, and the original denomination of *cercopithecus faunus* alone retained.

This species has all the upper parts of the body of the same mottled mixture of green, yellow, and brown which is observed in the common callitrix, but the under parts are greyish-white, and a band of the same colour passes over the eyes and spreads into large whiskers on the cheeks. The space round the eyes, the nose and the lips, are livid flesh colour; the eyes are large and dark, and the whole expression of the countenance milder and more open than we recollect to have ever seen in any other species of monkey. Yet the character of the animal does not altogether answer to these favourable indications. It is calm, circumspect, and inactive, but averse to familiarity, and always ready to resent the least encroachment upon its independence. Such, at least, was the character of the individual originally observed in the gardens of the Zoological Society, and other specimens which we have since seen, presented no difference. Even the young appear to be little inclined to the frolic and curiosity of some other monkeys, and are generally observed seated in a corner of their cage or on the perch, almost heedless of what passes around them. When disturbed or interfered with, however, they soon shake off their former apathy, and the wickedness with which they attempt to injure the assailant forms a singular contrast to the mildness and gentleness depicted in their countenances. The malbrouk described by M. F. Cuvier, on the other hand, exhibited a very different character and disposition. No animal could be more active and restless; it was continually in motion, and played a thousand different tricks: but it was extremely irritable in its temper, and always watched for an opportunity to make its attacks when its adversary was unguarded or had his attention directed elsewhere. It would then fly upon him suddenly, bite or scratch him severely, and as suddenly retreat beyond the reach of chastisement, but without ever losing sight of the object of its resentment, and only for the purpose of renewing the assault on the first favourable occasion. Those which we have seen in the gardens of the Zoological Society were less maliciously disposed. One in particular, though an adult male, was extremely gentle, and took great pleasure in being scratched and caressed by the visitors. The species is of a greyer colour than the callitrix, and browner than the grivet, and may be easily distinguished by the lighter colour of the arms and thighs, which are of a nearly pure ashy-grey, and without any mixture of the green and yellow which mark the upper surface of the body. The whiskers and under parts of the body are greyish-white, and the scrotum of a beautiful indigo or lapis-lazuli colour; but the chief distinction lies in the peculiar expression of countenance which has been already described, and which cannot be mistaken by any person who has seen a good figure of the species. No writer has mentioned the exact habitat of this species, nor have we ever been able to ascertain this point, with regard to the numerous specimens which we have seen. Buffon, who confounded his malbrouk with the bonnet-monkey, reported it to come from India; but in this he was certainly mistaken: there are, however, specimens in the museum of Leyden, said to be from the coast of Guinea, and this is no doubt the true habitat.

The PATAS, or NISNAS (*Cercopithecus ruber*).

We have now arrived at a monkey still resembling the callitrix in its comparatively large size, and in the general proportions of its members ; but differing materially in colour, the prevailing tints being red or reddish-brown, and without the mixture of speckled grey and green which distinguishes the group just described. The present section includes an animal which has latterly been described under two different specific names, the young having been long since described by Buffon under the name of the patas, or red monkey, and the adult having been recently brought from the interior of Darfur and Kordofan, by the Prussian travellers, Hemprich and Ehrenberg, and figured in the magnificent work called " Symbolæ Physicæ," now in course of publication by the latter author, under the new name of *C. pyronotus.*

With this exception, thanks to the singularity and brilliancy of its colours, the red monkey, *cercopithecus ruber,* has hitherto escaped the fate of many of its congeners, having never, that we are aware of, been confounded with any other species of cercopithecs. It is a very beautiful species, about the size of the callitrix, but with a rounder head and shorter face, which approximate it, in some degree, to the last subdivision of the present genus, though the superior development of its muscular powers and its bold and independent character, more properly associate it with the malbrouk and the tota. All the upper parts of the young animal are of a brilliant fawn or pale sandy-red colour, which becomes fainter on the arms and thighs; the breast, belly, and inner surface of the extremities are very pale grey, and the tail of the same colour as the body, only paler at the extremity than towards the root. The face is of a dirty or tawny-flesh colour, the end of the nose covered with very short black hairs, which are continued in a narrow line, like a small pair of moustaches, on the upper lip, and a band of the same colour passes over the eyes, like a black fillet tied

round the head. The ears and naked parts of the
hands and feet are livid-flesh colour, and the tail is
about equal in length to the body. The patas is occasionally, though not very frequently, seen in our
public menageries. It is a native of Senegal, where
patas is its name among the negroes. It is found
likewise in Senaar and Kordofan, as we shall presently see, and in all probability extends throughout
the whole of Central Africa.

In confinement the patas is restless and playful; but
full of distrust and little disposed to familiarity.
With the intelligence and penetration of the rest of
its congeners comprised in the present section, it is
equally capricious and inconstant in its temper, and
should never be trusted without great circumspection. Of its manners in a state of nature we have
the following account from the pen of Brue, an old
French traveller, who was formerly employed in
establishing the gum-trade along the banks of the
Senegal and Gambia, and who made frequent excursions up the former river for that purpose. It was
on one of these trips that he met with the patas,
which he describes as being possessed of a great
share of curiosity, and of such a brilliant red colour
that they almost appeared to have been painted. " I
have seen these animals," says he, " descend from the
tops of the trees to the lower branches to examine
and admire our boats as we passed beneath them ;
and after gazing upon us for some time, and appearing to be pondering deeply upon so strange a sight,
retire to make way for some new comers, who would
satisfy their eager curiosity in the same manner.
After some time, emboldened by experience, they became more confident, and began to pelt us with rot-
ten branches and other missiles, not always of the
most delicate description. This conduct the sailors
returned by a few musket shots, by which some

were killed and others grievously wounded. At first, however, our attack only emboldened them, and they renewed the assault with great clamour and determination ; but finally, perceiving that the odds were clearly against them, they scampered nimbly out of range of our guns, and contemplated us afterwards from a safer distance."

The *nisnas*, or *cercopithecus pyronotus*, of Hemprich and Ehrenberg is but the adult of the common red monkey, as we have ourselves ascertained by the examination of specimens of all ages, both from Senegal and Ethiopia. It is, however, an animal which derives no mean historical interest from the circumstance of its being occasionally represented on the tombs of the ancient Egyptians. The nisnas, as this animal is called by the Arabs of its native country, attains to as large a size as any of the cercopithecs. Its face is deep black, with a livid ring round the eyes, and a few white hairs upon the nose; the whiskers are large, bushy, and of a pure white colour; the back, sides, and upper parts of the body deep reddish-brown, which extends about half-way down the arms and thighs, all the remainder of the limbs, both outside and in, being of a pure white colour. There is a triangular spot of more intense ochre than the ground colour of the body, on the forehead, and another on each side at the root of the tail; the soles, palms, and tips of the fingers and toes are black, and the scrotum of a beautiful light verdigris colour. M. Ehrenberg says that the adult male, when in good health, is furnished with a copious mane, which, however, does not appear in his figure, as, according to his own account, the specimen from which that was taken, and which he had brought alive to Berlin on his return from his African travels, had been long in a declining state of health, and lost the mane previous to the drawing

being made. We have, however, seen various specimens of this animal, at Frankfort and Paris, from
both Eastern and Western Africa, and of both sexes,
without remarking this character; and, indeed, we
have considerable doubts as to the existence of a
mane in any species of cercopithec, at least in the
sense expressed by that term as applied to the *cynocephalus hamadryas* and *papio gelada;* but if it
really do exist in the nisnas, it will be a highly interesting fact, as being the third instance of such an
ornament existing among the very limited number of
known simiæ inhabiting Ethiopia, and, as far as at
present known, entirely confined to the quadrumana
of that part of Africa.

This species is unquestionably the cepus which
Ælian, on the authority of Pythagoras, describes as an
inhabitant of the countries bordering on the Red Sea.
The deep flame colour of the head and back, and
the pure white of the whiskers, belly, and extremities,
would be alone sufficient to identify it, if the detailed
description of the ancient naturalist, more minute
and elaborate than almost any other notice which ancient authors have left us of the animals which they
mention, did not agree in all essential particulars.
It is seldom, indeed, that we are able to identify an
animal so satisfactorily with any ancient description;
but here the size, colours, and habitat, are all too minutely described to admit of any mistake; and the
travels of Rüppell and Hemprich have made us sufficiently acquainted with the zoology of its native regions to assure us that there is no other species of
monkey in Ethiopia to which that description can
apply.

The cepus, cephus, or cebus, is mentioned by many
of the ancient classical authors, and the identification of the particular species to which they severally
referred has given rise to a good deal of conjecture

among modern naturalists and commentators. Baron Cuvier, in the notes to a late French edition of Pliny, has attempted to show, but not very successfully, that these notices refer to three distinct species of simiæ. He supposes that the cepus of Strabo and Diodorus refers to the common Ethiopian baboon, *cynocephalus sphinx*, whilst he identifies the *cynocephalus hamadryas*, another species of baboon inhabiting Ethiopia and Arabia, with the animal mentioned under the same name by Agatharcides, and that of Ælian, already mentioned, with the patas, or red monkey of Senegal. For these approximations no better reason can be assigned than the mere conjecture of the author, and this is sufficiently disproved, at least in one case, by Agatharcides himself, who, *apud Phocium*, expressly distinguishes the cepus from the cynocephalus. The cebus of Aristotle, indeed, appears to have been really a different animal, as we shall endeavour to show when speaking of the *papio gelada ;* but, on the other hand, the cepus, cephus, and cebus of the more modern Greeks and Romans most probably all referred to the present species. After the time of Aristotle, the Ptolemies occupied the throne of Egypt up to the period of its becoming a Roman province. The authors of that time had consequently better opportunities of becoming acquainted with the productions of Ethiopia than their predecessors enjoyed. Ælian, as we have seen, gives us a very recognizable description of the animal : Strabo relates that the Babylonians worshipped it in conjunction with the *cynocephalus* or baboon, and Juvenal informs us that it was equally an object of religious veneration among the ancient Egyptians. Here, however, both these authors appear to have been mistaken. The image of the nisnas certainly appears occasionally on the monuments and tombs of ancient Egypt, but only in relation to profane subjects, and never as a constituent part of their religious ceremonies—a situation which is exclusively occupied by the baboon. For instance, in the procession of a returning conqueror, represented in a painting discovered by the late Mr. Salt, and engraved by Minutoli (tab. xii. fig. 9), a monkey is introduced riding on the neck of a giraffe or camelopard; but this ' was manifestly intended merely to fix the locality of the country or people, whose subjugation the triumphal procession was meant to commemorate; and a few other instances might be adduced of the images of monkeys found upon sepulchral stones, as, for example, that represented by Denon, tab. xcvii. There is a very beautiful sculpture of this description deposited in the Royal Museum at Berlin; it was found among the tombs of Memphis, and represents the animal bound with a strap round the loins, in the same manner as we constantly see monkeys secured at the present day, thus intimating that it was a domestic pet and a favourite of its deceased master, whose tomb it is made to ornament.

The nisnas has been described or mentioned by many modern authors, from the days of Prosper Alpinus downwards; but previous to the travels of Hemprich and Ehrenberg it had not been satisfactorily ascertained to be a native of Eastern Africa. Ethiopian specimens are seldom or never brought alive to this country; at least we have never seen an individual either in any of our public menageries, nor is there even a preserved specimen in our British Museum. Dr. Rüppell assures us that it is less frequently tamed in Egypt than the tota or *cercopithecus griseus*, with which the Egyptian peasantry confound it under the common name of Abellan. Its native name in Kordofan, as we are informed on the same authority, is *nango*.

Cercopithecus Dilophos, Pogonias, and Temminckii.

The three monkeys included in the present section are in some respects intermediate between those of the second and third divisions of the cercopithecs; they resemble the callitrix and its allied species in the speckled or annulated character of the fur, and in the very considerable size to which they attain; but are more nearly related to the mona and Diana, by their gentleness and docility, and may very well commence the series of which these species may be in some measure considered typical. The first was described and figured by M. F. Cuvier, from the living animal, but under the wrong name of Diana, with which species he confounded it; the name of *dilophos*, here retained, is that given to it in the Leyden Museum, where we have had an opportunity of examining two fine specimens; the second species was described some years ago by the late Mr. Bennett, from a specimen in the collection of the Zoological Society; and the third is an unnamed species which we found in the Museum des Pays Bas, and which we propose to dedicate to the celebrated director of that national institution, as a mark of respect for the eminent position which he occupies among the cultivators of natural science, and of gratitude for the liberality with which he opens the treasures of the magnificent collection confided to his charge to foreign naturalists.

Of the *cercopithecus dilophos* M. F. Cuvier gives the following description from a specimen which lived for some years at the Jardin des Plantes. " On its first arrival the head, neck, shoulders, arms, forearms, hands, breasts, belly, and tail, were uniform black, only rather less intense on the under parts and a considerable portion of the tail than elsewhere; the back and sides were minutely speckled with white and black, from the hairs being individually annulated with these two colours; the whiskers were speckled with yellow and black, and there was likewise a slight tinge of yellow on the white crescent which passed over the eyes; the chin was covered with a few white hairs, but they did not form the long prominent beard of the roloway; there were no fulvous coloured hairs, except just under the callosities, and even there they were scanty; the face was violet, tinged with reddish on the muzzle and eyelids. The hands were black, and the eyes hazel. The only change which age produced in this individual was the augmentation of the yellow tinge on the whiskers, and its replacing the white rings on the hair of the back; the inner surface of the thighs above also assumed a soft greyish or dun colour. The whole animal was very densely covered above, but more scantily on the under surface of the body." This description agrees in all respects with the Leyden specimens. These are of large size, larger indeed than the generality of cercopithecs; they have all the under parts, as well as the crown of the head, the shoulders, limbs, and tail, intense black; the cheeks, sides, and back, are very finely and minutely speckled with black and grey, in the same manner as many species of squirrels, but much darker. In one specimen the lunated mark over the eyes is pure white, in the other speckled with brown.

The *cercopithecus pogonias* has the occiput, shoulders, outer face of the arms and hind hands black speckled with white; the back, croup, and tail pure black; the forehead is of a straw colour, speckled with black, particularly in the centre, and a patch of the same colour from the brows backwards to the opening of the ears; the whiskers are large and bushy, and of a beautiful clear straw colour, slightly speckled with black, and a long tuft of hair of the same colour grows from the interior of the ear; the hind thighs, legs, and indeed the whole of the posterior extremities, the paws only excepted, are pale dunnish grey, moderately grizzled with black; the tail is black throughout its whole length, both above and below, with the exception of the under surface of the half next the root, which, as well as the entire under surface of the body and inside of the limbs, is rusty yellow. The only known specimen is in the Zoological Museum.

The *cercopithecus Temminckii* is about the size of the Diana. The head, back, and cheeks are ash-coloured, slightly mixed with brown on the hips and rump, the hair being everywhere annulated with white, and thus partially speckled; the arms, fore-arms, thighs, legs, and paws are black; the whole of the chin and throat pure unmixed white; the cheeks, whiskers, and head grizzled ash, like the back and sides; the face apparently greyish-blue, and the belly ash-coloured. The tail is about the length of the body, but has lost the greater part of the hair; what remains, however, is of the same colour as the body. The only known specimen—that, namely, in the Leyden Museum—was purchased at Amsterdam in 1824, and said to have been brought from the coast of Guinea. The Zoological Society's specimen of *C. pogonias* came from Fernando Po; and it is probable that *C. dilophos* inhabits the same coast of Africa, though we have been unable to ascertain the origin either of M. F. Cuvier's specimen or of those in the Museum des Pays Bas.

THE DIANA MONKEY.

The Diana monkey, originally described by the celebrated Linnæus, and so named on account of a
lunated white mark across the forehead similar to that
with which the goddess of the chase is represented on
antique statues, commences the third and last group
of cercopithecs which comprises the smaller and gentler species of the genus. The real name of this
beautiful animal in its native country, on the Gold
Coast, is said to be *roloway*: Marcgrave, however,
informs us that it is called *erquima* in Congo, and it
has frequently been described under the name of the
palatine monkey, from the fancied resemblance which
Allamand saw between a lady's tippet and the collar and accidentally divided beard of the individual
which he figured and described in the Dutch edition
of Buffon's Histoire Naturelle. The divided beard

of the individual observed by Allamand, which appears to have been the result of pure accident, has given rise to the very general error of considering the roloway as a distinct species from the Diana; but this is altogether without reason, and we are well assured by the examination and report of subsequent authors that the *simia Diana* and *simia roloway* of the Linnæan system are really referable to one and the same species. The animal itself is not less remarkable for the singular form of its long peaked beard than for the beauty and variety of its colours, and the gentleness and playful activity of its manners and disposition. The ground colour of the body is of the most beautiful minever, or that intimate mixture of black and clear grey which characterizes many of the squirrels, such as the American grey squirrel and other allied species; but the colours are darker and more contrasted in the present case, and a broad stripe of the purest and most intense chestnut-brown passes down the animal's back from the shoulders to the root of the tail. The face, hands, and end of the tail, are deep black; the reversed crescent on the forehead, the whiskers, beard, breast, and throat, white; and the abdomen and inner surface of the thighs yellowish-grey. But the length and peculiar form of the beard are unquestionably the most singular character about this animal. The ornament in question consists of long white hairs, which spring equally from the cheeks and chin, and project outwards two or three inches beyond the latter, terminating in a point, and resembling the formal cut of the peaked beard which we see in some old paintings about the time of Henry VIII. This ornament the animal itself is very solicitous to keep properly trimmed and neat, and it is amusing to see it when about to drink, taking the beard in its hand and holding it back to prevent it from coming in contact with the water. The first time we observed this strange action was in the instance of an individual formerly kept at the rooms of the Zoological Society in Burton-street. We happened to be standing close to his pole when he came down to drink, and the ludicrous effect of the creature's solicitude about his beard made us laugh outright. He looked up at us for a moment, as if in seeming astonishment, and then, as if suddenly penetrating the cause of our risibility, and resenting what he no doubt considered as a personal insult, flew at us with great wickedness, and was only prevented, by the shortness of his chain and our hasty retreat, from punishing us severely for our ill-timed mirth. In general, however, the individual in question was extremely good-tempered and not indisposed to familiarity. It was confined next to a small species of American cebus, but at such a distance as just to prevent the two animals from injuring one another with their teeth. In this predicament it was highly amusing to see them at play, lying on their sides and clawing each other with their hind hands, the cebus making use of his prehensile tail to entangle his adversary, and the Diana every now and then revenging himself by seizing upon this supernumerary organ of assault and dragging its owner after him to the top of the pole.

The Mona, Moustache, and Talapoin Monkeys,

Are three species of the smaller and gentle cercopithecs, less frequently seen in this country than the callitrix and its allied species, but equally interesting on account of the innocence and playfulness of their disposition, and the brilliancy and variety of their colours. " If," says M. F. Cuvier, " elegance of form, gracefulness of movement, gentleness and sim-

plicity of character, united with penetration and intelligence of expression, can inspire affection or make
an animal admired and sought after, all these qualities are permanently united in the small group of
monkeys allied to the mona, itself distinguished not
less by the variety of its colours than by its temper
and disposition." The head of this beautiful species
is of a mixed green and gold colour ; the back and
sides of a brilliant chestnut pointed with black ; the
outer surface of the legs, thighs, and tail speckled
with black and grey; the throat, breast, belly, and
inner face of the members of the purest white ; and
the large and bushy whiskers of a beautiful straw
colour, slightly tinged with green.—The upper part
of the face is of a violet-blue colour, the under half,
about the end of the nose and mouth, flesh-coloured,
and on each hip, immediately in front of the tail, is a
conspicuous oval spot of the most brilliant white, a
mark altogether peculiar to the mona, and which renders it impossible to confound it with any other species.   M. F. Cuvier has drawn a very flattering picture of the manners and intelligence of the mona in
a state of confinement, of its docility, gentleness, curiosity, and good-nature; but here, as in other instances, we must beware of generalizing too rapidly,
or of ascribing to the whole species the good qualities
of a single individual.   The mona, it is true, is less
petulant and mischievous than the larger and more
powerful cercopithecs ; the females and young males
are at all times gentle and playful, but we have seen
the adults of the latter sex exhibit a marked degree
of caprice, and become as intolerant of familiarity as
the aged callitrix or macac.   The name of mona is a
misnomer as applied to the present species; the
word is generic among the Moors and Spaniards
for monkeys in general, and was first applied, but
arbitrarily and without a shadow of pretence or jus-

tice, to the present species by Buffon, who has, in a manner equally arbitrary and unfounded, identified it with the cebus of the Greeks and Romans, and assigned Barbary and Egypt as its native country, though he afterwards received a specimen from the coast of Guinea. The latter locality is, in fact, the true habitat of the mona; but, as we are unacquainted with the native name, and as that here given has been long applied exclusively to the present species, we have no choice but to retain it.

The beautiful species of cercopithec which Buffon first described under the name of *moustache*, and which that naturalist and M. F. Cuvier alone seem to have observed in a living state, is generally identified, but without sufficient authority, with the *simia cephus* of Linnæus, a species founded upon a vague description of Marcgrave. It is one of the smallest and most beautiful of the simiæ, the fullgrown animal measuring little more than a foot in length. The top of the head is green; the back and sides greenish-brown, the members and under surface of the body grey, sometimes tinged with light yellow; the latter half of the tail reddish-fawn colour; and the whiskers, which are thick and bushy, of a bright yellow on the upper half, and pale-white under the chin. The ears, hands, and scrotum are naked, and flesh-coloured; and the face of a uniform bluish black, with the exception of a remarkable bar of a dead or French-white shade, which passes backward over the upper lip, on each side, immediately under the nose, and, from its striking resemblance to a pair of moustaches, gives origin to the name by which the species is invariably designated. There was a fine specimen of the moustache some years ago in the Surrey Zoological Gardens; but the animal is not often seen in this country, and the individual in question was the only one we have ever had an opportunity of observing. Like other species of the present group, it was gentle, playful, and familiar, but did not live long enough to enable us to study its manners minutely. It was said to have been brought from the Gold Coast.

The *talapoin* is another pretty little monkey, which was first figured and described by Buffon and Daubenton, but which was not subsequently observed alive by any other naturalist till M. F. Cuvier met with it in the possession of a dealer in Paris, from whom he purchased it for the Jardin du Roi, and afterwards figured it under the name of melarine, without at the time perceiving its identity with the *cercopithecus talapoin* of systematic writers. The whole animal is of a bright yellowish green colour above, and light grey beneath; the whiskers pale yellow, the face flesh-coloured, and the nose and ears dark brown or black. The distribution and general shade of colours which distinguish this animal have some resemblance to those of the common callitrix, or green monkey; but the round form of the head, the shortness of the face, its livid flesh-colour, and the black mark on the nose, are at all times sufficient to differentiate it from that and the kindred species of cercopithecs. It is seldom brought to this country, nor are we aware of its precise habitat, but it may be presumed that, like the great majority of its congeners, it is an inhabitant of Guinea or some other part of Western Africa. At all events it is certainly not an Indian species, as Buffon was led to suppose from the name of talapoin, which he received with his specimen, and which properly belongs to an order of the priesthood among the Buddhists. It is in all probability a misnomer as applied to the animal, and might, perhaps with advantage, give place to M. F. Cuvier's name of melarine.

WHITE-NOSED MONKEYS.

The last of the cercopithecs of which it is necessary
for us to take particular notice are two, if not three,
species, belonging to the same group as the mona
and talapoin, and which are generally known by the
name of white-nosed monkeys, from having the tip
of the nose distinguished by a remarkable spot of
this colour, whilst all the rest of the face is deep
black or violet. These species, as we know, both
from the accounts of travellers and the arrival of
specimens, inhabit the coast of Guinea and the
neighbourhood of Sierra Leone.   Two are well
known to naturalists as distinct species by the names
of *cercopithecus nictitans* and *cercopithecus petaurista*, and a third, if it be not in reality identical with
the last-named animal, has been indicated by Audebert under the appellation of *cercopithecus ascanius*.
M. F. Cuvier and other French zoologists of the

present day have adopted the opinion of this identity, but suppress the Linnæan name of petaurista and substitute that of ascanius introduced by Audebert; but if the species be really the same, the former name ought certainly to be preserved on account of its priority of application. But, however this may be, Audebert has figured and described both the ascanius and the petaurista, which he expressly compares with one another; and he was too good a zoologist, at least on this part of the subject, to allow of his authority being arbitrarily disregarded in a matter which came under his own personal observation, and that by persons who have avowedly never enjoyed the same opportunities of comparing the two animals. He assures us that the species differ in the colour of the face, which is black in the petaurista and violet-blue in the ascanius; in a large tuft of white hair which the latter has on each temple, and which is not found in the former; and finally in the ears of the ascanius being small, naked, and flesh-coloured, whilst they are large and black in the petaurista. The upper parts of the body are, moreover, described as of an olive-green colour in the ascanius, the beard and under parts light brown or dark grey, and the external face of the limbs black; the petaurista, on the contrary, has the back of a greenish brown colour, the hands grey, and the outer face of the limbs olive green. Such is the substance of Audebert's own comparative description; and, if faithful to nature, it would certainly indicate a decided specific difference between the two animals; but it is to be observed that Allemand's description, to which he refers as the type of his petaurista, agrees more nearly with his ascanius than with that species; and the confusion, after all, may have arisen from his having figured the one from a living specimen,

and the other, as he himself informs us, from a prepared skin.

The disposition of the petaurista, or, as it is commonly called by English writers, the lesser white-
nosed monkey, is extremely gentle and even confid-
ing. Its manners are playful and engaging beyond
any other species we have ever observed, and it has
an amiability and innocence in its conduct and
expression, which, united to its lively and familiar
disposition, never fail to make it a prime favourite
with its visitors. An individual of this species, which
formerly lived in the gardens of the Zoological Society,
was confined in the same cage with a young hoonuman, *semnopithecus entellus*, whose gravity was
sorely disturbed by the unwearied activity and playfulness of its mercurial companion. Whilst the
white-nose was frolicing round the cage or playing
with the spectators, the hoonuman would sit upon the
perch, the very picture of melancholy and apathy,
with his long tail hanging down to the bottom; but
his attention was roused and his security endangered
every moment, by the tricks of the restless little
creature, which in its sports and gambols continually
caught by the hoonuman's tail, either to swing itself
out of the reach of the spectators, or, like a boy at his
gymnastic exercises, to assist it in climbing up to the
perch. All this, however, was done with great good-
nature on both sides, and it was highly diverting to
see the playful innocence of the one, and the gravity
with which the other regarded it, like a fond parent
enjoying the innocent follies of a favourite child.

The *cercopithecus nictitans*, or greater white-nosed
monkey, is easily distinguished from the petaurist or
lesser white-nose, not only by its larger size and the
greater prominence of its nose, of which the point is
equally white, but likewise by its much darker

colours, the whole of the body and whiskers being black with white specks, only rather lighter on the under than on the upper surface, and pure unmixed black on the neck, legs, and tail. The naked part of the face is bluish-black, the upper eyelids flesh-coloured, the ears dark brown, and the palms of the hands and the soles of the feet perfectly black. We have likewise observed this species in the gardens of the Zoological Society. Though lively and good-natured it was neither so gentle nor so familiar as the petaurist, but seemed more nearly to resemble the mona in its temper and character, and sometimes showed itself both petulant and capricious.

Chapter XI.

The origin of the common English word *Baboon* is a matter of some uncertainty. Skinner and other etymologists content themselves with deriving it from the common vernacular word *babe*, without considering that the German *pavian*, the Dutch *baviaan*, the French *babouin*, the Italian *babbuino*, and the Swedish *babian*, are manifestly but different modes of writing the same term, which must consequently have had a common origin in all these languages. It appears to be in reality a diminutive of the term expressing paternity, which, under the various forms *abba*, *babbo*, *papa*, &c., is found in most European and some Eastern languages; and seems to have been originally applied in derision. But however this may be, it is ageed on all hands that the vulgar Latin word *papio*, applied to the baboons by the writers of the fifteenth and sixteenth centuries, is a cognate and equivalent term, introduced after the corruption of the Latin language, and derived from the same barbarous, or rather Eastern, source as those above enumerated. In our own language the word has been invariably restricted to the simiæ of the present group, as we have already seen that the terms *ape* and *monkey* were respectively appropriated to the two preceding; and in this respect the nomenclature of ordinary language offers a rare and valuable coincidence with the principles of scientific classification. The baboons, in fact, as that name is usually understood

and applied in the English language, compose a
group of simiæ exactly co-ordinate with the apes and
monkeys already described; distinguished from the
former by the equality of their members, their cheek
pouches, and ischial callosities; and from the latter
by the short robust make of their bodies and extremities, their tubercular tails, too short to execute the
functions usually assigned to that organ, and the
mountain rather than sylvan habitat which this conformation necessarily induces. The most prominent
of these traits of structure, the abbreviated or tubercular nature of the tail, is the idea usually attached
to the word *baboon*, and it is certainly the most prominent and characteristic attribute of the group;
since, as we have frequently had occasion to observe,
the comparative development of this organ, if not
the immediate cause, is, at all events, the most certain index of the habits and economy of these animals. The baboons, thus defined, comprise two
distinct genera, *Papio* and *Cynocephalus*, respectively confined, with one or two exceptions, to the
continents of Asia and Africa.

In pursuance of the plan which we have hitherto
followed in the present work, of describing the quadrumanous animals according to the order of their
geographical distribution over the surface of the globe,
we have, then, to introduce to the reader's notice the
genus *Papio*, the last and lowest of the groups
which inhabit the Asiatic continent and the great
islands of the Indian archipelago, and which appear
to occupy in these regions the situation which the
cynocephals fill in Africa. The name of macac, or,
as the French write it, *macaque*, hitherto applied to
these animals, is of barbarous origin, and, as far as we
have been able to learn, appears for the first time in
" Marcgrave's Natural History of Brazil" as the native
appellation of a kind of monkey found in Congo and

along the coasts of the Gulf of Guinea. Its application to an Asiatic species of a genus totally distinct from that to which the animal properly bearing it really belongs, is one of the many similar errors of nomenclature committed by the celebrated Buffon, at that time indeed unavoidable, from the very limited knowledge which naturalists possessed on the subject of specific distinctions, and especially from the confusion which reigned in the geographical part of zoology; even the species to which he applied it, however, must, as we have already seen, be removed to a different genus; and it consequently becomes necessary to provide the present group with a more appropriate name, which shall be less liable to misapplication. We have for this purpose chosen the term *Papio*, which was originally used to designate some species of the present group and of cynocephals, and therefore serves very well to express the relations which subsist between these two genera of baboons.

The genus Papio is very distinct from the semnopithecs and other quadrumanous forms which, like it, inhabit the most eastern parts of the old world, and fill the forests of Asia and the Indian isles. Of all other Asiatic simiæ it is the only genus, the animals belonging to which are provided with cheek-pouches,—a natural character, as we have often had occasion to observe, of marked influence upon the habits and economy of these animals, and which is alone sufficient to distinguish the papios from all the Asiatic species which we have been hitherto describing. The organs in question are, as far as we at present know, common to all the African simiæ, except the chimpanzee. Among the Asiatic species, however, they are confined to the genus papio, and the few species of cercopithecs hitherto confounded with it under the common name of macacs; and it is not a little singular that the simiæ of the two neighbouring continents should be thus definitely characterized and distinguished from one another. Such facts, however, regarding the geographical distribution, not only of species but of entire groups of animals, are of constant occurrence in natural history; and as they are amongst the most curious and important results which the study of this delightful science furnishes, when it is pursued in a proper philosophical spirit, their prominent development has been our principal object in keeping together those groups which nature has herself placed in the same habitat, and describing them in succession according to their geographical distribution, rather than in the presumed and somewhat arbitrary order in which they are generally placed, according to the supposed perfection or degradation of their organic structure. Nor is it less worthy of remark, that this genus, the only Asiatic group that participates in the zoological characters of the African simiæ, should likewise be the only one that intermixes with them in its natural habitats and geographical distribution; two species of the genus, at least, being found in the northern and eastern countries of Africa, and some of the cercopithecs, or ordinary monkeys of that continent, exhibiting the minor characters of the Asiatic papios. These generalizations, of such high interest to the scientific naturalist, will be more fully developed when we come to treat of the history of the species which have more immediately suggested them; in the meantime we proceed with the general history of the papios.

The cheek-pouches of these animals are of very considerable capacity, and are capable of being made the repositories of an astonishing quantity of illicit plunder, for this is too frequently the proper appellation of their contents; they extend some distance

behind and beneath the gums, and although not
obvious externally, except when distended with booty,
are very apparent when the mouth is opened and
examined within. The teeth are of the same general form and number as in the other simiæ; the
molars, at the same time, differ from those of the
semnopithecs, in not being worn or ground down by
the effect of detrition; their crowns, on the contrary,
are tuberculous, as in the generality of the African
monkeys, though, like their congeners of the Asiatic
continent, the papios have the additional or fifth
lobe on the last inferior molar; a character, however,
by no means exclusively confined to the Asiatic
monkeys, nor even, as has been hitherto supposed,
to the baboons, among the African, being equally
found in the mangabey (*cercopithecus fuliginosus*),
and probably in various other cercopithecs. This,
though a very minor modification indeed, has been
much insisted upon by M. F. Cuvier and others, as an
important zoological character; but, without taking
into account its entire want of influence upon the
habits and economy of animal life, in the absence of
which it could scarcely be considered a scientific
character at all, its value, even as a practical diagnosis, is greatly impaired by the fact just stated,
and we must seek in other and more exclusive characters for a definite distinction between the papios
and the cercopithecs. Still we would not be understood as desirous to depreciate the character in
question beneath its actual value, or as anxious to
exclude it altogether from the generic diagnoses of
the genus Papio; our only wish is 'to reduce it
to its just and proper standard as a subordinate or
secondary character, and to deprive it of the exaggerated consequence which has hitherto attached to
it. In so far as we have any certain knowledge upon
the subject, it is universally found among the papios,

and but partially among the cercopithecs; consequently, if not absolutely exclusive, it is at all events
generally so, and may therefore be relied on, in most
cases, as a good practical distinction between the
species of these two genera. The canine teeth of the
old male papios acquire a very considerable development, and, as we shall presently see, combine with
their other characters to degrade them sensibly in the
scale of existence, and adapt them to a life more nearly
resembling that of the inferior quadrupeds.

But the principal distinction between these animals
and the cercopithecs consists rather in the general
but gradual modification of the whole structure than
in the predominant development of any one part or
organ. Their limbs are shorter and stouter, their
whole bodies more robust and powerful, than those
of the African genus; their faces, instead of being
short, round and flat, are prolonged as in the other baboons, only that the nose, instead of being similarly
produced and truncated, is formed like that of the ordinary simiæ; the eyes are surmounted by large and
prominent superorbital crests, which project markedly
beyond the orbits, and give them that deep-set, malicious cast, which distinguishes the baboons above all
other simiæ; their callosities are unusually large;
and their tails, instead of being long and muscular,
as in the semnopithecs and cercopithecs, serving, as it
were, the purpose of a rudder and balance to direct
and steady their motion or equilibrium, are, generally
speaking, tuberculous, or, at all events, short and lax,
and never enter as an efficient instrument into the
function of locomotion. Even those species which
have this latter organ of considerable length, as, for
instance, the rhesus and the wanderoo, never carry it
stretched out horizontally, as those species do which
make a constant use of it in the act of progression,
but keep it hanging down in a vertical direction

Y

like the tails of ordinary quadrupeds. Generally
speaking, however, the tails of the papios are short,
sometimes merely tuberculous, and at other times
altogether wanting; and this circumstance, combined
with their whole external figure, their squat, robust
bodies, and short, muscular limbs, was the reason why
the older systematic naturalists united them with the
cynocephals—a genus to which they unquestionably
bear a much nearer resemblance, as well in form as
in manners and intelligence, than to any other group
of quadrumana. Even in external form, their chief
distinction lies in the less truncated figure of the
snout, and in the nose not projecting beyond the
lips; but they have the same compact, powerful
make, the same short, robust members, the same prominent superciliary crests, the same deep-sunk eyes,
and, as we have just seen, the same abbreviated or
tuberculous tails.

The real difference which exists between the papios and cercopithecs, and the true nature and value
of the characters which distinguish these two genera
from one another, have been hitherto but vaguely and
imperfectly appreciated by zoologists; so much so,
that whilst some have questioned the propriety of
their separation at all, others have subdivided them
into numerous inferior or intermediate groups: few
or none could tell where the one genus ended and
the other began; and, indeed, the purely arbitrary
character of these groups, as at present constructed,
renders it a matter of impossibility to do so. We
have already had occasion to point out the insufficiency of the principles derived from the facial
angle and from the additional tubercle on the last
inferior molar tooth, as characters whereby to distinguish the different genera of simiæ, not only from
their entire deficiency of influence upon the habits
and economy of animal life, but likewise from the

error and confusion resulting from their practical application. Yet these have been, hitherto, the only characters employed to differentiate the papios from the cercopithecs; and it is to the prevalence of these vague and insufficient principles that we must attribute the very loose and confused ideas which still subsist among the best zoologists, with regard to the true nature and limits of these two genera. Naturalists, by that instinctive, but often indefinable, power of discrimination which resides in the eye, could at one glance perceive the generic difference of the magot (*papio inuus*) and the roloway (*cercopithecus Diana*), or of the maimon (*papio nemestrinus*) and the white-nose (*cercopithecus petaurista*), for example; but they have hitherto failed to embody this perception in a precise and logical definition, or indeed to detect the influential zoological character which is the true primary cause of the generic difference. Hence all the hesitation, doubt, and confusion with respect to these two genera; hence the unnatural and purely arbitrary genera *inuus, cercocebus*, &c. which have been successively proposed to be detached from either group as a means of removing the evil, and successively rejected as insufficient for that purpose, demonstrating at once the consciousness which zoologists entertained of the defects here mentioned, and their inability to remedy them. The truth is, however, that they had not carefully studied the habits and economy of the two groups, or the nature and value of the characters upon which their distinction depends. These do not consist in the greater or less opening of the facial angle; for, independent of the insufficiency and perfectly unscientific nature of that diagnosis, all the larger cercopithecs have the muzzle as much prolonged as any of the papios; neither do they depend upon the additional tubercle on the last inferior molar of the same genus,

since this character has been shown to exist in the
mangabey (*cercopithecus fuliginosus*), and is most
probably common to other species of the larger cercopithecs.

Where then, it may be asked, are we to find the
real distinction which exists between these two
genera ? Long and careful observation of the living
animals, and an attentive study of their habits and
actions, have at length enabled us to solve this difficulty, and to place the generic distinction of the
papios and cercopithecs on the purely scientific basis
of prominent and influential characters, respectively
peculiar and appropriate to either genus. It is, in
fact, in the function executed by the tail, and in the
consequent modifications which this organ necessarily undergoes in each of these genera, that the
real and zoological distinction between them actually
consists ; and it was a vague and confused apprehension of the influence and importance of this character that suggested to Baron Cuvier the idea of
his proposed genus *inuus*, which, by his own showing, differs from the macacs only in the tuberculous
nature of the tail. Upon the same principle Baron
Cuvier ought to have included in his genus *inuus* not
the magot alone, but likewise the *papio niger* of the
Philippines, the two species described by his brother,
M. F. Cuvier, under the names of *macacus maurus*
and *macacus speciosus*, and a new species (*papio Japonicus*), recently brought from Japan by Dr. Seibold. All these have tuberculous tails as well as the
magot : in the maimon and bhunder (*papio nemestrinus* and *papio rhesus*) that organ is but little
more developed ; whilst in the wanderoo and gelada
(*papio silenus* and *papio gelada*), the only species in
which it acquires any length, it never reaches beyond
the houghs, nor is it ever employed to assist the progressive motions of the animals, as among the cerco-

pithecs. These species, therefore, cannot be separated with any kind of propriety from the first-mentioned papios merely on account of their tails; that
organ, though rather more developed in the wanderoo
and rhesus than in the magot and papio niger, is
still greatly abbreviated, as compared with the tails of
the cercopithecs, and entirely devoid of influence as
an element in the habits and economy of animal life.
But there are other species, hitherto associated with
the papios above enumerated, and even considered as
the typical species of the genus *macacus*, in which
this organ acquires a much greater development and
executes much more important functions. In the
species, for instance, to which Buffon originally appropriated the name of macaque, the *macacus cynomolgus* of more recent writers, in the bonnet Chinois
(*macacus radiatus*) of the same author, and in the
two allied species, *macacus carbonarius* and *macacus
pileatus*, the tail is comparatively as long as in any
of the cercopithecs, and is equally influential upon
their actions as an efficient and powerful instrument
in guiding and steadying their motions during rapid
progression. There is, consequently, no real difference, in this respect at least, between these presumed
macacs and the larger cercopithecs; and an attentive examination and comparison of all these species
will show that their minor characters and habits are
in equal accordance; all have the same lengthened
muzzles and prominent superciliary crests, the same
long muscular and efficient tails, and the same irritable and petulant tempers : they are all of medium
size, none of them ever acquiring the massive proportions of the true papios and many of the acknowledged cercopithecs, as, for instance, *cercopithecus
albogularis*, *ruber*, and *dilophus*, being considerably
larger than the species in question, and all inhabit
the forests, live entirely upon wild fruits, and seldom

or never descend to the surface of the earth. The
real papios, on the contrary—those species, namely,
in which the tail, from its abridged dimensions, is
deficient in power to direct or control the motions
of the animal—are, more properly speaking, a terrestrial than an arborial genus; they reside among the
rocks and mountains more commonly than in
wooded localities, acquire massive and robust proportions, in old age especially, and devour frogs,
lizards, and large insects, as readily as vegetable substances.   In short, they perfectly resemble the cynocephals in their habits and economy, and are only to
be distinguished by the form of the nose and the
comparative elongation of the muzzle.   They are, in
reality, the baboons of Asia, as the cynocephals are of
Africa; and, with that genus, constitute a very
marked and natural group or sub-family of simiæ,
readily distinguishable from the monkeys by the tuberculous form and powerless character of the tail,
and from the apes by the equality of the pectoral and
abdominal members and the possession of cheek-
pouches and naked callosities.

Thus restricted and defined, the genus papio becomes at once simple, natural, and intelligible; its
characters embody a definite and tangible idea, instead of the vague and contradictory notions which
they have hitherto conveyed; and this is unquestion-
bly the best and most important test of a natural
group.   The genus papio, therefore, as here circumscribed and characterized, is as definitely and as readily distinguished from cercopithecus as from any of
the other genera of simiæ.   The confusion which has
hitherto prevailed in respect to these two groups
arose, as we have just shown, from a misapprehen-
sion of their respective influential characters, and the
consequent association of the common macac, bonnet-
monkey, and other species bearing all the characters

of true cercopithecs, with the real papios; the separation of these anomalous species, and their union
with their true congeners, the cercopithecs, at once
puts an end to the confusion, and establishes the respective genera upon a secure and natural basis.
Even the most minute and trifling characters of the
animals confirm the propriety of this approximation;
the hair of the cercopithecs is, generally speaking,
beautifully annulated with rings of different colours,
and the same character is very apparent, though perhaps not quite to the same extent, in the fur of the
macacus, or rather *cercopithecus cynomolgus* and the
other allied species; the hair of the true papios, on
the contrary, is perfectly plain and uniform. In this
respect, likewise, the papios differ from the cynocephals, which have the varied and annulated coats of
the cercopithecs; but the resemblance which they bear
to these animals, in their more important relations,
are more striking and material. Each group is divisible into two analogous subgenera, according to
the comparative development or tuberculous form of
the tail; thus the *cynocephalus papio*, *anubis*, *porcarius*, *sphynx*, and *hamadrias*, correspond to the
gelada, the *wanderoo*, the *maimon*, or pig-tailed
baboon, and the *bhunder*, among the papios; whilst
the tailless species of the latter genus are represented
by the drill and the mandrill of the former.

The habits and manners of the papios are in accordance with these physical characters, and correspond more nearly with those of the cynocephals than
with those of the cercopithecs and ordinary monkeys.
In youth they are sufficiently gentle, though at all
times irascible and ready to take offence at the slightest
provocation; even pointing the finger or laughing at
them is sufficient to rouse their anger, but they are as
readily appeased as excited, and as prompt to forget as
to revenge an insult. Less lively and playful than the

cercopithecs, they are equally petulant and mischievous ; less curious, they are equally intelligent, and are
more frequently employed as mimics by the itinerant
showmen than any other species of the monkey tribe.
The females and young males are sufficiently obedient and easily taught to comprehend and execute
any simple act, but in old age they become morose,
sullen, and malicious, lose their docility, if not their intelligence, and grow equally insensible to blows or caresses.   Indeed, they will permit neither the one nor
the other, but exhibit a frightful spectacle of savage
irritability and sulkiness.   To this very unamiable intellectual character they add the most disgusting
manners in other respects ; their lubricity is of the most
revolting description, and they would almost seem to
take a pride in displaying it in its most loathsome
form : in short, these animals offer an assemblage of
all the most unamiable and brutal qualities, developed
in their darkest and most repulsive colours, and it is
often difficult to say whether their persons or their
manners are more offensive to the spectator.   Even
the females, at certain periods, though always of a
more gentle and obedient disposition than the males,
assume the most disgusting appearances, and become,
if possible, more revolting in their manners and habits
than the other sex.   Thus we find that degradation
of physical structure is universally accompanied by a
corresponding degradation of the intellectual and
moral qualities ; and that the lower we descend in the
scale of organic life, the lower we likewise descend
in the scale of mental excellence.

    The papios, of all the other simiæ, are the only
ones which have propagated their species in confinement* ; another mark, probably, of their general infe-

    * We have since had an opportunity of seeing a young cy-
nocephal, which was recently brought forth in the menagerie
of the Jardin des Plantes.

riority to the rest of their tribe, and of their nearer approximation to the ordinary quadrupeds. The young, after a gestation of six or seven months, are brought forth with all their senses in considerable perfection. For the first fortnight they remain constantly suspended to the mother's breast, with the mouth continually applied to the nipple, and holding themselves firmly attached with their hands, by means of the surrounding hair. They soon afterwards begin to look about and take notice of what is passing around them, and, from the first attempts which they make at walking or leaping, display an address and agility which might well be mistaken for the result of long experience : they seem, especially, to have a wonderful facility of transferring to the eye, ideas of which we are generally in the habit of ascribing the origin to the sense of touch, and measure distances at a glance and with a precision which is truly astonishing to the student of mental phenomena. M. F. Cuvier supposes that this fact announces that nature has provided the young monkey with a peculiar instinct which she has denied to the young of the human species ; but there is really nothing in the action to countenance so extravagant a supposition, or which cannot be satisfactorily explained upon more ordinary and philosophical principles. The simple fact, as we apprehend, is, that the young monkey, like the young of all the other inferior animals, is brought into the world with its organs, both of sense and motion, more completely developed than those of the human infant, and consequently in a more fit state to execute their several functions, whether of acquiring a knowledge of the qualities and relations of surrounding objects, or of performing the acts of locomotion and prehension. This being the case, it follows, as a matter of course, that it will sooner learn to distin-

guish things and perform actions, simply because its
sensorial and muscular apparatus are so far advanced
towards perfection as to enable it to do so, and not
by virtue of any peculiar instinct or faculty in the
mind.　It is the rapidity alone with which the knowledge is acquired, and the actions performed, which
has surprised M. F. Cuvier ; and it must be admitted
that a fortnight's time is quite short enough for the
young monkey to obtain a degree of strength and intelligence which it requires many months to develop in
the human infant ; but here we apprehend there is an
error in the comparison, since man is in this respect
an exception to all other animals, inasmuch as he is
brought into the world in a much more imperfect
condition ; and this state of things would seem to
have been wisely arranged by the Almighty for the
purpose of affording time for the development of
that moral character, which, in his case, has been
superadded to the ordinary intellect of other creatures.
Were we, however, to examine the young monkey
immediately or shortly after birth, there is no doubt
but that it would be found as deficient in knowledge
as it unquestionably is in experience ; nor do we see
anything in the phenomenon, which has so much
surprised M. Cuvier, more extraordinary than may
be daily observed in a young calf or foal.

The papios, as they approach more nearly than
any of the monkeys to the form and structure of
ordinary quadrupeds, so likewise do they more nearly
resemble them in their habits and manners.　They
go more frequently on all-fours, and with greater
ease and facility, than either the semnopithecs or
cercopithecs ; this indeed seems to be their most natural and appropriate pace, as it is likewise of the cynocephals, so nearly related to them in other respects ;
and, like these latter animals, they are more frequently found upon the ground, or among the rocky

precipices of mountainous countries, than in the woods and forests, or among the branches of trees. Their habits are, of course, in both instances, the effects of organization; the robust, powerful forms, and short, muscular limbs of the animals qualifying them for a mountain, rather than for an arborial life; a circumstance farther promoted by the defect of the long movable tail which performs so conspicuous a part in the actions of the sylvan monkeys.

The habitat of this genus extends over the whole of Asia and the northern and eastern provinces of Africa. The former continent may, however, be considered as the head quarters of these animals, two species only being found in the latter, whilst there are no fewer than seven, if not more, spread over the peninsulas of India and Malacca, and the great islands of the Eastern Archipelago. Five species are said to be inhabitants of continental India alone, of which however, this habitat is doubtful as regards some of them; the wanderoo (*papio silenus*) is said to be found both on the coast of Malabar and in the island of Ceylon; another species is known to exist in Sumatra, and most likely in the neighbouring islands also; and one (the *papio niger*) has been brought from the Philippines. Other species doubtless exist, and may continue for ever unknown, in the impenetrable and hostile forests of Borneo, Celebes, and Sumatra. The papios are naturally divisible into two small groups, distinguished by the greater or less length of the tail, on the one hand, and its tuberculous form or total absence altogether on the other. To the former belong the gelada (*papio gelada*), the wanderoo (*papio silenus*), the bandar, or bhunder (*papio rhesus*), and the maimon (*papio nemestrinus*); whilst the magot, or, as it is often called, the Barbary ape (*papio inuus*), *papio niger*, *papio maurus*, and *papio speciosus*, are either

altogether destitute of this organ, or have it developed only in a tuberculous or rudimentary form.
We shall select some of the most interesting species
from each of these groups for the purpose of more
detailed description.

The Bhunder (*Papio Rhesus*).

We select the rhesus as an example of the short-
tailed papios, not only because it is necessary to
clear up a good deal of confusion which has crept
into the common works on natural history on the
subject of this animal, but likewise because it is one
of those species which enjoy a very high religious
veneration among the worshippers of Brahma, and
become, in consequence of their connexion with the

history of that singular people, particularly worthy of notice. It is at all times an ungracious task to engage in rectifying the synonyma, or correcting the numerous errors which are daily creeping into this branch of natural history, either from the haste or ignorance of describers who consider everything, unknown to themselves, as equally unknown to the rest of the world, and recklessly impose new names and imperfect characters, which serve only to embroil and confuse everything that had been done before ; but, however unpleasing, the task is highly necessary ; and he who would benefit science must not shrink from undertaking it, either on account of the labour and difficulty attending its execution, or of the censure of contemporaries thereby implied, and sometimes unavoidably expressed. Delicacy and good feeling will of course dictate the propriety of conveying censure, when it is unavoidable, in language free from offence : the discussion of plain scientific truths ought never to affect the passions of the disputants ; and if the vanity of affected superiority sometimes leads men to speak in disparaging terms of the labours of their contemporaries, they are themselves the real sufferers in the end, and the reflection that they are as liable to error as their neighbours, ought to make them extremely cautious of indiscriminate blame. These reflections have been naturally suggested by the necessity under which we feel ourselves placed, in relation to the animal which forms the subject of the present article, of calling to account the great and justly celebrated Baron Cuvier,—a philosopher whose critical acumen and just appreciation of specific differences seldom led him into such mistakes,—as the original author of all the errors which have prevailed regarding the history and synonyma of the rhesus.

Edwards had described and figured a papio under the name of the pig-tailed monkey, which was principally distinguished by its short tail, naked and attenuated something like that of a hog. Buffon had afterwards met with and figured the same species under the name of *maimon*, at the same time expressly referring to Edwards's description ; and the identity of the two animals was adopted by Geoffroy St. Hilaire, Audebert, and other naturalists, the animal being introduced into the system under the specific name of *simia nemestrinus*. Buffon, however, had, in the seventh volume of the supplement to his great work, figured and described, under the names of *macaque à queue courte*, and *patas à queue courte*, another species, somewhat allied to the maimon or pig-tailed monkey, by the shortness of the tail, but very different in most of its other characters. This species Audebert afterwards figured and described, from a living specimen, under the name of *simia rhesus*, referring to the *macaque à queue courte* of Buffon as specifically identical. Thus the matter rested till the publication of the first edition of the " Règne Animal," in which Baron Cuvier considered the maimon of Buffon to be the same species described by Audebert under the name of rhesus ; and the authority which that work quickly obtained, spread the error so rapidly and extensively, that even so judicious an inquirer as M. Desmarest has adopted it without question, and it has since prevaded almost every book subsequently published on the subject. M. Cuvier appears to have been at that period unacquainted with either of the species in question, in a living state ; and the specific characters of all monkeys, depending, as has been repeatedly observed, so much upon physiognomical expression, are so liable to be effaced in prepared specimens, that it is almost impossible to observe them in museums.

This was probably the origin of Baron Cuvier's mistake ; and his brother, M. F. Cuvier, who afterwards described both species from living specimens, seems to have been so completely imbued with the same error, that he can scarcely get rid of it even with the animal before him. Both species, however, are frequently brought into this country; and no one who has ever seen or examined them with ordinary attention, could fail to recognize their specific distinction, or the truth and fidelity of Buffon's description, as applied to the pig-tailed monkey. In fact, they have scarcely a character in common, except the shortness of the tail, which is, however, invariably slender, pointed, and almost naked in the one, and uniformly thick and covered with rather bushy hair in the other. Besides this, they differ widely in habitat; the maimon being confined to Sumatra, and the rhesus inhabiting Bengal and the upper provinces of India.

The specific name of rhesus was invented by Audebert as a substitute for the objectionable compound epithet of *macaque à queue courte*, applied to the species by Buffon. The proper native name of the animal in Bengal and Upper India, however, is *bhunder*, or as it is sometimes written, *bandar* or *bender;* and by this name we shall beg leave to distinguish it, as the proper native names are always of high importance both to the traveller and zoologist, being frequently the only means of distinguishing the animals mentioned in books or met with in foreign countries. The *bhunder*, then, is of a mixed greenish-grey colour, on all the upper parts of the body, arising from each hair being marked with alternate rings of light dun and dark brown; the throat, breast, belly, and inner face of the arms and thighs are light grey, and the buttocks and back part of the hips and thighs bright red; the hair on these latter parts is longer than elsewhere, and its colour contrasting strongly with the sombre hue of the

surrounding fur, has acquired for these animals the
local Indian soubriquet of lall-saunt or red-rumps.
The skin of the face, ears, and hands is naked, and of
a clear copper colour, and the tail, as has been already
mentioned, is short, thick, and rather bushy; it is
habitually carried closely pressed against the person of
the animal—a character common to all the papios and
cynocephals, and which distinguishes them at the
first glance from the semnopithecs, cercopithecs, and
colobs.

M. F. Cuvier observes that the skin of the *bhunder*
is by nature extremely flaccid. "Even young individuals," says he, "already exhibit those pendent folds
of skin on each side of the breast, which are more generally the marks of old age in other monkeys, and the
breasts themselves, as well as the belly, soon assume
the same characteristic appearance. Hence it arises
that when the animal is fat, it acquires a rotundity or
corpulency of person almost monstrous; the breasts
of the female then become full and globular as in
the human species, the belly increases, and the face
swells out to such a degree that it is difficult to
recognize the features. Itinerant showmen take advantage of their knowledge of these circumstances to
fatten up the rhesus, and exhibit it to the public as
an extraordinary species of pygmy or orang outan, a
deception which the full breasts and rose-coloured
nipples of the animal go far to countenance." The
females differ from the males only in being rather
smaller and of a gentler disposition.

Compared with many other species, however, the
bhunder is at all ages of an obstinate, intractable temper, and in this respect, as well as in others, differs essentially from the maimon, or, as it ought more properly to be called, the *bruh*, this being its native name
among the Malays of Sumatra. We have always
found the latter species, even in old age, more amena-

ble to discipline and sensible of kind treatment than any other papios. It seems more readily to resign itself to its situation in confinement, becomes serious rather than sulky, and exhibits neither the obstinacy nor malice of its congeners. It is possible that in extreme age it may become as sullen and morose as the other papios; it is certain that it acquires at that period an appearance of hideous deformity from its extreme corpulence of body and deeply-sunk eyes; for in this species, as in all the papios, the body seems to continue to increase in dimensions throughout the entire period of the animal's life; but in adolescence, and still more in youth, it is no less certain that the bruh is both good-natured and intelligent. These qualities have procured it a high degree of respect among the natives of Sumatra, who are fond of domesticating the bruh, and have even contrived to turn its intelligence and docility to a better account than we find authentically recorded of any other monkey. Sir Stamford Raffles informs us that they teach it to climb the cocoa palms for the purpose of procuring the fruit, and that it selects the ripe from the unripe nuts with admirable discrimination, and plucks no more than its master desires. In reference to this custom, Sir Stamford, in his valuable paper on the Animals of Java, published in the 13th volume of the " Transactions of the Linnæan Society," proposes the specific name of *carpolegus* for the bruh, not being aware of its identity with the maimon and pig-tailed monkey of naturalists; but as Sir Stamford's own specimens, now deposited in the museum of the Zoological Society, fully establish this identity, the name of *carpolegus* must consequently be suppressed in favour of *nemestrinus,* which the animal has always borne among systematic zoologists. The observations which we have here made in relation to the natural manners

and disposition of the bruh, and which are derived
from a careful study of more than a dozen individuals, which have been exhibited within these
few years in the different British menageries, are
fully confirmed by what M. F. Cuvier has recorded
of the specimens described in his " Histoire Naturelle
des Mammifères."

We now resume the history of the bhunder.
Both this species and the bruh have occasionally
bred in the menagerie of the Jardin des Plantes ;
and, with the exception of the common macac,
(the *cercopithecus cynomolgus* of a former article,)
and the magot, most of which, it will be observed,
belong to the present genus, they are the only
monkeys, or indeed the only simiæ, which have been
known to breed in confinement.* The following is
M. F. Cuvier's account of this interesting event :—
" The young *rhesus*," says he, " of which I have
here given a figure, was produced on the 18th
of December, 1824, with all its senses perfectly
developed. I could not exactly ascertain the period
of gestation, but presume it to have been about seven
months, which was about the period I had remarked
in the instance of other species. Immediately after
being born, this young rhesus fixed itself to the belly
of its mother, holding her firmly by the fur with its
hands and feet, and applying its mouth to the nipple,
which it never quitted for fifteen days, unless to
change from one breast to the other, never altering
its position during the whole of that time, sleeping
when the mother was quiet, but never quitting its
hold even when asleep. Thus passed the first
fifteen days of its life, during which it made no
movements, except those of its lips and tongue for
the purpose of sucking, and of its eyes to see ; for,

* We have since seen at Paris, in October, 1837, a young
cynocephal, brought forth in that menagerie.

from the first moment of its life, it appeared to distinguish objects and to regard them attentively: it followed with its eyes the different movements that were made around it, and nothing announced the necessity of touch to inform it, not only of the effort which would be required to reach a distant body, but of the greater or less distance of these bodies from itself.

" The care and attention of the mother, in everything relating to the nurture and preservation of her infant, were as devoted and as provident as can be well imagined. She could never hear a sound or observe a movement without having her attention excited and her solicitude roused for its protection; its weight never seemed to impede her movements, which she managed so adroitly, that, in spite of their complication and variety, its safety was never for a moment endangered. At the end of about fifteen days, the little creature began to detach itself from its mother; and, from its very first attempt, displayed an address and a precision which could result neither from exercise nor experience, and which proved that all the theories which have been propounded, as to the absolute necessity of touch for exercising certain functions of sight, are illusory and unfounded. At first it fixed itself to the vertical bars of its cage, and climbed and descended them at will; but the mother's eye always followed it, and her hand was ever ready to support or assist it; after thus enjoying its liberty for a few seconds, it returned to its original position. At other times it would advance a few steps along the bottom of the cage, and from its first attempts, I have seen it voluntarily precipitate itself from top to bottom, and light with the utmost precision on its feet, then leap upon the bars and seize them with an exactness which at least equalled that of the mother herself. Presently the mother might be seen at times attempting to get rid of the trouble of nursing, though she never forgot her solicitude for the young one's safety, for no sooner did danger threaten, than it was again pressed in her arms, and the burthen and the trouble equally forgotten.

" In proportion as its powers were developed, the leaps and gambols of this little creature became perfectly surprising. I took a pleasure in examining it during these moments of gaiety, and I may say that I never knew it to make a false movement or a false calculation, or fail to arrive with the utmost precision at the very spot it intended. From this observation, I had an evident proof that a particular instinct guided it in judging of distances, and determining the degree of force necessary to accomplish a particular action. It is certain that, with the intelligence of man, this animal would have required numerous trials and multiplied attempts to accomplish what it here did perfectly well from the first, yet it was now scarcely a month old.

" It was only at the end of about six weeks that a more substantial nutriment than milk became necessary for the support of this young animal ; and then it was that I observed a new fact in the intellectual nature of these creatures. This mother, formerly filled with such tenderness, and animated with such solicitude,—which supported her young one constantly at her breast, and exhibited so much maternal love and affection that one would have imagined her more likely to feed it from her own mouth,—yet would not permit it to touch the least morsel of food, deprived it of the fruit and other things given to it, drove it away whenever it approached the vessel containing their common provisions, and hastened to fill her cheek-pouches and hands that nothing might escape her. Nor could these actions be traced to any other sentiment than

pure gluttony; she could not have been desirous of
compelling it to suck, for her milk was already dried
up, nor could she have feared that the aliment would
injure the young one, for it sought it of its own
accord. Hunger, however, made this little creature
extremely bold and adroit; the blows of the mother,
which, indeed, were never very heavy, were disregarded, and whatever care she took to drive it
away and possess herself of the whole, it always
contrived to steal a portion, which it retired to
devour in the farthest corner of the cage, always
taking care to turn its back to the mother,—a
precaution by no means useless, since I have seen
her more than once quit her own place, and go to
the other end of the cage to take out of its very
mouth the morsel it was eating. Except at meal
times, the mother never displayed these unnatural
feelings, but attended to all the wants and actions of
her offspring with the utmost care and affection.
The little creature itself perfectly distinguished those
who fed and caressed it, and showed no signs of
malice, or any other character of the monkey, except
in its vivacity and address."

On this very interesting extract, we shall only
observe that the conclusions which M. F. Cuvier
deduces from the early intelligence and precision of
action displayed by the young rhesus, seem scarcely
warranted by the premises, since he makes no
allowance for the more perfect development of the
senses and physical powers of this little animal as
compared with the human infant. This development of physical power is necessarily accompanied
by a corresponding development of the mental
faculties, and the animal being thus possessed of the
means, will consequently acquire experience with a
rapidity altogether unexampled in the case of man;
the very power of clinging for fifteen days to

mother's body, and the experience of the space between its different extremities therein acquired, appears sufficient to account for the knowledge of distance which so much surprised M. Cuvier.

With the exception of the hoonuman or entellus, the bhunder appears to be the only monkey found in Bengal and the upper provinces of India. This is confirmed by various travellers, as well as by Indian officers, with whom we have conversed upon the subject; and the report of Mr. Hodgson, that the *toque*, or bonnet-monkey, *macacus radiatus*, inhabits the great Saul forest and the lower provinces of Nepaul, most probably originates in some mistake. The following account of the bhunder is given by Captain Williamson in his magnificent and valuable treatise on the "Wild Sports of India:"—"The common kind of monkey," says he, "which is found almost everywhere, is the bhunder, or woodman. These, when erect, may measure about two feet in height; they are docile and affectionate. Under the tuition of the jugglers, who, among many other curious matters, exhibit a variety of tricks done most naturally by the bhunders, it is very diverting to see these little mimics counterfeiting the gait and motions of various professions, and especially corroborating by their actions the deluge of flattery which the jugglers pour forth in praise of everything relating to the English character. Their antics are so excellently just on these occasions, that many human professors of the mimic art might, without the smallest disparagement, take a lesson from these diminutive imitators.

" In many places there are established revenues allotted for feeding whole tribes of bhunders. These generally depend on a *faukeer*, or mendicant priest, or on a *milky*, who has lands bestowed upon him by some bequest as an object of charity. These, having either a small hut, or being attached to some particular mausoleum, erected in honor of their bene-factor, maintain themselves and the bhunders by an appeal to the charity of travellers, who, pleased with the familiarity of the monkeys, rarely fail to bestow a few *pice*, or small copper coin, part of which is disbursed at the shop of a neighbouring vendor of provisions, who always resides near such a scene of regular consumption in that line. The monkeys are very orderly, coming when called, and never molesting any person. It has, indeed, happened that the pensioners have taken offence at mere trifles, and done some mischief; their bite is very severe, and they display uncommon unanimity and perseverance in their resentments."

This account is confirmed by Mr. Johnson in his " Indian Field Sports." We shall extract his ob-servations, because they are not only interesting in other respects, but likewise because they contain an example of the high veneration with which the natives regard these animals, and the danger which Europeans sometimes incur in imprudently molesting them. " At Bindrabun," says he (a name which I imagine was originally *Baunder-bund*, literally signifying a jungle of monkeys), " a town only a few miles distant from the holy city of Muttra, more than a hundred gardens are well cultivated with all kinds of fruit, solely for the support of these animals, which are kept up and maintained by religious endowments from rich natives. There are thousands of monkeys in and about that place; and it is rather strange that I should never have seen among them any of the hunaman tribe; they are all small brown monkeys, such as accompany jugglers, and which, I believe, are the most sagacious of any. When I was passing through a street in Bindrabun, an old monkey came down from the branches of a tree we were passing under, and, pulling off my *hurcharrah's* turban, as he was running in front of the palanquin, decamped with it over the roofs of some houses, where it was impossible to follow him, and was not again seen."

" I once resided a month in that town, occupying a large house on the banks of the river belonging to a rich native; it had no doors, and the monkeys frequently came into the room where we were sitting, carrying off bread and other things from the breakfast table. If we were sleeping or sitting in a corner of the room, they would ransack every other part. I often feigned sleep to observe their manœuvres, and the caution with which they proceeded to examine everything. I was much amused to see their sagacity and alertness. They would often spring twelve or fifteen feet from one house to another, with one or sometimes two young ones under their bellies, carrying with them also a loaf of bread, some sugar, or other articles ; and to have seen the care they always took of their young would have been a good lesson to many mothers. Whilst I was stationed at Muttra, two young officers on a sporting excursion at Bindrabun, imprudently fired at a monkey, which enraged the inhabitants, fakeers, and other Hindoos of the place, to such a degree, as to cause them to assemble in a large body : they pelted the gentlemen and the elephant on which they rode, with bricks and other missiles, and drove them into the river, where they were both drowned as well as the driver; the elephant was saved and landed about six miles down the river without the *howdah* or any of the tackling. It being well known that all Hindoos have a religious veneration for these animals, Europeans ought never to injure them ; humanity also dictates it, as the following circumstance which happened to myself fully shows.

" I was one of a party at Teecarry, in the Behar district; our tents were pitched in a large mango garden, and our horses picketed in the same garden, a short distance off from the tents. When we were at dinner, a *syce*, or groom, came to us complaining that some of the horses had broken loose, in consequence of being frightened by monkeys, and that, by their chattering and breaking off the dry branches of the trees in leaping about, the rest would break loose if they were not driven away. As soon as dinner was over, I therefore went out with my gun to drive them off, and fired with small shot at one of them, which instantly ran down to the lowest branch of the tree, as if he was going to fly at me, stopped suddenly, and coolly put its paw to the part wounded, covered with blood, and held it out for me to see: I was so much hurt at the time that it has left an impression never to be effaced, and I have never since fired a gun at any of the tribe. Almost immediately on my return to the party, the syce came to inform us that the monkey was dead; we ordered him to bring it to us, but by the time he returned the other monkeys had carried off the dead body, and none of them could anywhere be seen.... I have been informed by a gentleman of great respectability, on whose veracity I can rely, that, in the district of Cooch Bahar, a very large tract of land is actually considered by the inhabitants to belong to a tribe of monkeys which inhabit the neighbouring hills, and when the natives cut their different kinds of grain, they always leave about a tenth part piled in heaps for the monkeys;" (which would thus appear to have a prescriptive, at least, if not a divine right, to tithes; and it seems that they insist upon receiving them in kind, for it is added, that) " as soon as their portion is marked out, they come down from the hills in a large body, and carry

z

off all that is allotted for them, stowing it under and between the rocks in such a manner as to prevent vermin from destroying it. On this grain they chiefly live; and the natives assert that, if they were not to have their due proportion, in another year they would not allow a single grain to become ripe, but would destroy it while green."

The WANDEROO (*Papio silenus*).

The wanderoo, if the species to which that name is generally applied be really the same as that originally described by Knox, in his "History of Ceylon," of which there seems great probability, would appear to be an inhabitant of that island and the neighbouring peninsula of India, though it is rather singular that we have been unable to find it mentioned in the works of any modern

traveller. M. F. Cuvier informs us, on the authority
of M. Duvaucel, who, however, only saw the species in the menagerie of Barracpore, that the Indians call this animal *nil bandar*, or, perhaps more
properly, *nyl* or *neel bhunder*, signifying the dark-
blue or black bhunder, but this evidently refers
merely to the colour of the hair, and can scarcely be
the real name of the animal, which, not being a
native of Bengal, is not likely to have a Bengalee
name. The whole body of the wanderoo is of a jet
black colour, as are likewise the naked face and
paws; the tail is rather short and tufted at the
extremity, and the face and neck are surrounded by
a long dense mane of greyish-dun hair, which bears
some resemblance to a judge's wig, and gives the
creature a corresponding look of wisdom and importance, which, united to its habitual gravity, is
sometimes indescribably ludicrous. This mane
forms so remarkable a character, that the wanderoo
has never been either mistaken or confounded with
any other species; an advantage which, as we have
had abundant opportunity to remark, few others of
the simiæ can boast. It is very frequently brought into
this country, but is chiefly remarkable for its large
mane and deep black colour; it is certainly a
handsome animal, but in its manners and disposition
differs in no respect from the rest of the papios.
Father Vincent Maria gives the following account of
the wanderoo in a state of nature :—" Four species
of monkeys are found on the coast of Malabar; the
first is entirely black, with shining hair and a white
beard which surrounds the chin, and measures
upwards of a palm in length. The other monkeys
entertain so high a respect for this species, that they
humiliate themselves before it, as if they seemed
capable of recognizing its superiority. The princes
and grandees hold these bearded monkeys in high

z 2

estimation, and indeed they appear to possess more
gravity and intelligence than the other species:
they are educated for shows and ceremonies, and
acquit themselves admirably." The homage here
described as being rendered to the wanderoo by the
other monkeys of Malabar may be all very true ;
but the good father mistakes the cause, as it is no
doubt paid to the physical and not to the moral
superiority of the animal, and is the effect of tyranny
rather than respect.

Two other species of papios, remarkable for the
short tuberculous character of the tail, have been
described and figured by M. F. Cuvier, under the
specific names of *macacus maurus* and *macacus
speciosus*. They are distinguished from one another
by the colour of the face, which in the former is
black, and in the latter of a deep rose-coloured red.
Of the black species we have no farther knowledge
than what we derive from M. F. Cuvier's description,
in which the animal is identified with the wood
baboon of Pennant; a species which has given rise to
considerable discussion, but which, we are satisfied,
ought rather to be referred to the drill (*cynocephalus
leucophœus*), as we shall prove when we come to
speak of that animal. It is much more likely that
the *petit cynocephale*, figured by Buffon in the 7th
volume of the Supplement to his "Histoire Naturelle,"
may be *macacus maurus* of M. Cuvier, though it
has escaped that gentleman's notice. The *macacus
speciosus* we have twice seen alive in this country,
but without being able to ascertain the exact locality
from which it had been obtained. Both specimens
were but semi-adult, and remarkably mild and good-
natured. It is probably to this or the black-faced
species that Father Vincent Maria refers, when he
says, " The third species of monkey found at Malabar
is of a cinereous colour, without a tail, or at least

having but a very short one ; it is docile and familiar, and readily learns anything that is taught it ; I had one given to me, which I was one day in the act of correcting, when its cries collected such a vast number of its wild kindred from the neighbouring forests, that I became afraid of some bodily injury, and to avoid their anger, was obliged to let my pet escape to the woods."

The MAGOT (*Papio inuus*).

We have selected this species as an example of the tailless papios, not only on account of the celebrity which it obtained among the ancient Greeks and Romans, by whom it was called *pithecus*, and whose knowledge of human anatomy appears to have been principally inferred from the dissection of this animal, but because it is, with one exception, the only known papio found in Africa; and thus forms, as it were, the connecting link which unites the simiæ of that continent with those of Asia, as well in regard to their organic relations as to their geographical distribution.   M. Geoffroy St. Hilaire, in his "Tableau des Quadrumanes," published in the 19th volume of the "Annales du Museum," among many other similar divisions which he has himself since seen the necessity of suppressing, proposes to consider the magot as the type of a distinct genus, under the name of *inuus ;* but as the only distinction is to be found in the absence of the tail, an organ which, in the papios, has no specific function even where it is most developed, and which we have seen gradually decreasing in length, till it is reduced to a mere tubercle, in the *papio maurus* and *papio speciosus*, and finally vanishing altogether in the present species and *papio niger*, there can be no

z 3

question as to the propriety of the learned French professor's subsequent suppression of this and his other proposed genera of monkeys; though, with a resolution worthy of a better cause, these are the very things which modern compilers seems most obstinately bent upon retaining and perpetuating; and we daily find books issuing from the press, in which the genus *inuus* and the genus *lasiopyga* are put forward as prominently and as confidently as the genus *colobus* or *semnopithecus*.

The magot, or, as it is often called, the Barbary ape, from being principally found in Northern Africa, is perhaps more celebrated than any of the other species of simiæ, not even excepting the orang-outan. When full grown it is about the size of a middling dog, and of a compact, powerful make. The general colour of the body is yellowish green, brindled or marked here and there with irregular stripes of brown, which, however, are only accidental, and arise from the hair of the part being shaded on one side so as to show the brown colour of its root. The face is naked, and of a livid flesh colour, but much wrinkled even in the young, and blotched with dirty brown spots of an irregular form; the cheeks, chin, and under parts of the body, are uniform dirty grey. The animal, like the rest of its congeners, has short robust legs, and prefers going on all-fours, in which position its compact form and defect of tail give it much the look of a small bear. When young it is docile and intelligent, and readily learns to mimic various actions, which makes it a favourite with the mountebanks, and it is accordingly seen frequently in the company of these modern peripatetics. As it becomes adult, however, the male magot grows less and less tractable or amenable to instruction, and finally ends by refusing to submit to any authority. Kindness and blows are then equally without effect to overcome the apathy and sulkiness of his disposition; as incapable of confidence as he is insensible to fear, the desire of liberty is, so to speak, the only sentiment which can stimulate him to activity, and when too strongly reminded of his captivity by neglect or ill treatment, he soon falls into a state of sullen fretfulness, which quickly brings on disease and terminates his existence. " On the contrary," to adopt the words of M. F. Cuvier, " if left in peace and quiet, he habituates himself to his confinement, but all activity is at an end: seated on his hind feet, with the elbows rested on his knees, and the hands hanging down, he follows those around him with an incurious if not a stupid look, and if not roused from this state of lethargy by the cravings of appetite, passes his life in an intermediate state between that of an animal and a vegetable: his vegetative functions still operate, but, except sensation, everything connected with intelligence seems obliterated.

" On the contrary," continues M. Cuvier, " the magot is, in a state of liberty, perhaps of all other animals that which unites in the highest degree vivacity of character with variety of sentiment, nor is there perhaps any other possessed of greater petulance or whose intelligence is more active or penetrating; and these qualities, united to their powerful organic structure, give them so decided a superiority over the other animals of the forest, that they soon gain the ascendancy, and reign as absolute tyrants in the districts where they establish themselves. United in large troops they cover the trees of the forests, openly attack whatever enemy they find themselves in sufficient force to oppose, and by their cries and restless importunity frighten from their haunts the more formidable beasts of prey; nor have they any other enemies to dread besides the middle-

sized cats, (the leopard, caracal, and similar species),
which, stealing upon them during the silence of the
night, ascend the trees in which they sleep, and kill
them before they are aware of their danger.....
The food most grateful to the magot in a state of
confinement is fruit, bread, or cooked vegetables,
particularly carrots and potatoes; but it habituates
itself to all sorts of nourishment, always smelling
whatever it suspects, or has not previously known.
When enraged, its jaws move with surprising rapidity,
its gestures become quick and violent, and it emits a
harsh, loud noise; it is, however, sufficiently mild
on other occasions. The natural sentiment which
makes it live in the society of its fellows, when in
the enjoyment of liberty, induces it, in confinement,
to adopt such small animals as are given to it for
companionship; it carries them everywhere about
with it, embracing and hugging them most affec-
tionately, and becoming furious at any attempt to
take them from it. We are assured that these animals
attend their young with a care and affection not to
be surpassed by the tenderest mother, and that they
bestow the greatest pains in keeping them clean and
neat."

So much for the manners of the magot, as observed
in confinement; its habits in a state of nature are
well described by M. Desfontaines, who had an
opportunity of studying them in the native country
of the animal. "The pithecus," says this gentleman,
" is found in the province of Constantia, in the
regency of Algiers, nor have I ever heard of their
being observed in any other part of Barbary. They
live in troops in the forests of the Atlas mountains
nearest to the sea shore, and are so common at
Stora that the surrounding trees are sometimes
covered with them. They live upon the cones of the
pine, sweet chestnuts, and the figs, melons, pistachio

nuts, and vegetables which they steal from the gardens
of the Arabs, in spite of all the pains taken to exclude
these mischievous animals. Whilst in the act of committing these thefts, two or three detach themselves
from the general body, and keep watch from the tops
of the surrounding trees or rocks; and as soon as
these sentinels perceive the approach of danger,
they give warning to their companions, who presently
scamper off with whatever they have been able to
lay their hands on.....The pithecus can walk
upright for a short time, but it supports itself with
difficulty in this position, which is not natural to it.
Its face is naked and much wrinkled, which gives
it an air of extreme old age, even before it is a
twelve-month old. Its cheek-pouches are not very
extensive; its eyes are round, fiery, and of great
vivacity; it has large callosities; but, instead of tail,
there is only a small cuticular appendix, scarcely six
lines in length. The nails are flattened as in man,
and it makes use of its hands and feet with great
address to seize whatever is offered to it, or even to
untie knots, which I have seen it do with great
facility. The colour varies from tawny to grey, but
always with a shade of green; in all those which I
have seen, a part of the breast and belly were
invariably covered by a large black patch, the skin
itself and not the hair being of this colour. In the
wild state, they generally bring forth only a single
young one; which, almost as soon as it is born,
mounts on the back of its mother, which it embraces
by the neck with its arms, and is thus transported
securely from place to place; sometimes, however,
it remains firmly attached to the breast."

That the magot, or Barbary ape, the *simia
inuus* of modern naturalists, was the *pithecus* of the
ancients, admits not of a shadow of doubt. Aristotle
characterises it in his brief manner, and mentions at

the same time a second species of monkey, which he calls *kebos*, and describes as similar to the *pithecus* in all respects, except the possession of a long tail. This kebos has been the subject of much discussion both among naturalists and commentators; and, till very recently, it must be confessed that the different conjectures which had been thrown out upon the subject had no better foundation than the fancy of their authors. Dr. Rüppell's late "Journey into Abyssinia," however, has at length made us acquainted with an animal, a second species of African papio, in effect only differing from the papio of Barbary by the possession of a long tail, exactly as Aristotle has described, and agreeing in every other essential character, even to the colour of the fur. This species is described in the " Neue Wirbelthiere " of the traveller just mentioned, under the native name of *gelada*, which it bears among the Abyssinians, and agrees so perfectly with Aristotle's characteristic description, as well as with the habitat of Æthiopia assigned by Pliny, that we have not the slightest hesitation in referring it to the much-disputed *kebos* of the former philosopher, of whose wonderful accuracy and discrimination this furnishes a new and most remarkable example. Buffon and others have identified the mona (*cercopithecus mona*) with the animal mentioned by the Greek philosopher; but, independently of the small size and singularly varied colouring of that species, which could never allow it to be confounded with the magot, it inhabits a different part of Africa, and comes to us only from the west coast, with the productions of which the Greeks were totally unacquainted. The case is different with respect to the *gelada* of Dr. Rüppell: that animal agrees with the magot in size, colour, and generic character, and is found in a country with which the ancient Greeks and Egyptians had constant commercial intercourse; this, however, ceased entirely after the fall of the Ptolemies, which accounts for the fact mentioned by Pliny, namely, that the *kebos* had never been exhibited at Rome save once, and that by Pompey the Great. Thus it turns out after all, that Aristotle was a more accurate naturalist than M. de Buffon, and less given to confound generic characters than even the great French Pliny himself. Nor is this the only instance by many which we could adduce, in which that extraordinary man has proved himself a better philosopher than his commentators. M. de Buffon, for instance, commits the gross mistake of supposing the young and old magot to be different species; and from a false reading of the passage in which Aristotle mentions the pithecus and kebos, attributes the same error to the Greek philosopher, whom he makes to describe the *cynocephalus*, (also mentioned in the same passage,) as being without a tail,—a thing which Aristotle certainly does not advance, though perhaps his words are a little equivocal. But whatever doubt can be reasonably entertained concerning the tail of the ancient *cynocephalus*, none can possibly attach to the rest of the description; the projecting muzzle and dog-like head, from which, indeed, the Greek name is derived, prove that the animal was a true cynocephal and not a papio, and no doubt can be entertained but that it was the same species which we find figured on the monuments of the ancient Egyptians.

The only other papio which it is necessary to allude to, is a species which has been brought within the last few years from the more remote islands of the Indian Archipelago; it is commonly said to be from the Philippines, and has been already incidentally mentioned in the commencement of this article. It is the *macacus*, or *cynocephalus niger* of authors, and is perhaps the handsomest species of the whole genus. The hair, as well as the skin and naked parts of the face and hands, is of the most intense black, and the cheeks are distinguished by two large projections or swellings, one on each side of the nose, which assimilate it in some degree to the cynocephals, most, if not all, of which are similarly characterised, and which was probably Baron Cuvier's reason for associating it with these animals under the name of *cynocephalus niger*. This animal, however, is very different from the cynocephals both in organic structure and in character. We have seen six living specimens within the last seven or eight years, and though all young, the projections on the cheeks were already well developed and common to both sexes; in both which respects, the black papio differs from the cynocephals, which have these swellings confined to the male sex, and only acquire them in advanced age. All these animals were mild, gentle, and playful, serious indeed but active, and perfectly familiar without being petulant. Their colour, proportions, and defect of tail, gave them a strong resemblance to diminutive bears. Two very large specimens, preserved in the museum of Leyden, are said to have been brought from Celebes. The same collection contains specimens of a tuberculous-tailed papio, brought from Japan by Dr. Seibold, but confounded with the *papio speciosus*, or *macacus speciosus* of M. F. Cuvier. It is, however, a very distinct species, and may be properly called *papio Japonicus*. The hair is as long and shaggy as that of a goat, whereas it is short, sleek, and glossy in the *papio speciosus*, as we have observed in the living animal; the tail is a short bushy tubercle about two inches in length, and the general colour of the fur, deep brown. A young specimen in the Paris Museum, also obtained by Dr. Seibold, has fine woolly fur of a dark brown colour, without any appearance of the grizzled or speckled character of *papio speciosus*. This species was long since briefly but accurately described by Kæmpfer.

CHAPTER XII.

CYNOCEPHALS—General Characters of the Genus—Enumeration and
Description of the different Species.

THE second genus of baboons, or, as they are more
properly called by scientific zoologists, *cynocephali*,
from the Greek words *kunos*, a dog, and *kephalos*, the
head, because their prolonged truncated muzzles
resemble those of dogs, compose a group of quadrumanous mammals very distinct from the apes,
monkeys, and even from the papios, which have preceded them in our general description of the simiæ ;
more nearly related to the inferior animals in their
organic structure, passions, and appetites, but greatly
superior to all common quadrupeds in their intelligence and mental resources. They form, in fact,
the last link in the chain of gradation which unites
the simiæ, properly so called, with the inferior tribes
of mammals ; but though greatly changed and
modified, their organs are still essentially the same
as in the apes and monkeys : notwithstanding their
comparative approximation to the common quadrupeds, their influential zoological characters still
retain the true quadrumanous type ; and their
structure, habits, and actions allow them to be
associated only with the simiæ.

The zoological name of this genus, *cynocephalus*,
of which we have already explained the signification,
is employed by Aristotle and other ancient writers
to denote a particular species of baboon, which
inhabits the countries around the Red Sea, and is
known to modern naturalists by the name of *cyno-*

cephalus hamadryas. The resemblance which it was
intended to express is, however, not peculiar to the
species originally so designated; it constitutes in
truth the most distinctive character of the present
group of baboons in general, and it is therefore with
great propriety that systematic zoologists have extended its signification, and applied it to the whole
genus.

Though the cynocephals differ widely from the
other generic groups of quadrumanous mammals,
and may be readily distinguished at sight, even by
those who are not much in the habit of observing
them, yet it has been found not a little difficult to
form such a simple definition of the genus as will at
once comprehend all the species belonging to it, and
definitely distinguish them from those which appertain to the proximate genus *papio.* This difficulty,
which, indeed, we have already found to be common
to most of the genera of quadrumana, at least as they
have been hitherto defined, arises from the fact that
the zoological characters of these groups have been
made to depend, not so much on actual differences of
organic structure, as on the different degrees or
modifications of the same structure which each
exhibits, and which, though readily seized upon by
the eye, are not so easily made intelligible to the ear.
It is a difficulty, indeed, which meets us at every step
in natural history, and which has given rise to much
of the error and confusion which so notoriously
encumber the science and impede the progress of the
student. Qualities which naturally address themselves to one sense are obliged to be explained through
the medium of another; vague and indefinite notions
are the necessary consequence; nor is there any other
means of avoiding the resulting evils than by accurate and correctly coloured figures—a desideratum
still felt, and, we fear, long likely to remain, in most

parts of mammalogy. Yet, notwithstanding this
difficulty of defining their limits and nature in the
present instance, the modifications in question are
of the utmost importance in studying the history and
structure of these animals, and exercise a powerful
and obvious influence upon their habits and economy.

The most marked and prominent of the characters
which more immediately distinguish the cynocephals
from the other simiæ, consist in the great prolongation of the face and jaws, and in the truncated form
of the muzzle, which give the whole head a close
resemblance to that of a large dog, and from which,
as already observed, the Greeks and Romans very
appropriately denominated them *cynocephali*, or
dog-headed monkeys. In the ordinary simiæ, the
apes and monkeys for example, which have the head
and face round as in the human species, the nose is flat,
and the nostrils situated in the superior plane of the
face, about half-way between the mouth and eyes, the
whole bearing no inapt resemblance to the physiognomy of a person who has lost the greater part of
his nose through disease : but in the baboons this
organ is prolonged uniformly with the jaws ; it even
surpasses the lips a little in length, and the nostrils
open on the under side of it, exactly as in the dog.
Here, then, there is a marked difference, both in the
form and development of the organ, from what we
observe in the apes and others of the higher quadrumana. The great length of the face detracts from
the size and capacity of the skull ; the organs of
mastication are strongly developed, to the pre-
judice of the brain and intellectual functions ; the
appetites of the brute prevail over the docility and
intelligence of the more noble animal principle ; the
facial angle, which has been pretty generally regarded
as a tolerably accurate measure of the cerebral and
mental capacity, is reduced to 30°, whilst it is never

less than 45° among the monkeys and papios, and in
the apes amounts even to 60° or 65°; and the
character of the cynocephals, as might be readily
suspected from these indications, is less docile and
intelligent than that of the kindred genera. To the
same prolongation of the face and preponderance
of the anterior over the posterior part of the head is
to be attributed, at least in a great measure, the fact
that the cynocephals less frequently assume the erect
posture than any of the other quadrumana, and even
when they do, are less capable of maintaining it for
any length of time. The weight of the long face and
muzzle, to which the diminutive size of the skull
forms but a very inefficient counterpoise, fatigues the
muscles of the neck, and constantly tends to make
the animal seek for support on all-fours, as may be
observed in a dog or a bear which has been taught
to dance, and in fact the cynocephals are in no
respect superior to these latter animals in the facility
with which they can maintain themselves in an
upright posture. Nor, though decidedly terrestrial
in their habits, do they often assume the upright
posture in a state of nature. The bear, when he is
alarmed or threatened, will stand up upon his hind
legs to defend himself; so likewise will the cynocephal; but the position is manifestly as constrained
and unnatural in the one case as in the other, and
neither of these animals resorts to it voluntarily,
unless under the circumstances just mentioned, or
occasionally for a few moments, to look around them
more easily than they can do on all-fours. Their
curiosity satisfied, they again drop upon the fore legs,
and proceed in the manner of ordinary quadrupeds.
The monkeys, it is true, do exactly the same thing,
but it must be remembered that they are properly
arborial animals, whilst the cynocephals are essentially
constructed for terrestrial progression.

The compressed and robust form of the body, and the short, muscular, and powerful nature of the limbs, are other characters which broadly distinguish the cynocephals, and exercise a very sensible influence upon their habits and economy. Generally speaking, the quadrumana are of a slender and active make, with long arms and legs, which adapt them for climbing and residing among the branches of trees; but the shortness of their limbs, and the weighty and powerful make of their bodies, whilst they do not entirely exclude the cynocephals from grasping and climbing trees, nevertheless render the woods and forests a less agreeable habitat to them than the precipitous sides of rocky mountains, where they live in large families, and climb among the cliffs with great ease and security. Their whole habits, indeed, as well as their organic structure, approximate these animals to the ordinary quadrupeds: the great development of their organs of smell; the position of the nostrils, which are more conveniently placed for the exercise of that function than in the other simiæ; the robust make of the extremities, and their equality in point of length; their gait; their habitat; the size and power of their canine teeth, and the nature of their food; all indicate their inferiority to the apes and monkeys. And as the habits of animals are necessarily derived from their organization, as the functions of an instrument depend upon the component parts of its structure, in proportion as the cynocephals are degraded in the scale of nature by their organic conformation, in the same degree do they participate in the intellectual inferiority and, if we may be allowed the expression, in the moral debasement of the common quadrupeds. Still, however, with regard to the general outline of their organization, they preserve much of the character of the other quadrumana; but it is only the worst part

of the mental and physical character of the apes and
monkeys which is exhibited in the cynocephals ;—
it is their malice and mischief, still further heightened
by an increase of physical force, without their playful and amusing curiosity ;—their humiliating approach to humanity, without the gentleness and
docility of their disposition.

In their native mountains, the ordinary food of the
cynocephals consists of wild berries and bulbous roots,
birds' eggs, insects, and in fact whatever comes in
their way that can be made eatable, without even
excepting lizards and small reptiles; but in the
vicinity of human habitations, they make frequent
incursions into the cultivated fields and gardens, and
destroy a still greater quantity of grain and fruits than
they carry away with them. In well inhabited countries, where they are likely to meet with resistance,
their predatory expeditions are usually made during
the night, and travellers assure us that, taught by
experience of the risks to which they are necessarily
exposed on such occasions, they place sentinels upon
the surrounding trees and heights to give them timely
warning of the approach of danger : but in wilder
and more solitary districts, where the thinness of the
population and the want of fire-arms place them on
some degree of equality with the inhabitants, they
make their forays in the open day, and dispute with
the husbandman the fruits of his labour. " I have
myself," says Pearce, in his *Life and Adventures in
Abyssinia*, " seen an assembly of large monkeys
(*baboons*) drive the keepers from the fields of grain,
in spite of their slings and stones, till several people
went from the village to their assistance, and even
then they only retired slowly, seeing that the men
had no guns." Some travellers even assert that if
the troop happens to be surprised in the act of
pillaging, the sentinels pay with their lives for their

neglect of the general safety, and it is certainly no
more wonderful that they should be punished in case
of neglect, than appointed in the first place; but
however this may be, it is certain that individuals are
frequently met with, which bear marks of ill usage
from their companions, and which even sometimes
appear to have been expelled from their society.
Others assure us that the troop sometimes forms
a long chain, extending from the vicinity of their
ordinary habitations to the garden or field which
they happen to be engaged in plundering, and that
the produce of their theft is pitched from hand to
hand till it reaches their retreat in the mountains.
By this union and division of labour, they are
enabled to carry off a much larger booty than if
every individual laboured for his own peculiar benefit;
but notwithstanding this attention to the general
interest, each takes care, before retiring, to fill his
cheek-pouches with the most choice fruits or grain
he can select, and also, if not apprehensive of being
pursued, to carry off quantities in his hands.   Thus
loaded the whole troop retire to the mountains to
enjoy their plunder.   They likewise search with
avidity for the nests of birds and suck the eggs; but
if there be young they kill them and destroy the nest,
as notwithstanding the manifest approximation of
their structure and appetites to carnivorous animals,
they appear never to touch a warm-blooded prey in
a state of nature, and even in captivity will eat no
flesh but what has been thoroughly boiled or roasted.
In this state we have seen various cynocephals enjoy
their mutton-bone, and pick it with apparent satisfaction; but it was evidently an acquired habit, like
that of drinking porter and smoking tobacco, which
they are often taught for the amusement of their
visitors.
    Of all the quadrumana, the cynocephals are the

most frightfully ugly. Their small eyes deeply sunk
beneath huge projecting eye-brows, their low contracted forehead, and the very diminutive size of their
cranium, compared with the enormous development
of their face and jaws, give them a fierce and sinister
look, which is still further heightened by their robust
powerful make, and by the appearance of the
enormous canine teeth which they never fail to display upon the slightest provocation. The fierceness
and brutality of their character and manners correspond with the expression of their physiognomy.
These passions are most strongly displayed by the
adult males; but it is more epecially when, in
addition to their ordinary disposition, they are agitated by the passion of love or jealousy that their
natural habitudes urge them to the most furious and
brutal excesses. In captivity they are often thrown
into the greatest agitation by the appearance of
young females. It is a common practice among
itinerant showmen, to excite the fury of the cynocephals, and display the natural jealousy of their dispositions, by caressing or offering to kiss the young
women who resort to their exhibitions, and the
sight never fails to provoke in the animals a degree
of rage bordering upon phrensy. On one occasion a
large cynocephal, of the species which inhabits the
Cape of Good Hope (*cynocephalus porcarius*),
escaped from his place of confinement in the "Jardin
des Plantes" at Paris; and, far from showing any disposition to return to his cage, severely wounded two
or three of the keepers who attempted to recapture
him. After many ineffectual trials to induce him to
return quietly, they at length hit upon a plan which
proved successful. There happened to be a small
grated window at the back part of his den, before
which one of the keepers presented himself in
company with the daughter of the superintendent,

2 A 3

whom he pretended to kiss and caress within view of
the animal. No sooner did the baboon witness this
familiarity, than he flew into the cage in the greatest
fury, and shook the gratings of the window violently,
endeavouring to undo the fastenings which separated
him from the object of his jealousy. Whilst employed in this vain attempt, the keepers seized the
opportunity of fastening the door and securing him
once more in his place of confinement. Nor is this
a solitary instance of the influence which women can
exert over the passions of these savage animals:
generally intractable and incorrigible whilst under
the management of men, it frequently happens that
the baboons are most effectually tamed and subjected
to even more than an ordinary degree of obedience
in the hands of women, whose attentions they even
appear to repay with gratitude and affection. Travellers sometimes speak of the danger which women
incur who reside in the vicinity of situations inhabited
by these animals, and affirm that the negresses on
the coast of Guinea are occasionally kidnapped by
the baboons, and carried off to their fastnesses in the
woods and mountains : we are even assured by wit-
nesses who testify to having seen the individuals,
that certain of these females have lived among the
baboons for many years, and that they were prevented
from escaping by being closely watched or shut up
in caves among the mountains, where, however, they
were plentifully fed, and in other respects treated
with great kindness. It must be observed, however,
that these accounts rest upon authority which is by
no means unexceptionable ; credible and well informed modern travellers do not relate them, and
even their older and more credulous predecessors
profess to give them only from hearsay. Not that
the facts are to be absolutely discredited on that
account ; they are too consonant with what we

actually know of the natural disposition and appetites of the cynocephals to be arbitrarily rejected as mere inventions; and the belief in their truth is besides too prevalent among the negro nations to be altogether without foundation.

In addition to the mental and physical characters already mentioned, the cynocephals, like the other baboons, besides the great development of their canine teeth, are distinguished by having a fifth tubercle or heel upon the posterior molar of the under jaw, in which respect they differ from the chimpanzees, orangs, and cercopithecs, and agree with the gibbons, semnopithecs, and colobs. They are moreover furnished with large ischiatic callosities and capacious cheek-pouches, and their tails, always shorter than those of the ordinary monkeys, never enter as efficient instruments into the functions of progression; but, though carried erect at the root, are afterwards allowed to hang down perpendicularly, at a little distance from the buttock and thighs, like that of a horse which has not been docked. Those species which have very short tails carry them upright and erect, as for example, the drill and mandrill; for, as regards the length of this organ, the cynocephals, like the papios, may be divided into two distinct subgenera, the one characterized by its moderate development, the other by its tuberculous form. Baron Cuvier, with less propriety than marks the generality of his generic divisions, separates these two minor groups for the purpose of forming them into distinct genera, in which, however, he has not been followed by his brother, M. F. Cuvier, by M. Geoffroy St. Hilaire, or indeed by any other naturalist intimately acquainted with the real characters of mammals. The mandrill and drill, of which M. Cuvier makes his second genus, are only distinguished from the other baboons, as the magot and some kindred

species are from the rest of the papios, by the shortness of their tails; and as this organ does not enter
into the function of progression, nor in any other
respect influence or modify the habits and economy
of the animals, its comparative development is consequently no real generic character, however useful
it may be as a specific mark or practical diagnosis.
We shall therefore follow the example of the most
judicious mammalogists in rejecting, as arbitrary and
artificial, the proposed division of Baron Cuvier,
and consider the cynocephals as composing a single
natural genus, divisible for practical purposes, as in
the parallel instance of the papios, into two minor
groups, distinguished from one another by the comparative development or brevity of the tail.

The cheek-bones of the cynocephals are remarkably
protuberant, and form large swellings on each side
of the nose; and though this character is more
strongly marked in the drill and mandrill than in
most of the other species, yet all exhibit it in a greater
or less degree. The use of this extraordinary development appears to be, by affording room for the
greater expansion of the pituitary membrane, and
enlarging the cavities of the nose and face, to increase
the power of the sense of smell, already carried to
such a predominant extent in other parts of their
structure, as to become in fact the most influential
and characteristic principle of their nature. All the
other details of their organization appear to be sub-
servient to this one object, so conducive to the habits
and economy of animals, which frequently depend
upon the sense of smell to direct them to the roots
and bulbs upon which they principally subsist, or to
enable them to distinguish between such as are
wholesome and such as are poisonous. But the protuberance of the cheek-bones here mentioned is not
absolutely confined to the cynocephals. Some of the

papios which approximate most nearly to the present
genus likewise exhibit the same development of
these parts; and it was probably this appearance
which induced Baron Cuvier to enumerate the black
papio of the Philippine Islands (*papio niger*)
among the cynocephali, though it differs from these
animals in all the other details of its structure.

It is only since the labours of the MM. Cuvier
and others have developed the true generic characters of the different groups which compose the
family of quadrumana, that we have become acquainted with the geographical distribution of these
animals and the habitats of the different genera.
We have thus learned that the simiæ of the African
continent are as distinct from those of Asia in their
zoological characters as they are in the localities
which they inhabit. In fact, amongst upwards of
fifty species of apes, monkeys, and baboons, which
inhabit these two continents, there is but a single
known instance of an Asiatic species occurring in
Africa, or of an African species occurring in Asia.
The instance to which we allude regards a species of
the present genus, the *cynocephalus hamadryas*
of zoologists, which is found in Asia as well as in
Africa, and which forms the only indisputable example
of any quadrumanous animal being common to both
these continents. In other respects, the cynocephals
are a strictly African genus; they inhabit all the
great mountain ranges of this continent, from the
shores of the Mediterranean to the Cape of Good
Hope, and are capable of supporting a much lower
degree of temperature than any of the other simiæ.
The lofty mountains of Samen, in Abyssinia, and the
bleak and desolate range of the Sneeuwberg, in South
Africa, are each tenanted by numerous troops of
these animals, which even appear to prefer the more
rigorous climate of these elevated regions to the hot

and sultry forests of the lower plains. Fischer, the most recent writer upon this subject, enumerates eleven different species of cynocephals, in his *Synopsis Mammalium;* but it is evident that some of those which he describes are the females or young of other species; and in fact the most judicious naturalists, those who describe from their own original observations, do not reckon more than seven or eight. The females indeed differ so much from the males in size and other characters, that it requires to be well acquainted with the animals in a living state, to distinguish correctly between their specific characters. The following species are very distinctly marked, and have been observed both in this country and on the Continent.

THE CHACMA (*Cynocephalus Porcarius*).

The colour of this species is a uniform dark brown, almost black, mixed throughout with an obscure

shade of deep green, darkest on the head and along
the ridge of the back, and paler on the anterior part
of the shoulders and on the flanks. The hair over
the whole body is long and shaggy, more particularly
on the neck and shoulders of the adult males, where
it forms something approaching to a mane; each
hair is of a light dun colour for some distance from
the root, and afterwards annulated throughout its
entire length with distinct rings alternately black and
dark green, sometimes, though but rarely, intermixed
with a few of a lighter or more yellowish shade.
The green predominates on the head more than on
the other parts; the face and ears are naked, as are
likewise the palms of the hands and soles of the
feet; the inner face of the arms and thighs is but
thinly covered with hair, which is, however, long and
of a uniform dark brown colour; the hair on the
feet and hands is short, bristly, and of an intense
black colour; and the cheeks are furnished with small
whiskers, directed backwards and of a greyish colour.
The tail is rather better than half the length of the
body, and terminates in a tuft of long black hair;
the skin of the hands, face, and ears is of a very dark
violet blue colour, with a paler ring surrounding each
eye; the upper eyelids are white as in the mangabey
(*cercopithecus fuliginosus*); the nose projects a little
beyond the upper lip; the nostrils are separated by a
small depression or rut, as in the dog and other
carnivorous mammals, and the callosities are less
strongly marked than in some other species of the
genus. In the adult animal the muzzle is extremely
prolonged in comparison to the skull, which is proportionally contracted and flattened: the young, on
the contrary, have the region of the brain much
larger in proportion to the length of the face, the
head considerably rounder, and in form more nearly
resembling that of the adult cercopithecs.

The chacma, so called from the Hottentot word *t'chackamma*, the aboriginal name of this baboon in South Africa, is one of the largest species of the present genus, and when full grown is equal in size, and much superior in strength, to a common English mastiff. It inhabits the mountains throughout the colony of the Cape of Good Hope, and associates in numerous families. Troops of three or four hundred individuals are often met with in the *kloofs*, or rocky mountain-passes of the country, stretched upon the sward and basking in the sun, or are heard screaming and howling from their dens among the rocks ; and it is amusing to see them, when disturbed by the approach of the travellers' wagons, scampering up the precipitous cliffs, yelling and chattering all the time, as if complaining of the unwonted intrusion upon their solitudes. Should the travellers *outspan*, or rest for the night, in their vicinity, they redouble their yells and clamour, and keep up such an incessant discord of screams and howls, as to banish rest, and make both men and cattle glad to get rid of the annoyance by renewing their journey with the peep of day. At other times they may be seen seated quietly on the tops of the distant rocks, gravely contemplating the train of the wagons, which pass beneath, or scrambling out of reach of the long *roer*, or rifle, with which the Dutch Cape boor is usually armed, climbing with facility up the face of cliffs to all appearance perpendicular, or hanging in mid-ascent suspended from the tough fibrous runner of a wild vine or some other creeping plant, whilst they look back upon what is passing beneath. These wild creepers abound everywhere in the precipitous dells and passes of the rocky mountains, frequently covering the entire surface of the cliffs by interlacing with one another like net-work, and, from the purpose which they serve the baboons in climbing the mountains, are in many places called monkeys' ladders. In the proper season they are clothed with the richest foliage and the most brilliant flowers; and there cannot be a more amusing or animating sight on a fine summer's evening, than to see the chacmas, like a troop of boys practising their gymnastic exercises, running up their slender stems, interspersed with innumerable proteas, geraniums, and other glories of the vegetable kingdom, whose varied and brilliant hues enliven the plains and mountains of South Africa. It is not always, however, that the pleasure of contemplating the movements of the baboons can be indulged without some degree of danger. These mischievous animals, if they observe the party to be unarmed, or as soon as they get beyond range of the guns, rally, and, in their turn, become the assailants, rolling down and throwing stones at the travellers, and sometimes rendering it not a little difficult to escape with safety.

There is no animal which the Cape dogs attack more wickedly, or against which they display so much real malice and hatred as the chacma. Whether it arise from the example of their masters, whose antipathy towards this disgusting caricature of humanity is extreme, or whether it be owing to personal ill-will towards a powerful, active, and malignant enemy, it is difficult to say; but the fact is indisputable, that the dogs will rather hunt the baboon than any other species of game: and yet they seldom escape from the encounter without paying dearly for their temerity. The sagacious and nimble animal, whose strength and powerful teeth make him more than a match for the largest mastiff, without taking into account his prowess and determined resolution, and the superiority which he derives from the prehensile power of his hands, either severs the carotid artery, which he well knows where to find, or seizing

the dog by the hind legs, swings him round till he is
quite giddy: if permitted to escape with his life after
such discipline, there are few dogs desirous of
renewing the experiment. Nay, the panther himself
is often foiled in his attack upon the chacma. Both
these animals live among the rocky and scrubby
mountains, and the females and young baboons are
the ordinary prey of the panther; but if he happen
to fall in with an adult or old male, he runs a great
chance of losing his supper and getting well thrashed
into the bargain. These qualities make the boors
cautious about hunting the baboon; indeed they
would, generally speaking, rather set their dogs upon
a lion or a leopard than upon one of these wily and
active animals.

Chacmas are still found upon the Table Mountains, above Cape Town, though they do not appear
to be so numerous as they were formerly. Still,
however, they pay occasional visits to the gardens
situated immediately at the foot of the mountain, and
conduct their enterprises with so much skill and
caution, that even the most watchful dogs, as we are
assured by Professor Lichtenstein, cannot always
prevent them or give intelligence of their presence.
" Although," he remarks, " Kolbe sometimes exagge-
rates the regular and concerted manner in which
their robberies are carried on, yet it is very true that
they go in large companies upon their marauding
parties, reciprocally to support each other, and carry
off their plunder in greater security." Their common
food consists of the bulbous roots of the *ixias
babianas*, a genus which derives its botanical name
from this circumstance, and other similar plants,
which are amazingly abundant among the flora of
South Africa; but they do not refuse the succulent
leaves of different vegetables, nor even young and
tender blades of grass, which we have ourselves seen

both this and other species of cynocephals, as well as papios, select and greedily devour. They dig up the roots with their fingers, and peel them carefully before eating them ; and heaps of these parings are frequently found near the large stones upon which they delight to sit for the purpose of sunning themselves or of viewing the surrounding prospect. Nor are they confined to a purely vegetable regimen. On the contrary, they greedily search after and devour different insects, such as locusts and scorpions, and it is highly amusing to witness the tact and cleverness which these intelligent animals display in depriving the last-mentioned dangerous insects of their formidable stings, before venturing to eat them. Even small reptiles are not rejected, and birds' eggs, grubs, and worms are a dainty treat. In short, their food and manner of life differ in no respect from that of the Bosjesmans, or original natives of the country which they inhabit; but with this advantage, that they do not feel the moral debasement and gross injustice which the unfeeling white men have exercised towards the poor outcast and persecuted savages.

It is of an individual of this species that LeVaillant, in his " *Premier Voyage dans l'Intérieur de l'Afrique*," has given so amusing and, in some instances, perhaps, so apocryphal an account, under the name of *Kees*. Kees was a young animal, and a deserved favourite with his master, whom he accompanied on his travels, amused by his tricks, and sometimes essentially served by his intelligence and sagacity. We must present our readers with a leaf or two out of the biography of Kees, in the words of the lively and entertaining French traveller, because, as far as we are aware, he has not been hitherto introduced to the English reader. " An animal," says M. Le Vaillant, " which often rendered me essential

services, whose presence has frequently interrupted or
banished from my memory the most bitter and harass-
ing reflections, whose simple and touching affection
even seemed on some occasions to anticipate my wishes,
and whose playful tricks were a perfect antidote to
ennui, was a monkey of the species so common at the
Cape and so well known by the name of *bavian*.   It
was very familiar, and attached itself particularly to me.
I conferred upon it the office of my taster-general ;
and when we met with any fruits or roots unknown
to ·my Hottentots, never ventured to eat them till
they had been presented to and pronounced upon by
Kees ; if he ate, we fed upon them with confidence and a good appetite ; if he rejected them, we
did so likewise.   The baboon has this quality in
particular, which distinguishes him from the lower
animals, and approximates him more nearly to man ;
he has received from nature equal portions of curiosity and gluttony ; without appetite, he tastes every
thing you give him ; without necessity, he touches
whatever comes in his way.   But in Kees I valued
a still more precious quality.   He was my best and
most trusty guardian ; night or day, it mattered not,
the most distant approach of danger roused him to
instant watchfulness, and his cries and gestures
invariably warned us of any unusual occurrence, long
before my dogs got scent of it.   Indeed, these otherwise faithful guardians became so habituated to his
voice, and depended so implicitly upon his instinct,
that they became utterly careless of their own duty,
and instead of watching our encampment, went to
sleep in full confidence ; but no sooner had he given
the alarm, than the whole pack were up and on the
alert, flying to defend the quarter from which his motions directed them to expect the threatened danger. ...
I often took him out with me on my hunting and
shooting excursions ; on the way he amused himself

by climbing the trees in search of gum, of which he was passionately fond : sometimes he would discover the honey-combs which the wild bees deposit in the hollows of decayed trees, but when neither gum nor honey were to be found, and he began to be pressed by hunger, an exhibition of the most comic and amusing nature took place. In default of more dainty fare, he would search for roots, and above all for a particular kind which the Hottentots call *kameroo* (*babiana?*), which he greatly admired, and which, unfortunately for him, I had myself found so refreshing and agreeable that I often contested the possession of the prize with him. This put him upon his mettle, and developed all his talents for *ruse* and deception. When he discovered the kameroo at any distance from me, he commenced devouring it, without even waiting to peel it, according to his usual custom, his eyes all the while eagerly fixed upon my motions; and he generally managed matters so adroitly as to have finished the banquet before I reached him : occasionally, however, I would arrive rather too soon for him; he would then break the root and cram it into his cheek-pouches, from which I have often taken it without his displaying either malice or resentment, at what he must have considered as an act of great injustice. To pluck up the roots, he resorted to a most ingenious method, which greatly amused me. Seizing the tuft of leaves with his teeth, he dug about and loosened the root with his fingers, and by then drawing his head gently backwards he commonly managed to extract it without breaking; but when this method failed, he would seize the tuft as before, and as close to the root as possible, and then, suddenly turning a somerset he would throw himself head over heels, and the kameroo rarely failed to follow.

" On these little expeditions, when he felt himself

fatigued, it was most ludicrous to see him mounting
upon the back of one of my dogs, which he would
thus compel to carry him for hours together. One of
the pack, however, was more than a match for him,
even at his own weapons, cunning and finesse. As
soon as this animal found Kees upon his shoulders,
instead of trying to shake him off or dispute the point,
which he knew by experience to be useless, he would
make a dead halt, and with great resignation and
gravity stand as immoveable as a statue, whilst our
whole train passed by and proceeded on their journey.
Thus the two would continue, mutually trying to tire
out one another's patience, till we were nearly out of
sight; this had no effect upon the dog, who, to do
him justice, possessed a most praiseworthy firmness
of character, and an obstinacy which would have
done honour to a logician: but with Kees it was a
different matter; he saw the distance increasing
without any better chance of overcoming his adversary's resolution than at first. Then commenced a
most ludicrous and amusing scene. Kees would
alight, and both follow the caravan at full speed; but
the dog, always distrusting the finesse of the monkey, would adroitly allow him to pass on a little
before him for fear of a surprise, running alongside
and a little behind him all the way, and never for a
moment taking his eye off him. In other respects
he had gained a complete ascendant over the whole
pack, which he undoubtedly owed to the superiority
of his instinct, for among animals, as among men,
cunning and address are frequently more than a
match for physical force. It was only at meal-times,
however, that Kees ever showed any ill-nature
towards the dogs; but when any of them approached
him on that important occasion, the administration
of a sound box on the ear warned him to keep at a
more respectful distance, and it is singular that

none of the pack ever disputed the point or resented the affront.

" A singularity in the conduct of this animal, which I have never been able to account for, was that, next to the serpent, he had the greatest dread of his own species—whether it was that he feared a partner in my affection for him, or that his domestication had impaired his faculties for a life of freedom. Yet, notwithstanding his manifest terror at their appearance, he never heard the other baboons howling in the mountains without replying ; but no sooner would they approach in answer to his voice, than he would fly, in great trepidation, and trembling in every limb, to the protection of his human companions. On such occasions, it was difficult to restore him to his self-possession, and it was only after the lapse of a considerable time that he recovered his usual tranquillity. Like all monkeys, he was incorrigibly addicted to petty larceny, and had he been an Englishman, would have been long since tried at the Old Bailey and transported to Botany Bay; but being a free-born Africander, for such is the name by which the Cape Colonists delight to be called, he committed his depredations with impunity, or only fled for an hour or two to the woods, to escape immediate chastisement, always, however, taking good care to return by nightfall. Never but on one occasion did he absent himself during the night. It was near dinner-time, and I had just prepared some fricasseed beans on my plate, when suddenly the cry of a bird which I had not before heard called off my attention, and I seized my gun and set off in pursuit of it. I had not been more than a quarter of an hour absent when I returned with my bird in my hand ; but Kees and my dinner had both disappeared in the meantime, though I had severely chastised him for stealing my supper on the previous evening.

I concluded, however, that, as usual, he would return on the approach of night, when he thought that the affair would be forgotten, and so thought no more of it; but for once I was mistaken in him; evening came without any appearance of Kees, nor had any of my Hottentots seen him on the following morning, and I began to fear that I had lost him for good. I really began seriously to feel the loss of his amusing qualities and watchfulness, when, on the third day after his disappearance, one of my people brought me the welcome intelligence that he had encountered him in the neighbouring wood, but that he concealed himself among the branches upon seeing that he was discovered. I immediately proceeded to the place indicated, and after beating for some time about the environs to no purpose, at length heard his voice, in the tone which he usually adopted when supplicating for a favour or a remission of punishment. Upon looking up, I perceived him half-hid behind a large branch, in a tree immediately above me, and from which in fact he had been watching our encampment ever since his departure; but all my persuasions could not prevail upon him to descend, and it was only by climbing the tree that I finally succeeded in securing him. He made no attempt to escape me, however, and his countenance exhibited a ludicrous mixture of joy at the meeting and fear of being punished for his misdeeds."

Kees, like many people of more rational pretensions, had his taste greatly perverted by civilization, and could drink off his glass of brandy with the *gusto* of an accomplished toper; but a trick of M. Le Vaillant effectually cured his addiction to the bottle, and rendered his after-life an example worthy of the most rigid " tee-totaller :" it would have delighted the president of a Temperance Society, had such excellent institutions existed in his days. " On one occasion,'' continues his biographer, " I had resolved to reward my Hottentots for their good conduct ; the pipe went merrily round, joy was pictured in every countenance, and the brandy-bottle was slowly circulating ; Kees, all impatience for the arrival of his turn, followed it with his eyes, holding his plate ready for his allotted portion, for I had found that in drinking out of a glass, his impatience generally caused some of the liquor to run up his nose, which greatly incommoded him, and kept him coughing and sneezing for hours afterwards. I was engaged at the moment in sealing a letter ; he had just received his share of the brandy, and was stooping down to drink it, when I adroitly introduced a slip of lighted paper under his chin : the whole plate suddenly burst into flame, and the terrified animal, with a yell of indescribable horror, leaped backwards at least twelve or fifteen feet at a single bound, and continued, during the whole time the brandy was burning, to chatter and gaze intently at a phenomenon which he no doubt considered of preternatural occurrence. He could never afterwards be prevailed upon to taste spirits of any kind, and the mere sight of a bottle was at all times sufficient to frighten and alarm him."

The Common Cynocephal and its allied Species.

The common cynocephal, *cynocephalus papio*, is of a uniform reddish brown colour, slightly shaded with yellow upon the head, shoulders, back, and extremities ; the whiskers alone are of a light fawn colour ; the face, ears, and hands are naked and entirely black ; the upper eyelids white ; and the tail about half the length of the body ; the hair on the occiput and neck is rather longer than that on the

back and shoulders, but not so much so as to form a
mane; the nose is advanced rather beyond the
extremity of the lips; the cheeks are considerably
swollen immediately below the eyes, after which the
breadth of the face contracts suddenly, giving the
muzzle or nose the appearance of having been
broken by a heavy blow. The whiskers are not so
thickly furnished as in some other species; they are,
however, similarly directed backwards, but do not
conceal the ears, which are black, naked, and rather
pointed. The under parts of the body, the breast,
belly, abdomen, and inner face of the arms and
thighs are very sparingly covered with long hairs of
a uniform brown colour. The females and young
differ in no other respect from the adult males, except
in being of a lighter and more active make.

This species inhabits the coast of Guinea, and is
that most commonly seen about the streets, and in
the menageries and museums of this country. In
youth it is good-tempered, curious, gluttonous, and
incessantly in motion, smacking its lips quickly and
chattering when it would beg contributions from its
visitors, and screaming loudly when refused or tan-
talized. As it grows old, however, it ceases to be
familiar, and assumes all the morose sulky disposition and repulsive manners which characterize the
baboons in general. The specimen observed by
Buffon was full-grown, and exhibited all the ferocity
of disposition and intractability of nature common to
the rest of its kind. "It was not," says he, "altogether hideous, and yet it excited horror. It appeared to be continually in a state of savage ferocity,
grinding its teeth, perpetually restless, and agitated
by unprovoked fury. It was obliged to be kept shut
up in an iron cage, of which it shook the bars so
violently with its hands as to inspire the spectators
with apprehension. It was a stout-built animal,

whose nervous limbs and compressed form indicated great force and agility; and though the length and thickness of its shaggy coat made it appear to be much larger than it was in reality, it was nevertheless so strong and active that it might have readily worsted the attack of several unarmed men."

Of the habits of this animal in a state of nature we are totally ignorant: though from the numbers brought to this country it must be very common on the western coast of Africa, yet no traveller in those parts has mentioned it, or at least not in such terms as to make it recognisable. From its familiarity, good nature, and the comical gravity with which it conducts itself, it is a general favourite with the visitors of exhibitions of animals, and generally manages to secure more than its just share of the nuts, apples, or cakes distributed on such occasions. Though inordinately addicted to gluttony and gor-mandizing, we have observed that the stronger do not bully the weaker, or deprive them of their food, so generally as we have seen other cynocephals and papios do; and when maltreated by larger animals of a different species, they make no defence, but com-plain by loud querulous cries. We have seen two of them sit for hours together, hugging, kissing, and chattering to one another, and, in short, exhibiting more true affection than we ever remember to have observed in any other species of simiæ. It was probably these good qualities that procured for a specimen of the present species the especial favour of one of that much-traduced class of her majesty's subjects called "spinsters of a certain age," who might be seen some two or three years ago taking her daily "constitutional" in the neighbour-hood of Baker-street, with a baboon wrapped care-fully up in the corner of her shawl, his smutty face and nose alone visible, as he rested his muzzle upon her arm, and gazed with becoming gravity at what was passing around him.

But the most ludicrous anecdote which we ever remember to have heard of the common baboon happened some years ago in the south of Scotland : a gentleman, the wall of whose domain ran for some way along the public road, which was, besides, overshadowed by some thick hedge-row timber, and rendered rather lonely by the absence of any cottages or farm-houses in the immediate vicinity, had one of these baboons, a good-tempered fellow, who was allowed to enjoy his liberty and roam about the grounds at will. One Saturday evening, in the dusk, or, as it is there called, the gloamin', he happened to be sitting on the top of the wall, screened from observation by the shade of a large tree whose branches projected over the road, when a countryman returning from market, and jogging slowly homewards on his weary nag, passed immediately beneath him. Jocko, who was a general favourite with the farm-servants, and dearly loved a ride, did not hesitate a moment, but dropped down behind the countryman, and clasping his arms around his neck, put his black face over his shoulder, and commenced chattering and grinning in his usual familiar manner. Hodge, however, was frightened out of his senses ; he put spurs to his horse, but the faster he galloped, the faster Pug chattered, and the closer he clung to save himself from falling. In the mean time, however, he had discovered a paper of cakes which the farmer was taking home to his children, which having secured, and finding that the ride was likely to lead him farther from home than was agreeable, he slipped quietly off by the tail, and scampered back to his accustomed haunts. It may be easily supposed that the countryman did not linger by the way that night ; in fact he arrived at home half-dead with terror, and fully persuaded that it was the foul fiend himself whom he had encountered, and who had come to seduce him from his faith.   How to account for the loss of the cakes was another matter; but it ought to be remembered that devils of all kinds, whether carnate or incarnate, have a special *penchant* for petticoat tails,* and cannot at all times be easily prevented from running after them.

The *cynocephalus anubis,* and *cynocephalus sphinx,* or *babouin* of the French authors, are two species closely allied to the common baboon; but being natives of Dongola and Senaar, they are less frequently seen in this country.   M. F. Cuvier is the only naturalist who has hitherto figured and described these animals from original observation; but we have occasionally seen them both in the menageries of this country, and can fully confirm the accuracy of that gentleman's descriptions and the propriety of the specific distinction; for there seems to be some hesitation among zoologists about admitting the species.   The sphinx is of a dark greenish colour above, mixed with long black hairs thinly scattered, and nearly naked on the under parts, the skin of the belly being of a light bluish white colour, and the hair of the thighs having a tinge of yellowish red; the face is pale violet brown, as are likewise the ears, palms of the hands, and soles of the feet, and there is a tan-coloured circle about the eyes.   The animal is of a slender make, and longer in the limbs than the common cynocephal—in form, indeed, approaching towards the semnopithecs; its nose does not extend beyond, or even as far as the lips, and the inside of the nostrils is white.   This description was taken from a semi-adult specimen that lived for two or three years in the Surrey Zoological Gardens. It was a strong animal, notwithstanding its slender

* A kind of Scotch cakes so called.

make, and kept two or three common cynocephals and some monkeys which were in the same cage with it in complete subjection. There was another specimen in Wombwell's travelling menagerie which agreed with it in every respect, but was older and larger. The hair of this specimen, particularly on the head, was longer than in the common species; it was rather thin, but stood almost erect, which was likewise the case in the individual just described, and gave the animal rather a shaggy appearance. The face was light brown, except round the eyes and on the tip of the nose, which were flesh-coloured; the cartilage of the latter organ did not extend so far as the upper lip, and the physiognomy of the face altogether bore a not very distant resemblance to that of Dr. Rüppell's *papio gelada*. In fact, these two animals appear to be the connecting links in the chain which unites the cynocephals and papios; and indeed, after all, the gelada might perhaps be included in the former genus with almost as much propriety as in the latter. The scrotum was large and flesh-coloured. The French naturalists call this species by the very barbarous name of *cynocephalus babouin;* but it is better in this, as in all other cases where it can be done, to preserve the original name of Linnæus, whom no subsequent naturalist has equalled in the propriety or elegance either of his generic or specific appellations. The *simia sphinx* of the great Swedish philosopher is a species which it is now impossible to determine with certainty; for though M. Geoffroy identifies it with the *papio*, or common baboon, he has no sufficient authority for the assertion. It is probable that more than one species, perhaps all the three included in the present article, were confounded together in the Linnæan term; and, since the other two have been provided with appropriate specific names, the best thing that can be done is to reserve the name of sphinx exclusively for the present species. The propriety of the application of this term to an animal common in the countries bordering upon Upper Egypt is obvious in other respects.

The *cynocephalus anubis*, another Nubian species, is of a much more sombre green than the sphinx, and has a longer muzzle and flatter skull. The whiskers are pale yellow, and the interior face of the members silvery grey. All the anterior parts of the face are black; the cheeks, and a circle round the eyes, flesh-coloured; the ears and feet black, and the callosities violet-coloured. There were two full grown specimens, a male and female, in the Surrey Zoological Gardens some time ago; the hair was very long, dark, and with only an obscure shade of green, and the cartilage of the nose rather prolonged beyond the extremity of the upper lip. We could not ascertain whence they had been obtained, but think it probable that they came from Egypt. Dr. Rüppell brought specimens of this species from Abyssinia, which are now deposited in the fine museum at Frankfort on the Maine, which has been formed almost entirely by the exertions of that eminent traveller and zoologist: there can consequently be no doubt as to the habitat of the *cynocephalus anubis;* that of the *sphinx,* however, is not so well authenticated. M. F. Cuvier, upon the very insufficient authority of Brisson, identifies it with the cynocephal so commonly sculptured upon the monuments of Egypt, and therefore appears to consider it as a native of Nubia and the adjacent countries, but we are rather inclined to consider it indigenous to Western Africa, as it could scarcely have escaped the notice of Rüppell, Hemprich, and Ehrenberg, had it existed in the countries which they so carefully explored. The probability, therefore, is,

that the species which played so important a part
in the mythology of the ancient Egyptians, whose
image is so constantly reproduced upon their
monuments, and to which the ancient classical
writers so frequently refer under the name of *cynocephalus*, is in reality the *cynocephalus anubis* of
modern zoologists. We have just seen that Dr.
Rüppell found it in Abyssinia; Caillaud observed it
occasionally in Senaar, and very commonly in ancient
Meroe; and the sculptures on the monuments are in
all respects more like the figure of the present animal
than the *cynocephalus hamadryas*, which is likewise
a native of the countries surrounding the Red Sea,
and has, apparently on that account alone, been
sometimes taken for the animal intended to be
represented.

This species, the derrias, or *cynocephalus hamadryas* of zoologists, has characters too prominent and
obvious to be mistaken. It inhabits the mountains of
Arabia and Abyssinia, and grows to the size of a large
pointer, measuring upwards of four feet in height
when standing erect, and two feet and a half when in
a sitting posture. The face is extremely elongated,
naked, and of a dirty flesh-colour, with a lighter ring
surrounding the eyes; the nostrils, as in the dog,
are separated by a slight furrow: the head, neck,
shoulders, and all the fore part of the body as far as
the loins, are covered with long shaggy hair; that
on the hips, thighs, and legs is short, and, contrasted
with the former, has the appearance of having been
clipped, so that the whole animal bears no unapt
resemblance to a shaved French poodle. The hair
of the occiput and neck is upwards of a foot in
length, and forms a long mane which falls back over
the shoulders, and at a distance looks something like
a full short cloak. The whiskers are broad and
directed backwards so as to conceal the ears; their

colour, as well as that of the head, mane, and fore part of the body, is a mixture of light grey and ashy brown, each hair being marked with numerous alternate rings of these two colours; the short hair of the hips, thighs, and extremities is of a uniform cinereous brown colour, paler on the posterior surface of the thighs than on the other parts; and there is a patch as large as a man's hand on each side of the callosities, and nearly naked. The tail is about half the length of the body, and is carried drooping as in the other baboons; it is terminated by a tuft of long hair; the callosities are large, and of a dark flesh-colour; the palms of the hands and soles of the feet dark brown. The females, when full-grown, are equal to the males in point of size, but differ considerably in the length and colour of the hair. This sex wants the mane which ornaments the neck of the male, and is covered over the whole body with short hair of equal length, and of a uniform deep olive brown colour, slightly mixed with green. The throat and breast are but sparingly covered with hair; and the skin on these parts, as well as on the face, hands, and callosities, is of a deep tan colour. Hemprich and Ehrenberg, who have given a very complete history and description of the derrias in the " *Symbolæ Physicæ*," compare the female to a bear, whilst the copious mane which adorns the fore quarters of the male gives that sex much of the external form and appearance of a small lion. The young of both sexes resemble the female; and the large manes and whiskers of the males only make their appearance when the animals arrive at their full growth and mature age, that is, after they have completed their second dentition. At this period they undergo a great change in their mental disposition as well as in their physical appearance. While young they are gentle, docile, and playful; but as soon as

they have acquired their full development they become morose, sulky, and malicious.

This species is common in Arabia and Abyssinia,
but is not found either in Egypt or Nubia. Hemprich and Ehrenberg found large troops of them in
Wadi Kanun, and the mountains near the city of
Gumfud, in the country of the Wahabees, as well as
in the mountains above Arkeeko, on the Red Sea;
and we learn from Salt and Pearce that they are
extremely common on the high lands in Tigre. The
travellers above mentioned found troops of a hundred
and upwards in the neighbourhood of Eilet, in the
chain of the Taranta. These were usually composed
of ten or a dozen adult males, and about twenty
adult females, the remainder of the troop being made
up of the young of the four or five preceding years.
When seen at a short distance approaching a small
stream for the purpose of quenching their thirst,
they bore a close resemblance to a flock of wild hogs;
and it was observed that the young ones always led
the van, whilst the old males brought up the rear,
probably for the purpose of having the whole family
continually under their immediate inspection. They
did not appear to pay the slightest attention to the
Gallas and Abyssinians; but when the European
travellers approached, whom they probably mistrusted
from the appearance of their fire-arms, the old males
abandoned their station in the rear, and placed themselves between the troop and their pursuers, so that
it was found extremely difficult to procure specimens
of either the females or young. When they first observed the travellers approaching they all stood upon
their hind legs, for the purpose of examining them;
the old males, having driven away the females and
young animals, remained in this position till the near
approach of the party compelled them also to retire,
when the whole troop scampered up the sides of the

mountains, making them resound with their shrill
clamour. The Arabic name of this animal is *robah*,
or *robbah ;* the Abyssinians call it *derrias,* according
to Pearce's orthography, or *karraï,* according to the
spelling of Hemprich.

The eminent traveller last mentioned has supposed
that the derrias was the baboon which occupied so
important a station in the miscellaneous mythology
of the ancient Egyptians, and of which the image is
so continually reproduced upon their public and pri-
vate monuments. In this opinion, however, we
conceive that he is clearly mistaken. Had the derrias
been the animal intended to be represented, the
remarkable contrast produced between the anterior
and posterior parts of the animal, in consequence of
the dense flowing mane which clothes the neck and
shoulders, would never have been overlooked by
artists who attended so minutely to the external outline of the figure as the Egyptian sculptors; nor is
there any other support for the opinion than the
mere vicinity of the habitat. It is much more probable that the animal really intended to be represented was the *cynocephalus anubis,* a species
which, as we have already seen, Caillaud observed
to be very common in ancient Meroe, the original
fountain of the Egyptian worship, and therefore
much more likely to have attracted the attention of
the natives than an animal inhabiting the distant
mountains of Abyssinia and Arabia. Besides, there
are no traces of the mane in the representations on
the Egyptian monuments ; the outline of the figures,
on the contrary, is perfectly straight and uniform, as
in the common maneless cynocephals, nor have we
ever observed a single instance in which the fore-
quarters were represented as larger or fuller than the
hind. It is therefore fair to conclude that these
figures are intended to represent the *cynocephalus*

anubis, the only other species which inhabits these countries, and of which the characters correspond with the representations. The figures on the tombs and monuments are generally represented in a sitting posture, and small metal images are sometimes dug up among the ruins of Memphis and Hermopolis: mummies containing the embalmed body of the animal have also been found among the catacombs. It appears to be the only species of the *simiæ* actually worshipped by the Egyptians: Strabo, indeed, (p. 812,) in mentioning Hermopolis as the centre of the adoration paid to the *cynocephalus,* says that the Babylonians in the vicinity of Memphis paid divine honours to the *cepus;* yet, though the geographer makes use of very different names, and though these in reality apply to very different animals, there is good reason to believe that they both refer in the present instance to the same species. No quadrumanous animal is ever found represented upon the sacred monuments of the ancient Egyptians, except the cynocephal, nor have the images or mummies of any other species ever been discovered in searching for antiquities. One or two instances indeed occur in the representations of profane subjects, such as the triumphal procession in honour of a returning conqueror, in which monkeys (*cercopithecs*) are introduced; as, for instance, the painting discovered at Thebes by the late Mr. Salt, and represented by Minutoli (tab. xii. fig. 2), in which a monkey is represented riding on the neck of a camelopard; but this was manifestly intended merely to fix the locality of the country or people whose subjugation the triumph was meant to commemorate, and by no means indicates a participation in the divine honours which were paid to the baboon.

The MANDRILL and DRILL.

These two very remarkable species, the last of the baboons and the lowest of all the simiæ, compose a small group or sub-genus of cynocephals analogous

to that which the magot and other short-tailed species form among the papios, participating in all the essential characters of the genus to which they properly belong, but distinguished from their congeners by the tuberculous form of the tail. In this respect the two small groups in question may be considered as the most typical forms of their respective genera, since, as we have repeatedly had occasion to observe, the tail exercises no important or essential function among any of the baboons; the absence of the organ should consequently be regarded as the normal rule, and its presence, where partially developed, as a mere accidental circumstance, or in the

2 c

light of a casual exception. But as the general law among the simiæ is the development of this organ, and not its absence, it so happens that nature, in conformity with this general law, has bestowed the organ upon the majority of the baboons, even whilst she has deprived it of the corresponding function which it exercises in other groups ; and this we conceive to be the true explanation of an anomaly which at first sight appears to place nature in apparent contradiction to herself.

The mandrill (*cynocephalus mormon*), when full-grown, is the largest of all the cynocephals, and may be readily distinguished from other species of the genus by the enormous protuberance of its cheeks, by its short tuberculous tail, and the brilliant and varied colours which mark its face and nose. The adult male measures upwards of five feet when standing upright; the limbs are short and powerful, the body thick and extremely robust, the head large and almost deprived of forehead, the eyebrows remarkably prominent, the eyes small and deeply sunk in the head, the cheek-bones swollen to an enormous size, and forming projections on each side of the nose of the size of a man's fist, marked transversely with numerous prominent ribs of light blue, scarlet, and deep purple ; the tail not more than a couple of inches in length, and generally carried erect, and the callosities large, naked, and of a blood-red colour. The general colour of the hair is light olive brown above, and silvery grey beneath, and the chin is furnished beneath with a small pointed beard of deep orange. The hair of the forehead and temples is directed upwards, so as to meet in a point on the crown, which gives the head a triangular appearance ; the ears are naked, angular at their anterior and posterior borders, as if they had been cropped, and of a bluish black colour ; and the muzzle and lips are large, swollen, and protuberant. The former is surrounded above with an elevated rim or border, and truncated very much like the snout of a hog— a character which we have observed in no other baboon, and which at one time induced us to suspect that the mandrill might possibly be the species incidentally mentioned by Aristotle under the name of chœropithecus, (χοιροπιθηκος, Hist. Anim., lib. ii. cap. 2,) and which might have been brought into Egypt or Greece by the Phœnicians and other merchants who traded between these countries and Western Africa. Other considerations appeared at the time to give some degree of probability to this conjecture. The tuberculous character of the tail, for instance, might have readily induced Aristotle to compare the mandrill with the *pithecus* (πιθηκος), or magot of Barbary; and thus sufficiently account for one part of the compound epithet by which he designates the animal in question, whilst the truncated form of the snout would easily suggest the similarity to the hog (χοιρος). Thus both mem·bers of the name employed by the Greek philosopher might be satisfactorily accounted for from the characters of the mandrill; but the main difficulty attending the hypothesis regarded, not the physical characters of the animal, but its geographical habitat; the civilized nations of antiquity had little or no communication with the countries surrounding the Gulf of Guinea, where alone the mandrill is to be found; and it might therefore be fairly asked by what means the Greeks of the time of Aristotle could possibly have acquired any knowledge of an animal inhabiting that distant and unknown region. This is certainly a grave, and we now believe an insurmountable, objection to the identification then sought to be established between the mandrill and the chœropithecus of Aristotle: but at the period when that opinion

was first promulgated, the force of the objection
arising from the geographical habitat of the mandrill
appeared to be much weakened by the reliance which
we placed upon Baron Cuvier's identification of the
catoblepas of ancient authors with the modern gnu, an
animal which inhabits a still more distant part of Africa,
and which has been hitherto found only to the north of
the Cape of Good Hope. More extended investigation
has since convinced us that Baron Cuvier was mistaken in this identification, and that the catoblepas
of the ancients referred really to the wild buffalo of
Abyssinia, of the native mode of hunting—which
Bruce has given so amusing an account in the
last volume of his celebrated travels to discover the
sources of the Nile, and of which the characters
agree equally well with the ancient description of the
catoblepas, without violating the geographical pro-
babilities of the question.   The support which our
original attempt to identify the chœropithecus with
the mandrill formerly derived from this circumstance
is consequently annihilated, and we must seek for the
animal of Aristotle in some other species of simia
more likely to come under his notice.

In pursuing this inquiry it must be observed that
little reliance is to be placed upon arguments derived
from the more minute characters of the animals
whose names are joined to form the compound
epithet : the Greeks, when ignorant of the native
names which animals bore in their own country,
frequently designated them by compound names
derived from very faint and often arbitrary resem-
blances, as camelopardalis, from the fancied resemblance of the giraffe to a camel on the one hand and
a leopard on the other ; hippelaphus, from the supposed similarity of the nyl-ghæ to a horse and a
stag, the name being justified, in the first instance,
by the spotted colour of the animal, and in the second

by the presence of a mane; so, in respect to the chœropithecus, it is impossible to fix upon the exact character in any species of simia which could induce Aristotle to compare it to a hog. The name chœropithecus occurs only once in his writings, and that is when, in describing the muzzle of the chameleon, he compares it to that of the chœropithecus. This shows that the animal must have been well known to the Greeks, or he would never have selected it as an object of comparison; it must therefore have inhabited the countries in the vicinity of the Red Sea: and the most probable conjecture which we can form, after a mature consideration of all the circumstances, is, that the Greek philosopher refers to the derrias, or *cynocephalus hamadryas* of modern zoologists, a species which has, in reality, a much more attenuated and lengthened muzzle than any of the other cynocephals, and which, when going in troops to drink at the mountain-streams, even Hemprich and Ehrenberg compare to a flock of wild hogs. If this conjecture be admissible, and there is very strong probability of its truth, we shall have succeeded in satisfactorily identifying well nigh all the species of simiæ mentioned by classical authors: the pithecus ($\pi\iota\theta\eta\kappa o\varsigma$) has invariably been referred to the magot, or common Barbary ape (*papio inuus*), and indeed it is impossible to mistake the descriptions of ancient writers in regard to this animal; the cebus ($\kappa\eta\mathcal{E}o\varsigma$) of Aristotle has been shown, in a former part of this volume, to agree only with the *papio gelada* lately discovered by Dr. Rüppell in the mountains of Abyssinia and ancient Meroe; the cepus ($\kappa\eta\pi o\varsigma$) of Ælian and some others of the later Greek writers has been shown to correspond in description with the *cercopithecus ruber* of modern zoologists; the calithrix ($\kappa\alpha\lambda\iota\theta\rho\iota\xi$) was proved to be in all probability the beautiful species of colobus known in Abyssinia under the

name of guereza; the cynocephalus (κυνοκεφαλος)
has been shown to be without a shadow of doubt the
baboon now known to naturalists by the specific name
of *cynocephalus anubis;* and we have just rendered
it at least highly probable that the chœropithecus of
Aristotle referred to the only other species of quadrumanous animal known to inhabit that part of the
globe.   No reasoning of this kind can be more
satisfactory than these identifications : all the ancient
names evidently referring to distinct species have
been accounted for, and every species of simiæ known
to inhabit the countries bordering on the Red Sea,
with one single exception, has been referred to its
ancient appellation.   The exception in question
relates to the *cercopithecus griseus,* described and
figured by M. F. Cuvier, and of which Dr. Rüppell
brought various specimens from Nubia and Kordofan,
and we think it highly probable that this may have
been the animal which the ancients intended to designate under the name of cercopithecus (κερκοπι-
θηκος), though it has hitherto been usual to consider
this term as employed generically among the Greeks
and Romans, as well as by modern authors.   It
seems to have been forgotten, however, that the
Greeks and Romans were acquainted with only two
species of cercopithecs, viz., that here alluded to,
and the *C. ruber,* for which, moreover, they had an
appropriate name; it is therefore highly improbable
that they should have had a generic term for these
two animals, and we therefore consider it most likely
that the word cercopithecus really referred to the
species of grey monkey figured by M. Cuvier.

We now resume the history of the mandrill.   The
females and young of this species differ from the
adult males, in the shorter and less protuberant form
of the muzzle, which is moreover of a uniform blue
colour; the cheek-bones have little or no elevation

above the general plane of the face, nor are they marked with the longitudinal furrows which give the aged individuals of the other sex so singular an appearance; at least they are far from being so prominently developed. It is only indeed when they have completed their second dentition, that these characters are fully displayed in the old males, and that the extremity of the muzzle assumes that brilliant red hue by which it is afterwards so remarkably distinguished.

The mandrill is often mentioned by travellers on the west coast of Africa, and bears the different names of *smitten, choras, boggo, barris*, &c., according to the language or dialect of the tribes or nations in whose territories it has been observed. It is described as being amazingly powerful and mischievous; but many traits of its character and habits have been confounded with those of the chimpanzee; and even the same names have been occasionally applied to both these animals in such a manner as to involve their history in almost inextricable confusion. The mental resources and habits of the mandrill do not differ materially from those of the other cynocephals, except that it becomes in advanced age still more morose and malicious. Those which have been observed in a domestic state readily acquire a decided taste for spirituous and fermented liquors, which indeed is common to other species of the same genus. A remarkably fine individual, which was long kept at Exeter Change, and afterwards at the Surrey Zoological Gardens, drank his pot of porter daily, and evidently enjoyed it; he had even learned to smoke, though this habit did not appear to be so congenial to his taste as his tippling propensities; and it was a very amusing sight to see him seated in his little arm-chair, with his pot of porter in one hand, and smoking away at his little short pipe with all the gravity and perseverance of a Dutchman.

In a state of nature his great strength and malicious disposition render the mandrill a truly formidable animal. As they generally move about in large troops they prove more than a match for the other inhabitants of the forest, and are even said to attack and drive away the wild elephants from the districts in which they have fixed their quarters. The very inhabitants of the countries where they reside are themselves afraid to pass through the woods, unless in large companies and well armed; and it is said that the mandrills will even watch their opportunity when the men are abroad in the fields to attack the negro villages, plunder them of every thing eatable, and sometimes even attempt to carry off the women into the woods.

The drill (*cynocephalus leucopheus*) is a species closely allied to the mandrill, and on that account long confounded with it by the generality of zoologists. It was, however, very distinctly figured and described by Pennant, under the name of the wood baboon, from a specimen in the Leverian museum; but it was only after the description and figure of M. F. Cuvier, taken from the living animal, and the detailed comparison which that eminent naturalist instituted between it and the mandrill, that its characters became fully known, and its specific distinction established. It is a native of the Coast of Guinea, and, like the mandrill, is distinguished by a short erect stumpy tail, scarcely two inches in length, and covered with short bristly hair. The cheeks are not so prominent as in that species, neither are they marked with the same variety of colours; and the size and power of the animal are rather inferior. The colours of the body bear some resemblance to those of the mandrill, but they are more mixed with green on the upper parts, and are of a lighter or more silvery hue beneath. The head, back, sides, outer surface of the limbs, a band across the lower part of the neck, and the backs of the fore-hands, are furnished with very long fine hair of a light brown colour at the root, and from thence to the point marked with alternate rings of black and yellow, the two last colours alone appearing externally, and by their intermixture giving rise to the greenish shade which predominates so much upon the upper parts of the head and body. The under parts of the body are equally covered with long fine hair, but of a uniform light brown or silvery grey colour, and more sparingly furnished than on the back and sides; the whiskers are thin and directed backwards; there is a small orange-coloured beard on the chin; the hair on the temples is directed upwards, and, meeting from both sides, forms a pointed ridge or crest on the crown of the head; and the tail, short as it is, is yet terminated by a small brush. The face and ears are naked, and of a glossy black colour, like polished ebony; the cheek-bones form polished elevations on each side of the nose, as in the mandrill, only that they are not nearly so large; neither are they marked with the same series of alternate ridges and furrows, nor with the brilliant variety of colours which render that species so remarkable; the palms of the hands and soles of the feet are also naked in the drill, and of a deep copper colour; the colour of the skin, when seen beneath the hair, is uniform dark blue, and that of the naked callosities bright red. The female only differs from the male by her smaller size, shorter head, and much paler colour; and the young males exhibit the same characters up to the period of their second dentition.

The wood baboon, the yellow baboon, and the

cinereous baboon of Pennant, are all manifestly
referable to this species, and differ only in the characters proper to the age and sex of the specimens from
which he took his descriptions. The habits and
manners of the drill have not been observed in a state
of nature, nor do we find the animal itself indicated
in the works of any West African traveller. In its native country it may probably be confounded with the
mandrill, at least by casual and passing observers, and
the similarity of its size, form, and characters, probably
also of its habits and dispositions, render this supposition extremely probable; but it is now frequently
brought to Europe, and is well known to zoologists
as a very distinct species. Its habits, in a state of
confinement, do not appear to differ materially from
those of its congeners. The individuals which we
have had opportunities of observing in the gardens
of the Zoological Society and in other collections,
were all of immature age and growth, and consequently exhibited none of that fierce and intractable
spirit which usually characterises the adult baboons.
They were, generally speaking, silent, sedate, and
sufficiently gentle, when not tantalised by withholding
food, or otherwise strongly excited : but the gloomy
ferocity of their natural disposition was nevertheless
gradually beginning to show itself in those which
had acquired a certain size and strength ; and there
can be little doubt but that the adult males exhibit
all the repulsive and malicious character of the
kindred species.

THE END.

London: Printed by W. CLOWES and SONS, Stamford Street.

46

CPSIA information can be obtained
at www.ICGtesting.com
Printed in the USA
BVHW011213140821
614282BV00024B/179